The King of the Great Clock Tower and *A Full Moon in March*

Manuscript Materials

THE CORNELL YEATS

PLAYS

The Countess Cathleen, edited by Michael J. Sidnell and Wayne K. Chapman
The Land of Heart's Desire, edited by Jared Curtis
Diarmuid and Grania, edited by J. C. C. Mays
Collaborative One-Act Plays, 1901–1903, "Cathleen ni Houlihan," "The Pot of Broth," "The Country of the Young," "Heads or Harps," edited by James Pethica
The Hour-Glass, edited by Catherine Phillips
The King's Threshold, edited by Declan Kiely
Deirdre, edited by Virginia Bartholome Rohan
"The Dreaming of the Bones" and "Calvary," edited by Wayne K. Chapman
"The Only Jealousy of Emer" and "Fighting the Waves," edited by Steven Winnett
The Words Upon the Window Pane, edited by Mary FitzGerald
"The King of the Great Clock Tower" and "A Full Moon in March" edited by Richard Allen Cave
The Herne's Egg, edited by Alison Armstrong
Purgatory, edited by Sandra F. Siegel
The Death of Cuchulain, edited by Phillip L. Marcus

POEMS

The Early Poetry, Volume I: "Mosada" and "The Island of Statues," edited by George Bornstein
The Early Poetry, Volume II: "The Wanderings of Oisin" and Other Early Poems to 1895, edited by George Bornstein
The Wind Among the Reeds, edited by Carolyn Holdsworth
"In the Seven Woods" and "The Green Helmet and Other Poems," edited by David Holdeman
Responsibilities, edited by William H. O'Donnell
The Wild Swans at Coole, edited by Stephen Parrish
Michael Robartes and the Dancer, edited by Thomas Parkinson, with Anne Brannen
The Winding Stair (1929), edited by David R. Clark
Words for Music, Perhaps, edited by David R. Clark
"Parnell's Funeral and Other Poems" from "A Full Moon in March," edited by David R. Clark
New Poems, edited by J. C. C. Mays and Stephen Parrish
Last Poems, edited by James Pethica

The King of the Great Clock Tower and *A Full Moon in March* Manuscript Materials

BY W. B. YEATS

EDITED BY

RICHARD ALLEN CAVE

Cornell University Press

ITHACA AND LONDON

The preparation of this volume was made possible in part
by a grant from The American Philanthropies.

First published 2007 by Cornell University Press

Printed in the United States of America

Library of Congress Cataloging-in-Publication Data

Yeats, W. B. (William Butler), 1865-1939.
[King of the great clock tower]
The King of the great clock tower ; and, A full moon in March : manuscript materials / by W.B. Yeats ; edited by Richard Allen Cave.
p. cm. -- (The Cornell Yeats)
Includes bibliographical references.
ISBN 978-0-8014-4611-5 (cloth : alk. paper)
1. Yeats, W. B. (William Butler), 1865-1939. King of the great clock tower--Criticism, Textual. 2. Yeats, W. B. (William Butler), 1865-1939. Full moon in March--Criticism, Textual. 3. Yeats, W. B. (William Butler), 1865-1939--Manuscripts--Facsimiles. I. Cave, Richard Allen. II. Yeats, W. B. (William Butler), 1865-1939. Full moon in March. III. Title. IV. Title: Full moon in March. V. Series: Yeats, W. B. (William Butler), 1865-1939. Works. 1982.

PR5904.K35 2007
822'.8--dc22

2007011167

Cornell University strives to utilize environmentally responsible suppliers and materials to the fullest extent possible in the publishing of its books. Such materials include vegetable-based, low-VOC inks and acid-free papers that are recycled, totally chlorine-free, or partly composed of non-wood fibers. For further information, visit our website at www.cornellpress.cornell.edu.

1 3 5 7 9 cloth printing 10 8 6 4 2

The Cornell Yeats

The volumes in this series present all available manuscripts, revised typescripts, proof-sheets, and other materials that record the growth of Yeats's poems and plays from the earliest draftings through to the lifetime published texts. Most of the materials are from the archives of Senator Michael Yeats, now in the care of the National Library of Ireland, supplemented by materials held by the late Anne Yeats; the remainder are preserved in public collections and private hands in Ireland and around the world. The volumes of poems, with a few exceptions, follow the titles of Yeats's own collections; several volumes of plays in the series contain more than one play.

In all the volumes manuscripts are reproduced in photographs accompanied by transcriptions, in order to illuminate Yeats's creative process—to show the poet at work. The remaining materials—such as clean typescripts and printed versions—are generally recorded in collated form in an apparatus hung below a finished text. Each volume contains an Introduction describing the significance of the materials it includes, tracing the relation of the various texts to one another. There is also a census of manuscripts, with full descriptive detail, and appendixes are frequently used to present related materials, some of them unpublished.

As the editions seek to present, comprehensively and accurately, the various versions behind Yeats's published poems and plays, including versions he left unpublished, they will be of use to readers who seek to understand how great writing can be made, and to scholars and editors who seek to establish and verify authoritative final texts.

THE YEATS EDITORIAL BOARD

For Chris Burgess

Contents

Acknowledgments

The largest debt of gratitude must be expressed to Senator Michael Yeats for his kind permission to examine and publish all this material relating to *The King of the Great Clock Tower* and *A Full Moon in March*. Second, I express grateful thanks to the Arts and Humanities Research Council (formerly the Arts and Humanities Research Board) for the award of a sabbatical extension grant; to Royal Holloway, University of London, for granting me the initial term's sabbatical, which made an application to the AHRC possible; to J. S. Bratton, then head of the Department of Drama and Theatre Studies at Royal Holloway, for extending my leave to a full academic year; and to June Layson (University of Surrey) and Christopher Murray (University College, Dublin), whose letters of recommendation for this project were in large measure responsible for the AHRC's generosity.

I have benefited considerably from the kind help and advice of staff in numerous libraries but especially wish to mention the unfailing support of Tom Desmond and his colleagues (Manuscript Department of the National Library of Ireland); David Ward (formerly of the library at Royal Holloway); Charles Benson (Trinity College, Dublin); Katharine Salzmann and her colleagues (Special Collections Department of the Morris Library, Southern Illinois University, Carbondale); Molly Wheeler (Harry Ransom Humanities Research Center, University of Texas at Austin); John Attebury (John J. Burns Library, Boston College); Sandy Roscoe (Special Collections Research Center, Joseph Regenstein Library, University of Chicago); Russell Maylone (McCormick Library of Special Collections, Northwestern University Library); Sarah Woodcock (Theatre Museum, London); Mairéad Delaney (archivist at the Abbey Theatre); Francesca Franchi (archivist at the Royal Opera House, Covent Garden); Anna Meadmore (archivist and librarian at the Royal Ballet School, Richmond Park); and Audrey Harmon, former librarian at the Royal Ballet School, who introduced me to Jill Gregory, one-time student at the Abbey School of Dance. I also wish to offer grateful thanks to John Kelly, editor of the *Collected Letters*, for sharing his unrivaled knowledge of Yeats's correspondence and for drawing my attention to a body of hitherto unpublished letters relevant to the two dance plays, the subject of this volume. To Sam McCready I am indebted for giving me access to his copy of Arthur Duff's music included in the appendix and to George Duggan for his kind permission to put this work in the public domain. Theo Snoddy offered invaluable help in tracking down the executors of the late Victor Brown, who designed the broadside of Yeats's poem, "The Wicked Hawthorn Tree"; and Tony Brown graciously gave me permission to include it in the volume.

Like all editors in the Cornell Yeats series, I am at a loss to convey my gratitude for the considerable help, encouragement, and valuable criticism offered me over the years by Stephen Parrish and Ann Saddlemyer as General Editors, from whom the invitation came to be involved in the project; and to Jared Curtis as Coordinating Editor for all his assistance with the layout of the finished volume. I have benefited too from the work of my predecessors in the series in setting clear and precise ground rules to follow and such impeccable standards to emulate; and I wish to express a special debt of gratitude to Warwick Gould, who not only introduced me to Stephen Parrish but, by inviting me to review for *Yeats Annual* the first volumes in the series, enabled me to learn so much from the work of those earlier editors before I engaged in completing a volume of my own.

There are numerous friends who over the years have shared with me their expertise in Yeatsian studies and insight into the plays as texts for performance and with whom I have discussed aspects of this book as it took shape: Ann Saddlemyer, again, who took time away from her own projects to answer endless questions about George Yeats and Lennox and Dolly Robinson and put a wealth of material in my way that helped to confirm my hypotheses; Colin Smythe (who also kindly photographed for me his copy of the Cuala *Broadside*, which features in the appendix); Katharine Worth, that indefatigable proselytiser for the staging of Yeats's plays; Brian Singleton of the Samuel Beckett Centre for Drama Studies, who continually arranged accommodation for me in Trinity College, Dublin, to facilitate my visits to libraries and archives; Janet Lansdale, who over many years' theatregoing and lively debate has taught me so much about dance analysis; and David Leonard of Dance Books, whose remarkable knowledge of publications about dance and dance history proved a never-failing resource. The late Dame Ninette de Valois roused my interest in these plays many years before her death, and to her I give thanks too for the gift of the photograph included in the appendix. I wish to place on record my particular indebtedness to the group of eighteen undergraduate students who, on a Performance Research Project under my guidance and that of my postgraduate fellow Jonathan Statham, staged recreations of the Abbey's 1934 production of *The King of the Great Clock Tower*, putting to the test my theories of how much of the extant material relating to the play may be considered as constituting a performance text. Rigorous critics and thinkers, their work was a continual joy. Finally to Chris Burgess, to whom this volume is dedicated, I offer my deepest thanks for giving unflagging and ever-patient support throughout all stages of the work.

RICHARD ALLEN CAVE

Royal Holloway, University of London

Abbreviations and Short Titles

HEOP	*The Hen's Egg and Other Plays* (London: Macmillan, 1938).
FMIM	*A Full Moon in March* (London: Macmillan, 1935).
FMIM (Chicago)	*A Full Moon in March* in *Poetry* (Chicago, 1935).
FMIM(K)	The verse version of *The King of the Great Clock Tower* in *A Full Moon in March* (London: Macmillan, 1934).
FMIM(M)	*A Full Moon in March* in *A Full Moon in March* (London: Macmillan, 1935).
KGCT	*The King of the Great Clock Tower, Commentaries and Poems* (Dublin: Cuala Press, 1934).
KGCT(C)	"Commentary on 'The Great Clock Tower'" in *The King of the Great Clock Tower* (Dublin: Cuala Press, 1934).
KGCT(K)	The prose version of *The King of the Great Clock Tower* in *The King of the Great Clock Tower* (Dublin: Cuala Press, 1934).
KGCT(L)	The prose version of *The King of the Great Clock Tower* as it appeared in the November 1934 issue of *Life and Letters* (London).
KGCT (prose) *KGCT* (verse)	Used in commentary to distinguish the two forms of the play.
Letters	*The Letters of W. B. Yeats*, ed. Allan Wade (London: Rupert Hart-Davis, 1954; New York: Macmillan, 1955).
NLI	National Library of Ireland archives
P	*Poetry* (Chicago), March 1935 (first appearance of *A Full Moon in March*).
VPl	*The Variorum Edition of the Plays of W. B. Yeats*, ed. Russell K. Alspach, assisted by Catharine C. Alspach (London: Macmillan, 1966).

Census of Manuscripts

The history of Yeats's composition of *The King of the Great Clock Tower* and *A Full Moon in March* is a complex one. Though three distinct works (including both the prose and verse versions of the first play) were the final outcome of a period of creativity that lasted some two years, stages of their evolution frequently overlapped, as I discuss in detail in the introduction. The chronology is intricate. Composition of *A Full Moon in March* grew out of an attempted revision of the earlier play. Lyric material that was eventually to find its proper place in *A Full Moon in March*, but which was completed while the prose version of *The King of the Great Clock Tower* was being revised for production at the Abbey, was incorporated (not at all successfully) into both the staging and early published editions of that play. Revision of that first (prose) version of *The King of the Great Clock Tower* for publication continued alongside the drafting of *A Full Moon in March*; and final revisions for an intended production of that second play were effected while *The King of the Great Clock Tower* was being rendered into verse (for eventual publication in the same volume with *A Full Moon in March*). The design of a census of manuscripts is consequently fraught with problems. Given the compositional history, should one devise a single census, despite the fact that three separate published texts and two distinct plays emerged from the endeavor? Should one create a census in two sections or even three? Good arguments could be sustained to support any of these possibilities. In the end I decided on the first option of a single alphabetical run to minimize overlap and consequent confusion. However, the resulting census is augmented by a second listing of all the materials in chronological order of composition, so far as that can be accurately determined, to help clarify the stages of the creative process. All materials in the following census bearing the prefix NLI are from the collections of the National Library of Ireland; the current whereabouts of other listed manuscript materials are stated in the specific descriptions. Where measurements of materials are given, height precedes width. Hereafter, in place of full titles of the several works, along with titles of publications in which they first appeared, the abbreviations listed on p. xiii are used.

BC A notebook (usually referred to as the "Rapallo notebook") in an octavo album format with leather boards imitating a medieval design with a series of three mock "hinges," embossed with stylized flowers, to front and back covers. The leaves are of cream laid paper, measuring 24.1 by 15.8 cm, and bear no watermark but some foxing; the endpapers carry a floral design in green and brown; and on the verso of the front endpaper are written Yeats's London address at the Savile Club and that of Riversdale, his home in Rathfarnham. The album itself measures 25 by 17.2 cm and appears to have been used predominantly between June and December 1934. Yeats chiefly deploys a dark, blue-black, or black ink for the entries, though there are occasional revisions or entries in pencil, while between 27^{v} and 28^{v}, he uses a lighter toned ink that shades into a mid-blue. The volume contains the following materials relevant to this edition: revisions to *KGCT* (prose) in response to Pound's dismissal of the play as "putrid" (1^{r}, 2^{r}, 2^{v}, 3^{r}, 3^{v}, 4^{r}); revised "Song for the Severed Head" (1^{v}, 4^{v}); further attempts at revising *KGCT* (prose) with intimations of the refrain, "desecration and the lover's night" (5^{r}); drafts of "Why must those holy, haughty, feet descend" (5^{v}, 6^{r}, 6^{v}, 7^{r}); drafts of "A Prayer for Old Age," which was to be included at close of the Preface to *KGCT* (prose) in the Cuala text (7^{v}, 8^{r}); drafts of "He had famished in a wilderness" included at the close of the Commentary on *KGCT* (prose) in the Cuala text (8^{v}, 9^{r}); draft of the Preface to *KGCT* (prose) for the Cuala text (9^{v}, 10^{r}, 10^{v}); more drafts of "He had famished" (11^{r}, 11^{v}, 12^{r}); draft of "Every loutish lad in love" for *FMIM(M)* (25^{v}, 26^{r}); draft prose scenario of "The Great Clock Tower" in a "New version for private room," which is a prose outline for *FMIM(M)* (26^{v}, 27^{r}, 27^{v}); diary including meetings with Group Theatre personnel to discuss their staging *FMIM(M)* (27^{v}); scenario of *FMIM(M)* continues (30^{v}, 31^{r}, 31^{v}, 32^{r}, 32^{v}); initial idea for "Song for the Severed Head" in *FMIM(M)* (32^{v}); draft of "Every loutish lad" (33^{r}); draft revisions to "Saddle and ride" to be included as "Alternative Song for Severed Head" in *FMIM(M)* (40^{r}); drafts of "Clip and lip and long for more" for *KGCT* (verse) (40^{v}, 41^{r}, 41^{v}, 42^{r}); two lines only of revision for *KGCT* (verse) (42^{v}); draft version of *KGCT* (verse) (43^{r}, 43^{v}, 44^{r}, 44^{v}, 45^{r}, 45^{v}, 46^{r}, 46^{v}). Some fifty-three pages in all contain draft material, densely packed on recto and verso; these entries relating to composition for the plays have interspersed between them draft manuscript materials of the poems and "Supernatural Songs" that are contained in the Cuala text of *KGCT* and the Macmillan text of *FMIM* together with some astrological calculations and hitherto unpublished poems addressed to Margot Ruddock. For a discussion of the remaining pages of manuscript, see *"Parnell's Funeral and Other Poems" from "A Full Moon in March": Manuscript Materials*, ed. David R. Clark (Ithaca: Cornell University Press, 2003). The remaining fifty-five pages of the album are left blank. The Rapallo notebook is in the Yeats Collection of the John J. Burns Library, Boston College.

The British Library, London:

Add. MS 55003 Holograph letter, dated July 18, 1939, from Arthur Duff accompanying a manuscript copy in blue ink on printed staves of his music for the "Song for the Severed Head" as performed in the Abbey Theatre production in July 1934. Included are (a) the vocal line with the words of the lyric arranged for singing ("For convenience I have written the tune in treble clef") on the recto and verso of p. 247 and the recto of p. 248; and (b) the same with piano accompaniment, but with the vocal line arranged in the bass clef on the recto and verso of pp. 250–251 and the recto of p. 252. Later in the volume the printed proof of the vocal line of the song, as set for inclusion in volume 5 of the projected but abandoned Coole edition of Yeats's collected works, is included on pp. 275–276. In his letter Duff points out that Yeats revised ll. 4–6 of the third stanza of the song before the performance but after he had completed his composition. Consequently in blue ink he gives the words for this stanza as they appear in NLI 29,551(2), and above these in pencil the lyric as it appears in the published Cuala edition, showing how each might be fitted to the melody. (Duff's tune for the final song, "The Wicked Hawthorn Tree," was printed along with Yeats's lyric and a drawing by Victor Brown as *Broadside*, no. 2, n.s., by the Cuala Press in February 1935.) Macmillan Archive: Yeats/Macmillan Correspondence.

Add. MS 55885 Page proofs of *FMIM*, headed on each verso "More Plays for Dancers" but revised to *Wheels and Butterflies*; stamped by Clark of Edinburgh "8 Feb 1939"; text appears to have been set from or to be an unbound gathering of that published by Macmillan in 1935 (the Preface is identical with the 1935 printed text, including, significantly, the final paragraph, referring to "the hermit Ribh in 'Supernatural Songs,'" though appropriately this is heavily scored through). Corrections in ink and pencil involve the insertion of omitted letters, punctuation, or spacing between stanzas of the lyrics; realigning of short stage directions when they relate to a particular character's movements; the centering of the lyrics on the page to distinguish them from the dialogue. An issue appears to have been how precisely to set the short lines that comprise the Attendants' dialogue; an instruction to "treat these as broken lines of blank verse" is followed. After these fall page proofs of *KGCT* (verse). These are similarly headed on each verso "More Plays for Dancers" but revised to *Wheels and Butterflies*; stamped by Clark of Edinburgh "8 Feb 1939"; text again appears to have been set from that published by Macmillan in 1935. Corrections in ink and pencil involve a repositioning of the dedication to Ninette de Valois from a separate page to the verso of the title page and the resituating of the list of "Persons in the Play" from the verso of the dedication to immediately before the start of the text. On the verso of the final lyric is printed the "Alternative Song for the Severed Head" as in the text printed in *HEOP*, which is not its placing in *FMIM(M)*, where it is included in the section headed "Parnell's Funeral and Other Poems." None of the corrections revise the actual text of either play. Macmillan Archive, volume MC.

Add. MS 55889 Page proofs of *FMIM* intended for volume 5, *The Collected Plays*, of the projected but abandoned Coole edition of Yeats's collected works; these are stamped by Clark of Edinburgh as "Third Proof" and dated "12 July 1936." The title page includes in penciled holograph the note, "Marked by Mrs Yeats." The list of "Persons in the Play," which had been set on the verso of the title page, has directions for its repositioning under the title that heads the actual play text; subsequent pencil markings show how the pagination will consequently be affected. Corrections throughout appear in ink (Thomas Mark) and pencil (George Yeats), the latter often answering questions posed by the former. While not exact replicas in terms of how they are effected, the corrections are virtually identical in substance to those that would be made later to Add. MS 55885, which suggests a wholly new set of proofs was created and checked some three years after those comprising Add. MS 55889 were completed. The most notable issue again involves a difficulty over how to set the Attendants' speeches, whether as verse or prose. For example, alongside the dialogue that introduces the lyric, "He had famished in a wilderness," Thomas Mark has questioned in ink: "Are these blank verse[s] broken and should they be set thus?" and he then lays out the speeches in the margin as blank verse, beneath which George Yeats responds in pencil with a terse, "Yes." This pattern of question and answer is repeated whenever speeches by the Attendants recur in the rest of the drama. Twice Thomas Mark questions an actual reading (in respect to the line, "How can she laugh / Loving the dead" and the word "eyelids" in the second line of the second stanza of the final lyric); to the first Mrs. Yeats responds, "Yes no other text exists," and to the second, "no other text." These are followed by page proofs of *KGCT* (verse), also intended for inclusion in volume 5, *The Collected Plays*, of the projected but abandoned Coole edition of Yeats's collected works; and are again stamped by Clark of Edinburgh as "Third Proof" and dated "12 July 1936." The title page includes provision for a date of composition but only "193" is printed, to which "5" has been added in ink. A substantial note in pencil on the title page in what appears to be George Yeats's hand has been erased to the point of being virtually unreadable, except for the final line, which appears to read, "before Full Moon in March," suggesting that her comment was about the precise ordering of the plays. Very few corrections are recorded. The dedication is here left undisturbed on the recto of the page following the title; and the list of "Persons in the Play," printed on the verso of the dedication, is not repositioned. None of the corrections revise the text of either play; none are by Yeats. Macmillan Archive, volume MCIV.

Add. MS 55892 Page proofs of *FMIM* for a projected volume of *Collected Plays* (possibly the later abandoned Coole edition), stamped as "Third Proof" by Clark of Edinburgh and dated "12 JUL 1939." The preceding gathering contains the text of *The Cat and the Moon*, but the final pages consist of a new title page headed "1935-1939 / LAST PLAYS" (a correction in ink reverses these lines), which are then listed as *A Full Moon in March*, *The King of the Great Clock Tower*, *The Herne's Egg*, *Purgatory*, and *The Death of Cuchulain*, with a marginal note, "This is not chronological but is the order of the volume form." There follows a title page for *FMIM(M)* with the date, "1935," appended in ink, and the Preface from Macmillan's 1935 printing of the play but without the final paragraph referring to the "Supernatural Songs." The next gathering begins with a second title page for *FMIM(M)* with a printed date, with two marginal notes in pencil. The first reads, "Add to Coll. Plays / after / The Words Upon the / Window-Pane," the position the play took in the *Collected Plays* that was eventually published by Macmillan in 1952. The second note reads, "Some markings / by Mrs Yeats." While not exact replicas in terms of how they are entered, the corrections, all in pencil, are nearly identical in substance with those that were made to Add. MS 55885 and Add. MS 55889. The heading, "Last Plays," on the verso of each page is consistently deleted. These are followed by page proofs of *KGCT* (verse) also for a projected volume of *Collected Plays* (possibly the later abandoned Coole edition), stamped as "Third Proof" by Clark of Edinburgh and dated "12 JUL 1939." As in Add. MS 55885, the date on the title page is given in print without a final digit, which has been added in pencil, and there are directions for moving the dedication to the verso of the title page and the list of "Persons in the Play" to immediately above the beginning of the play text. In that opening list "The Stranger" is corrected to "The Stroller." As with *FMIM(M)*, the corrections are virtually identical in substance to those that were made to Add. MS 55885 and Add. MS 55889; most of these relate to layout, especially of the songs; there are no revisions to the text. Macmillan Archive, volume MCVII.

LCP An eight-page carbon copy on flimsy cream paper of *A Full Moon in March*, submitted to the Lord Chamberlain's Office by the Phoenix Ballet and Dramatic Club for a licence to perform the play at the Everyman Theatre, Hampstead, London. The text is a copy of *FMIM(M)* with holograph additions in blue ink (brackets around each of the stage directions and seven cues for music and movement of the curtains). The licence (no. 1701) was given on June 15, 1950, on the recommendation of the reader, C. D. Heriot. LCP 1950/30 British Library.

CDML A folder containing first page proofs of the *KGCT*, starting from p. 1 of the playtext and concluding on p. 26 with the final words of section V of the "Commentary on A Parnellite at Parnell's Funeral" (but omitting what were eventually to become the last twelve lines of the poem, though these appeared in the Cuala volume at the close of the commentary). In the portion containing *KGCT* (prose), there are revisions in diverse hands, including holograph corrections in black ink by Yeats. These generally are concerned with correcting faulty spacing, punctuation, and cases. The most substantial revisions are to the directions concerning the movements of the Queen once she rises and begins to dance, though these are not always in Yeats's hand. The revisions also include the direction for her final appearance within the half-closed curtains. The penciled addition in parentheses of a first draft of the latter half of the concluding note (about omitting "this last song" lest there be "too much music between the end of the dance and the descent of the curtain") is not in Yeats's holograph. There are also penciled indications for repaginating, substantially reducing the content of each page, which were carried through into the revised proofs (NLI 30,020) and the published Cuala text. One correction by Yeats is autographed by him. The individual sheets are the same size (21 by 13.2 cm) as the final proofs but of flimsier paper. The material is now in the possession of the Charles Deering McCormick Library of Special Collections, Northwestern University Library, Evanston, Illinois.

HRC Ten numbered pages of typescript (ribbon copy) of *FMIM(M)* on thin cream foolscap copying paper, bearing the watermark Swift Brook / Bond (the top copy of which JRL1 and NLI 30,186 are carbon copies). The stage directions are underlined in red throughout. Marks in the top left-hand corner of the first, second, and last pages indicate that the sheets were once held together with a paper clip, which rusted with time but is since removed. There are extensive corrections and revisions in Yeats's holograph in black or blue/black ink; most notably, the original title "*The Lover's Night*" is heavily crossed through and replaced with the title by which the play is now known. Within the stage directions, any reference to a curtain or to staging conditions in a conventional theater are crossed through, leaving directions only for a ritual involving the unfolding and folding of a cloth, indicating a preferred production in the manner of Yeats's earlier *Four Plays for Dancers* (London: Macmillan, 1921), modeled on Japanese Noh drama. The material is now located in the Harry Ransom Humanities Research Center, University of Texas, Austin.

JRL1 Ten loose, numbered pages of typescript of *FMIM* (Chicago), a carbon copy in black type of HRC on thin, cream foolscap copying paper bearing the watermark Swift Brook / Bond. Some deletions and rephrasings within the stage directions achieved by overtyping the copy text. Some corrections to the text and reassignment of speeches in holograph in black ink but not seemingly in Yeats's hand. In all these details this copy is an exact match of NLI 30,186. Throughout there are additional markings in pencil, presumably by Morton Zabel, the acting editor of *Poetry*, preparing this text for publication. With the exception of "William Butler Yeats" added in parentheses to the top right-hand corner of p. 1 and "March 1935," a little lower but positioned in the top left-hand corner of the same page, the remaining penciled marginalia relate to such matters as size of font, capitalization of characters' names, italicizing and centering on the page of stage directions, the setting of the Attendants' speeches as prose, etc. The material is housed in box 41, folder 10, of the *Poetry* papers in the Joseph Regenstein Library, University of Chicago.

JRL2 Three long galley proofs of of *FMIM* (Chicago) on flimsy white paper of the text as set for publication in *Poetry*. All three measure 9.0 cm in width but are of varying lengths: the first galley, which runs from the title to line 69 (*VPl*) measures 49.2 cm; the second, which covers ll. 70–150 (*VPl*), measures 51.3 cm; and the third, running from the stage direction that precedes l. 151 to the end of the play at l. 197 (*VPl*), where Yeats's name is appended as author, measures 45.0 cm. There are numerous penciled corrections in Yeats's holograph and in a hand that appears to be Zabel's. Many of the corrections concern punctuation, the changing of cases for certain letters, the printing of the Attendants' speeches as prose instead of verse. However, a number of substantive revisions of note are by Yeats, but, as Zabel did not wait for receipt of the corrected galleys in his haste to have the play published (appropriately) in the March edition of *Poetry*, these were not incorporated into the printed text. (None occurs in the Macmillan text of *A Full Moon in March* in 1935.) The galleys are found along with other Yeats materials in box 3, folder 24, of the Morton Dauwen Zabel Papers in the Joseph Regenstein Library, University of Chicago. Also in this file are both the envelope in which Yeats returned the proofs, date-stamped "9.III.35", and a correspondence card bearing his signature but no message. A penciled date on the envelope records that the proofs arrived in Chicago on March 18, 1935.

NLI 8769(i) An envelope containing thirteen unbound sheets of white, three-holed, loose-leaf paper (measuring 20.3 by 16.5 cm) with rounded corners, bearing the watermark WALKER'S / LOOSE / LEAF / MADE IN GT. BRITAIN. Each sheet carries thirty-one faint green lines (spaced 0.5 cm apart) with a close, double red rule at 0.5 cm from the top, designed to carry a title; the rectos are numbered but with corrections after page "10" to maintain a proper sequence. The relatively clean text in Yeats's holograph in black ink is of *KGCT* (prose), including the framing lyrics (but without "Why must those holy, haughty feet descend," which was added later). On 2^{v} and 5^{v} are penciled redraftings of the King's opening speech (for that on 5^{v}, the sheet has been inverted); both are heavily deleted in pencil, the second further with thick lines in black ink. The envelope also contains NLI 8769(ii).

NLI 8769(ii) Twelve unnumbered sheets of loose leaf white paper with curved corners, measuring 22.9 by 18.2 cm, which bear the watermark WALKER'S / LOOSE / LEAF / MADE IN GT. BRITAIN. There are thirty-five pale green lines (spaced 0.5 cm apart) to a page and a close, double red rule 2 cm from the top, designed to carry a title. Throughout, the sheets are inverted, so that the rule is at the base of the page. The rectos of seven sheets offer a relatively clean copy of *KGCT* (verse) in Yeats's hand in blue-black ink, but the opening and closing lyrics are absent (they were to remain unchanged from the version in prose). The text ends (6^{r}) with the King's line "O; O; they have begun to sing" (l. 130 in *VPl*) followed by the speech prefix "First Attendant (singing as head)." On 7^{r} is the curt instruction: "Then stage directions as in Great Clock Tower & / First Attendant's song, which ends play." There follows a heavily revised manuscript draft of two pages for the Preface to *FMIM* (Macmillan, 1935) in blue-black ink. On 10^{r}–11^{v}, Yeats explores possible orderings of the contents for the Macmillan volume; the final sheet is left blank. In the envelope with NLI 8769(i).

NLI 8906 Thirteen numbered sheets of cream paper bearing three holes on the left-hand side of each sheet as designed for use within Walker's (larger) loose leaf ring binder. The pages each carry the watermark Walker's / Loose / Leaf / Made in Gt. Britain and measure 23 by 18 cm. There are thirty-five pale green lines (spaced 0.5 cm apart) to a page and a close, double red rule 2 cm from the top, designed to carry a title. Pages 1, 5–7, and 10 are deployed the correct way up and on the recto of each; the remaining sheets, as in NLI 30,336, are inverted so that the red rule appears at the bottom of the page. The text, headed "The Swine-herd," is throughout in black ink in Yeats's holograph with revisions and deletions (often extensive) by him in the same shade of ink. There are some underlinings, corrections, and revisions in dark pencil. On the verso of the first page Yeats attempts (with the page inverted) a different spelling of the title: "The Swine-Heard."

NLI 29,550(1) From the Abbey Theatre Collection, a bound, ribbon typescript of *KGCT* (prose)—possibly a prompt copy or actor's script—with stiffened paper cover, measuring 25 by 20 cm. The cover, badly charred round the edges presumably from the Abbey fire, bears a title and autograph in Yeats's hand in dark pencil. Seventeen sheets of cream paper carry the watermark Swift Brook / Bond, but the page numbering begins only after two title pages, the second with list of characters and notes on Queen and Stranger, so the numbered pages actually run to 15. A few penciled corrections are in Yeats's hand; notes on music in medium blue ink, which has faded to mauve, are by another. One of six copies that Yeats asked to be made of the corrected typescript, SIUC 76/1/7.

NLI 29,550(2) Also from the Abbey Theatre Collection, a carbon copy of *KGCT* (prose) running to eight sheets on white paper now aged to gray with charring at edges, measuring 25.5 by 20.3 cm. A hole in the top left corner of every sheet indicates that they were once stapled together. The sheets carry no watermark; the script has the characteristic purple tone of a carbon copy. The numbering commences after two title pages as in NLI 29,550(1). A few penciled revisions correct typographical errors or omissions; others indicate additional stage directions and positioning of actors on stage. There follow two sheets of a thicker cream paper, measuring 26.0 by 20.5 cm, bearing the watermark Swift Brook / Bond. In black ink (seemingly in Yeats's hand) occurs the cryptic note: "O'Mahony / inner garment." Between the second title page carrying the list of characters and the opening page of text is inserted a single sheet of gray-lined, cream-white paper, bearing no watermark but measuring 22.7 by 17.4 cm., on which is a pencil sketch (with annotations in Lennox Robinson's hand) of a floor plan of the setting for the Abbey production (the sheet is foliated 2bis^{r} to indicate an insertion).

NLI 30,020 Unbound printed pages, marked "Final proof," of *KGCT* (prose) as published in *KGCT*. The text now includes the additions marked into CDML. The thin, cream paper, measuring 21 by 13.2 cm, carries no watermark; the typography has been prepared throughout as for the published volume. A few corrections by Yeats in pencil relate to errors in layout or typographical slips, punctuation, or italicization. Corrections to the Commentary are initially in pencil but change after p. 17 to blue-black ink.

NLI 30,186 Ten loose, numbered pages of typescript of *FMIM(M)* a carbon copy in black type of HRC. The thin, cream paper (measuring 33 by 20.2 cm) bears the watermark SWIFT BROOK / BOND. Generally clean text but some deletions or rephrasings within the stage directions achieved by overtyping the copy text. Several revisions or insertions in holograph in black ink and reascriptions of speeches between the two Attendants immediately before the central lyric, "He had famished in a wilderness," but these are not in Yeats's hand. Indications also in holograph, showing how single lines of verse divided between two speakers should be repositioned to preserve a visual sense of the verse line, suggest that this copy may have been prepared for an intended published version, as was the case with JRL1.

NLI 30,306 In envelope: a single sheet of gray-lined, cream/white paper, measuring 25.5 by 20.3 cm. with twenty-six light blue-gray lines, spaced 0.8 cm apart (the same paper as NLI 30,800). It contains in Yeats's holograph in black ink a draft with some few revisions of section IV of the Commentary on the play, in preparation for *KGCT*. The fragment is headed "iv" to confirm its link with the Cuala text.

NLI 30,336 a–e In envelope: a loose-leaf notebook (Walker's Loose Leaf Books, refill size 860, measuring 21 by 19 cm) with red leatherette cover and dark green inner boards, holding some thirty-two pages of disparate manuscript drafts in an inner metal file. Each of the three-holed pages of white paper (measuring 20.4 by 16.5 cm) carries thirty-one faint gray-green lines, spaced 0.5 cm apart, with a close, double red rule 2 cm from the top, designed to carry a title; but Yeats generally inverts the file so the rule appears at the base of the page. (a) On 2^r is a revised opening speech for the King for *KGCT* (prose), developing material explored in BC, 1^r–4^r (see above) in a relatively clean copy. (b) On 3^v–4^r is a draft for the program note Yeats devised for the 1934 Abbey production of *KGCT* (prose), an expanded version of which was eventually to form section IV of the Commentary on the play in the Cuala edition (see NLI 30,306). Both these drafts are in holograph in black ink. (c) Among the ensuing drafts of various prefaces, essays, and commentaries is a version in black ink of the song for the severed head in *FMIM(M)* considerably developed from the five lines in the Rapallo notebook (see BC above), and a version in pencil of the Queen's song. (d) Fourteen pages of manuscript materials relating to *FMIM(M)*, under the title "The Severed Head," comprise three different attempts at expanding on the scenario completed in BC. The second of these is completely crossed through. The group of materials starts with two separate attempts at an opening sequence for the Attendants. The first attempt at drafting the main body of the play, covering some eight sides, approximates what in *VPl* are designated lines 1–123; the second, deleted attempt, covering five sides, approximates lines 29–87, and the third, covering some four sides, approximates lines 33–87. (e) A version of the first lyric, "Every loutish lad in love," occurs between the second and third drafts of the dialogue, running over one-and-a-half pages. The text and all the revisions and deletions are in blue-black ink (sometimes shading to black) in Yeats's holograph. It is by no means certain that the ordering of the items within this notebook now follows the original sequence.

NLI 30,546 One of two companion album-style notebooks, measuring 27.3 by 22.5 cm, handsomely bound in light tan leather with gilt decoration, marbled endpapers, and pages of cream, unlined paper bearing the watermark BASKERVILLE / VELLUM / WOVE. On the spine (2.2 cm wide) in gilt letters is stamped "W. B. / YEATS / PROSE" (the companion volume, NLI

30,547, is titled "POETRY"). Only the first eight leaves (measuring 26.5 by 20.3 cm) have been used on recto and verso, and the ninth solely on the recto; the rest remain blank. The contents include several diary-like entries and private musings; drafts headed "Note to Three Songs" and "Note upon the Great Clock Tower"; further prefatory material (signed and dated "March 1934"); some astrological musing; and notes on costuming in *The Resurrection* and a sketch of a setting for that play. The "Note upon the Great Clock Tower" occurs on the verso of 4^v–7^v and on both recto and verso of 8. Revised, this "Note" was to form the "Commentary on 'The Great Clock Tower' " in *KGCT*, pp. 15–20.

NLI 30,800 In envelope: a single sheet of gray-lined, cream/white paper, measuring 25.5 by 20.3 cm (the same paper as NLI 30,306) has holograph version in black ink by Yeats of the stage direction for *KGCT* (prose): "When the inner curtain is closed, the attendants stand upon either side, singing"; this precedes the final lyric, "Why must those holy, haughty feet descend," which was added to the performance text during the final rehearsals. There are some revisions to the first and last stanza, and to the initial direction. The manuscript is headed: "(Continue on p. 11 as follows)."

RI-SM A set of twenty-five photocopied sheets of Arthur Duff's settings for the four songs in *KGCT* (prose), giving the vocal line (with text) and a piano accompaniment. The score is in manuscript on printed staves. These pages, now in the collection of Sam McCready, were copied from originals owned by Robert Irwin, who sang the role of the First Musician in the initial staging of the play at the Abbey Theatre in 1934. The present whereabouts of Irwin's manuscript copy is not known. Though the words "dance follows" are written at the conclusion of the song for the severed head, the music for the dance is not included; neither it nor any orchestrated version of the accompaniments appear to be extant. There are some variant readings in the texts as set by Duff when compared with the published versions of the various lyrics.

SIUC 76/1/7 In folder: nine pages of typescript of *KGCT* (prose), revised by Yeats in black ink (pp. 1–7) and later in heavy pencil (pp. 7–9). The text, a ribbon copy on cream, flimsy, foolscap paper, is close to the performed and published texts. The title is in red, underlined in black, while in the "Note" describing how Queen and Stranger should wear masks, the characters' titles are underlined in red. The characters' names in the dialogue are normally in capitals, except in the final lyric where all but the initial letter are in lower case. The type throughout is in black with fading in some letters, particularly "g." The heaviest revisions are on pp. 1, 2, 5, and 7. On the top right corner of the first page in Yeats's hand appears the instruction: "6. Copies," two of which are extant as SIUC 91/16/10 and NLI 29,550(1). Inverted on the verso of p. 9, there are four small sketches in ink of designs for thrones, getting progressively more stylized until they end with the "cube" form that is incorporated into the stage directions. The inventory of the H. Lytton Wilson Collection of William Butler Yeats, where the manuscript is situated, describes the drawings as follows: "On the back of page 9 there is a little sketch that Yeats made for Mrs. Wilson of his idea for the scenery." The material is now in the possession of the Special Collections of the Morris Library, Southern Illinois University.

SIUC 91/16/10 A carbon copy of *KGCT* (prose): seventeen pages bound in light brown card, held together with three staples and darker brown binding tape; the fifteen pages of text are numbered but not the preliminary pages with title, list of characters and the "Note" on the masks for Queen and Stranger. The flimsy, cream/white copy paper bears the watermark Swift Brook / Bond and measures 25 by 20 cm. One of six copies that Yeats asked to be made of the corrected typescript, SIUC 76/1/7 (see NLI 29,550[1] above), it bears holograph corrections by Yeats in black ink throughout, who in addition to penning the title of the play on the front cover has noted just below the top binding: "Corrected / April / 1934." This item is now catalogued in the Lennox Robinson Collection in the possession of the Special Collections of the Morris Library, Southern Illinois University.

WBY/NLI 1606 and 1606(a) Two copies of *Poetry* (Chicago), vol. 45, no. 6 (March 1935); the text of the play runs on pp. 299–310 and opens the issue. Text as in JRL2 but with minor divergences regarding the setting of the Attendants' speeches. Neither copy carries revisions by Yeats. From Yeats's library, formerly in the possession of Anne Yeats and now in the collections of the National Library of Ireland.

WBY/NLI 2351 Copy of *A Full Moon in March* (London: Macmillan, 1935). On dust jacket in Yeats's holograph in ink: "Copy corrected by WBY," but there are no corrections to the text of either *FMIM(M)* or *KGCT* (verse), only to the poems "Three Songs to the Same Tune" in black ink, while each of the "Supernatural Songs" is dated in pencil. From Yeats's library, formerly in the possession of Anne Yeats and now in the collections of the National Library of Ireland.

WBY/NLI 2372 Copy of *The King of the Great Clock Tower, Commentaries and Poems* (New York: Macmillan, 1935). The one penciled annotation relates to "Ribh Considers Christian Love Insufficient"; there are no revisions to the text of the play. From Yeats's library, formerly in the possession of Anne Yeats and now in the collections of the National Library of Ireland.

WBY/NLI 2422 a–g Boxed collection of four copies (rather than seven as is implied by the catalog number) of a poem titled "The Singing Head and the Lady," which is actually "He had famished in a wilderness" in final form; they were printed by Frederick Prokosch at his press in Bryn Mawr. "Xmas 1934" is given as the date of publication on the title page. Most copies are of twelve unnumbered pages, measuring 16.4 by 11.3 cm, including a title page, text over two pages, and a colophon, which reads: "Twenty copies of this poem were printed for the author; six on Oland; numbered 1–6; six on Dresden, numbered I–VI; six on rice paper, numbered a–f; and two on Imperial vellum, numbered A and B. This is number . . . ." The copies on Imperial vellum run to only four pages, given the thickness of the paper. All are bound rather amateurishly in differently patterned paper covers with white labels printed in black (duplicate labels are tipped in at end); the vellum copies have gold and black labels. This collection comprises copies 6; IV; e; and A. None contains any holograph revisions. The poem had first appeared with this title in *The Spectator* for December 7, 1934, and was included without a title at the end of the commentary on *The King of the Great Clock Tower* in the Cuala edition of that play, which was issued exactly one week later. From Yeats's library, formerly in the possession of Anne Yeats and now in the collections of the National Library of Ireland.

Chronology of Manuscripts

Given the complexities of the composition of the plays, a possible chronological ordering of the materials included in the census of manuscripts seemed advisable. This chronology, therefore, follows the gestation of each of the three related plays in a tabular format. Known dates of particular items are given in bold. Both the reasoning behind the particular ordering and the provenance of the dates assigned to particular periods of composition are in the introduction. Where two carbon copies of an earlier typescript are extant, the catalog numbers are given together linked by ***and*** (in bold and italic). Where a particular listed item has major import for one of the three plays but also has traceable influences on one or both of the other two, then the catalogue number of that item appears in two or more columns but is given in square brackets in relation to the play(s) where the significance is less pronounced. In the case of published texts, the presence of square brackets around an item indicates that only a part of that particular play (such as a song or lyric chorus) was included in the publication. Items listed in the census that relate to publishing and censorship matters occurring after Yeats's death have not been included in the chronology.

***The King of the Great Clock Tower* (Prose)**	***A Full Moon in March***	***The King of the Great Clock Tower* (Verse)**
Letter to Olivia Shakespear (dated **November 11, 1933**)		
NLI 8769(i)		
SIUC 76/1/7		
NLI 29,550(1) ***and*** SIUC 91/16/10 (latter dated **April 1934**)		
NLI 29,550(2)		
BC (1^r, 1^v, 2^r, 2^v, 3^r, 3^v, 4^r, 4^v, 5^r initially dated **June 1934**)	[BC (1^r, 2^r, 2^v, 3^r, 3^v, 4^r, 4^v, 5^r initially dated **June 1934**)]	[BC (1^r, 2^r, 2^v, 3^r, 3^v, 4^r, 4^v, 5^r initially dated **June 1934**)]
NLI 30,336 a	[NLI 30,336 a]	
	BC (5^r, 5^v, 6^r, 6^v, 7^r)	BC (1^v)
NLI 30,800	[NLI 30,800]	
NLI 30,336 b		

The King of the Great Clock Tower **(Prose)**	***A Full Moon in March***	***The King of the Great Clock Tower*** **(Verse)**
Performed July 30, 1934		
[BC (7^{v}, 8^{r}, 8^{v}, 9^{r}, 11^{r}, 11^{v}, 12^{r})]	BC (7^{v}, 8^{r}, 8^{v}, 9^{r}, 11^{r}, 11^{v}, 12^{r})	
BC (9^{v}, 10^{r}, 10^{v})		
NLI 30,546 (4^{v}, 5^{v}, 6^{v}, 7^{v}, 8^{r}, 8^{v})		
NLI 30,306		
CDML *and* NLI 30,020 (proofs printed on **August 24, 1934**;	[CDML *and* NLI 30,020]	
setting was completed by **September 3**;	BC (25^{v}, 26^{r})	
full printing was completed by **October 20**)	BC (26^{v}, 27^{r}, 27^{v} dated **October 1934**)	
	BC (30^{v}, 31^{r}, 31^{v}, 32^{r}, 32^{v}, 33^{r})	
	NLI 30,336 c, d, e (probably **October/early November 1934**)	
Publication in *Life and Letters* **(November 1934)**	NLI 8906 (**mid-November 1934**)	
	HRC	
	NLI 30,186 *and* JRL1	
		BC (40^{r}, 40^{v}, 41^{r}, 41^{v}, 42^{r}, 42^{v}, 43^{r}, 43^{v}, 44^{r}, 44^{v}, 45^{r}, 45^{v}, 46^{r}, 46^{v} dated **early/mid-December 1934**)
Cuala edition (published **December 14, 1934**)	[Cuala edition of *The King of the Great Clock Tower* (prose)]	
	[WBY/NLI 2422 a-g (dated "**Xmas 1934**")]	NLI 8769(ii) (completed by **December 26, 1934**)
	JRL2	
[Final song appeared as Cuala *Broadside* (**February 1935**)]		
	Publication in *Poetry* (**March 1935**)	
	[WBY/NLI 1606 *and* 1606(a)]	
Macmillan edition, New York (published in **May 1935**)		NLI 8769(ii) draft of Preface dated May [30, 1935]
	Macmillan edition, London (published **November 22, 1935**)	Macmillan edition, London (published **November 22, 1935**)

Introduction

"It takes years to get my plays right."[1] So Yeats informed Margot Ruddock from Rome on October 11, 1934, where between sessions of an international theater conference (organized as the Fourth Congress of the Alessandro Volta Foundation) he had begun to redraft *The King of the Great Clock Tower* to give her a role to act. In fact, in June of that year he had begun to rewrite his first prose version of the play before it had even been staged (it was performed most successfully at the Abbey Theatre from July 30 that summer). Two versions of *The King of the Great Clock Tower* (one in prose and one in verse) and a wholly new play derived from the first, titled *A Full Moon in March*, were to emerge out of a period of gestation that had started early in November 1933,[2] and ended with the publication of *A Full Moon in March* by Macmillan in November 1935. The composition of each play was fueled by intense feeling for a woman. Both were performers: Ninette de Valois elected only to dance on stage and not to speak; Margot Ruddock was an actress possessed of a rich contralto voice who preferred not to dance (despite Yeats's most enduring description of her as his "sweet dancer"). Yeats devised strategies for each of his dance plays to meet these prescriptions.[3] While admiration for de Valois's artistry helped to shape the first play, the second for Ruddock was the product of a deepening personal infatuation. The structure and content of the two plays and the differences between them reflect the wholly different emotions that stimulated their creation.

Yeats frequently gave as his motive for embarking on this new dance play his desire to prove to himself that he was not too old to write poetry. In the Preface to the 1934 Cuala edition of *The King of the Great Clock Tower* he admits realizing twelve months earlier that he had written no verse for two years ("I had never been so long barren")[4]; and ponders whether the death of Lady Gregory and the consequent loss to him of Coole Park with all its associations with past

---

[1]*Ah, Sweet Dancer, W. B. Yeats, Margot Ruddock: A Correspondence*, ed. Roger McHugh (London: Macmillan, 1970), p. 23. Hereafter cited as *Ah, Sweet Dancer*.

[2]Yeats sent a copy of what he saw as the opening lyric of a new "dance play" to Olivia Shakespear on November 11, 1933. See *The Letters of W. B. Yeats*, ed. Allan Wade (London: Rupert Hart-Davis, 1954), pp. 816–818. Hereafter cited as *Letters*.

[3]Ninette de Valois was the stage name of Edris Stannus. Margot Ruddock acted under the surname of her first husband as Margot Collis. At the time of her relationship with Yeats, she was married to the actor Raymond Lovell. The image of Margot dancing is central to both poems about her included in *New Poems*: "Sweet Dancer" and "A Crazed Girl." See W. B. Yeats, *New Poems: Manuscript Materials*, ed. J. C. C. Mays and Stephen Parrish (Ithaca: Cornell University Press, 2000) pp. 44–47 and pp. 102–105, respectively. Both poems were included by Mrs. Yeats and Thomas Mark in *Last Poems and Plays* (London: Macmillan, 1940), and they both appear in the section headed "Last Poems" in *Collected Poems* (London: Macmillan, 1950).

[4]W. B. Yeats, *The King of the Great Clock Tower* (Dublin: Cuala Press, 1934). The Preface is unpaginated.

poetic and theatrical endeavor had cost him his "theme."[5] The play was initially devised as a structure following the pattern of his Noh-inspired "Plays for Dancers," as he called them, since this would require him to frame several choric lyrics: these would test whether there were still a creative sap to flow. But sometime early in 1934 circumstances gave Yeats a more concrete reason for completing a dance play: Ninette de Valois had informed him that after July she would have to end her association with the Abbey because of her growing commitments in London; and pressing financial considerations prompted the Abbey board of directors in consequence to plan the closing of the School of Ballet, which she had founded. Her departure brought to an end an era that had offered Yeats a particularly fruitful period of collaboration with a practitioner whose absolute dedication to her art (so akin to his own) had won his lasting respect. The occasion required marking in a special way, and the completed play (subsequently dedicated to de Valois in its later versified form) can be seen as at once gift, celebration, thank-offering, and memorial. It was fitting that its staging was an unqualified success.

Yeats had met de Valois in Cambridge in May 1927 at the Festival Theatre on the Newmarket Road, which was the brainchild of her wealthy cousin, Terence Gray. It was, as Yeats rightly informed his wife, "the one centre of scenic & lighting experiment now in England."[6] Fired by his reading about and experience of German expressionist theater, Gray had acquired the old Theatre Royal, a Georgian structure that retained most of the original architectural features, and had transformed it with the addition of a cyclorama, revolve, and a Schweibe lighting system into one of the best equipped theaters in England. With a regular undergraduate clientele to call on in term time, Gray had the ideal audience for the kind of experiment in presentational theater that he was devising. Following in the wake of such German practitioners as Leopold Jessner, he sought to test the extent to which the expressionist style of staging might be applied to the whole gamut of the classic repertoire of non-naturalist plays as well as to the modern German drama for which the style was created. Actors appearing in non-naturalistic settings under matching lighting effects while deploying non-naturalistic modes of vocal delivery obviously needed to learn forms of non-naturalistic movement if a unified aesthetic effect was to be achieved on stage in a production; and so Gray had invited de Valois to join the company to teach appropriate movement techniques and choreograph sequences of dance, mime, or tableau when these were required. The Festival had opened in the autumn of 1926 with a staging of Aeschylus's *The Oresteia* and the following January Gray himself directed a production of Yeats's *On Baile's Strand*, for which de Valois had devised the staging of the oath-taking ritual between Cuchulain and Conchubar and, more importantly, stylized angular movements for the Blind Man and the Fool to offset their disturbingly grotesque masks. Gordon Bottomley, the poet-dramatist, was so impressed by the staging not only of his own verse tragedy, *King Lear's Wife*, but also of *On Baile's Strand*, that he encouraged Yeats to attend a projected production of *The Player Queen* at the Festival, which was scheduled to open May 16, 1927. Fortunately in England that month, Yeats attended the Saturday matinee and liked what he saw so much he stayed for the evening performance too, since Gray offered to put him up for the night. His account of the whole experience to his wife, while it offers details of de Valois's background

[5]As early as September 7, 1933, Yeats had confided to Sturge Moore, "For a year now I have written little but prose, trying for new foundations." See *W. B. Yeats and T. Sturge Moore: Their Correspondence, 1901–1937*, ed. Ursula Bridge (London: Routledge and Kegan Paul, 1953), p. 177.

[6]Letter from Yeats to his wife (May 23, 1927), courtesy of John Kelly. The text is partly quoted in Ann Saddlemyer, *Becoming George: The Life of Mrs. W. B. Yeats* (Oxford: Oxford University Press, 2002), p. 362. Hereafter cited as *Becoming George*.

and career, gives no indication that they had had what proved a momentous meeting for them both during the ensuing Sunday morning:

> The acting [in *The Player Queen*] was as a whole good amateur acting – very good sometimes – but one man – the man who played the old man who wants straw [the Old Beggar] gave a beautiful performance – grotesque, phantastic & distinguished. However what impressed me was the staging, that was just what I had dreamed of. The beasts – they streamed in through the audience – were a delight.[7] After my play came dancing, the work of a woman who has, I think, inventive genius.[8] She is Irish and a friend of Maud's – her people have a place at Bessington [*sic*] – & has spent some years with the Russian ballet. I travelled up with her brother & got his address – as we might want her in Dublin if we continue to prosper.[9]

Yeats and de Valois had met in the theater foyer, where he had urged her to come to Dublin to help restage his plays for dancers and to found a school of dance at the Abbey.[10] It was an offer she eagerly accepted, since it fitted her current agenda perfectly.

The Abbey would be the third repertory theater in which she and dancers from her private school would display their expertise and she her gifts as a choreographer. By the autumn of 1926 de Valois was committed to working not only for Gray in Cambridge but also for Lilian Baylis at the Old Vic in London, to whom she had offered her services as arranger of dances in plays and operas, which made up the repertory of her theater. These three theaters with their decidedly different audiences would challenge her creative skills but also considerably extend her expertise as a performer, based largely until now in classical ballet. The three theaters she chose to associate herself with were also in their different ways at the forefront of the repertory theater movement and working alongside such diverse managerial and directorial talents as Baylis, Gray, and Yeats would, or so she hoped, teach her essential principles of running a large-scale theatrical enterprise. Already her ambition was to run a dance company, modeled on Serge Diaghilev's Ballets Russes, which she had joined from 1923–1925. As the younger Yeats had wished to establish a stage for poetry, so she wished to create a permanent stage in England for dance. Baylis required her to recreate traditional and period styles of dancing for her drama productions and suitable divertissement for the interludes of ballet needed in many nineteenth-century operas; Gray worked almost entirely in the expressionist mode and gave her numerous opportunities of working with masks; and now Yeats invited her to enter as collaborator into the world of myth, ritual, and symbolism that found embodiment on his stage.

Given the array and volume of demands upon her energy and invention, de Valois insisted on

---

[7]Gray had taken out the original proscenium architecture at the Festival and built out a deep forestage, which descended by steps to join two aisles that traversed the auditorium from the rear of the stalls. His productions frequently deployed the aisles for entrances and exits, breaking down the customary barrier between performer and spectator. For this and further information about the Festival Theatre during the period of Gray's tenure (including Yeats and Bottomley's visits), see Richard Allen Cave, *Terence Gray and the Cambridge Festival Theatre* (Cambridge: Chadwyck-Healey, 1980), pp. 19–23; and Norman Marshall, *The Other Theatre* (London: John Lehmann, 1947), pp. 54–55.

[8]It was part of de Valois's agreement with Gray that once a term half the program in a chosen week would be given over to her and her dance school to perform a divertissement of short varied pieces. The performances of *The Player Queen* were coupled with such a display of dancing.

[9]Yeats to his wife, May 23, 1927. (See note 6 above.) Baltiboys, de Valois's home, was near Blessington, Co. Wicklow; the brother referred to here was the theater photographer, Gordon Anthony.

[10]See Ninette de Valois, *Step by Step* (London: W. H. Allen, 1977), pp. 181–182. Hereafter cited as *Step by Step*.

one change in the contract with the Abbey: while she would set up and supervise the School, its daily running should be in the hands of one of her own trained assistants. As at the Cambridge Festival there would be evenings when dance would share the program with drama, when pupils from the school would assist her but also be supplemented where necessary by more senior students or staff from her Academy of Choreographic Art in South Kensington.[11] The first performance of the Abbey School was on January 30, 1928, completing a bill that began with a revival of William Boyle's *The Eloquent Dempsey*; de Valois danced four of the ten items she had choreographed; and the program ended with a recreation for her Dublin pupils of *The Curse of the Aspen Tree*, an improvisatory piece deploying masks, which had been first performed at the Cambridge Festival in the dance recital that followed the staging of Yeats's *The Player Queen.*[12] Thereafter, dance performances were given at irregular intervals. This was a remarkable record to sustain in terms of the continual demand for new work, even allowing for the fact that de Valois could (and did) recreate material she had composed for the other theaters where she was engaged.[13]

It was the prospect of a revival of his dance plays at the Abbey in the hands of a sympathetic choreographer that most excited Yeats: the work of the school, though admirable and welcome in itself, would create the taste by which his own most innovative theater work would finally reap its critical reward. Appropriate choreography had been the one seriously missing element in staging those plays for dancers to date: Ito, who performed in *At The Hawk's Well* in 1916, had trained with Dalcroze but had little experience of creating dance as distinct from interpreting the invention of others; and Norah McGuinness, though her designs for *The Only Jealousy of Emer* in 1926 were exquisite and apt, was on her own admission a nerve-wracked amateur in the role of Fand, since she had no skill in improvising movement. Yeats would appear to have supposed that these two, spurred on by his confidence in their abilities, would be inspired to devise movement extempore simply by the context and mood of the plays in which they found themselves. (Yeats, though expert in later years at making and remaking himself, was less

---

[11]The Academy was based at 6A Roland Houses, Roland Gardens, London, SW7. From 1928 advertisements for the school in dance journals announced "*New Branch*: ABBEY THEATRE, DUBLIN"; after 1930 under the main heading there is the simple statement: "LONDON AND DUBLIN," and the name of the current director of the Abbey School is always listed with de Valois and her London assistants as the teaching personnel of the Academy. The advertisements often contain photographs of recent work and include several images of performances at the Abbey. The initial director of the Abbey School from November 1927 was the actress-dancer, Vivienne Bennett, who had been a member of the 1921 Group, de Valois's first attempt at creating a company; Bennett gave a fierce recitation of Ernst Toller's poem, *Rout*, to accompany de Valois's expressionist ballet of the same title to music by Sir Arthur Bliss; the ballet shared the bill at the Festival in January 1927 with Yeats's *On Baile's Strand.* After Bennett left Dublin to pursue her career as an actress at the end of February 1928, her place was taken by Sara Patrick; later from the autumn term of 1931, Nesta Brooking presided until the demise of the school in the summer of 1934.

[12]Lennox Robinson wrote to George Yeats on January 13, 1928, prior to that opening performance: "Ninette de Valois . . . is coming over here on the 23rd to rehearse for a week and do a ballet all the week after at Abbey, she'll bring two people with her [Freda Bamford and Marie Neilson] and of course really it will be all the work of these people plus herself and la Bennett but the Dublin class will be used and we'll pretend to the press and public that this is what we can do after 2 months training!" (courtesy of Ann Saddlemyer). Yeats missed the occasion as he was seriously ill in Cannes. Those first performances were so successful that the houses got larger by the night and seven new pupils enrolled for the classes.

[13]Sometimes the strain was too much: a letter from Lennox Robinson to Yeats (most likely dated November 21, 1929) informs him of "complaints that the ballet is repeating itself. Miss de Valois says, and with justification that without men she can't do much – and the Gaelic Leaguers have been a failure, she is now trying to get young men from the School of Art – still she has pushed up as one of her solo dances 'A Daughter of Eve' which she has done at least twice here before. Anyhow she is penitent and very upset by the notices and it will not occur again" (courtesy of

successful at refashioning others to the image he had of them.) De Valois was to prove the exception, however: she was prepared either to perform to her own previously set choreography or to improvise, as the occasion demanded. She was something of a poet herself and found onstage that she could respond *physically* to the imagery and rhythms of verse or prose that were being spoken around her. From her published accounts of her experience of performing for Yeats, it is clear that she possessed a heightened sensitivity to the poetic dimension of the plays, which by some internal alchemy she could transmute into an embodiment of their aesthetic import: dancing, she *became* symbol.[14]

Her commitment to come to Dublin immediately stimulated Yeats's inspiration. He had seen at Cambridge examples of her solo work and three substantial but strikingly diverse ensemble pieces for students of the London Academy (*Rhythm*, set to music by Beethoven; *Poissons d'Or* set to Debussy; and *The Legend of the Aspen Tree*, set to an arrangement of Hebridean songs by Marjorie Kennedy-Fraser and staged in Dublin in January 1928 as *The Curse of the Aspen Tree*).[15] Here was potential for a danced chorus. With this in mind and de Valois's stricture that, though she was willing to be involved in the dance plays, she would not speak on stage, he set about redesigning *The Only Jealousy of Emer* as their first collaboration in the weeks while the school was being established and he was wintering in Cannes (1927–1928). *Fighting the Waves* was sufficiently drafted by mid-January 1928 for Lennox Robinson to give de Valois a copy for her comments and input. That performances were delayed until August 13, 1929, proved beneficial, since it allowed the collaboration to extend to include a special score by George Antheil and masks by the Dutch sculptor Hildo Krop.[16] Poet, choreographer, composer,

---

Ann Saddlemyer). Shortly after this, programs and the prospectus began to advertise twice weekly evening classes "for business men" on "Wednesday and Friday at 7 o'c" and men were subsequently listed in the casts (though de Valois tended to bring in experienced performers such as Hedley Briggs from England and Arthur Hamilton from Belfast to undertake more demanding roles).

[14] "[Y]ou had to feel more than understand; you had to allow yourself to be absorbed into the whole, never to exist as an isolated part, only as a part of the whole. It became more and more a question of feeling the play rather than intellectually trying to understand every line. In the end there was a fusion; you felt your body and your emotions take part in the spirit of the general production" (*Step by Step*, p. 183). The whole chapter on Yeats in this volume of autobiography contains details of how de Valois prepared to perform in one of the dance plays. For information about Yeats and Michio Ito, see Liam Miller, *The Noble Drama of W. B. Yeats* (Dublin: Dolmen Press, 1977), pp. 224–231. Hereafter cited as *The Noble Drama*. For an account of Yeats's instructions to Norah McGuinness concerning her performance as Fand, see her article, "Young Painter and Elderly Genius," *The Irish Times* (supplement for the Yeats centenary), June 10, 1965.

[15] See the programs for the Festival Theatre for the week beginning May 16, 1927, and for the Abbey Theatre for the week beginning January 30, 1928.

[16] The delays were largely provoked by Antheil's illness, which prevented him from completing the score and its orchestration on time. George Antheil, an American composer championed at this time by Ezra Pound, was possessed of a certain notoriety on account of his flamboyant nature and the iconoclasm of his compositional style (his autobiography was aptly titled *The Bad Boy of Music*); he was later to compose music for Martha Graham's choreography. See *Becoming George*, pp. 416–417 and passim; and George Antheil, *The Bad Boy of Music* (London: Hutchinson, 1947), pp. 180–181. Hildo Krop's sculptures were in a monumental Expressionist mode akin to Jacob Epstein's style and often featured mask-like motifs in his decorative designs for institutional buildings and bridges throughout Amsterdam. Krop designed a number of masks for Dutch productions throughout the 1920s; those deployed at the Abbey were copies of ones he had created for a Dutch production of *The Only Jealousy of Emer* (*Vrouwe Emer's Groote Strijd*) commissioned by the dancer Lili Green and the director Albert Van Dalsum in Amsterdam in 1922. The production had been revived in 1923, 1924, and (with changes of casting) in 1926. Photographs sent to Yeats by Pieter Nicolaas van Eyck of the last revival and of the bronze casts that subsequently Krop had made from the masks prompted Yeats to request Krop to reproduce his work for the Abbey. (See *The Noble Drama*, pp. 272–275 and plates XVIII–XXII, which reproduce the bronze replicas of the masks; and E. J. Lagerweij-Polak, *Hildo Krop: beeldhouwer* [Den Haag: SD / Openbaar kunstbezit, 1992], pp. 52–53 and p. 122.)

artist and scene designer (Dorothy Travers Smith) pooled their expertise to perfect a theater work under Robinson's direction that united all the arts of performance. It was a triumphant vindication of Yeats's aesthetic tenets for the staging of his plays, and vindication too of de Valois's coming to Dublin: that so much had been achieved in a little under two years was impressive.[17]

As if to prove the point but from a more personal perspective, de Valois at her own expense revived the production at the Lyric Theatre, Hammersmith, on March 28, 1930, but with Robinson now directing an English cast, always excepting herself as Fand. Sets, masks, costumes, and music were borrowed from the Abbey, and Constant Lambert conducted Antheil's score. *Fighting the Waves* formed the final item in a program that also included a Festival Theatre production of Gordon Bottomley's *So Fair A Satrap* and two ballet items choreographed by de Valois that had been staged previously at the Old Vic and the Festival (*Les Petits Riens* and *The Picnic*). The single performance at once demonstrated to a London audience the range of de Valois's invention and how firmly she had established herself and the dance in the British theatrical scene.[18] The performance also introduced spectators to an aspect of Yeats's dramaturgy (his plays for dancers) that they had not encountered during touring visits by the Abbey, where the repertoire tended to focus on the more popular of his earlier dramas. While clearly designed to enhance the reputation of herself and her academy, de Valois's event, if only for the space of an afternoon, boldly reclaimed the stage for poetry.

Reviewing the Dublin production of *Fighting the Waves*, the critic for the *Irish Statesman* (August 17, 1929) opined: "This adaptation of Irish material to ballet form is a new graft upon the old Abbey stock which, properly cultivated, will grow ever more fruitful. . . . The experiment as a whole shows that the Abbey is setting its face in the right direction." This must have been gratifying for Yeats and de Valois, but they chose to bide their time before attempting a second experiment, perhaps because of the complexities involved in organizing the required muster of creative talents. In any event *The Dreaming of the Bones* was not staged until December 6, 1931, in a production by Udolphus Wright; de Valois's contribution was confined to devising the general, stylized movement work for the cast and the choreography for the final dance of the agonized, fleeing ghosts. Yeats was attending to the dying Lady Gregory at Coole but made two expeditions to Dublin to start the rehearsals and then oversee the final (dress) rehearsal and attend the single performance. (The play was given during an evening called "Mainly Ballet: the Abbey Directors' Sunday Entertainments," which, as Yeats informed Olivia Shakespear, were designed "to keep our audiences together until the company returns from America.")[19] What is revealing (and, to the theater historian, annoying) about all reviews of the dance performances

---

[17]*The Irish Times* of August 14, 1929, noted that "at the fall of the curtain the audience gave free rein to its enthusiasm," while the review in the *Dublin Evening Mail* the same day described the production as an "experiment, but an enthralling and, indeed, noble one." Hildo Krop attended the performance and afterward, when addressing the audience, an unusually modest Yeats (according to the same *Times* review) asserted: "Your thanks are due to the actors, the producer, the musician, the dancers and the mask-maker. My part has been but small." The house, according to Lily Yeats, was crowded, with numerous people left standing (letter from Lily Yeats to Ruth Lane-Poole, dated August 18, 1929, courtesy of Ann Saddlemyer).

[18]Though billed to appear in the lead role in *Les Petits Riens*, de Valois withdrew from that performance as she had injured her foot, but she did undertake the role of Fand.

[19]The letter is dated by John Kelly as written on November 22, 1931 (Wade records the postmark as November 23. See *Letters*, p. 785.) In its review of the performance *The Irish Times* (December 7, 1931) recorded that Yeats addressed the audience at the close, informing them "that it was the intention of the Abbey Theatre to present a few similar programs on Sunday evenings during the absence of the Abbey Company in America. Miss de Valois had found a large

at the Abbey is a total inability on the part of critics to *read* movement language in a manner that would allow them to write informatively on the subject. The article in the *Irish Independent* (December 7, 1931) mentions appreciatively that "the play was magnificently performed"; praises in general terms the contributions of Joseph O'Neill as the Singer and W. O'Gorman as the Young Man; goes into more detail about the melodic qualities of John Stephenson's voice (in the role of Diarmuid, the male ghost), and its aptness for the demands of Yeats's dramatic verse; but the sole comment on the movement is praise of Stephenson's "graceful miming with Nesta Brooking" (Devorgilla) as demonstrating "his versatility in dramatic art." Earlier the dance content of the evening's program overall is loosely described as possessing a "rare beauty and interest." But there was no denying the success of the venture and the production was revived for a longer run from April 12, 1932.

No new production or restaging of one of the dance plays occurred for over a year (Lady Gregory died May 22, 1932; the Yeatses moved to Riversdale during July; and from mid-October to late the following January Yeats was lecturing in America). The next full-scale collaborative venture, a revival of *At The Hawk's Well*, ran from July 25, 1933; though the first staged of the plays for dancers, this was its first public performance (two earlier productions had been held in private drawing rooms: Lady Cunard's in Cavendish Square, London, in 1916 and Yeats's in Merrion Square in 1924). De Valois inherited (and actually fitted perfectly) Ito's costume as the Hawk/Guardian of the Well, but she devised her own choreography. She had had considerable experience over her years as performer and choreographer of how dance can advance even a quite intricate narrative, define psychological nuances or shifting power relations between characters, and bring a disturbing immediacy to the invasion of a mundane world by a metaphysical dimension of reality (to be seen perhaps at its finest in her ballet, *Job*, inspired throughout by William Blake's illustrations to that book of the Old Testament). Unlike many creators of the role, including Ito, de Valois worked for a more complex effect than merely imitating the aggressive wing-beat and swooping power of a hawk: the dance must evoke at once a bird of prey *and* the supernatural powers of a woman of the Sidhe, who is also in some measure the young Cuchulain's daemon or destiny. (Cuchulain himself is unsure of the identity of the figure who confronts him: "I am not afraid of you, bird, woman or witch,"[20] and she appears to him both threatening and alluring.) In his later dance plays (*The Death of Cuchulain*, *The King of the Great Clock Tower*, *A Full Moon in March*) Yeats tends to offer a scenario in his stage directions, which the dance must follow; or one of the performers outlines the scenario in an introductory speech (*Calvary*); or one who watches the event gives a rapt account even as it is played out before his gaze (*The Dreaming of the Bones*). But in *At The Hawk's Well* there is no directly articulated schema; the significance of it all has to be inferred from the dance itself read in conjunction with the terrified reactions of the chorus of Musicians and the comments of Cuchulain, as he is steadily drawn from the role of spectator of a solo to participate in a duet of what are increasingly dueling bodies. That Yeats envisaged a sustained interlude of dance moving through a gamut of emotional moods and psychological tensions can be deduced from

---

audience for ballet in London, and he hoped that an audience for such programmes could be gathered in Dublin." Was the intention modeled on the work of the Camargo Society in London, in which de Valois played an active part? This group held irregular gatherings, usually at the Mercury Theatre and generally on Sunday evenings, with the aim of promoting the art of the dance (and ballet particularly) in England. Its most significant achievement was to give early choreographic opportunities to Frederick Ashton as well as to de Valois, who that very same year had created *Job* under their auspices (first staged July 5, 1931).

[20] *VPl*, 409.

his reiterated direction: "*The dance goes on for some time. . . . The dance goes on.*"[21] De Valois interpreted the text as requiring her to devise three distinct phases of movement: "an evocation of brooding power, through suggestive seduction to the violent ecstasy of a wild bird" and the resulting choreography was by turns threatening, erotic, exhilarating.[22]

Of special note is the context in which this revival was situated: *At The Hawk's Well* shared a triple bill with two other dance works, *The Drinking Horn* and *Bluebeard*, which were also choreographed by de Valois. The first, to music and a scenario by Arthur Duff, was a fairytale ballet, danced by the pupils of the Abbey School, involving an elf, lovers, a mysterious flute player, and an armed knight guarding a sacred well. It clearly dealt in a lighthearted way with similar motifs to Yeats's dance play; but, being couched in terms of a more traditional balletic fantasy, it nicely offset the Noh-inspired rigor, refined stylization, and developed stage symbolism of his work. *Bluebeard*, described by its author (Mary Devenport O'Neill) as a "ballet poem," was a reworking of the familiar tale as a dance drama but one shaped to a structure very different from that which Yeats had been perfecting.[23] Though not wholly successful, *Bluebeard* was a valuable experiment at this point in time, partly because it contrasted so pointedly with the powerfully allusive economy and psychological intensity of the Yeatsian form, but also because it showed that other dramatists were being attracted by revivals of this aspect of his dramaturgy, by the success of the Abbey School of Dance, and by the innovative skills of de Valois as choreographer and performer, to respond to the specific challenges of the genre. Had de Valois not resigned the following year, it is conceivable that, building on such strong foundations, a tradition of movement-based, poetic drama might have been established steadily at the Abbey with the trained personnel necessary for its staging.

But de Valois tendered her resignation in the early months of 1934 at a meeting with Yeats in Liverpool: "'And who,' he said, gazing elsewhere as usual, 'will do my Plays for Dancers?'"[24] To anyone closely following de Valois's career over the preceding months, her decision should not have come as a surprise. Her work with Gray at the Festival Theatre had ended during the summer of 1933, when he quit theater business for good; her responsibilities had largely been taken over by Hedley Briggs and Sara Patrick in recent seasons, though the periodic evenings of dance performances by her school continued. Her work for Lilian Baylis had, however, flourished: both women had quickly come to respect each other's crusading vision and indefatigable stamina in realizing objectives. When by the end of the decade Baylis had acquired Sadler's Wells Theatre in addition to the Old Vic, she was persuaded to incorporate into the renovations there provision for a dance studio to house de Valois's school. Sadler's Wells reopened on January 6, 1931; and the following May 5 a first full evening of dance was offered

[21]Ibid., pp. 409–410.

[22]Kathrine Sorley Walker, *Ninette de Valois: Idealist without Illusions* (London: Hamish Hamilton, 1987), p. 131. Hereafter cited as *Ninette de Valois*. The same ideas were reiterated by de Valois (almost verbatim) in an interview with me in August 1976.

[23]Arthur Duff was a Dublin composer, organist, and one-time first bandmaster of the Irish Army School of Music; his orchestral works, impressionistic in feeling, were noted for the tonal coloring he achieved with wind and brass instrumentation and for his inventive use of the idioms of Irish folk music. A prompt copy of Mary Devenport O'Neill's *Bluebeard* is in the National Library of Ireland. This shows that the dramatist's focus was on the discoveries of the Duke's seventh wife, Ilina (played by de Valois), about the fate of her predecessors and her attempts to resist with the help of her brothers what she foretells is to be her fate. The drama pursues a linear development in which sequences of mime and dancing are framed by verse commentaries or meditations by a male and female attendant (Joseph O'Neill and Ria Mooney) to the accompaniment of a vocal quartet.

[24]*Step by Step*, p. 186.

at the Old Vic. By the end of that year the Vic-Wells Ballet had come into existence, realizing de Valois's cherished dream of founding an English dance company.[25] Though she had established her company's early reputation chiefly with new choreography, she promptly set herself the task of building up and extending her dancers' expertise to enable them to take into the repertoire the major full-scale "classics": *Coppelia, Giselle, Casse-Noisette, Le Lac des Cygnes*.[26] All this, while managing a company and continuing to choreograph herself: it was clear where the focus of her energies and future commitment had to lie. But she honored one last appearance for Yeats and in a program where she alone featured as dancer without the school in attendance: *The King of the Great Clock Tower* concluded a triple bill comprising also a revival of Lennox Robinson's *Church Street* and the first production of Yeats's *The Resurrection*.

The Composition of *The King of the Great Clock Tower*: Manuscripts, Revisions, and a Performance Text

That Yeats had begun writing a new dance drama by early November 1933, long before de Valois gave him the occasion for its staging, is evident from a letter he wrote to Olivia Shakespear on November 11; he enclosed two stanzas, which were designed to be sung at "the opening of the curtain." Noticeably there was to be no repetition of the ritual folding and unfolding of a cloth, which had signaled the ceremonial beginning of the plays for dancers; from the first (presumably as a consequence of the success of the recent stagings of those earlier plays) Yeats appears to have intended his new work for the Abbey. The lyric reads as follows:

First musician (singing)
I wait until the tower gives forth the chime;
And dream of ghosts that have the speech of birds;
Because they have no thoughts they have no words;
No thought because no past or future; Time
Comes from the torture of our flesh, and these
~~Their spires of smoke about the sacred grove,~~
Cast out by death and tethered there by love,
~~Make but one ghost whenever fancy please.~~
Touch nerve to nerve throughout the sacred grove
And seem a single creature when they please

[25]Having proved herself as an arranger of dances for Shakespeare and opera, de Valois had been invited to stage short works to accompany short operas. Steadily de Valois encouraged the ever-cautious Baylis to increase the frequency of occasional evenings of choreography: first one and then two evenings of the week's program at her two theaters were soon devoted wholly to dance.

[26]Several one-act pieces created for Diaghilev by Russian choreographer Michel Fokine were already on offer: these included *Les Sylphides*, *Le Spectre de la Rose*, and *Carnaval* as vehicles, respectively, for dancers Markova, Dolin, and Helpmann. *Coppelia* had been mounted in March 1933; then in rapid succession *Giselle* opened at the Old Vic on January 1, 1934, and *Casse-Noisette* at Sadler's Wells on January 30, while *Le Lac des Cygnes* was planned for November 20. (This was a full staging of the work; the company had performed act 2 since October 1932.) De Valois's own choreographic output was prodigious: in 1934 before crossing over to Dublin to rehearse for Yeats's play in July, she had completed the choreography and staging of two markedly contrasting ballets: *The Haunted Ballroom* for her own company (Sadler's Wells, April 3) and *Bar aux Folies-bergère* for Marie Rambert (Mercury Theatre, May 15).

Second musician (singing)
I call to mind the iron of the bell
And get from that my harsher imagery,
All love is shackled to mortality,
Love's image is a man-at-arms in steel;
Love's image is a woman made of stone;
It dreams of the unborn; all else is nought;
To morrow and to morrow fills its thought;
~~It keeps all tenderness~~
~~All tenderness reserves~~ for that alone.
All tenderness reserves

Yeats indicates to Olivia Shakespear that "the chiming bells" referred to in the opening line are to be a central feature of the ensuing drama and, after the stanzas, he observes that the "inner ideas in these lines" will provide the theme of his play: "One might say the love of the beloved seeks eternity, that of the child seeks time."[27] Allan Wade in editing the letter identifies the lines as intended for *The King of the Great Clock Tower*, then concludes his footnote with the comment: "By the time the play came to be published they had been completely rewritten."[28] This is not strictly true. Phrases from the First Musician's speech are carried over into the final version of the play: the idea of lovers or enamored ghosts having "the speech of birds" because, being beyond thought, they have no need for words; they are beyond the need for thinking because they are free of the constrictions of time ("No thought because no past or future") and are free of time, because they exist in a state of complete ecstasy ("Touch nerve to nerve throughout the sacred grove"). Where the published text differs is in its sustaining this evocation of amatory bliss, which is now deliberately compared with the experience of Oisin with Niamh in the Danaan Land of Promise. This intertextual reference to *The Wanderings of Oisin* (1889) is the first of several relating to his early narrative and dramatic writings that, as composition advanced, Yeats would introduce into the play. What would in time be excised is the Second Musician's depiction of an alternative world where "love is shackled to mortality" by the lover's awareness of the demands of time ("I call to mind the iron of the bell"); yet some degree of the threat that dominates this stanza lingers in the final text as a dark undertone to the celebratory mood. There the First Attendant's opening speech concludes by depicting the absolute transcendence of lovers through the image of them as "bobbins where all time is bound and wound," the Second Attendant promptly transmutes the metaphor into an allusion to the thread of an individual's destiny which, were it once to "run loose," might casually be severed by the Fates (the Norns). Later the First Attendant's evocation of Oisin's joyful play in the world of the Sidhe records the distant "beating of a bell"; it may go unheeded now, but we recall from Yeats's poem that the sound of a bell will eventually bring the hero memories of the human world to which fatally he will choose to return. The two central lines of the draft for the Second Musician's speech ("Love's image is a man-at-arms in steel; / Love's image is a woman made of stone;") are not carried over directly into subsequent versions, but they do recur, embodied now in the stage tableau revealed to spectators as the Attendants open the inner curtains: a King, who must be armed at least with a sword, and a Queen who, unnervingly still

[27]Transcribed from a copy of the original provided by Special Collections and University Archives, Frank Melville Jr. Memorial Library, Stony Brook University. See *Letters*, p. 817.

[28]Ibid.

and silent, is soon to be cruelly harassed by him for being "an image of stone or wood." The formative influence of these sixteen lyrical lines may perhaps end there in respect of the play, but their fusion of the metaphysical and the erotic within the context of a fierce opposition of the transcendent with the temporal anticipates the thematic focus of several of the poems that in time will comprise the *Supernatural Songs* (especially, "Ribh at the Tomb of Baile and Aillinn"), which were all conceived in the period when Yeats began revising *The King of the Great Clock Tower* and transforming it into *A Full Moon in March.*

The letter to Olivia Shakespear gives no indication what the content of the ensuing play was to be, beyond vague, overly abstract intimations about its theme, so one cannot be certain at what point in the composition Yeats began developing the narrative of the conflict of King and Stroller for the attentions of the Queen and its powerful central image of the dance with the severed head, which then miraculously sings of its gratitude. In line with several motifs in the play where Yeats seems intent on drawing informed spectators' awareness to his own earlier writings, the narrative recalls the story "The Binding of the Hair" in the 1897 edition of *The Secret Rose* in which (as Yeats states in his Commentary on the play) "a certain man [Aodh] swears to sing the praise of a certain woman [Queen Dectira], his head is cut off and the head sings."[29] Yeats admits that dramatizing this story brought him "close" to Wilde's *Salome* but tries to shrug off possible charges of plagiarism with the observation that "in his [Wilde's] play the dance is before the head is cut off."[30] While this is undeniably true, the plays do have much in common nonetheless. Yeats had seen his friend Charles Ricketts's production of *Salome* in 1906 when the lighting scheme in particular excited him to attempt something similar at the Abbey some weeks later when he and Robert Gregory staged Yeats's *The Shadowy Waters.*[31] It is equally possible that Ninette de Valois, to whom the versified form of the play was dedicated, was (consciously or unconsciously) an influence on the subject matter. Over the period of their working relationship she had devised choreography for three differently accomplished actresses in the role of Salome: Vivienne Bennett and Beatrix Lehmann (1929 and 1931, respectively, at the Festival Theatre, Cambridge) and Margaret Rawlings (1931 at the Gate Theatre, London). She had herself danced as Salome in a version of the choreography devised for Rawlings titled *The Dancer's Reward* (December 15, 1931) for a Camargo Society Midnight Ballet Party at the Carlton Theatre.[32] However, this had been simply what has come to be known from Wilde's stage direction as "the dance of the seven veils." The full role would have suited de Valois in many ways (she was noted for her soubrette performances in ballet, and her stage persona also embraced an earthy lyricism and tragic intensity), but she resolutely refused to speak on stage. She and Yeats met regularly at this time in Dublin or London, and it is difficult to imagine

---

[29]*The Secret Rose* (London: Lawrence & Bullen, 1897); *The King of the Great Clock Tower*, pp. 19–20.

[30]*The King of the Great Clock Tower*, p. 20.

[31]Ricketts had died in 1931, but two of Yeats's friends had kept his memory alive: Gordon Bottomley had published an extended obituary with illustrations, "Charles Ricketts R. A." in *Theatre Arts Monthly* in 1932; and Sturge Moore had edited with a detailed introduction, *Charles Ricketts, R. A.: Sixty-Five Illustrations* for Cassel in 1933. For an account of Yeats's work with Robert Gregory on *The Shadowy Waters*, see Richard Allen Cave, "Robert Gregory: Artist and Stage Designer" in *Lady Gregory: Fifty Years After*, ed. Ann Saddlemyer and Colin Smythe (Gerrard's Cross: Colin Smythe, 1987), pp. 382–383.

[32]A photograph of de Valois in what appear to be rehearsal clothes for this performance was included in the *Daily Express* for December 14, 1931; it shows her accompanied by Ursula Moreton and Marie Nielson, who had played Salome's "slaves" throughout the month-long run of the play with Margaret Rawlings at the Gate Theatre from May 27, 1931. Performances of Wilde's play were followed each evening by *Danses Divertisements* given by de Valois with Hedley Briggs.

them not discussing her activities on the English scene, given his avid interest in all forms of experimental or alternative theater. *The King of the Great Clock Tower* was the only new play to emerge from their creative partnership of six years. Is it possible to view the play as a witty theatrical conceit that reworks *Salome*-related material while respecting de Valois's self-imposed veto about speaking? The result is a play, constructed around a great silence, in which the power of the body as a medium of intense expressiveness becomes ultimately the dominant means to shape meaning.

Nothing remains extant of that initial draft other than the version of the opening lyric copied for Olivia Shakespear. The surviving manuscript or typescript materials reveal the full play already in a developed form, with the opening lyric thoroughly revised and the thematic opposition of two styles of loving (the one transcending time, the other constricted by it) now fully embodied in the action and in the contrasting figures of King and Stranger/Stroller. How long a period of time elapsed between the initial sketch and the extant full versions of the play is difficult to determine precisely. Some help with dating is proffered by the cover of what appears to be the third item in the sequence, the typescript (SIUC 91/16/10). This is one of two surviving copies of the six that Yeats asked to be made after he had revised the typed version (SIUC 76/1/7) of his holograph text (NLI 8769); it is bound into a light brown cardboard cover on which in his hand is penned "Corrected April 1934." Also three letters to friends dated earlier in 1934 refer to his working on *The King of the Great Clock Tower* after his return to Dublin in the New Year. To Edmund Dulac (January 13) he states he has been "putting the last touches to a new dance play which will be danced this year at the Abbey," while to Olivia Shakespear (January 27) he announces that, despite having to proceed slowly because of a lingering cold, the play has now been finished, adding the detail that "there are four lyrics including the one I sent you though altogether rewritten" before contextualizing his intentions with an intimate admission: "I made up the play that I might write lyrics out of dramatic experience, all my personal experience having in some strange way come to an end. They are good lyrics a little in my early manner." To John Masefield (February 2) he confesses to the same motive for writing and adds further details about a potential staging:

> I have been writing verse again. I found that all my personal material seemed to have disappeared and so, to find out whether age had finished me or not, I made a little dramatic structure which required four lyrics, a dance play. I think they are as good as anything I have done lately; a musician [Arthur Duff] is now at work on the play which will be done at the Abbey some time this year.[33]

(Reference to his fears about his creativity were in time to inform the opening paragraph of Yeats's Preface to the Cuala edition.) Revisions to the play, however, did not end with that "corrected" copy in April. Subtle but significant changes were made both during rehearsals and later when he came to prepare the text for publication in the journal *Life and Letters* and by the Cuala Press.

The relative neatness of the surviving manuscript (NLI 8769) suggests that this may in large part be a copy by Yeats of earlier "foul papers." The narrative advances through its various stages at roughly the same pace as in the final version; some deletions tighten the expression

---

[33]I am indebted to John Kelly for drawing my attention to this information in the letters to Dulac and Masefield. The letter to Olivia Shakespear is published in full in *Letters*, p. 819.

dramatically; the most substantial changes are first to the title page with its list of characters and initial stage directions, as Yeats envisages the demands of mounting the play at the Peacock Theatre as an alternative to the main stage at the Abbey; and secondly to the opening lyric (already much altered from the version sent to Olivia Shakespear) where phrases are reworked to achieve greater clarity of definition or for better euphony. The handwriting gets larger and slacker as the pages advance but this seems the result of tiredness at copying a substantial text, rather than provoked by an excited burst of inspiration.

The typescript copy of the manuscript (SIUC 76/1/7) is revised throughout to correct lineation, punctuation, and spelling. The major revisions relate to staging and to the details of the Stranger's oath, where the original claim made in the tavern that the Queen will dance for him is extended to include the further idea that in return he will sing. And when the claims are confidently repeated, the sequence of prophesied events (including the further detail sanctioned by the god Aengus that the Queen will kiss him) are now enumerated and accompanied by a direction requiring the actor to count each stage upon his fingers. The insolent challenge in this now motivates a new stage direction marking the Stranger's exit, where "(THE STRANGER goes out Right)" is changed to "(The king forces the stranger out to R.)" before the verb is altered to the yet more violent "thrusts." Yeats is beginning to sharpen the individualizing traits of the two men and is finding in consequence ways of using the language of gesture to heighten the contrast. This whole version shows him visualizing the play in performance to a remarkably powerful degree: most of the substantive changes or, more usually, additions to the text relate to the appearance of the characters, their costumes and masks, and to the setting and spatial organization of the stage and the actors within it. Gone here are the references to a staging in the Peacock, and a complex series of curtains and screens are envisaged as framing the action, while the major characters are now boldly distinguished in red, orange, and black against a background of blue, shading upward from dark to light. All references to an orchestra are cut, as is the mention of specific instruments "drum, gong, zither and flute"; but the directions for the positioning of the severed head in relation to King and Queen and for the Queen's dance with the head are becoming more fully realized in his imagination. That Yeats wished to avoid any cultural reference that might carry specific temporal or ethnic resonance (evident in his deploying only abstract color relations in the décor) is further supported by four small sketches for the thrones on the back of this copy, where baroque extravagance gives place rapidly to the stark formalism of a simple cube. Though the first mention of the cubes in the stage directions (copied from the manuscript version) posits them ("may be") as a stylistic choice, all subsequent references, which are added to this text, make their use prescriptive ("should be . . . are"). A final detail, which also relates to performance, is the decision to assign the opening lyric differently between the two Musicians/Attendants. In the manuscript version they were each initially assigned a complete stanza, but Yeats had second thoughts and crossed this through. In the typescript the opening line of each stanza has been assigned to one performer and the remaining seven lines to the other. In the revisions to the list of characters the two male Attendants are distinguished as to vocal range: one is to be bass and one tenor. Yeats, however, had trouble, both in the initial listing and in the ascription of the actual lines, in deciding which performer should possess which particular timbre. Clearly the choice would impact on how especially the isolated line was received and interpreted by an audience. Once it was decided that the Second Attendant should be the tenor, then the ascription of the lines later in the action where one of the attendants speaks for the Queen had to be given to him, while the song of the severed head had to be assigned to the bass. It is not surprising, given the performance-oriented nature of his holograph revisions to this typescript, that Yeats should have been sufficiently satisfied with the result to demand that "6 copies" be made in readiness for the play going into rehearsal.

What is remarkable about the sequence of manuscript materials for *The King of the Great Clock Tower* (unlike those for most of Yeats's other plays) is that they allow one to watch a *performance text* steadily come into being. Of the two surviving copies of the six that he asked to be made of the typescript SIUC 76/1/7, both NLI 29,550(1) and SIUC 91/16/10 contain information about the use of music in the production: one in relation to the moment that the Queen stirs into movement; the other giving instructions for the placing on stage and use of a drum and gong by the two Attendants. This suggests, as indeed was the case, that the eventual production used both the orchestral music composed by Duff (included in the appendixes) and percussive accompaniments to certain moments in the action created by two of the actors (the stage directions are revised to require the drum to indicate the knocking of the Stranger "upon the great door" and the gong to mark the striking of midnight in the Great Clock Tower). And Yeats changed his idea about the disposition of the vocal ranges for the opening lyric, reversing the assigning of the lines so that the gnomic introductions to each of the two stanzas were now given to the bass voice while the dominant voice overall was to be the tenor. This second copy (SIUC 91/16/10) also incorporates the addition ("sat there an image of stone or wood") to the King's opening address to the silent Queen, which exactly crystallizes his utter exasperation. More searchingly Yeats begins in this same copy to revise the last three lines of the final stanza of the song for the severed head. These had remained unchanged since the manuscript version, but in that first formulation the expression and its constituent idea lack focus: it seems as if the head is urging the one-time Stranger, now a ghostly phantom, to join with the legendary beings listed earlier in the song, who have all achieved immortality in art because their lives exemplified "heroic wantonness." (To be precise, this is by virtue of Yeats's own artistry, since the "images" are all drawn from his own early poetry, drama, and fiction.) The particularized injunction, "Grip the saddle tight with your knees" is replaced here by an evocation of urgency, "Image, image, up and away," if the phantom is to join the host in its eager flight. There is greater clarity, energy, and drama in the expression now, but it is still in a different stylistic vein from the pithy and immediately recognizable portrait studies of Cuchulain, Niam, Hanrahan, and the rest contained in the preceding lines. Yeats remained unsure of the appropriateness of the change and was to revise the lines yet further. This text forms the copy bearing the cover with the annotation "Corrected April 1934." All the versions discussed so far, therefore, were the fruit of an intense period of creativity during the months from January to April of that year.

Accurately dating the typescript NLI 29,550(2) is not easy. The two bound copies that precede it in the overall sequence may have been designed for circulation among the personnel to be involved in staging the play (director, choreographer, composer, designer, mask maker) rather than at this stage for use in the rehearsal room; several of the annotations, especially those incorporated into NLI 29,550(1), would suggest that this was the case; the presence of SIUC 91/16/10 in a collection of Lennox Robinson's papers at Carbondale, which includes a number of other play scripts, supports this idea. (A more heavily annotated script used in rehearsals would most likely have been kept in the theater as prompt copy for use during the run of performances and to assist in staging any subsequent revivals.) The typescript would seem to have been prepared from SIUC 91/16/10, since it incorporates all the revisions made to that "corrected" copy, but it also bears traces (not always in Yeats's hand) of having been used in rehearsal; it may therefore be the sole survivor of several intended for the cast. Given the nature of the annotations made on it, this typescript must have been completed by the time rehearsals started in mid-July (Yeats himself first attended a rehearsal on his return from Rapallo on July 24).[34] The most important inclusion with this version is a penciled sketch in the form of a floor plan of the stage showing the disposition of the sets of curtains, the screens, the four cube-shaped thrones, and an entrance for the Stranger situated downstage right (which is also where the King will move to retrieve the mask which represents the severed head); the placing of the two Attendants before the inner curtain; the positioning of King and Queen at the start of the play; and of the severed head and the King immediately before the dance commences. The sketch is most likely the work of Lennox Robinson (what are clearly his annotations later in the text are made with the same heavy, broad-pointed pencil), but it realizes Yeats's prescriptions exactly and adds immeasurably to one's sense of how the play appeared in performance.

Though the play had gone into rehearsal, the text had by no means taken its final shape: NLI 29,550(2) is not an accurate record of the actual performance text. Some significant changes and additions were made, which can be gauged only by comparing that typescript with the two texts published later in 1934, first in *Life and Letters* in November and then by the Cuala Press. Yeats often revised plays in light of his experience of them in performance before he submitted the texts for publication, but the printed texts here for once appear to record what actually happened on stage at the Abbey on the opening night of July 30 and throughout the play's run. The Cuala text prints a surprising addition in the form of a bracketed note after the final song in which Yeats states first that what one has just read is what was enacted, but then records his dissatisfaction with the closing lyrics as performed and makes suggestions about what to him is a fitting compromise. The penciled note "Insert 2 new verses" at the end of the typescript NLI 29,550(2) anticipates what had occurred. Yeats frequently at this time mentioned a fear that his creativity was at an end; and the play, as discussed above, had been conceived in part to test whether his powers were indeed on the wane, the drama being an occasion for writing verse lyrics. Four such lyrics had been required for *The King of the Great Clock Tower* and their completion seemed proof that his powers were intact. Throughout June, which he spent in Rapallo, he had put his inspiration to further testing, spurred on by the acquisition of a new, leather-bound notebook. Though Curtis Bradford has argued that "Yeats seldom used his bound manuscript books methodically, starting on page 1 and going to the end," every indication (sustained choice of writing medium, sequences of pages devoted to a given work until its virtual completion has been achieved rather than its composition being dotted about within a notebook) suggests that this volume was handled for the most part systematically and in chronological order as regards the composition of specific items.[35]

The first sustained lyrical composition in the Rapallo notebook is what in time became "Why

[34] So Yeats informed Olivia Shakespear in a letter dated July 25. I am indebted to John Kelly for this information.

[35] Curtis Bradford, *W. B. Yeats at Work* (Carbondale: Southern Illinois University Press, 1965), p. 114. In the Rapallo notebook, if composition of a particular work is disrupted by what seems to be a more pressing demand on Yeats's attention, then he takes up drafting the first work again on the next page after the completion of the second. For example, on 8^{v} he starts drafting what will become the lyric, "He had famished in a wilderness" but leaves off composing this from 9^{v} to 10^{v}, while he completes on those pages a version of the Preface to the Cuala text of *The King of the Great Clock Tower.* The lyric is taken up again and virtually completed on 11^{rv} and 12^{r}. Similarly the prose scenario for *A Full Moon in March* runs from 26^{v} to 32^{v} but is interrupted between 28^{r} and 30^{r} for a series of astrological readings and calculations for the months of October through December 1934. One possible exception to this is the composition of the "New Song for the Severed Head" that was included in the versified version of *The King of the Great Clock Tower*, but this will be dealt with later in this introduction.

must those holy, haughty feet descend," the closing song from *A Full Moon in March*. The drafts begin in earnest on the verso of page 5 and continue to the recto of page 7, though on the verso of page 4 and again at the base of the recto of page 5, there are scraps of verse ("What is makes those haughty feet descend," "Has mixed the delicate raddle into white," "What thing they seek," "For desecration and the lover's night" and finally "Out of the marble nitches [*sic*] they descend / Painted by some great masters") which remarkably form the heart of the poem that was to emerge. The lyric clearly sprang from the same flow of inspiration as the play, and, though Yeats was ultimately to position it differently, his first decision was to include it as a continuation of the final lyric of *The King of the Great Clock Tower*. Though the two published texts include all three stanzas and Arthur Duff set three stanzas to music, Yeats's note in the Cuala edition intimates that only two were actually performed at the Abbey, undoubtedly the "2 new verses" referred to in a penciled note found on the final page of NLI 29,550(2).[36] Experience taught Yeats that in performance, if this further lyric were included, "there was too much music between the end of the dance and the descent of the curtain" and he recommended its omission.

There is a problematic manuscript in the collections of the National Library of Ireland (NLI 30,800) that comprises a single sheet of paper headed "(continue on page 11 as follows)"; it gives a direction about "the inner curtain" and the position of the Attendants relative to it before writing out a reasonably clean version of "Why must those holy, haughty feet descend," which assigns the lines between two Attendants. There are some significant variant readings from the Cuala text, especially in the first, third, and fifth lines of the first stanza; and the penultimate line of the third stanza is revised to be phrased as it ultimately appeared in print. The problem is to which later version of the play was it to be attached as page 11? SIUC 91/16/10 runs to fifteen pages, while NLI 29,550(2) runs to only six, and so too does the text in *Life and Letters*.[37] The Cuala text alone ends the lyric "O, but I saw a solemn sight" on page 10. The Cuala Press Time Book, covering the period March 1934 to October 1938, in the Cuala Archive at Trinity College, Dublin (Press. A, box 1, no. 5) shows that the setting of *The Great Clock Tower* volume began on May 21, which is well before the play went into rehearsal at the Abbey, and that a first set of proofs was taken precisely one month later (June 21–23); two further sets of proofs labeled "Revised Proofs B & C" were taken on August 24; but correcting was not undertaken until September 1–3. The long gap in time between the taking of the first set of proofs and proofs B and C would allow for changes to be incorporated in consequence of Yeats's experience of the play in production. Two sets of page proofs (CDML) and the revised proofs (NLI 30,020)

---

[36]One might suppose that the third, most difficult stanza was the one omitted in performance and that stanzas one and two only were performed, but the evidence suggests otherwise. Duff's melodic line and its harmonic accompaniment is virtually identical for each stanza so it would have been possible to move from the concluding phrase of the second stanza straight to the short musical refrain that ends the composition. However, though Duff set three stanzas to music, the text he used for the third stanza is not that which Yeats designated his preferred version but the stanza that is printed in the Cuala edition as an alternative for use in performance. For the reasons given above, it would be equally as easy to move from the closing phrase of stanza one to the short musical introduction to the alternative version of stanza three, omitting stanza two in its entirety. That this was what happened in performance seems likely, since the alternative version would appear to have been composed by Yeats as antiphonal to the opening stanza, answering many of the questions that are posed there. There are a number of variant readings in the words for this lyric that Duff set to music, which differ from either of the printed texts.

[37]It could not be easily attached to any of the drafts of *A Full Moon in March* for similar reasons concerning pagination; and moreover the revised stage direction is closer to those for the earlier play than the later at this stage of the action.

survive; both contain the full three stanzas of "Why must those holy, haughty feet descend"; in both they run over from page 10 to page 11. CDML exactly reproduces the opening stage direction as written in the manuscript (NLI 30,800), but it is corrected there to read as it appears in the revised proof and the published Cuala text. (This evidence would suggest that CDML is to be identified as proof B and NLI 30,020 as proof C; no copy of the first proof survives.) More importantly, a first (incomplete) attempt at phrasing the two questions that comprise the fifth line of the first stanza of the lyric ("~~What thing they seek and wherefore they~~") is heavily scored through in its entirety in NLI 30,800, while a second attempt is heavily emended too; most of the first question is canceled ("What ~~do they seek~~") and the alternative reading ("What are they seeking") is crammed tightly between these two cancellations. This may account for the complete omission of the line in CDML, which necessitates a penciled insertion by Yeats to give the reading ("What do they seek for? why must they descend?"); this is copied into the revised proof and published text. There is a further complexity. In the *Life and Letters* text, the whole fifth line of the stanza is omitted, exactly as in CDML; also the phrasing of the third line of the song ("Ran such a delicate raddle . . . ") shares a reading common to NLI 30,800 and CDML, which was revised to "Ran that delicate raddle . . . " for the Cuala edition. Was the *Life and Letters* text of *The King of the Great Clock Tower* set from the proof B of the Cuala edition, corrected and revised (a non-extant copy of CDML to which similar emendations had been added)? The evidence would suggest that this was so. The text of NLI 30,800 ends with the direction, "The stage curtain falls," after the third stanza of the lyric. No manuscript draft survives of the note Yeats subsequently added at this point, which offers an alternative final stanza; but the text of the note as printed in CDML is considerably extended by penciled additions to reach a version akin to that which appears in the revised proof, NLI 30,020 (though it differs in some details). What the existence of NLI 30,800 suggests is that Yeats was undecided whether or not to include the three stanzas of "Why must those holy, haughty feet descend" in the printed text of *The King of the Great Clock Tower,* given his dissatisfaction with them in performance. Opting to include them prompted him then to draft the note admitting to his dissatisfaction and suggesting the omission of the last song in any future staging. The decision to include the song at all may have been motivated by the same impulse that led to his finding a place within the Cuala publication for all the lyrics he had completed since beginning work on the play: as certain and reassuring proof that his lyrical inspiration had not dried up with age. NLI 30,800 may be something of an enigma, but its existence may help to explain a number of curious features concerning the publishing history of *The King of the Great Clock Tower*. It also supplements the body of surviving evidence determining what the performance-text actually comprised.

Situated earlier than the drafting of the lyric "Why must those holy, haughty feet descend" in the Rapallo notebook (and therefore possibly earlier in time of composition) are two other experiments that had an impact on the published text. On the verso of the first page under the heading "A new song for the severed head in Clock Tower" appears a first attempt at what would in time become the song for the Stroller's head in the versified format of *The King of the Great Clock Tower*. Yeats's sudden dissatisfaction with his original song, and particularly with its concluding stanza, had not been assuaged by his corrections to SIUC 91/16/10, and, once resident in Italy, this was interestingly one of the first creative matters he addressed. If the material seemed sufficiently intractable to be abandoned at this stage, it was perhaps because it embraced a whole new set of ideas about the potential for erotic contact between the living and the dead. But on the verso of page 4 he turned his attention back to the original lyric and amidst various half-developed ideas found the emblem he was searching for to conclude his parade of "images": a figure suggestive of both mad King Sweeney from mythology and the protagonist of Yeats's own story "The Wisdom of the King" from *The Secret Rose* (1897):

> That king that made the people stare
> Because he had feathers instead of hair
> And all the rest are waiting there

With some minor adjustments including the elimination of that weak last line, this was inserted into both printed texts. Whether these revised lines were actually performed is doubtful: the copy of Duff's music for the song that belonged to Robert Irwin, who played the First Musician and so sang this lyric, does not include the changes to the final stanza. The manuscript of Duff's music for the song in the version with piano accompaniment (in the Macmillan Archive in the British Library, Add. MS 55003) gives Yeats's original words under the vocal line in the same ink as that used for the scoring, but the revised words have been added later in pencil above these, most likely at the time of Duff's correspondence with Macmillan in 1939.

There are a number of small but significant changes to the directions for the Queen's dance, if one compares those given in SIUC 91/16/10 with the Cuala proof sheets and the published texts: the nature of these suggests that the latter more faithfully indicate what was performed by de Valois. In the printed versions the Queen rises not just before her dance begins but earlier when, after the first, brief intimation of her song, the King bids her "sing out loud." This would allow a more extended mime between the first movement of the Queen's head, through her gazing at the King to the performance of the strange and haunting lyric defining her dread of losing her beauty with the loss of her chastity. (De Valois was well trained in traditional theater mime and made extensive and original use of its vocabulary in many of her own ballets, while work at the Festival Theatre on Gray's productions of classical Greek tragedy and expressionist dramas had provided her with contexts that considerably augmented her command of the medium.) Yeats's original concept had been that the Queen should take the head in her hands as the dance progressed and steadily raise it with outstretched arms above her head, eventually coming to sustain that pose in the center of the stage for the duration of the sequence where the head sings. The printed texts offer different directions, requiring the Queen to take the head as she dances and to place it before her "on the ground" while standing motionless and gazing at its features. Her stillness is now what motivates the King's order that she continue to dance, his jeering recall of the Stroller's words describing the Queen and his insistence that she display her beauty to the full. When she next comes to rest, the head is to be placed on her shoulder for the duration of the song. All these corrections are added (not always in Yeats's hand) to the set of Cuala proofs (CDML) and incorporated into the revised proofs (NLI 30,020). The new directions concerning the movements of the Queen are all found in the text printed in *Life and Letters* but not the final parenthetical note.

These changes meticulously integrate the dance more purposefully into the development of the action and the dialogue, while the situating of the head on the dancer's shoulder relieves her of the difficulty of sustaining the posture of holding an object of some weight aloft for a marked period of time, which would be highly taxing on her arms and shoulders and rapidly exhaust her stamina. This position, giving much of the weight of the head to her shoulder, would allow the performer from time to time to free one arm and hand to gesture expressively and so develop a relation between the Queen and the severed head. This in turn would make for a smooth transition when "the dance begins again" as the song ends: the gesturing hand and arm could lead the whole body back into movement. There is a further period of dancing prescribed in the printed texts (but not in SIUC 91/16/10) before the clock begins to strike. From this point on, the directions in typescript and printed texts are identical, as the dance rises to a climax when the Queen kisses the mouth of the severed head as the last note of midnight strikes. Clearly in the performance this has to be a moment of complete empowerment for the Queen, since her ensuing posture with the head now upon her breast overawes the King and frustrates his attempts at violence.

What the revisions show is a finer awareness of the need for pacing within this long episode to allow moments of repose for the dancer, which would offer her brief pauses to recover her stamina and to mark the stages in what is a complex psychological and emotional journey of self-discovery for the character of the Queen. (In a letter to Olivia Shakespear, Yeats described the dance as moving between horror and fascination.)[38] Through the dance she moves from the posture of abject stillness, which she has sustained since the start of the play, to that stance of supreme self-possession and command with which she ends it. The revisions could only have been effected in response to de Valois's artistry, as she steadily improvised and built up her contribution to the performance, making compromises with Yeats's original imaginings in the interests of practicality and her impeccable sense of how long to pace episodes of movement if their intent is to be fully communicated to an audience. Once again the revisions bring us closer to an appreciation of the play as performed.

There are two further revisions that require comment: one seems to have been effected during rehearsal, the other in preparing the play for publication. In SIUC 91/16/10 the two Attendants' final lyric is sung while the curtains slowly close on the tableau of the prostrate King at the feet of his Queen, who now cradles the Stroller's head upon her breast. A wholly new direction is added (but not in Yeats's hand) to the set of Cuala proofs (CDML) after the third stanza: "THE QUEEN *has come down stage and now stands framed in the half-closed curtains.*" (The revision is included in the text published in *Life and Letters.*) This is a brilliant theatrical conceit to end the play, as Yeats finds a stage image that graphically embodies how the Queen, as a consequence of her experience within the play, now stands poised between two dimensions of reality, having a profound communion with the worlds of both the living and the dead. What might have inspired this addition? *The King of the Great Clock Tower* played each night directly after a first staging of Yeats's *The Resurrection* and both plays were in rehearsal together under Robinson's direction. In his account of the performances for Olivia Shakespear, Yeats remarks how at the profoundest level the two plays share a common theme: "the slain god, the risen god."[39] At the climactic moment of *The Resurrection* there comes the stage direction: "*The figure of Christ wearing a recognizable but stylistic mask enters through the curtain,*" a curtain that we have just been informed by the Hebrew has "nothing behind it but a blank wall."[40] Did Robinson or, more likely, Yeats during the rehearsals decide to point up the parallel between the plays by replicating the dominant stage image from the first play at the

[38]The letter is dated August 7, 1934. See *Letters*, p. 827. I have been considerably influenced in my interpretations of the danced sequences by discussions held with Ninette de Valois in the mid-1970s, when she frequently lectured for me on the University of London's International Summer School. Much of what I then noted down has been confirmed by Jill Gregory, one of the surviving members of the Abbey School of Dance, who possessed a sufficiently sharp memory for choreographic detail to be invited by de Valois to become the ballet mistress for her London company.

[39]Ibid, p. 826.

[40]See *VPl*, 929.

close of the second? In *The Resurrection* the world of the seeming dead penetrates the world of the living; in *The King of the Great Clock Tower* the living Queen holds mystical converse with the world of the dead and through the language not of the mind but of the body. In each case the moment defines an inspired image, at once simple and succinct in terms of its realization yet profound in its allusive potential.

It was right that on further reflection Yeats decided also to emend the stanza that concludes the final lyric when he came to revise the proofs for the Cuala edition: "I have stopped so long a gap in the wall" is descriptively evocative of a common enough scene in the Irish countryside focused on the siting of a hawthorn within the landscape; but it is too specific, too mundane in its resonances adequately to form a bridge between what one hears and what one observes and so carry the weight of a complex symbolism. (This is the reading that Duff set to music and was performed.) The simple revision of the line to "I have stood so long by a gap in the wall" at once conjures up the image of the hawthorn but also allows entry to more challenging metaphysical possibilities such as are suggested by the particular placing of the Queen within the stage picture just as the curtains are about to close. It is a moment of stasis, of illumination, so intense that it would have rendered quite redundant the added verses from the lyric "Why must those holy, haughty feet descend?" These lines with their refrain about "desecration" would have needlessly troubled the exquisite poise, which the collaborative artistry of poet and dancer had expertly created.

Ezra Pound's Intervention and Its Consequences: The Rapallo Notebook

It would be naïve to suppose that Yeats's work on *The King of the Great Clock Tower* moved along a simple trajectory from the prose version and its performance text through a recreation of this in verse to the steady transformation of the material into a new drama, *A Full Moon in March*. Already it has been observed how freshly written, additional lyrics (not at all appropriately) were inserted into the performance text of *The King of the Great Clock Tower* during the later stages of the rehearsal process. Further completed lyrics were to appear at the conclusion to the Preface of the Cuala edition of the play (the poem subsequently called "A Prayer For Old Age" but here left untitled) and as a coda to the Commentary ("He had famished in a wilderness," which was eventually to find a place in the text of *A Full Moon in March* as the interlude between the spoken and danced sections of the play). Yeats would appear to have achieved a satisfying version of *The King of the Great Clock Tower* ready for staging before his departure for Rapallo in June of 1934. That he began suddenly to continue working at the play resulted from his showing a copy to Ezra Pound, whose reaction was vehement, unexpected, and damning. An irate Yeats recorded the episode as the first entry in his new notebook:

> Rapallo. June, 1934
> Gave "Clock Tower" to Ezra to read. He condemned it "Nobody language." At first I took his condemnation as a confirmation of my fear that I am now too old. I have ~~hardly~~ written little verse for three years. But "nobody language" is something I can remedy. I never write in verse, but first in prose to get structure.

What is striking about this account is how decidedly different it is from that given in the Preface to the Cuala edition, which is altogether more detached and witty at Pound's expense. This later version of events offers a detailed character study of Pound as critic and political thinker before revealing that his judgement of the play was confined to a single word: "Putrid." Interestingly Yeats makes no attempt to defend himself against this criticism of the play's moral tone: the cumulative details of the pen-portrait of Pound as eccentric iconoclast cleverly destabilize any pretensions to authority he might claim on ethical or literary grounds. Yeats records the episode chiefly as an illustration of Pound's absurdity.[41] The Preface makes no mention of the issue of language, though that is clearly what rankled most deeply with Yeats in the heat of the moment of Pound's attack; and that cruel opinion, "nobody language," had a remarkable impact. Yeats drew a thick line under the entry in his notebook and promptly began to redraft the opening of the play. He starts to characterize the King as O'Rourke of Breffny, attempting to make him a "somebody" by giving him an ancestry that includes a great-grandfather of the same name, who married a woman called Dervorgilla. It was Dervorgilla whose elopement with Diarmuid MacMurrough in time brought about the invasion of Ireland by the English (a subject already treated by Yeats in *The Dreaming of the Bones* and by Lady Gregory in *Dervorgilla*), and that name causes O'Rourke to muse on a genetic inheritance that prompts him like his ancestors to be attracted to "women worthy death," women who are distant, their faces expressionless, their bodies seemingly "made of marble or of hollow bronze." O'Rourke's words steadily characterize in this way the still presence and unmoving features of his Queen, which provokes in him a mounting anger and desperation. Over some seven pages of the notebook Yeats wrestled with this new approach, trying to adapt it in different ways to his existing text, but, as the constant deletions and repeated startings over again attest, the new intractably refused to meld into the old, even when in a seemingly calmer mood he tried to transcribe a clean copy into the loose-leaf notebook (NLI 30,336), which he was also deploying at this time (it peters out with an unfinished sentence). This is hardly surprising when one considers the care with which in creating the performance text of *The King of the Great Clock Tower* Yeats removed from the design concept and the dialogue all specificity of reference, which might rob his invention of a certain myth-like quality. This had resulted in an extreme simplicity coupled with an intense allusiveness. References to the adulterous relationship of Dervorgilla and MacMurrough and her abandonment of O'Rourke would risk restricting the play to the confines of Irish history and, possibly with Irish spectators, rouse expectations that Yeats was writing to a political agenda; this would seriously jeopardize the communicating of his metaphysical theme about the slain but risen god, and bring unwelcome pejorative associations to any interpretation of the Queen's role. The strength of *The King of the Great Clock Tower* theatrically lies in its heightened abstraction, which enables the play to move effortlessly toward its conclusion through dance, mime, tableau, and choric song. The success of the first production a month later made that strength abundantly clear.

This frantic response to Pound's strictures was not, however, a waste of creative energy. When in time Yeats came to write a version of the play in verse, he found ways of subtly distinguishing between King and Stroller through rhythm and syntax in ways which the

[41]Yeats chose not to send the *Sunday Times* review of the Abbey production of *The King of the Great Clock Tower* to Pound himself. But because he felt the review exonerated the play and proved Pound wrong, he instructed Olivia Shakespear to forward the newspaper cutting to her daughter "to show to Ezra that I may confound him. He may have been right to condemn it as poetry but he condemned it as drama. It has turned out the most popular of my dance plays" (*Letters*, p. 827.) For further comment on this episode, see R. F. Foster, *W. B. Yeats: A Life*, vol. 2: *The Arch-Poet: 1915–1939* (Oxford: Oxford University Press, 2003), pp. 500–501; and *Becoming George*, p. 477.

medium of prose did not so readily allow: in this version he achieved resonances of character within a prevailing abstraction. More importantly, O'Rourke's efforts to *read* the character of his Queen and the complexity of his response to her presence, veering between attraction and repulsion, began to generate some powerful, if disturbing, images: Yeats was effecting not the revision of an old play but the genesis of a new one. While many lines in these opening pages of the notebook work over the theme of O'Rourke and his ancestry, as large a body of lines struggles to define his perception of his Queen's presence, and it is here that a constellation of words and images comes steadily into prominence. Images drawing on masks and puppets alternate with invocations (recto of page 2 of the Rapallo notebook) of statues "fashioned of marble or of hollow bronze," which transmute into O'Rourke's hope, "I married her, content if I might love / As palmers love their holy images" (recto of page 3). Significantly that last line was immediately revised to read: "As palmers some old image in a niche." The Queen's emotional coldness and detachment also suggest pride and behind all O'Rourke's agonizing lies the question of why such superior beings should choose to relate to "our common pleasant life" (NLI 30,336). Suddenly the potential of these gestures is realized in the four single-line scraps of verse quoted above (p. xlii). Together they gave Yeats not only the theme for a wholly new lyric but also his subject for a new drama: adulterous Dervorgilla is promptly abandoned as a more challenging heroine hesitantly takes shape in his imagination.

The Composition of *A Full Moon in March*: Manuscripts and Revisions

The extant materials defining the various stages of the composition of *A Full Moon in March* are remarkably full, far more so than is the case with *The King of the Great Clock Tower*. The Rapallo notebook contains drafts for the three songs to be sung by the Attendants (they appear and therefore presumably were created in the following order: "Why must those holy, haughty feet descend"; "He had famished in a wilderness"; "Every loutish lad in love") together with a rough outline for the song for the severed head of the Stroller ("I sing a song of Jack and Jill"), while a fuller version of that lyric and a draft for the Queen's song ("Child and darling, hear my song") appear in the loose-leaf file, NLI 30,336. Interestingly the song for the severed head arises from and indeed concludes the development of the prose scenario for the complete play in the Rapallo notebook. Initially the new play still bears the title "The Great Clock Tower," but this is qualified as a "New version – for private room." The composition of the scenario is disrupted over several pages by a series of astrological calculations and Tarot readings (all in Yeats's hand) and a brief diary for a period spent in London in late October 1934. After it recommences, the scenario steadily moves into a prose version of the dialogue of Stroller and Queen. This section of the Rapallo notebook ends with drafts of poems relating to Margot Ruddock. Significantly on the verso of page 34 the last of three drafts of the poem "To Margot" is titled differently from the preceding two: "I ~~When~~ Old Pythagoras fell in love." This draft differs somewhat from the version published by Roger McHugh in *Ah, Sweet Dancer*;[42] it reads:

---

[42]See *Ah, Sweet Dancer*, where a photograph of a later manuscript draft is included opposite p. 80. The pages of the Rapallo notebook containing the drafts of "To Margot" were not transcribed by David R. Clark because, though that poem was conceived during the same period as many of the poems included in "Parnell's Funeral and Other Poems," it was not published in either that volume or in *Collected Poems*. See *"Parnell's Funeral and Other Poems" from "A Full Moon in March": Manuscript Materials*, ed. David R. Clark (Ithaca: Cornell University Press, 2003).

Life was running out & then
Generous eyes on mine were cast
I like other aging men
Sat & gazed upon a past
In seeming all compounded of
Lost opportunities in love

What is remarkable is how closely the private poem to Ruddock follows ideas, images, phrasing, and ultimately meaning of the lyric "Every loutish lad in love," a draft of which immediately precedes (on the recto of page 33) the first attempt at "To Margot." The significant difference is that, whereas in the lyric Pythagoras is a *type* of old man, in "To Margot" Pythagoras has become Yeats's own self as a pathetic old man who, suddenly graced with the gift of love that shines from Margot's eyes, is transformed. This juxtaposition of lyric and poem endorses an interpretation of "Every loutish lad in love" as also stressing the transforming power of love, which is important in understanding the logic that Yeats steadily built into the play, as it matured through the various drafts. Composition of the full play next shifts to the loose-leaf file (NLI 30,336) under the new title of "The Severed Head," where verse steadily replaces prose in the writing. In the several reworkings of the opening of the dialogue between Stroller and Queen in this manuscript, their distinctive character-traits begin to emerge and be strengthened: he, uncouth and cockily confident; she, aloof, outwardly cold but inwardly yearning. A first holograph attempt at combining songs and dialogue into the dramatic structure that was to become *A Full Moon in March* is found in NLI 8906; this version carries yet another attempt at a suitable title: "The Swineherd." However, the ending after the Queen's sinking "slowly down – holding the head against her head" is abbreviated to the curt direction: "Song of the closing of the curtains or of the unfolding & folding of the Cloth. The song at the end of Clock Tower with the lines Their desecration and the lovers night." A fourth try at a title, "The Lover's Night," heads the ten-page typescript (HRC) prepared from the foregoing manuscripts, but this is heavily emended to the title by which the play is now known. Two carbon copies of this typescript exist (NLI 30,186 and JRL1), which contain the revisions made to the top copy; in both cases these have been achieved by erasing the carbon and overtyping with the new readings. One of these (JRL1) served as copy text for the first publication of the play by Morton Zabel in *Poetry*. Throughout, it contains penciled instructions for the typesetter, presumably in Zabel's hand, concerning layout, size of type, and italicization of the stage directions. We learn from a letter that Yeats wrote in response to a request from R. A. Scott-James for possible lyrics to publish in his magazine, *London Mercury*, that "excited by the appropriateness of the month" the editors of *Poetry* published the play precipitately in March 1935 "without waiting for my proofs or letting me know the proposed date of publication."[43] Those three long columns of galley proofs, containing Yeats's corrections in heavy pencil, did arrive in Chicago and survive among Zabel's private papers (JRL2); but the revisions are mostly concerned with layout and contain nothing of substance. The text published by Macmillan later that same year (along with

[43]March 19, 1935 (courtesy of John Kelly). Scott-James had recently published sizeable extracts from *Dramatis Personae* in *London Mercury* and clearly wished to build the relationship with Yeats, who rightly supposed, however, that "Prior publication in America probably excludes it [*A Full Moon in March*] from your consideration."

the version in verse of *The King of the Great Clock Tower*) offers a number of markedly different readings from the two revised carbon copies and the galleys. Unlike the situation obtaining with *The King of the Great Clock Tower*, that final version was not reached after taking the play through a rehearsal process in which further changes might have been effected in order to create a performance text, though one major change (to be discussed later) was incorporated into the Macmillan text when Yeats thought the play might be staged by Nancy Price (an actress and director who had founded the People's National Theatre Company in 1933). Though there were protracted schemes for a production involving Margot Ruddock, none was realized, and the play remained unstaged at Yeats's death.

What is immediately apparent from this summary of the stages of the play's composition is that it gives the lie to Yeats's oft-repeated claim that by this stage of his career he devised prose dialogues to act as stimuli for the writing of lyrics. Here the ordering is reversed in large measure with lyrics preceding the drafting of the dialogue. Of course, to some degree he had the dramatic content in hand, since he saw *A Full Moon in March* as a revision of *The King of the Great Clock Tower*. Yet, given his dissatisfaction with the inclusion of "Why must those holy, haughty feet descend" as the ending for the earlier play in performance,[44] it is not surprising that the new play should in time pursue a markedly different theme, resulting in a different characterizing of the roles of both Stroller and Queen. Consequently *A Full Moon in March* followed a dramatic logic that would make that same lyric, newly situated, a fitting conclusion.[45] It would appear that he found that logic by devising the choric lyrics in the *reverse* order to that in which they appear within the play's structure. A major difference between the two plays is the inclusion of a centrally placed lyric ("He had famished in a winderness")[46] to mark on the narrative level a passage of time between the two halves of the action and on a practical level an interval in which a dancer might substitute for the actress in the role of the Queen. At no point did Yeats envisage that Margot Ruddock would be capable of dancing effectively: from the first he had seen the necessity of creating a structure in which Ruddock would perform the first half of the play and de Valois the second (danced and mimed) section. For all his growing infatuation with Ruddock, he was still a shrewd enough man of the theater to create a means whereby de Valois might repeat her success in negotiating the demanding ending of *The King of the Great Clock Tower*. Hence, quite early in the composition came the image of the *veiled* Queen, a climactic unveiling that still does not reveal the actress's face to the audience and, along with that, the devising of an interlude in which the substitution of the dancer might take place (Yeats described the substitution to Ruddock as being "quite easy as

---

[44]When (in a letter dated November 29, 1934) Yeats offered Morton Zabel *A Full Moon in March* for publication in *Poetry* (Chicago), he described this first siting of the lyric as seeming "out of place."

[45]Comparing the two plays in the letter to R. A. Scott-James dated March 19, 1935 (see footnote 43), Yeats observed of *A Full Moon in March* that "the fable is quite different."

[46]This lyric too was completed to Yeats's satisfaction by the time that *The King of the Great Clock Tower* went to press with Cuala. It was not incorporated, however, into the text of the earlier play, as "Why must those holy, haughty feet descend" had been, but was placed as the conclusion to his "Commentary on 'The Great Clock Tower.'" There it immediately followed his disclaimer that Wilde's *Salome* had had any influence on the composition of his play, suggesting instead that a story in *The Secret Rose* and a related poem, "He gives His Beloved Certain Rhymes" (see *Collected Poems*, p. 71), were more precise stimuli to his creativity. Reference to that story is carried over into the Attendants' speeches that lead into the lyric in *A Full Moon in March* ("An ancient Irish Queen / That stuck a head upon a stake"), but Yeats immediately asserts that he is here developing the trope differently ("But that's a different queen, / A different story").

you will both wear masks").[47]

Where the two choral lyrics that frame the action of *The King of the Great Clock Tower* remain firmly on a metaphysical plane, the three that introduce, develop, and conclude *A Full Moon in March* are decidedly different in tone and import: they focus more on ways of breaking out of the limits of stereotypical character traits, of transcending the self. "Every loutish lad in love" introduces the fundamental qualities of the man who is soon to intrude into the Queen's presence but suggests how the transfiguring power of love may displace his loutishness. The central sung lyric, "He had famished in a wilderness," carries the transformation further: what initially appeared to be brashness is steadily converted into heroic wantonness. However, the introductory dialogue of the Attendants invites an audience to perceive the lyric as applying to the Queen; and indeed that conversion of the Swineherd from lout to hero requires as profound a shift in her modes of perception too, extending her awareness beyond the limitations of snobbery and rank to the extent that she can apprehend the value of his daring and the resultant sacrifice of his life. The final lyric explores the compulsions of the psyche that bring about that poignant change within the Queen: the need to embrace everything that is antithetical to her known self the better to achieve emotional and spiritual wholeness. Turning away from a life defined by rules and contracts and determined by aesthetic and intellectual choices, she finds a new mode of living in the body, where a night of love and its consequence mark the desecration of all that the Queen once prized as of sovereign value. Appropriately the competitive, vocal reasoning, which is Yeats's prime mode of representing the Queen at first in the play, is displaced by a dancer's expressive physique, invariably for him an emblem of inner unity. The transformation the Queen undergoes is also most eloquently evoked by the new song composed for her: gone is the terror of sexual invasion defined by the song for the Queen in *The King of the Great Clock Tower*, and instead she proffers an apology for the cruelty of her past self and her icy self-possession. In the song and the accompanying image of her arms raising the head on high (at once her "child" and her "darling"), her past, her present, and her future selves are held in a delicate equipoise, as her once haughty tone gives way to a new tenderness. Equally remarkable for its tone is the new song for the severed head, which plays with the naïve idioms of nursery rhyme (which often mask disturbing emotional complexities) to define the Swineherd's mystical appreciation beyond death of the changes undergone by the Queen's psyche: Jill's seemingly wanton aggression is now perceived as a necessary means to effect Jack's apotheosis as a

---

[47]See *Ah, Sweet Dancer*, p. 23. This comment from a letter to Ruddock dated October 11, 1934, is the earliest reference to the new play; it was sent from Rome where Yeats was attending the theater conference organized by the Alessandro Volta Foundation. On October 26 he wrote to his wife of his plans to have the new play, "sketched in Rome," staged in London and Dublin (the latter performance being for the benefit of the Irish Academy and to be held in Lady Londonderry's drawing room), and adds the details "music by Dulac, Miss De Valois as dancer." He made no mention of Ruddock's potential involvement. (Ann Saddlemyer drew my attention to this letter.) By early December when there were plans afoot for a staging of *A Full Moon in March* Yeats confided in a letter to Edmund Dulac that he supposed "that Ninette will want to substitute *The Clock Tower*," adding that he had himself come to dislike the original play (see *Letters*, p. 830). In conversation with me, de Valois claimed that she found it particularly helpful that the plays for dancers required her to be a silent presence on stage absorbing the atmosphere and the dramatic rhythm of the given performance for a good while *before* she was required to dance; it was for her a deeply meditative time, which inspired her subsequent improvisations. Given that intensely personal response, it is not surprising that she would prefer *The King of the Great Clock Tower* to *A Full Moon in March*, where the calculatedly late arrival on stage of the dancer would rob her of that preparatory engagement with the play in performance. (For similar comments from de Valois about the necessity for her of "feeling the play," see *Step by Step*, pp. 183–185.)

brilliant star.[48] The chosen idiom allows Yeats to suffuse the Swineherd's known grossness with a newfound generosity of spirit, while the simple, near-predictable rhymes indicate a degree of acceptance of the inevitable as absolute. Remarkably (given their tonal intricacies) both lyrics appear to have been completed at a sitting at least in outline with scant need for revision.

The drafting of the body of the play appears to have been accomplished in three stages: the material found in the Rapallo notebook; that contained in the loose-leaf notebook (NLI 30,336); and a relatively clean manuscript copy of the full play (NLI 8906), which formed the basis of the first typescript (HRC). Further local revisions were attempted as the play went into publication, but the main creative dynamic was completed with the holograph revisions to the typescript. The Rapallo album contains both the initial scenario (covering some three pages) and a first attempt at developing this into a structured dialogue between Queen and Stroller (covering some five pages); five pages of astrological readings separate these two otherwise sustained entries. There is no mention yet of the Attendants or the role they will play in the action, though there are demands in the scenario that a Captain of the Guard should take the Stroller to his death, and he is given an opening exchange with the Queen before the entrance of the Stroller as in the final text, when Yeats began to flesh out his schema. The scenario begins as a mix of stage directions with passages of reported speech ("Is it true what she has announced . . . "), but, as the situation begins to get a hold on his imagination, Yeats begins sliding in and out of direct speech. The scenario establishes the basic narrative elements: the song contest and its reward; the Stroller's gross appearance; the threat of death for failure to win the hand of the Queen; the Stroller's alternative proposal for action involving the Queen dancing for him before he will deign to sing to her; the Queen's shocked retreat into protestations about her beauty; her commanding his death; his fearless insistence that the terms of the contract he has established be fulfilled as midnight strikes with the added detail that "when the last stroke has struck / you shall kiss me upon the lips"; her further demands for his death ("The ax [*sic*], the ax"); then a ritual "folding and unfolding of the curtain," before the play ends with "a version of desecration & the lovers night." There is no reference as yet to the use of a mask as representing the severed head or to the dance, though Yeats presumably envisaged these elements at this stage as roughly imitating the final sequences of *The King of the Great Clock Tower*.

When Yeats returned to the material, he clearly had a powerful sense of the Queen's sexual languor and longing as prompting her emotional shifts between a firm style of command and a hesitant mode of entreaty. The addition of that brief episode with the Captain of the Guard

---

[48]One recalls the "reward" offered many of the victims of their cruelties by the Greek and Roman gods, as recorded in classical myths. It is difficult to gauge whether Yeats's reversion to the nursery rhyme was mere coincidence or an instance of creative intertextual referencing. The choice of the nursery idiom may be a possible further influence from de Valois. When the original production of *The Dreaming of the Bones* was revived for a full week's run at the Abbey on April 12, 1932, it was framed by a different repertoire of danced items from the works performed in December 1931. Yeats's play was followed on that later occasion by a recreation of the work based on Edward Elgar's *Nursery Suite*, which had first been staged by de Valois for her London company at Sadler's Wells earlier that year on March 19. The penultimate sequence (and the last of the nursery rhymes to be performed before the climactic "envoy" of the fairytale characters) was "Jack and Jill went up the Hill," where the role of Jill was performed by the noticeably talented Jill Gregory. It is not certain that Yeats saw one of these performances: he had been in London for a BBC broadcast on April 10 but would have received as always a detailed account of the proceedings from Lennox Robinson. Interestingly de Valois had earlier choreographed a pas de deux on the same nursery theme for three of her Dublin pupils but to music by Bach (Toni Repetto-Butler had danced Jack throughout the run, while Jill was shared by Eileen Hare and Muriel Kelly); this version had been staged in the week beginning April 22, 1929. Kathrine Sorley Walker argues that this early version "probably contained ideas used by her [de Valois] three years later" (see *Ninette de Valois*, pp. 91 and 120–121).

establishes that complexity succinctly and precisely. The Stroller's character traits have changed somewhat too: there is less insistence now on his foulness as swineherd (though that motive is not lost) while more weight is given to the danger and endurance of his journey in quest of the Queen. The account of the death awaiting those who fail the Queen's test is elaborated with a degree of relish, but there is a new irony in her discovery that the Stroller's silence is not the product of fear at her information but deep composure as he inwardly meditates on the nature and circumstance of their "marriage night." Prompted to explain why he has come to her, he speaks of the fascination of her cruelty as "the white / skin of desire," which Yeats promptly revised to the more explicit "I see your cruelty and desire it," a concept that was to undergo considerable refinement. The Queen tries to refocus his interest in her beauty and in the kingdom her love would bestow on him, but the Stroller resists her tactics, offering an alternative outcome to their meeting, based not on inequalities of power, status, or appearance but on physical union and compatibility (she is to honor him with a dance and he honor her with a song). Her renewed threats of violence set the Stroller laughing: as he envisages the future with greater clarity he sees her kneeling now as well as dancing before earning his gift of a song, which will end with their coupling and sinking into "the bridal sleep." The summoning of the Captain ends the scene. But this draft continues first with a detailed instruction for the symbolically bloodied appearance of the dancer-as-Queen so that, as she holds the head above her, "blood seems / to drop over her body" and next with an outline of the danced sequences which involve the Queen kneeling to sing her song, raising the head aloft as it sings to her, and shuddering "at her loins," which some lines for an Attendant explain as the Queen conceiving "of his blood" before succumbing to "the bridal sleep," all as the Stroller predicted. The whole dramatic impact of the scene is then tersely summarized: "The dance the / kiss – the shudder. She sinks down in sleep." This version ends with an attempt at the song for the severed head ("Jack must sing a song of Jill"), which confidently reaches for the right idiom and tone: it is startling, audacious, yet wholly in character with the Stroller, as this draft is beginning to define the role. Most of the elements of the dialogue and the ensuing danced action are in place now (except for the songs), though the characters of Queen and Stroller need the subtler definition that Yeats's growing sense of their purpose in the action will achieve. One major detail, however, has still to be introduced: the concept of the Queen's mystical conception through the touch of blood. Though the lines for the Attendant at the close of the dance begin to sketch in the idea, this particular situating of the material, if carried through to performance, would not have the dramatic impact that comes from the Stroller voicing it as a folk-myth from his country, which the dance will then realize in all its strangeness. Situated at the end of the first half of the play, it becomes the organizing principle on which the second sequence is structured, where a body dancing (and not language) becomes the prime medium of communication.[49]

The material contained in NLI 30,336 includes some crucial new material along with attempts to revise sections already substantially worked. The first draft runs to eight pages and comprises a very full coverage (still in prose) of the opening half of the play, ending with a first sketch of the Stroller's story of the woman who bathed in blood and conceived, which is notable for specifying (as no subsequent versions were to do) that the blood is that of an "old man."

---

[48]There is a small anticipation of the image of the Queen all bathed in blood on the second page of the scenario, when the insulted Queen, urging the Captain of the Guard to decapitate the Stroller so she will be rid of his presence, starts a threat with the words, "when I bathe my hands / in his blood." Noticeably the phrase is dropped from the fuller draft at this moment in the action. It is likely that the image continued to resonate in Yeats's imagination.

Reference has been made above to the significant placing in the Rapallo notebook of drafts for the poem "To Margot" immediately after the earliest work on *A Full Moon in March* and to Yeats's identifying in one version of the poem with the figure of the elderly Pythogoras from the opening lyric of the play. "To Margot" investigates the difficulties and discrepancies inhering in the trope of January falling in love with May. That Yeats continued for some time to view the central pairing in *A Full Moon in March* in these terms (of an elderly Stroller/Swineherd and a young Queen) is apparent from this reference to "an old man's blood." Later drafts of the play abandon references to age and augment (once the character is called "The Swineherd") the references to his craft and his foulness, as if Yeats suddenly decided to change the dominant trope to that of Beauty and the Beast, as less explicitly self-referential. It is, however, for the opening of the play that most of the wholly new material is conceived, as Yeats begins to design speeches for the Attendants to frame the action. Two attempts are made at a short introductory sequence, though little of this material will find its way into the finished text beyond reference to a stage manager who has been consulted about the content of the action and the significance of the timing at a full moon in March (he will later become the anonymous "he" who will instruct the attendants how to introduce the play). This version both offers symbolic references to support the idea of the date as mystical, as ushering in a profound reversal of circumstance (there are slight echoes here of the lyrics framing *The Resurrection*), and intimates that a woman dancing will be emblematic of this transformation. The second version is preoccupied with the Queen as image and as "player" and with the resulting complexities that must be read into her character. That both these versions were ultimately omitted is not surprising, as they are overly prescriptive of how spectators are to interpret the ensuing action: being too anticipatory, they rob that action of surprise and the audience of any sense of creative discovery.

The second draft, which covers the next five sides of paper, is an initial attempt to work all the material in verse but it is largely scored through; it runs from the Queen's questioning of the Captain through to the Stroller's terse rebuffing of the Queen's offer of kingship ("What do I know of kingdoms?"). Much of the verse is routine as yet: a wrestling to fit a steadily elaborated content into the constriction of verse lines. But there are notable exceptions to this prevailing quality such as the Stroller's expanded description of himself as foul in origin and appearance to test how impartial the Queen will be in judging his song on its merits. This draft is also the first to contain the telling phrase "Cruel as the winter of virginity" in the Queen's frank self-appraisal. There follows in the notebook a version of the Attendant's opening lyric, "Every loutish lad in love," before the third draft begins, which is numbered over four pages and headed "B." Again in verse, the material runs from the Stroller's questioning whether it is true that the man who sings best to her shall take the Queen as wife to "What do I know of kingdoms?" Though occasional details are still to be added, overall the speeches follow the exact ordering of the published texts. What further revisions will do is to pare away redundant matter until the dialogue has a remarkable terseness and implacable momentum. Of twenty-two exchanges only two extend beyond at most three verse lines: his account of his foulness; hers of her cruelty. Great dramatic and psychological power accrues around this display to each other of the worst facets of their individual natures, as if they are challenging each other to find the better self that hides behind surface appearance. For the first time in the process of drafting, the text becomes drama.

An unusual feature of this third draft in NLI 30,336 is that, whereas in all earlier versions the characters are designated "Stroller" and "Queen" (once reduced to the initials "S" and "Q"), here they are referred to as "He" and "She." The drafts of the Supernatural Song, which was eventually titled "He and She" but headed in one version significantly as "Bride & Bride-Groom," immediately precede (22v–26r) in the Rapallo notebook the scenario for *A Full Moon in March* (26v–27v).[50] In a letter to Olivia Shakespear dated August 25, 1934, Yeats quotes the poem, describing it as one of a series "of a personal metaphysical sort . . . on the soul" and concludes, "It is of course my centric myth."[51] To what extent can the poem be seen as a valuable commentary on the play, since both are rooted deeply into the same private myth? Both deploy moon symbolism to explore a woman's fear for loss of selfhood (and one projected title for the poem explicitly situates the experience in the context of the marriage night). The letter to Shakespear ends with a postscript, which refers to his wife commenting on their daughter Anne's preoccupation with death and recalls how George Yeats's "spirits once spoke of . . . the centric movement of phase 15 (full moon) as the kiss of Death."[52] A major difference from the time scheme of *The King of the Great Clock Tower* is that, where that text stresses how the climactic action is to be understood as occuring during the tolling of midnight, the new play from this set of manuscripts onwards emphasizes how it takes place instead at the full moon with all the more intricate symbolic import that this implies for Yeats.

The manuscripts that comprise the thirteen pages of NLI 8906 show Yeats bringing together for the first time the whole range of what until now had largely been composed as disparate elements. (It is a matter for conjecture when precisely during the chronology of the redraftings that comprise NLI 30,336 he composed the songs for Queen and severed head, since they are found at some distance from the work on the body of the play and in both cases on the verso of other material, as if he had turned to a convenient blank or half-used page to try out an idea. To complicate matters, it is by no means certain that the ordering of the items in this notebook now follows the original sequence.) What is remarkable is how close NLI 8906 is to the finished text. In a number of places Yeats substantially revises the dialogue or directions as he proceeds, bringing that closeness even nearer. But much of the manuscript is surprisingly clean, as if the revising were going on in his imagination before he committed pen to paper; and the revisions that are on the page seem an immediate response to a phrasing that is not quite sharp enough. Most of the changes (other than the renaming of the Stroller as the Swineherd) involve the elimination of lines or the condensation of the content to achieve as terse an expression of an idea as possible, continuing a process that began with the third version in NLI 30,336. The opening exchange for the Attendants still toys with a listing of symbolic resonances associated with a full moon in the month of March (though the Second Attendant curtly dismisses such speculation as "nonsense") and is generally more prolix than this sequence was to become. The directions that a ritual "unfolding & folding of the cloth" accompany the opening lyric imply that Yeats still at this stage envisaged a staging akin to that for his plays for dancers. When, however, he offers similar directions involving a ritual with a cloth later in the manuscript at both the moment the Queen drops her veil when the Attendants sing "He had famished in a wilderness" and before the singing of the final lyric, he noticeably now includes an alternative "or close the stage curtain." The text, as first published in *Poetry*, refers only to the ritual with

---

[50]The final draft of "He and She" in the Rapallo notebook (26r) actually shares the page with the opening stanza of a draft of the lyric "Every loutish lad in love." For the drafts of the poem with transcriptions, see *"Parnell's Funeral and Other Poems" from "A Full Moon in March": Manuscript Materials*, ed. David R. Clark (Ithaca: Cornell University Press, 2003), pp. 190–205.

[51]*Letters*, pp. 828–829.

[52]Ibid, p. 829.

the cloth throughout the stage directions, whereas the later Macmillan text assumes the use of both a main stage curtain and an inner curtain, which are deployed in the same manner as the two sets of curtains required for *The King of the Great Clock Tower*; all references to the ritual are excised from the Macmillan text.

It is in this version that Yeats finally hits on the right phrasing of the initial line of the opening lyric, where the specific instance ("A loutish lad that . . . ") broadens into a confident generalization ("Every loutish lad in love"). Some more extended sequences (as distinct from individual speeches) go through a complete redrafting: a notable instance of this is the point at which several of the earlier drafts ended, when the Swineherd scoffs at the idea of being a king. Yeats now makes that dismissal the stronger by having the Swineherd snap his fingers as he reiterates his scorn ("That for kingdoms") and cutting his comment about preferring to return to his swine when married so that it is the Queen who is prompted in response to ask what will become of her if they wed and he lead her away from the luxuries of her palace. The sheer contrast of his promising a night of passion amid the dung of swine with the lovingly enumerated symbols of the Queen's power (throne, corridors, servants) now more logically propels her into furious denunciation of his insults. The resulting action up to the moment when the Queen drops her veil is considerably elaborated here compared with previous versions that included this sequence; the revision that gives greater motivation for her vehemence now makes possible these new developments (her wish for the Swineherd's immediate death; her relief that he has not desired to see and therefore sully her face with his gaze). The Swineherd's story of the woman "bathed in blood" and the Queen's reactions to it are drafted twice; but, though the second is scored through (leaving the first as preferred), neither has yet achieved the psychological complexity of the final text where the Queen is both fascinated and repelled by what the tale conjures in her imagination. Here she longs only to be rid of him and pointedly refuses to touch any part of him when dead. Why she should then drop her veil rather defies credibility.

Only the stage directions for the dancing in the second half of the play appear to have given Yeats trouble. Partly, as is evident from this manuscript, this derived from his attempting to fit the pattern of de Valois's dance from the earlier play in performance to the sequence of spoken and sung passages, when it became clear to him that a different ordering and a decidedly different tone and atmosphere were required for the new work. The difficult pose with the head held aloft now comes at the start of the sequence when the dancer's stamina would be at a peak; she next moves to set the head upon her throne where appropriately it sings for her of violence and transformation. The final lengthy direction outlines a scenario in which the queen's relation to the head, which she has now laid on the ground, is at first both inviting and refusing; but then, as the accompanying drum taps grow ever more insistent and rapid, she gives herself up to its rhythm in a manner that Yeats for the only time in all the draft materials describes categorically as expressing "the sexual act." She then kisses the head and sinks to the ground cradling it to her breast. Later revisions will observe the ordering of what is to date the fullest account of Yeats's conception of the dance and its pacing but will refine the explicitness of this version to subtle implication. This manuscript ends abruptly calling for "the song at the end of Clock Tower."

The typescript, HRC, could not accurately be described as a straight transcription of the revised manuscript, NLI 8906, but it comes close to being so. Many of the differences are a matter of silently correcting spelling, adding appropriate punctuation, adjusting the phasing or grammar in minor ways to improve the rhythm and euphony of the decasyllabic lines in which the dialogue is composed. There are some compressions or inversions of words to give a line greater dramatic energy (as, for example, when "If by my tears or by the trembling of my limbs" of the manuscript is revised in the typescript to read: "If by trembling of my limbs or sudden tears"). More extended revisions are made to the stage directions for the dancing, especially to the final sequence that leads to the kissing of the severed head and the sinking of the body as if in sleep. Generally these involve fusing what were originally rapid bursts of short sentences into longer syntactical units, thereby creating a clearer sense of the dance as an evolving organic entity, a physical and psychological journey for the Queen. The only sustained major revision is to the opening dialogue for the Attendants. Noticeably, Yeats calls for three performers as Attendants, although the dialogue and the division of the songs is throughout assigned to only two. The fact of there being three appears to have been forgotten after the opening stage direction, except that Yeats in his mind's eye was still clearly envisaging a staging akin to that prescribed for his earlier dance plays modeled on the Noh and deploying a ritual with a cloth to frame the action and instill a suitably elevated tone in the playing space; and three performers ideally are required for such a ritual, if the cloth is to be of a size to make a fitting impact and the handling of the unfolding and folding is to remain clean and precise. (This anomaly of a third, silent Attendant is carried over into the text printed in *Poetry*.) The most striking change is to the Attendant's opening dialogue where all reference to any symbolic import the play may carry is cut; instead we are confronted by the players' uncertainty about what they are to do and the casual instruction they have been given about joining in "wherever we thought it necessary." This introduces a sense of the casual and the makeshift, as if the performers are being invited to improvise, which contrasts markedly with the energy and polished verbal precision of the songs they sing. Final revisions to the opening for the Macmillan text were to make that distinction even sharper. It is as if, once the Attendants move from everyday speech to lyric verse, they enter a different dimension of reality where they acquire profounder levels of perception. This contrast of the perfunctory with the exacting endows the visionary nature of their songs with a consummate authority.

Yeats revised the typescript thoroughly, retitling the play in the process, inserting the occasional word omitted in the transcription, correcting the layout of half-lines of verse, and cutting from the stage directions all reference to a mode of staging within curtains that imitated the Abbey's production of *The King of the Great Clock Tower*. Three small but effective emendations to the text were effected; each rendered a relatively flat expression more vivid in its dramatic context. Substituting "rags" for "clothes" in the line, "My flesh seems scarce less ragged than my clothes" powerfully endorses the Swineherd's disheveled appearance and the utter lowliness of his status. Revising the Queen's satirical attitude to men's belief that "woman's beauty is a melting thing" to " . . . a kindly thing" stresses by contrast how much she relishes seeing herself against type as wholly "cruel." The somewhat dated use of "kindly" rather than the simpler form of the epithet, "kind," brings with it a wealth of Shakespearean resonance, where the word carries more the significance of "human" and "humane." A line that had repeatedly until now eluded the succinct expression Yeats sought, "That he has brought an insult not his love" (itself a correction of a line first typed here as "But he came here to insult not to love") is now changed to "he has brought hither insult and not love"; but in its ordinariness this still seems to vitiate rather than provide a climax to the Queen's fury that will goad her to demand the Swineherd's death. (Only the Macmillan text was to match tone and emotional context with an apt expression.) All these holograph revisions were typed as corrections into the two extant carbon copies of HRC (NLI 30,186 and JRL1), and it was this corrected text that Morton Zabel published precipitately in *Poetry* to Yeats's chagrin. His set of proofs (JRL2) show him mostly concerned with getting the dialogue of the Attendants set as prose, not verse, with changing the case of certain letters and with tidying up the punctuation. Two changes are of note: in the Swineherd's description of his hair, "ragged" replaces "matted" (a change that prompted further revision and compression for the Macmillan printing until every aspect of his appearance is defined by that epithet); however, another attempt to rework the penultimate line of the first stanza of the final lyric to read "What are they seeking? Why do they descend?" was not subsequently taken up.

Some seventeen revisions were effected in the text before Macmillan published the play. A major change, immediately apparent from the opening stage direction is that Yeats has now wholly abandoned the idea of the Noh-type staging as set out in the directions printed in the text in *Poetry* and reverted to the requirement that the play be performed like *The King of the Great Clock Tower* within two sets of curtains. The Attendants have in consequence been reduced to two and these characterized as "*an elderly woman and a young man.*" The timbre of their voices will now more accurately represent those of the Queen and the Swineherd in the latter half of the action, while the difference in age endows the woman, given the lines assigned to her, with a wonderful knowing authority to offset the man's apparent naïveté. It is she who now fittingly understands the import of the play, which they have observed, and so can properly give voice to the refrain of the final lyric with its insight into the need for "desecration and the lover's night." Several of the remaining changes involve minor adjustments to compress the syntax to make lines more vivid ("But that's a different queen, / A different story"), or the former ordering of lines is reversed to bring greater subtlety to the psychological progression of the dialogue. Both techniques, for example, are evident in the revising of the Queen's speech ("Some I reject, / No man abhorrent to these eyes can sing / Some I have punished for their impudence."), where the second and third lines are reversed in the revision and the new final line compressed to emphasize a finality and callousness in the expression: "Some I reject, / Some I have punished for their impudence. / None I abhor can sing." The Swineherd immediately picks up the threat implicit in this and courageously draws attention to his foulness as if challenging the Queen to find him abhorrent. His ensuing speech is again modified and compressed while new patterns of repetition stress the likely foulness of how he must appear to her perceptions.

There is now a play of tensions to be detected in the flow of the dialogue, as if the characters are measuring up to each other, sizing each other up as potential combatants; but what adds to the drama for an audience is the uncertainty of whether they are both of them in a swaggering, assertive mood, on the defensive, or just being quite open about themselves. The insertion of a new line a little later in the action, which is divided between the two characters, builds on this effect. The Swineherd announces the terms of the song contest (that the Queen offers herself for the winning every full moon in March) and observes that he is "here alone." Whereas previously the dialogue moved straight into the Queen's elaborately phrased decision not to harm him, now the Queen confirms his observation ("No other man has come") and he repeats that it is now the allotted time ("The moon is full"). This provides a wonderful caesura in the action as they both accept the full implications of the situation in which they find themselves: the outcome must either be their marriage or his death. That the Queen's immediate response is to try to send him away undermines all her previous aloof behavior and coldness, her seeming inability to care for anyone. Later in the early stages of her dance, the directions require the Queen to move before the Swineherd's severed head as if alternately "alluring and refusing"; the revisions and the added line begin to establish a pattern of mood swings in the Queen between attraction and repulsion, which introduces a stronger sense of organic cohesion and growth to the play's development. That the Queen is entering new psychological territory where she is steadily losing her one-time self-possession is nicely caught by the redrafted line, which climaxes her furious condemnation of the Swineherd's seeming rudeness: " . . . he came hither not to sing but to heap / *Complexities* of insult upon my head" (my emphasis). After so many half-hearted attempts, the line finally provides a complete outburst for the Queen's anger (implying as it does the accumulating wave of enormities that she has had to suffer); but the ambiguity of the word "complexities" also hints at the deep, inner disturbance that the experience has provoked in her. The complexities she has tried to find the means to read in him has made her aware of complexities in herself.

All this sensitively prepares for what is a completely new handling of the dialogue that leads up to the Swineherd's exit to his death. Where formerly the Queen expressed sheer disgust at the Swineherd's story of the woman bathed in blood ("Oh, foul, foul, foul") and longed only to be rid of him, now she repeats phrases from the Swineherd's lines as if mesmerized by his tale; but noticeably she transforms his story in the retelling until it is no longer simply a folk myth but directly applied to their immediate predicament. It is she who envisages a severed head held in her hands as the source of the blood, which envelops the woman. The speeches now teach the alert spectator how to *read* the later dance as it evolves. With this connected sequence of revisions the psychological and emotional structuring of the play is greatly strengthened.

Dating the Composition of *A Full Moon in March* in Relation to Plans for Its Staging

The first reference we possess that dates the redesigning of *The King of the Great Clock Tower* as a wholly different kind of dance play comes in a letter to Margot Ruddock of October 11, 1934, where Yeats observes that "the old version of the play is bad because abstract & incoherent. This version is poignant & simple – lyrical dialogue all simple."[53] Throughout the period of its composition he always intended that the play would be staged with Ruddock as the Queen; plans were made with her to this effect, but their efforts were continually frustrated. There were many reasons for this, some of Yeats's creating, some Ruddock's. As the diary-like entry for the week beginning October 23 in the Rapallo notebook substantiates (verso of page 27), Yeats had become interested in the activities of the Group Theatre during the autumn of 1934; the entry is situated significantly at the end of his first attempt at a scenario for *A Full Moon in March*. He saw and admired their production of T. S. Eliot's *Sweeney Agonistes*, directed by Rupert Doone; the use of masks and stylized, rhythmical, or danced movement throughout (Doone was a dancer by training) particularly appealed to him. Also he was excited by their choice to perform not in a theater but in the company's base, situated on the top floor at 9 Great Newport Street, and wrote to his wife that the premises were a large room "which suits my no [*sic*] plays."[54] That experience presumably made him immediately favor a proposal from Ashley Dukes, the dramatist and theater critic, that he should join with Eliot and W. H. Auden in a season of poetic drama to be staged by Doone and actors from the Group Theatre at Dukes's small club theater, the Mercury in Notting Hill. Yeats was promised an evening to himself (the

[53]See *Ah, Sweet Dancer*, p. 23.

[54]The letter is provisionally dated October 26 (courtesy of Ann Saddlemyer). For a history of the Group Theatre and Yeats's involvement with it, see Michael Sidnell, *Dances of Death: The Group Theatre of London in the Thirties* (London: Faber and Faber, 1984). Hereafter cited as *Dances of Death.*

plan at first was to stage *Fighting the Waves* and *The Player Queen* with *A Full Moon in March*), while Eliot and Auden would share the second bill; the plays would be performed in repertory. Dulac was to design costumes for *The Player Queen* and compose a score for *A Full Moon in March* (still at this stage referred to as "the new version of The Clock Tower"); Constant Lambert (de Valois's conductor and musical arranger for her Vic-Wells Ballet Company) was to write new music for *Fighting the Waves*, and the scheme was to involve working again with de Valois and with Frederick Ashton.[55]

Over the next few months various complications arose. Eliot and Auden had no new short dramatic works to offer for production and Dukes objected to their suggestion that the Group Theatre productions of *Sweeney Agonistes* and Auden's *The Dance of Death* be revived, since both works were already familiar to the kinds of audience the scheme was likely to attract. Yeats meanwhile continued to work on his drafts of "the new play about the severed head": writing to Dulac on November 6, he confided that he had "finished a first draft in prose & almost finished a draft in verse, digging down through thought to find passion. It has grown into a most audacious thing. If I succeed with it it will [be] the most powerful & strange of my dance plays."[56] This letter would suggest that Yeats was referring to what comprises the drafts in NLI 30,336. If this is so, then progress on the play must have extended so far in less than a month, since he first wrote of the project to Margot Ruddock. By November 17, he was writing to Ruddock that "Until yesterday I was still correcting my dance-play," while three days later he wrote to Patrick McCartan, apologizing for not communicating "ten days ago," but pleading his need to finish a dance play "& could think of nothing else."[57] This would seem to imply that progress on the play had reached what now comprises NLI 8906, since it was a further nine days before Yeats wrote to Morton Zabel (November 29) offering him the text of *A Full Moon in March* for publication in *Poetry*. This would allow a suitable period of time for him to revise the typescript (HRC) and for the carbons to be corrected. Given the seeming urgency of that letter and Yeats's determination stated within it to find an American publisher as quickly as possible, one can but suppose that he would have written to Zabel sooner, had the corrected carbons been ready at the time he wrote to Ruddock and McCartan. This means that the major creative work on the play was completed in a little over six weeks (though it was to be a further ten months before *A Full Moon in March* reached its finished form).

It was presumably another of the carbon copies that, shown to Dulac after Yeats traveled to

[55]This is the substance of a letter written to George Yeats on October 30, 1934, in which Yeats delightedly reports that Ashley Dukes "has undertaken all expenses." Yeats had met Dukes earlier in that October at the Theatre Congress in Rome, where Dukes was the English representative. It is interesting that, despite his involvement with Margot Ruddock, Yeats was planning the repertory to foreground de Valois's artistry (Ruddock one can but suppose would feature in *The Player Queen* and *A Full Moon in March*). Lambert and Ashton were two of de Valois's most trusted helpers in establishing her London-based company. No further mention of the involvement of de Valois or Lambert, however, occurs beyond this date; Ashton stayed the course for a short while longer. While introducing Ashton to the venture of working with a poet-dramatist ultimately failed on this occasion, later in the decade he was to enjoy a fruitful creative partnership with Gertrude Stein in staging the American production of the operatic version of her *Four Saints in Three Acts* (1934) and when choreographing *A Wedding Bouquet* to her scenario (1937).

[56]Courtesy of John Kelly. The confidence offered to Dulac here is ironic, since his friend was highly critical of the "blood symbolism" in the play when he was shown a draft a month later. Yeats wrote that he expected the piece to be "opposed to the clear, bright dry air of your genius" (*Letters*, p. 830).

[57]For the letter to Ruddock, see *Ah, Sweet Dancer*, p. 26; for that to McCartan see John Unterecker, "Yeats and Patrick McCartan: A Fenian Friendship," *The Dolmen Press Yeats Centenary Papers 1965* (Dublin: Dolmen Press, 1968), p. 372.

London again on December 7, excited his shocked reaction: "The 'Love and blood' theme I find unpleasant; many people may find it so . . . the Queen is not remote enough and the swineherd too vehement, they seem to have been forced into a kind of realism that is out of tune with the otherwise symbolical spirit of the play." He advised against including it in the projected program of productions for the Mercury Theatre, recommending instead *The Resurrection* and *The Player Queen*, separated by an interlude (this is presumably a sop to Yeats's feelings) of poems to be recited by Margot.[58] Yeats ignored the advice: by December 19 a meeting with Eliot, Dulac, Ashton, and Yeats, a self-styled "controlling board," had agreed on *The Resurrection*, *The Player Queen*, and *A Full Moon in March* as Yeats's contribution to a season at the Mercury Theatre, planned for the period of April 29 to May 19, 1935. On December 23, Yeats interviewed Doone with a view to his directing *A Full Moon in March.* Though on this occasion he considered that Doone "made most strange & imaginative suggestions," he was soon to have his doubts about Doone's suitability for staging his plays and he threatened to direct his plays himself; this produced consternation amongst the "board" and much settling of feathers and injured dignities was required of Dulac. By January 30 Yeats was even proposing the compromise that Doone might prefer to stage his *Fighting the Waves* instead of *A Full Moon in March*, which would be dropped from the program forthwith. Throughout this period in several letters to his wife, Yeats mentioned having "properly typed" copies made of *A Full Moon in March* for his agent, A. P. Watt.[59] These are less likely to be the corrected carbons taken from HRC than wholly fresh typescripts (none of which is seemingly extant) based on one of those carbons; they were certainly in his possession by early January before he returned to Dublin on January 11. From mid-January to early March he suffered renewed congestion of the lungs, which caused a general collapse and his confinement to bed; negotiations over the London season were left in Ruddock's hands.

Ruddock quickly got out of her depth: Yeats was too far away and too ill to offer support and Auden, Eliot, Dukes, and Doone were powerful individualists (too powerful for Ruddock's voice or presence to carry much authority). Ashton's name disappears out of the venture at this point, while Tyrone Guthrie's surfaces suddenly as a possible director; Doone grew uncertain about how much of the program he was to be responsible for and threatened to resign. Yeats, now convalescent, understandably became confused about who was directing what; he opined he was happy for Guthrie to direct *The Resurrection* and *The Player Queen* but (in a surprising *volte face*) insisted that Doone was the man for *A Full Moon in March* along with the Eliot and Auden pieces; and to Dulac he began to express grave doubts about Dukes as the Machiavel behind all the upsets ("I am told he is very flighty until tied down by his wife"). On one point Yeats was adamant: "What I care about is that I must approve the cast, producer & method & production of my own plays. A play is written for a certain method of production."[60] In mid-April the whole project "went Smash," or so he informed his wife. Eliot had just completed *Murder in the Cathedral* and Dukes had discovered that he could present it simultaneously in London and Canterbury, so the planned season of poetic dramas by various hands was

[58]The full text of this letter is in R. J. Finneran, G. Mills Harper, and W. M. Murphy, eds., *Letters to W. B. Yeats* (London and Basingstoke: Macmillan, 1977), pp. 567–568.

[59]See especially letters to George Yeats dated December 26, 1934, and January 3, 1935 (John Kelly kindly allowed me access to these letters).

[60]Letter to Edmund Dulac dated March 19, 1935. Dukes's wife was the dancer Marie Rambert.

quickly jettisoned in Eliot's favor.[61] Though at another's prompting Dukes offered to mount a fortnight's run of Yeats's plays to celebrate his seventieth birthday, nothing came of it. Instead, Nancy Price staged the celebratory birthday productions at the Little Theatre in late October. It was the opinion of Robert Medley, Rupert Doone's partner, that the project was doomed to failure from the first, because everyone involved was pursuing a private agenda, which made clashes inevitable. Doone suspected that Dukes was trying to take over the Group Theatre for his own ends and he felt he was losing control of a situation in which he was increasingly in name only the overall director; Auden considered (along with Doone) that there was a risk the Group Theatre's left-wing credentials would be compromised through involvement with Dukes; Yeats, abetted by Dukes and Dulac, to some degree feared being associated with Doone and Auden, given those very credentials; Eliot did not wish to mar the chances of his Canterbury commission; and Dukes, for all his seeming altruism over staging a season of poetic drama, fundamentally was after a financial success for his theater and was seeking (as Doone rightly surmised) to create an acting ensemble of his own. There was always too the embarrassing problem of Margot Ruddock, whom Yeats imposed on them all. Medley relates that Yeats took Doone to hear Ruddock read his poems; but the experience, far from advancing her career as Yeats clearly hoped, led to Doone's "private determination that the 'sweet dancer' should never be allowed on the boards."[62] Presumably Nancy Price shared Doone's opinion of Ruddock's talent. She did not include a production of *A Full Moon in March* in her "birthday offering," staged at matinees on October 28, 29, and 31, even though Ruddock sent her a copy of the final version of the play (before its publication) in the hope of acting the part of the Queen; instead, Price wickedly enquired about staging *The King of the Great Clock Tower*, which offered no role for Margot (Yeats in seeming innocence offered to send Price his newly completed version in verse).[63] Despite Ruddock's efforts to secure the role of Decima, the Player Queen, Price cast her as the timorous, withdrawn, and ascetic real Queen, in what were virtually her last performances as an actress, as she had begun to lose all confidence in her technique.[64]

Though Yeats was repeatedly frustrated by the London theatrical scene over a staging of *A Full Moon in March*, the play had been published by Zabel in his Chicago-based journal in March 1935, for which Yeats was paid thirteen guineas. In early September he was prompted to make the final important revisions to the play, which are included in the Macmillan text. It would appear to be the act of searching out a copy that Ruddock might forward to Nancy Price, which provided the occasion for him to return to the text critically and make what was the last

---

[61]Letter to George Yeats dated April 15, 1935.

[62]See Robert Medley, *Drawn from the Life: A Memoir* (London: Faber and Faber, 1983), pp. 153–154. Medley's account of the Group Theatre is covered in chapters 9 and 10. For the Poets' Theatre and its relation to the activities of Doone and the Group Theatre, see also *Dances of Death*, pp. 266–269.

[63]Letter to Margot Ruddock dated September 24, 1935. See *Ah, Sweet Dancer*, p. 51.

[64]Yeats wrote to Ruddock on October 29, 1935, praising her performance in *The Player Queen* as "magnificent" and confiding that, beside her, the actress in the title role [Joan Maude, Nancy Price's daughter] "for all her beauty, faded out," because Margot possessed "precision and passion." He concluded by asking Ruddock to wire him immediately "if Miss Price's conscience awakes and decides that you are to be Player Queen," which suggests that he had attempted yet again to influence Price to favor Ruddock. There is a possibility that the two actresses exchanged roles for the Thursday matinee, but, if so, Yeats did not see the performance. (See *Ah, Sweet Dancer*, pp. 56–57.) Interestingly, as Ann Saddlemyer has kindly pointed out to me, he offered a rather different account of the relative merits of the two actresses when writing about the production to his wife on October 31: "The Player Queen (Nancy Prince's daughter) was beautiful, never less than a picture postcard of the most popular sort but not a trace of talent. Margot was accomplished, distinguished flawless, & will be no more praised by the weekly reviews, than by the daily."

but in many ways the most important of changes. The note he included with a transcription he sent to Margot Ruddock makes it clear which were the lines that he had redrafted so late in the creative process:

> I send a revised copy of *The Full Moon in March*. If you look at it you will find it better dramatically. It makes the play turn on stronger hinges. Only a few words are changed however. The bit where she is told that a woman conceived from a drop of blood is much more actable . . . [65]

What in effect Yeats had added was the keystone that perfected the whole structure of the piece. Macmillan's edition was published on November 22, 1935.[66]

Reworking *The King of the Great Clock Tower* in Verse

Though Yeats's first reference to his rewriting *The King of the Great Clock Tower* in verse occurs in a letter to his wife dated December 13, 1934, tentative efforts at reworking the prose material had begun with his response to Pound's vehement criticism of the original play back in June of that year.[67] Significantly, when Yeats tried to impose *character* on his stylized portrayal of the king, he quickly resorted to verse as well as inventing a history and a perverse, inherited psychology for O'Rourke of Breffny. That attempt was soon abandoned, hardly getting beyond the king's opening speech; but, when Yeats returned to the task of redrafting the play in verse, echoes of that initial exercise reverberated in the phrasing of the king's first speech. Much of this draft, which is found in the Rapallo notebook between the verso of page 42 and that of page 46, follows Yeats's pattern of cycling back over sequences of lines to refashion them as his imagination senses new potential to develop within first inspirations or he perceives a need to improve the euphony of an expression or aim at a more exact and concise verbal formulation. These features are all typical of Yeats's working methods with an early draft. Yeats described his process in a letter to Frank Pearce Sturm, dated January 7, 1935, as "following the exact dramatic scheme of the Clock Tower."[68] On a factual level this is true, but it does not account for the emerging of a remarkable difference between the two versions of the play: the steady

---

[65] Letter to Margot Ruddock dated September 9, 1935. See *Ah, Sweet Dancer*, p. 46.

[66] Though *A Full Moon in March* went unperformed in Yeats's lifetime, it was given its first professional performance in 1950 by the Phoenix Ballet and Dramatic Club at the Everyman Theatre, Hampstead, who submitted a copy for licensing to the Lord Chamberlain's Office. The report of the reader (C. D. Heriot), who recommended the award of a licence (granted June 15, 1950), gives an excellent summary of the action, before concluding: "The whole play is very stylized and 'poetic' and—for my taste—pretentious and empty. The head is a stylized mask, previously worn by the Swineherd, and the costume of the Queen stylistically patched with red cloth."

[67] "Little here to report except a pleasant life. I am rewriting 'The Clock Tower' in verse, substituting a new and more philosophical lyric for that containing 'What says the Clock' which becomes a separate poem. I dine with Ashley Dukes tonight to talk over details" (courtesy of Ann Saddlemyer). Yeats wrote again three days later (December 16) from the Savile Club: "Nothing to report except that I am writing poetry & recovering from it by conversation and idleness. In about two months I should have a new book of verse, without including any of the prose parts of "The Clock Tower" – that play I am writing in verse." On Boxing Day, 1934, he reviewed the work done over his month in London and informed her: "I have written three lyrics & put The Clock Tower into verse," which intimates that the redrafting by then was completed to his satisfaction.

[68] For a longer quotation from this letter giving the context for this phrase in detail, together with bibliographical information on its source, see footnote 72.

characterization of King and Stroller through distinguishing rhythms assigned to their several speeches. Rhythm, especially rhythm in its precise relation to syntax, allows Yeats to create profound differences of character without any need to resort to personality traits displayed through the kind of trivial details that made his attempts to portray O'Rourke so frustrating and futile an experiment. Here a fundamental, character-driven contrast between the two men is effected without disrupting that high degree of stylization that gives the play its unity. Rhythms define the two men's contrasting modes of expressing their masculinity: the King's forthright and insistent in its veering between commands and questions; the Stroller's expansive, lyrical, questing, and passionate. As one turns from the Rapallo notebook to the cleaner copy, which comprises NLI 8769(ii), the contrast becomes more evident and the result is to give greater definition to the focal role of the Queen and the nature of her silence. She retreats from the King's questions, which seek to fix her in time as his possession and subject of his power, into the depths of self where she can preserve her integrity by brooding on silence. However, she responds to the Stroller's praise and daring, which honor her femininity, and chooses to communicate with him through the metaphor of her body dancing. Attention to the dramatic possibilities inherent in rhythm gives the new version a more complex narrative logic and coherence than the earlier prose version by rooting the play now more firmly in issues of gender. The changes are often minimal (sometimes simply a matter of lineation), but the results are profound in their implications.

Collating the two manuscript drafts with the text eventually published by Macmillan shows only two of the Stroller's speeches as causing Yeats ongoing difficulty: his description of his wife, which leads into the account of his being derided by fellow diners in a tavern; and his story of his ritual fasting and meeting with Aengus beside the Boyne. They are the only passages that extend and amplify the original prose version. The problem with the first instance was to find terms that were not overly dismissive, snobbish, or crude. Initial attempts at evoking an image of the wife ("country clown," "slut," or "turnip to scare children") were presumably abandoned as too harsh, though the last of these prompted Yeats to carry the image on into the Stroller's description of the diners, providing a running metaphor to define his sense of alienation from his kind. A later revision in the Rapallo notebook hits on the image of the goose to evoke pictures of the woman's size and gait, which are not overly judgmental. Wittily extending this image to the diners so they become "ganders" instantly transforms them into a loud, jeering mob, a flock of honking geese, driving the Stroller away to a shamed exile. The laugh now is momentarily on the Stroller, displacing any tendency to judge him as precious or superior. The running metaphor provides the necessary motivation to propel the Stroller into his penitential famine by the river Boyne. Revisions to the second sequence seem more a matter of negotiating a suitable pace to transform the atmosphere from boorish farce to metaphysical awe: too quick a transition would risk bathos at the very moment when the strange begins to take possession of the stage. The augmentation of detail with the inclusion of the sea mew, the salt sea wind, and the green hillock suggest an intensifying of the Stroller's sensibility with his fast, while the reduction of his famine from a prosaic month to the magical resonance of "nine days" expertly prepares for the arrival of the gods and Aengus's fateful prediction. Yeats's command of tone is masterly: this is particularly evident in his decision to cut the Stroller's aside to the King during his recall of Aengus's promise about the Queen's kiss ("drink in the words"), which is cocky and insidious and at odds with the prevailing mystical tenor of the moment.[69] The reading in the

[69]See NLI 8769(ii), p. 295, l. 13.

published text ("his very words") is less charged, less of a sexual challenge.

Though the text in verse follows the prose version in remarkable detail, there is one insertion that merits comment. At the moment that the Queen begins her dance, the King, mistakenly believing that she is following his instructions as to her behavior, urges her on in the Cuala prose text with the words: "Dance! Display your beauty!" From the draft in the Rapallo notebook through to the published verse text Yeats chose to expand these words: "Dance, give him scorn for scorn, / Display your beauty, spread your peacock tail."[70] The reference to "scorn" defines the King's sense of the Queen's motive for dancing and exposes the extent of his misapprehension, while "spread your peacock tail" may be read in this context as an injunction for the Queen to exhibit an hauteur befitting her status. But the version in verse was dedicated to Ninette de Valois, and it may be that there is a delicate intertextual reference to be detected here. "Pride" was a solo work danced to a Scriabin score, which became a popular staple of de Valois's personal repertoire. It had been created initially for performance at Gray's Festival Theatre in May 1927; it was included in the divertissements that made up the first program given by the Abbey School of Dance on January 30, 1928, and repeated in Dublin on several occasions. The choreography showed off de Valois's wit and satirical skills to perfection: she preened and flaunted *en pointe* about the stage in a manner suggestive at once of a modish "flapper" and of that traditional emblem of pride, the peacock. Her dress enhanced the peacock reference, being a dark blue leotard over which she wore a thigh-length skirt of light green, extending into a wide train to the rear, while on her head she sported a tight skullcap matching the blue skirt, from which in the center of her forehead flourished a high, green, feather-like decoration. In addition the train was cut and wired to suggest the characteristic shapes of peacock feathers.[71] It was a daring piece in its subtle intimations of a certain calculated license and louche, physical display: in some ways "Pride" was a representation of precisely the kind of woman that the King wants his Queen to be (though the reality, as he is soon to discover, is very different). Had de Valois ever performed in this version of the play in Dublin, the reference would have directed informed spectators to read her dancing before the Stroller's head as carrying a far more profound significance than the flirtatious and seductive choreography of "Pride." Characteristically the images that Yeats's words would have called to mind on such an occasion would have invited appreciation too of the rich variety of de Valois's choreographic invention, by drawing attention to the stylistic difference of what was actually being performed from what was being conjured momentarily into spectators' memories.

The thorniest problem with this version of *The King of the Great Clock Tower* obtains with dating of the drafts of the "New Song for the Severed Head." As was demonstrated above, the concluding stanza of the song for the prose version had continually taxed Yeats's invention and was even being revised in Rapallo after the play had been handed over to Robinson for

---

[70]See *The King of the Great Clock Tower*, p. 8; also *A Full Moon in March* (London: Macmillan, 1935), p. 38.

[71]A fine photograph of de Valois in this dress is included in *Ninette de Valois*, p. 83. The "flapper" associations are beautifully suggested by the carriage of her arms and the framing of her face with her hands. De Valois informed the present writer that she had sewed more material to the hem of her skirt for performances in Dublin, as Lennox Robinson was afraid its brevity would provoke accusations of impropriety! A later photograph of de Valois performing the piece in a "Sunshine Matinee" at the New Scala Theatre in July 1930, shows her wearing a different dress of a heavier material but cut to a similar design, except that here the skirt is brocaded or oversewn with designs evocative of peacock feathers, which de Valois is "displaying" with an elegant turn of the hand. (This can be seen in the de Valois file in the archives of the Royal Ballet School, White Lodge, Richmond Park.)

staging. However, no sooner had Yeats solved his difficulties with the song than he began devising a replacement. What prompted this is not clear. While the first song is about "heroic wantonness," the second explores the potential for mystical communion between the living and the dead. The later theme may have been inspired by his seeing the prose version in performance alongside *The Resurrection*; the staging confirmed his sense of the two plays as sharing a common metaphysical subject, and Yeats through the revised song may have wished to make the connections stronger. But, if that were so, one cannot but question why he made no attempt to include the new song in the printed texts of the prose version published later that same year. Much depends on how one dates the composition of the new song. The problem one faces is the separation in the Rapallo notebook of what appears to be its initial draft (the verso of page 1) from the main body of work on its development (from the verso of page 40 to the recto of page 42). This would appear to make it an exception to the practice Yeats adopted within this notebook (commented on above) of working at specific projects in defined groups of pages. Internal evidence would suggest that, after effecting the initial draft sometime in June 1934, he deferred further work on the new song, preferring instead to rework the final stanza of the original lyric to his satisfaction (on the verso of page 4). Justification for this view would be that the draft tends flatly to expound the theme of the intensifying of love's pleasures in the realm of the dead rather than gnomically and sometimes teasingly evoking the idea as a marvel beyond human comprehension, which the later drafts work to achieve. There are few phrases in consequence that one can trace through from the initial draft into the finished song, but there are echoes of motifs and phrasing from the O'Rourke of Breffny material contained in the pages that frame that draft.

If this interpretation is accurate, then Yeats did not return to the lyric for the severed head until after he had completed a sizeable body of work relating to *A Full Moon in March*, many of the "Supernatural Songs" (including in seeming order of composition: "A Prayer for Old Age," "Ribh Denounces Patrick," "Ribh at the Tomb of Baile and Aillinn," "The Four Ages of Man," "Ribh Considers Christian Love Insufficient," "He and She," "Whence Had They Come?" and "The Magic Drum"), and two unpublished poems addressed to Margot Ruddock. Most of these works deal with the mysteries and marvels of transcendental experience or with intuitions of such possibilities. Completing the new song over three drafts with a further page of revisions is accomplished with far greater confidence, speed, and rigor in the wake of such a tide of compositional brilliance; and its completion seems to have led Yeats into recreating *The King of the Great Clock Tower* in verse.[72] What is remarkable is how close, compared with the initial draft, all these attempts are to the finished lyric; revision is now a matter of fine tuning, of fully releasing the potential already perceived in ideas and images. The strange is rendered so immediate that it engrosses the imagination because of the sheer linguistic precision with which it is conveyed; much of the revising is bound up with sharpening that very quality and with drawing a palpably felt difference between the "marvel" being evoked and the lewd fantasies of adolescents or the frenzy of visionaries. The Queen as recipient of the song is being taught how

[72]Though his correspondence with his wife over the Christmas period of 1934 refers only to his involvement in rewriting the play, a letter dated January 7, 1935, to Frank Pearce Sturm offers more precise details: "I have rewritten that play in verse, following the exact dramatic scheme of the Clock Tower, and keeping that name, but changing the central lyric ("Images ride"), for that lyric was too vaguely connected with the central idea. I keep it, however, as a separate lyric." See *Frank Pearce Sturm, His Life, Letters and Collected Work*, ed. Richard Taylor (Urbana: University of Illinois Press, 1969), p. 105.

to discipline her mind so that it may become attuned to the secrets of the dead; her kissing the head is a token of her commitment to a union beyond the constraints of time, as emblematized by the tolling of midnight, a commitment that subdues and marginalizes the King in what had once been his space to shape and order as he chose. Where the first song ("Images ride") had invited the Queen to enter the eternal present of the world of art and story, the new song invites her into a far more challenging metaphysical terrain. It is tempting to question whether, after completing this new song, Yeats had not finally given *The King of the Great Clock Tower* the spiritual coherence that he deemed it previously lacked.[73]

Preface and Commentary: Manuscripts and Revisions

The prefatory materials for the published texts of the plays and the commentary that follows *The King of the Great Clock Tower* in the Cuala edition were largely achieved without substantial revision. All attempt to define the contexts in which the plays are best sited. The Preface to the Cuala publication informs the reader of Yeats's fears for his productivity, of his reasons for writing *The King of the Great Clock Tower* to revive what he thought was his failing creative inspiration, his consulting with Pound who was so preoccupied with his own obsessions that his sought-for critique proved unhelpful, hurtful, and inaccurate but had the benefit of spurring Yeats to trust more to his own instincts. Instinct and the body are celebrated in the short poem with which the Preface concludes, "God guard me from those thoughts men think," which he subsequently titled "A Prayer for Old Age." The "Commentary on 'The Great Clock Tower'" sets that play in the wider contexts of Yeats's changing styles as a playwright and his lifetime preoccupation as a poet-dramatist with the relation between words and music in sung lyrics, an account that demonstrates how widely over the years his attitudes changed as to which should have precedence in performance.

The essay finishes with a defense of his play against potential accusations that he has plagiarized his subject from Wilde's *Salome* (1894), a defense he couches first in terms of the different sources, which they severally drew on as inspiration (Wilde looking to Heine and Jewish legend, while Yeats turned to wholly Celtic material and the story he had first told as "The Binding of the Hair" in *The Secret Rose*),[74] and second in terms of the different placing of the dance within their narrative structures in relation to the severing of the head. That the possible resemblance with Wilde's play was a lingering source of anxiety is evident in the fact that this paragraph (itself an extended version of the program note Yeats wrote for the Abbey staging in 1934) is repeated verbatim in Macmillan's 1935 edition of *A Full Moon in March* and the 1938 American edition of *The Herne's Egg and Other Plays*. There are possible connections with Wilde's play, but they are far subtler than the ones Yeats outlines here, such as the creative use of stage space to define the changing power relations of the various characters. For all Yeats's breast-beating, no one seems to have made much of the issue. Joseph Holloway, one-time architect of the Abbey Theatre and inveterate recorder in his voluminous diaries of his and his friends' impressions of the Irish theatrical scene, makes no mention whatever of

---

[73]Yeats described *The King of the Great Clock Tower* as "theatrically coherent, spiritually incoherent" in a letter to Edmund Dulac (dated December 10, 1934) when defending *A Full Moon in March* against Dulac's criticism of its violence and disturbing blood symbolism. See *Letters*, p. 830.

[74]W. B. Yeats, *The Secret Rose* (London: Lawrence & Bullen, 1897), pp. 1–10.

Wilde in his various entries about the performances, which he surely would have done had hints of plagiarism been a subject of Dublin gossip.[75] Because of a strike in the printing trade that effectively silenced newspapers in Dublin the week of the production, only English papers (*The Times* and *The Sunday Times*) carried reviews of the Abbey's staging of *The King of the Great Clock Tower*, though *The Weekly Irish Times* carried a retrospective appreciation in its first October edition.[76] The reviewer for *The Times* quoted the whole program note with its references to Wilde but made no adverse comment. The critic for *The Sunday Times* described the play as "an adaptation to an Irish legendary setting of the theme of Salome" before again quoting most of the program note; and, though he viewed de Valois's dances as "macabre," he admitted she performed with "wonderful grace and expression"; most importantly, there is sustained praise for the extreme formality of Yeats's dramaturgy. The short notice in *The Weekly Irish Times* focused not on content but on his imposition of "very strict restrictions on his art . . . to clear the ground of all but the essentials," which the critic argued gave the new play the "grace and perfection" of the earlier plays for dancers; he concluded: "it was as charming, and seemed as artless, as a fairy-tale." A review in January 1935 of *Wheels and Butterflies* and of *The King of the Great Clock Tower* in the *Times Literary Supplement* makes a comparison in Yeats's favor, not with Wilde, however, but with "the *Surréalistes*" for a shared tendency "towards the night-side of life . . . though, unlike them, Mr. Yeats works with a great intellectual control."[77] A further review in the *T.L.S.* of the 1935 edition of *A Full Moon in March* refers to Yeats's "preoccupation with a rather Ninetyish fable" but makes no mention of Wilde, preferring to praise Yeats's "personal use of words" as "speaking an ever-young longing and an ageing anguish."[78]

The terms that recur here ("fairy-tale," "Ninetyish fable," surrealism) intimate, without ever spelling out, another potentially more fundamental influence than Wilde's tragedy: Maeterlinck's *Pelléas and Mélisande* of 1892. It was the one play by Maeterlinck that Yeats continued to admire into later life, and he had seen it performed by Sarah Bernhardt and Mrs. Patrick Campbell. In Maeterlinck's drama two men compete for the attentions of a woman to whom they are each deeply attracted and their styles of approach define two contrasting styles of masculinity: Golaud, the elder brother, with his heavily insistent questions from the very moment of his meeting with Mélisande seeks to *know* every last detail of her existence, even setting his child to spy on her movements; Pelléas seeks only the pleasure of her company and delights in allowing her simply to *be*. Mélisande is the unknown one, found lost in a wood, whose enigmatic answers to Golaud's questions imply her life was formerly regal and tragic. When (idling in the forest with Pelléas) she fails to catch a ring she has thrown into the air, a distant bell tolls noon as the jewel falls into a deep lake; the ring is Golaud's gift and the menacing bell intimates forthcoming tragedy. Golaud kills Pelléas out of envy of the union of sensibilities that

---

[75]See Robert Hogan and Michael J. O'Neill, eds., *Joseph Holloway's Irish Theatre*, vol. 2: *1932–1937* (Dixon, California: Proscenium Press, 1969), pp. 35–36. This is, however, a shortened edited text of what Holloway wrote about the production over several days (and several viewings) during the week of the run. At no point, even when recording the relaxed gossip of his circle of friends about the play and Yeats does he intimate that anyone considered plagiarism was involved in Yeats's conception.

[76]See "The Abbey Theatre, two new plays by W. B. Yeats," *The Times*, July 31, 1934, p. 12; "Mr. Yeats's New Plays: Irish Free State Notes. Memorable First Night," *The Sunday Times*, August 5, 1934, p. 5; and "The Dublin Theatre: New Productions," *The Weekly Irish Times*, October 6, 1934, p. 12.

[77]See "The New Poetic Drama," *The Times Literary Supplement*, January 24, 1935, pp. 1–2.

[78]See "The Mind of Mr. Yeats in Verse," *The Times Literary Supplement*, December 7, 1935, p. 833.

the younger man shares with Mélisande; she retreats into the scared vulnerability in which he found her; and Golaud loses both brother and wife. Here is the whole narrative structure of Yeats's play and many of its particular details and symbols (the questions, the brooding woman with an enigmatic past, the marked contrast of the two men, a woman celebrating her unique sensitivity, the clock striking twelve, the marginalizing of the man of power, and his attempt at revenge) and yet to draw attention to such similarities is immediately to sense how completely Yeats has transcended whatever influence in the depths of his imagination Maeterlinck's play may have had on him. He has made every last detail his own, investing it with his particular symbolic intent; and, above all, has transformed the philosophical defeatism shaping Maeterlinck's work into an endorsement of the possibility of metaphysical transcendence. Where Mélisande fades away in pathos, the Queen comes into the power that attends complete self-possession.

When Yeats redesigned *The King of the Great Clock Tower* as *A Full Moon in March*, it was the fable of Turandot that now shaped the action; this was a story that had previously attracted dramatization by Gozzi, Klabund, and Puccini in the European tradition; but again Yeats transformed the underlying ideology, making it less a stereotypical, masculinist fantasy about an aloof woman succumbing to the heat of a man's passion than a rigorous investigation into the power of seemingly antithetical psyches to come into a union where both find a necessary complement to their innermost selves. His play is not about a struggle for sexual supremacy, but about the psychological forces that enable his characters to surmount the impulse to promote that struggle. In both cases it was that process of clearing the ground "of all but the essentials," described by the reviewer for *The Weekly Irish Times*, that paring away and refining to get to the core of a story, which enabled Yeats to shift his and his audience's perspective onto a known archetype and to see it afresh. Freed from its constricting traditional interpretation, it begins to yield wholly original insights. The stages of that process are what a study of the extant manuscript materials of both plays reveals.[78] Macmillan's publishing of *A Full Moon in March* on November 22, 1935, brought to an end a period of compositional activity that had lasted some twenty-four months (taking the starting date as sometime before the letter of November 11, 1933, in which Yeats informed Olivia Shakespear of his commencing work on a new dance play). The narrative of those two years, as told by the manuscripts, demonstrates the focused integrity, at first threatened but ultimately strengthened by Ezra Pound's intervention, that motivated Yeats's determination to get his plays "right."

---

[78]Working on the manuscripts has quite changed my own interpretation of the play. For an earlier somewhat dismissive critique of *A Full Moon in March*, see *W. B. Yeats, Selected Plays*, ed. Richard Allen Cave (London: Penguin Books, 1997), pp. 362–363.

Transcriptions Principles and Procedures

Yeats's hand in manuscript drafts from his later years is difficult at best; over the period when he was engaged in composing the two plays featured in this volume, he was frequently ill and, on at least one occasion, profoundly irate; and so the quality of the holograph suffers. When writing for himself, prior to preparing relatively clean drafts for his typist, Yeats was frequently slapdash when moved with inspiration: words are left unfinished or hardly defined except by a brief line or flourish with his pen; letters were formed carelessly or inconsistently, spelling and punctuation were idiosyncratic; cancellations might be a simple crossing through of a sequence of text or be so heavily marked for deletion as to render his initial thoughts all but indecipherable. The photographic reproductions will enable readers to see what Yeats actually inscribed on the page; the transcriptions, given the obscurities mentioned above, offer therefore what at times can only be an approximation, an interpretation, or "translation" of the original; but the endeavour has been to achieve as accurate a reflection of each possible page as the limits created by the legibility of Yeats's holograph and the accuracy of the editor allow. The principles followed in recording the transcriptions are those adopted throughout the series and these are rehearsed below.

Where there is little doubt over Yeats's intentions, words are transcribed in full, even where some of the letters may be missing or represented by his characteristically vague flourish to denote word endings, such as "ing" or "ed." His idiosyncratic spelling is preserved, without editorial comment if his intent is clear; so too his own versions of Irish names and words, wherever the writing is legible, but the commonly accepted spelling is given in the annotations. On occasion he starts a word but leaves it largely incomplete ("orche" for "orchestra"); such words are transcribed as written and commented on in the annotations.

Illegible words and editorial conjectures are represented as follows:

[?]	an illegible word
[?] [?] [?]	a run of illegible words
[~~?~~]	a canceled illegible word
[?often]	a conjectural reading
[?ivory/every]	equally possible conjectural readings

The ampersand is used where Yeats deploys it and overwriting without cancellation of the original reading is represented by bracketing both readings with the revised reading above the initial one:

$\left\{\begin{array}{l}\text{is}\\\text{are}\end{array}\right.$

Accidental ink blots or other markings are not reproduced but often commented on in the annotations where they render meanings conjectural.

Cancellations of single words, phrases within a line, or of whole lines are indicated by a horizontal line through the words involved. No word that Yeats did not in part cancel is canceled in the transcriptions. The canceling of entire passages is shown by a vertical bracket in the left margin. Hid underlinings and "stet" markings are preserved. The transcription of typescripts does not preserve minor typographical slips if he has corrected them by hand, though on occasion these may be commented on in the annotations. Every effort has been made in the layout of individual pages in the transcriptions to preserve the position of words on the original manuscript page. Yeats's brackets and arrows showing how he wished a phrase or passage to be relocated have been reproduced.

The conventions used in presenting the resultant readings are listed below. Beneath the first transcription of each piece of writing (play, lyric, or commentary) are two kinds of information:

(1) Under *found in* are listed the manuscripts in the census in which each draft appears.
(2) Under *published in* are listed the separate publications to which the manuscript or typescript leads.

The following typographical conventions are used to indicate the medium in which the text occurs in the manuscript material:

roman type	ink
italic type	pencil
boldface type	typescript or print
italic boldface type	italic print

The following variants are not normally recorded in the apparatus:

(1) variants of type face, spacing, underlining, or punctuation in titles
(2) variants involving the exchange of single and double quotation marks
(3) variants involving the placement of punctuation inside or outside quotation marks
(4) involving the exchange of "&" and "and"

In the apparatus the following abbreviations are used:

del	deleted or deletion
ital	italics
rev to	revised to
sd	stage direction

Abbreviations and short titles of publications cited in the apparatus are listed on p. xiii above.

In some manuscripts, foliation numbers and letters inscribed on the page are the work of a cataloguer and these are omitted in the transcriptions. Only Yeats's pagination is transcribed, even when it is somewhat wayward and subject to his own corrections. All holograph revisions to typescripts are recorded.

Line numbers are assigned to each line of dialogue, often when the line is incomplete or canceled, if it merits comment. If a line is divided between two speakers, the number is not repeated. In both verse and prose texts, speaker tags and stage directions that are written on a separate line from the dialogue are not assigned numbers. The heading of each page of transcription bears, to the left, the name and leaf number of the manuscript that is being transcribed below and, to the right, a reference to the corresponding lines of text to which they relate, as numbered in *The Variorum Edition of the Plays of W. B. Yeats* (London: Macmillan, 1966), or, on occasion, in another closely related manuscript:

[BC, 4^r] [*VPl*, 23–49]

The King of the Great Clock Tower
and
A Full Moon in March

Manuscripts, with Transcriptions and Photographic Reproductions

Part I. *The King of the Great Clock Tower* (Prose)

A. Earliest Extant Manuscript: NLI 8769(i)

The earliest extant manuscript for the prose version of *The King of the Great Clock Tower*, NLI 8769(i), consists of materials of nearly finished condition that contrast markedly with the extensive and complex evolution of *A Full Moon in March* that appeared in 1935. Its relative neatness may suggest that it derives from late in the cycle of composition: the opening lyric, for example, has moved a long way from the sketch of two stanzas, which Yeats sent to Olivia Shakespear (cited in the introduction, pp. xxxv–xxxvi). In this draft, Yeats is already beginning to conceive of the play in production, adding details relating to a possible staging, which he generally leaves until quite late in his dramaturgical process. For example, on 2^r the idea for the cubes to represent thrones is present, though the prescriptions for the four types of instruments to accompany the action were in time to be reduced to drum and gong. In the stage direction on 3^r he offers the option of using the instruments on stage to accompany the action or of assigning the role to the Abbey orchestra, as was eventually the case for the opening production. Yeats's entertaining of possibilities is evident in other ways: in pencil on 4^v, he attempts to redraft the King's opening speech, toying with whether to make the speech formal or a direct personalized address to the Queen.

[NLI 8769(i), 1r]

The King of the Great Clock Tower 1

~~When the stage curtain rises there is an inner curtain~~
~~a musician~~

Characters

The King of the Great Clock Tower

The Queen

A Stranger

Three musicians

The Queen should wear a beautiful, impassive mask.
If played in an ordinary theatre when the stage curtain rises, there is an inner curtain which may have a pattern representing ~~dancers~~, dancers, A musician stands on either side, ~~The singer & dancer~~ they sing, and during the second verse slowly part the curtains

If played at The Peacock Theatre where the stage curtain parts in the middle no inner curtain is necessary

[NLI 8769(i), 1r] [*VPl*, title, preliminaries, and initial stage direction]

1

The King of the Great Clock Tower
The King of the Great Clock Tower

[When the stage curtain rises there is an inner curtain
A Musician

Characters
The King of the Great Clock Tower
The queen
A stranger

Three musicians
The queen should wear a beautiful, impassive mask.
if played in an ordinary theatre
When the stage curtain rises ^ there is an inner
curtain which may have a pattern representing
~~If Ple played at The Peacock Theatre where there~~
~~dancers, a~~ dancers,. ^A musician stands
one at either side, ~~The sing & durin~~ they sing
and during the second verse slowly part
the curtains

If played at "The Peacock Theatre" where the stage curtain
parts in the middle no inner curtain is necessary

---

found in NLI 8769(i) *transcribed above and below, pp. 3–29*
SIUC 76/1/7 *transcribed below, pp. 33–51*
SIUC 91/16/10 *transcribed below, pp. 55–70*
BC, 4v *transcribed below, pp. 73–75*
published in *Life and Letters* (November 1934) *transcribed below, pp. 77–86*
KGCT

Alternative sets of directions reflect Yeats's uncertainty over which of the Abbey stages is likely to be preferred for his new dance play.

2

They dance all day that dance in Tir-nan-Og!
There every lover is a happy rogue
And should he speak it is the speech of birds
Nothing has he & there has no words
No thought because no clock, no clock because,
If I consider deeply, lad & lass,
Nerves lonely nerves upon the nipping ground
Are [illegible] where all time is loud & warm

O never may the dismal head run loose
For there the hound that Oisin saw pursues
The hornless deer that runs in such a fright;
And there the woman clasps an apple tight
For all the clamour of a famished man;
They run the forever & [illegible] in forever;
They run
Nor can they stop & [illegible] a breath they still
Hear in the forever the beating of a bell.

(When the curtain is drawn one sees to left the King, Queen, upon two thrones which may be two cubes. There is a third cube to R. A musician sets forth ground to R beside him drum, gong, zither & flute. The two musicians sit down beside him. If instead of drum, gong, etc the orchestra of the theatre be used the two musicians are sufficient. They sit to R side by side.)

[NLI 8769(i), 2^r] [*VPl*, 1–16 and stage direction]

2

~~First Musician~~

I

1 They dance all day that dance in Tur-nan-Oge!
2 There every lover is a happy rogue
3 And should he speak it is the speach of birds
No thought has he
4 ~~He has no thought~~ & [?then/thus] has no words
clock clock
5 No thought because no ~~time~~, no ~~time~~ because,
6 If I consider ~~deep~~ly, lad & lass,
Nerve
7 ~~Neve~~ touching nerve upon that happy ground
8 Are bobbins where all time is bound & wound

II

~~Second Musician~~

9 O never may that dismal thread run loose
the hound that Oisin saw
10 For there ~~upon the foam the hound~~ pursues
11 The hornless deer that runs in such a fright,
12 And there the woman clasps an apple [?] tight
all
13 For the clamour of a famished man;
They run the foam & ~~there in foam~~ there in foam
14 ~~In foam there & there in fright~~ ^ they ~~run~~ ran
15 Nor can they stop to take a breath that still
16 Hear in the foam the beating of a bell.

(When the curtain is drawn one sees to left the King
There is a third cube to R.
queen upon two thrones which may be two cubes. ^ A Musician
on the ground to R
sits ~~to right~~ be^side him drum, gong, zither & flute. The two musicians
~~set~~ sit down beside him. If instead of ~~gong~~, drum, gong etc
the orcestra of the theatre be used then two musicians are sufficient
They sit to R side by side.)

At this question once more — I
ask you before the courtiers here
assembled where your country lies
(~~[cancelled]~~) you
I do not know why but your silence
has grown unendurable to all here
The Queen

3

The King. A year ago this night ~~[cancelled]~~
~~my queen~~ you came into this house. I made
You my queen yet neither I nor any other
Man know from what country you came. And
now before our friends & courtiers here
assembled I ask you once more ?
where that country is, who & what you were
before you became my queen. You have kept
silence long, though that silence has
become unendurable to all here & to me.
(There is a pause. The queen neither speaks
nor moves. A musician beats three times
upon the gong, ~~or strikes three times~~ or
~~[cancelled]~~
or it may be struck off stage)

The King. Captain of the guard.

Musician (speaking as captain of the guard) King, I am here.

The King. Some one has struck three times upon the great door
admit him.

[NLI 8769(i), 2v] [*VPl*, 21–28]

And yet I question once more – I ask you to tell the courtiers & friends here assembled where your country lies – ~~(?A pause & three knocks~~ you I do no know why but your silence has grown unendurable. A pause this know they

[NLI 8769(i), 3r] [*VPl*, 17–29]

3

The King. A year ago this night ~~I made you my queen,~~ you walked into this house. I made you my queen yet neither I nor any other man know from country you came, and now before our friends and courtiers here assembled I ask you once more I where that country is, who & what you were before you became my queen. You have kept silence long enough, this silence ~~be~~ has become unendurable to all here & to me.

(There is a pause. The queen neither speaks nor moves. A musician beats three times upon the gong~~). or strikes three times upon the~~ or ~~three blows are struck upon a drum in the orces~~ or they may be struck off stage)

The King. Captain of the guard.

Musician (speaking as captain of the guard) King I am here.

The King. Some one has struck three times upon the great door admit him.

2v, 1–7 In pencil Yeats attempts a more compressed restatement of 5–10 of 3r opposite, to which it is keyed, then canceled.

4

~~A Man~~ The Stranger enters, who has a wild, slight grotesque mask. It covers the upper part of his face, the lower part is hidden by a beard.

The King. What is your name?

The Stranger. It is enough that I am a stroller & a fool and that you are the King of the Great Clock Tower

The King. I am the King. What do you want?

The ~~Man~~ Stranger. A year ago somebody told me that you had married the most beautiful woman in the world & from this moment I have had her image in my head & month by month it has grown more & more beautiful. I have made poems about it & sung them everywhere but I have never seen her

The King. Have you no wife or sweetheart of your own.

[NLI 8769(i), 4r] [*VPl*, 32–44]

4

The Stranger wild,
~~A Man~~ enters, who has a^slightly grotesque mask. It covers the upper part of his face, the lower part is hidden by a beard.

The King. What is your name?

The Stranger. It is enough that I am a stroller & a fool and that you are the King of the Great Clock Tower

The King. I am the king. What do you want?

Stranger
The ~~Man.~~ A year a go somebody told me that you had married the most beautiful woman in the world & from this moment I have had her image in my head & month by month it has grown more & more beautiful. I have made poems about it & sing them everywhere but I have never seen her

The King. Have you no wife or sweet heart of your own.

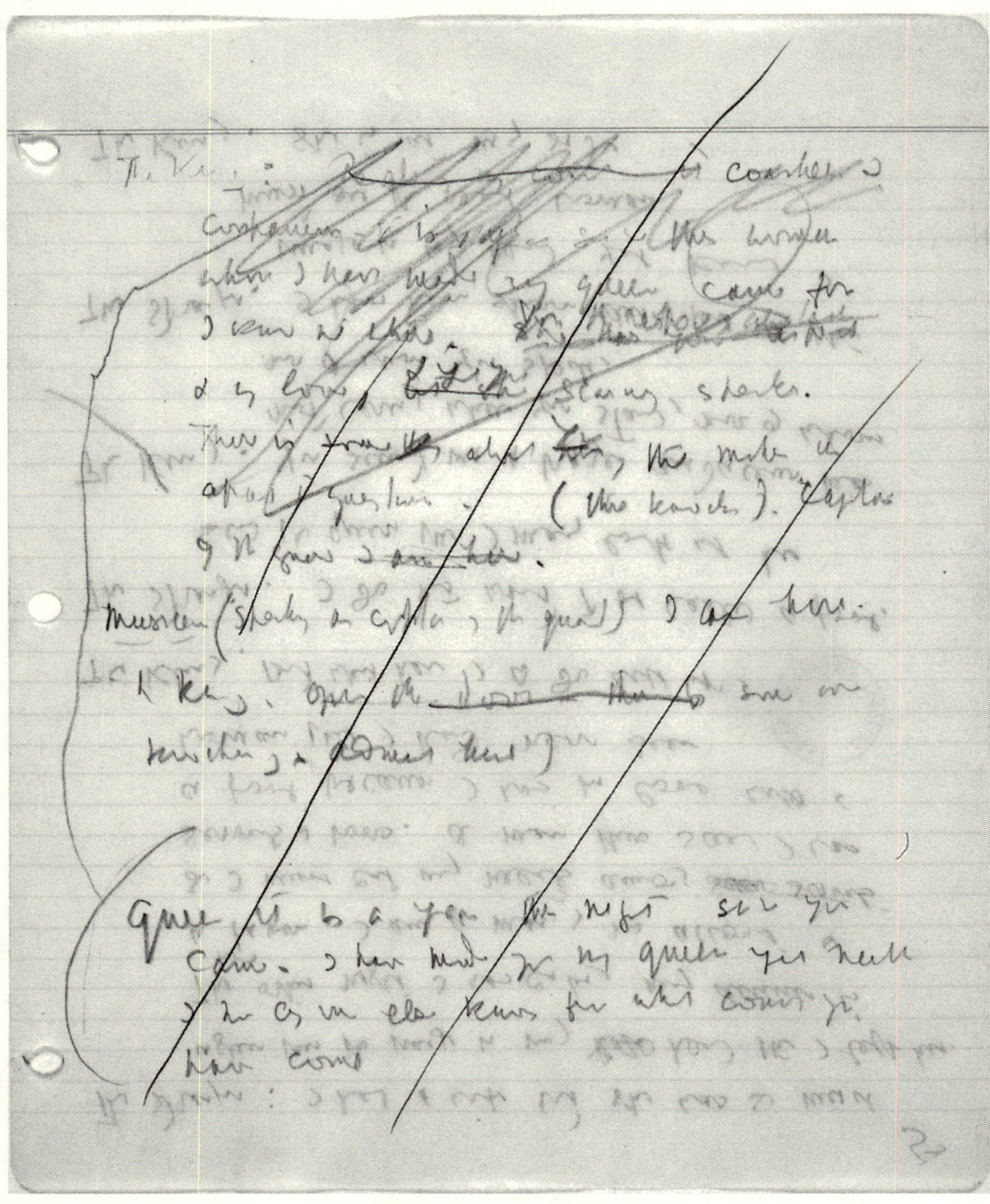

[NLI 8769(i), 4[v]] [*VPl*, 17–29]

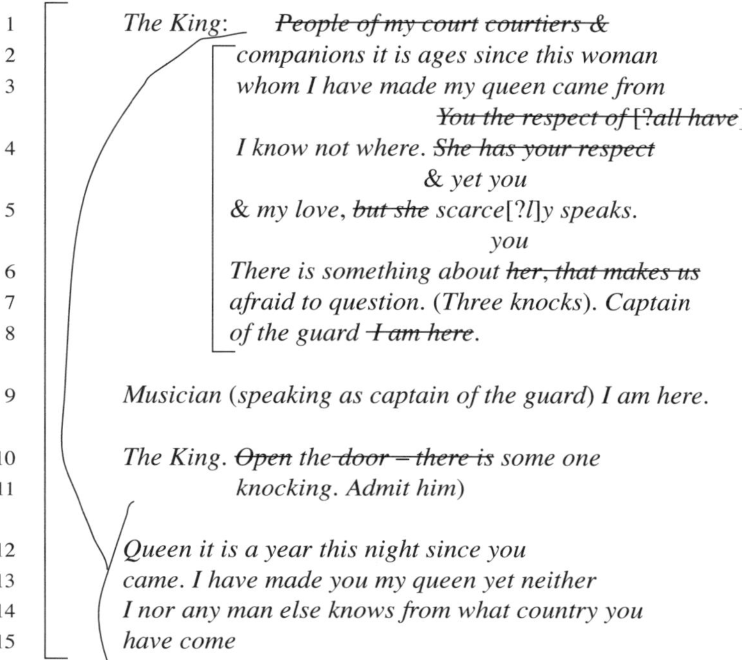

The King: ~~*People of my court*~~ ~~*courtiers &*~~
companions it is ages since this woman
whom I have made my queen came from
~~*You the respect of*~~ [~~*?all have*~~]
I know not where. ~~*She has your respect*~~
& yet you
& my love, ~~*but she*~~ *scarce*[*?l*]*y speaks.*
you
There is something about ~~*her, that makes us*~~
afraid to question. (Three knocks). Captain
of the guard ~~*I am here*~~*.*

Musician (speaking as captain of the guard) I am here.

The King. ~~*Open*~~ *the* ~~*door – there is*~~ *some one*
knocking. Admit him)

Queen it is a year this night since you
came. I have made you my queen yet neither
I nor any man else knows from what country you
have come

Punch holes on the left and the double line at the top give the appearance of a recto, but Yeats turned the sheet over and reversed it before writing on it. The illegible words after the King's speech-prefix were canceled first; ll. 2–8 were canceled next and replaced by ll. 12–15; finally, the entire page of text was struck out.

5r

The Stranger: I had a wife but she was so much
uglier than the image in my [cancelled] head that I left her.
The other night I was eating my dinner in
a Tavern. I am a man of no account &
so I must eat my meals among ~~[cancelled]~~ servants
servants & boors. A man there said I was
a fool because I was in love with a
woman that I had never seen

The King. But what have I to do with it.

The Stranger. I do not want to be called a fool,
send the queen that I may look at her

The King. You seem to me a brazen audacious man
not caring where you stand, nor of whom
nor to whom you speak,

The Stranger. I have never shown disrespect to this
image in my head yet know I
must see the real woman

The King. She is at my side

[NLI 8769(i), 5r] [*VPl*, 45–59]

5

The Stranger: I had a wife but she was so much uglier than the image in my ~~had~~ head that I left her. The other night I was eating my dinner in a tavern. I am a man of no account & so I must eat my meals among ~~seav servants~~ servants and boors. A man there said I was a fool because I was in love with a woman that I had never seen

The King. But what have I to do with it.

The Stranger. I do not want to be called a fool. Send the queen that I may look at her

The King. You seem to me a brazen audaceous man not caring where you stand, nor of whom nor to whom you speak.

The Stranger. I have never shown disrespect to the image in my head yet knew I must see the real woman

The King. She is at my side

[NLI 8769(i), 6r]

6

The Stranger. Is this the queen of the Great Clock Tower

The King. She is the queen

(The Stranger stands in front of her. A pause)

The Stranger. She is not so tall as I had thought
nor as white & ~~[illegible]~~ red but what does it
matter, I shall proclaim wherever I go
that I have seen her & that she is the
most beautiful woman in the world.

The King. Then go. You have seen her.

The Stranger. Not yet. I was a little drunk that night
when they mocked me & I swore that not only
would I see the queen & that — O I must
have been very drunk that she would dance
for me.

The King. ~~I shall have the silence~~ I will have
you flogged

The Stranger. Then you flog a sacred man

[NLI 8769(i), 6r] [*VPl*, 60–76]

6

The Stranger. Is this the queen of the Great Clock Tower

The King. She is the queen

(The Stranger stands in front of her. A pause)

The Stranger. She is not so tall as I had thought nor as white or ~~read~~ ^red^ but what does it matter, I shall proclaim wherever I go that I have seen her & that she is the most beautiful woman in the world.

The King. Then go. You have seen her.

The Stranger. Not yet I was a little drunk that night when they mocked me & I swore that not only would I see the queen & that – O I must have been very drunk that she would dance for me.

The King. ~~I shall have Be silent or~~ I will have you flogged

The Stranger. Then you flog a sacred man

[NLI 8769(i), 7r]

7

The King. A secret then

The Stranger. I will tell you a great secret.
I went to the Boyne where the old gods live.
I lay there for a month eating nothing.
Then I saw Aengus & all the gods. I told
them of my oath & all the gods shouted.
After that there was silence & then Aengus spoke
& listen well for these are the very words he
spoke. "Upon the last night of the year
when the great clock strikes the last note
of midnight the queen will kiss you upon
the mouth!"

The King. Captain of the guard

Musician (speaking as captain of the guard) I am here

The King. I give this man to you. Strike his head from
his body

The Stranger. I go yet all things I saw will happen. The
gods have spoken. (He goes & K)

[NLI 8769(i), 7r] [*VPl*, 77–95]

7

The King. A sacred man

The Stranger. I will tell you a great secret. I went to the Boyne where the old gods live. I lay there for a month eating nothing. Then I saw Aengus & all the gods. I told them of my oath & all the gods shouted. After that there was silence & then Aengus spoke & listen well for these were the very words the spoke. "Upon the last night of the year when the great clock strikes the last note of midnight the queen will kiss you upon the mouth."

The King. Captain of the Guard

Musician (speaking as Captain of the Guard) I am here

The King. I give this man to you. Strike his head from his body

The Stranger. I go yet all this I said will happen. The gods have shouted. (He goes to R)

8 For "words the" read "words he".

[NLI 8769(i), 8r]

8

The King. Stop. That tale is all lies. You knew
the queen before she came to this country. You
are somebody that she has made mad
as she has made me mad. (To queen)
Speak. ~~Speak~~. Who is this man? If perhaps
if you tell me this I will spare her life.
(The queen remains remains silent & immovable)
So be it. Whether her tale be true or not
it is plain that he wishes to sacrifice her life.
To lay it down at your feet. Take
him captain of the guard. (The stranger goes
out ~~at~~ R) Bring me his head that
I may know that he is dead. (He
stands at R looking at stage) If he was not
your lover before you came to this country,
if he is nothing to you, if he is nothing
but a shuttle & fool, if he is nothing but
a man who has insulted you, laugh or sing
I do not care which it is. Sit at here her knee

[NLI 8769(i), 8r] [*VPl*, 101–114]

8

The King. Stop. This tale is all lies. You knew the queen before she came to this country. You are somebody that she has made mad as she has made me mad. (To queen) Speak. ~~Speak~~. Who is this man? ~~If~~ Perhaps if you tell me this I will spare his life.

(<u>The Queen ~~reamins~~ remains silent & immovable</u>)

So be it. Whether his tale be true or not it is plain that he wishes to sacrifice his life. To lay it down at your feet. Take him Captain of the Guard. (The Stranger goes out ~~ri~~ R) Bring me his head that I may know that he is dead. (He stands at R looking off stage) If he was not your lover before you came into this country, if he is nothing to you, if he is nothing but a stroller & fool, if he is nothing but a man who has insulted you, laugh or sing I do not care what it is. Let all ~~her~~ here know

9

(The queen moves for the first time)

Why do you fix your eyes upon me.

Musician. (sings as queen in a low voice)

O what may come
Into my womb.

The King.

Oh this is better: sing out till all here may
know that you rejoice in the death

Musician (sings as queen)

He longs to kill
My body until
That sudden shudder
And limbs lie still

O what may come
Into my womb
What caterpillar
My beauty consume

[NLI 8769(i), 9r] [*VPl*, 115–127]

9

1 ~~know that you rejoice in his death~~

(The queen moves for the first time.)

2 Why do you fix your eyes upon me.

~~The que~~
~~Mus~~
Musician. (singing as queen ~~a~~ in a low voice)
3 O what may come
4 Into my womb

The King.
5 Oh that is better. Sing out that all here may
6 know that you rejoice in his death

~~Qu~~ Musician (singing as queen)
He
7 ~~The~~ longs to kill
8 My body until
9 That sudden shudder
10 And limbs lie still

11 O what may come
12 Into my womb
13 What catterpillar
14 My beauty consume

10

I do not know what would mean but this seem scornful.
He goes out & returns & returns with the head, & he stoops
~~upon a sheet he fixes the spear in the floor & the right~~
which he lays upon the cabinet throne of R.

The King, Now I shall know of their life
(He sits on the throne of L)
sir: I shall sit here beside the queen
You have our attention, sir, shall stand
(The queen rises). Why do you rise. (The
queen ~~has stood~~ begins, to dance) That is good, the ghost
dance, leave him not mocking with a dance
a good the ghost (he laughs) ~~dance, dance~~
~~I tell~~ (The queen stands motionless before the
the head) dance, dance, you were nothing
to him but an image in his head, &
now he is nothing to you but, & what
is the good of lovers that is but a head.
(He laughs) ~~queen~~ dance (The queen dances,
this like the head between her hands & stands
in the centre of the stage

[NLI 8769(i), 10r] [*VPl*, 128–139]

10

1 I do not know what words mean but they seem scornful.
the
He goes out at right & returns with head of the stranger
~~upon a spear he fixes the spear in the floor to~~ the right
which he lays upon the cubical throne to R.

2 The King. Now I shall know if these lips
(He sits upon the throne to L)
3 sing: I shall sit here beside the queen
4 You ^ have our attention. Sing stroller fool
5 (The queen rises). Why do you rise. (The
~~then stands~~
6 queen begins to dance.) That is good thought
7 dance, turn him into mockery with a dance
8 A good thought (he laughs) ~~dance, dance~~
9 ~~I like~~ (The queen stands motionless before the
10 the head) dance, dance you were nothing
11 to him but an image in his head, &
12 now he is nothing to you but, and what
13 is the good of a lover that is but a head.
14 (He laughs) ~~Que~~ dance (The queen dances,
then lifts the head between her hands & stands
in the centre of the stage

---

1 For "what words" read "what those words".
6 For "That is good" read "That is a good".
12 For "to you but, and" read "to you but a head, and".

11

of the centre of the stage
The King. The lips are stirring, the eyes move, 'Imagine riding'
Musician (singing as head in a low voice) ' ~~I heard~~ a man say)
The King, O listen it has begun to sing (He covers down covering his face

Musician (singing as head)
Imagine riding I heard a man say —
Out of Ben Bulben and Knocknarea,
What says the clock in the great Clock Tower.
Out of the grave, saddle and ride
But lovers from Rosses crowding tide
The meet in upon the mountain side,
A slow low note and an iron bell

"
What made them mount & what made them ~~[illegible]~~ couple
Cuchulain that fought night-long with the foam;
What says the clock in the great clock Tower;
Niam that rode on it; Lad and Lass
That sat so still and played at the ~~[illegible]~~ chess
Heard deep heroic wantonness;
A slow low note & an iron bell;

'''
Aleel, his countess; Hanrahan
That seemed but a wild wenching man;
What says the clock in the great clock tower

[NLI 8769(i), 11[r]] [*VPl*, 140–160]

~~11~~

11 1~~N3~~

~~at the centre of the stage.~~

1 The King. The lips are opening. The ~~ye~~ eyes move

Images ride"

2 Musician (singing as head in a low voice) '~~I heard a man~~ say'

3 The King. O terrors it has begun to sing (He cowers down covering his face

Musician (singing as head)

I

4 Images ride – I heard a man ~~sta~~ say–
5 Out of Benbulben and Knocknarea,
6 What says the clock in the Great Clock Tower
7 Out of the grave, saddle & ride
8 But turn from Rosses crawling tide
9 The meet's upon the mountain side,
10 A slow low note & an iron bell

II

come
11 What made them mount & what made them ~~ride~~
12 Cuchulain that fought night-long with the foam;
13 What says the clock in the Great Clock Tower;
14 Niam that rode on it; lad and lass
15 That sat so still and played at the ~~ele~~ chess
16 Heart's deep heroic wantonness;
17 A slow low note & an iron bell;

III

18 Aleel, his countess; Hanrahan
19 That seemed but a wild wenching man;
20 What says the clock in the great Clock tower

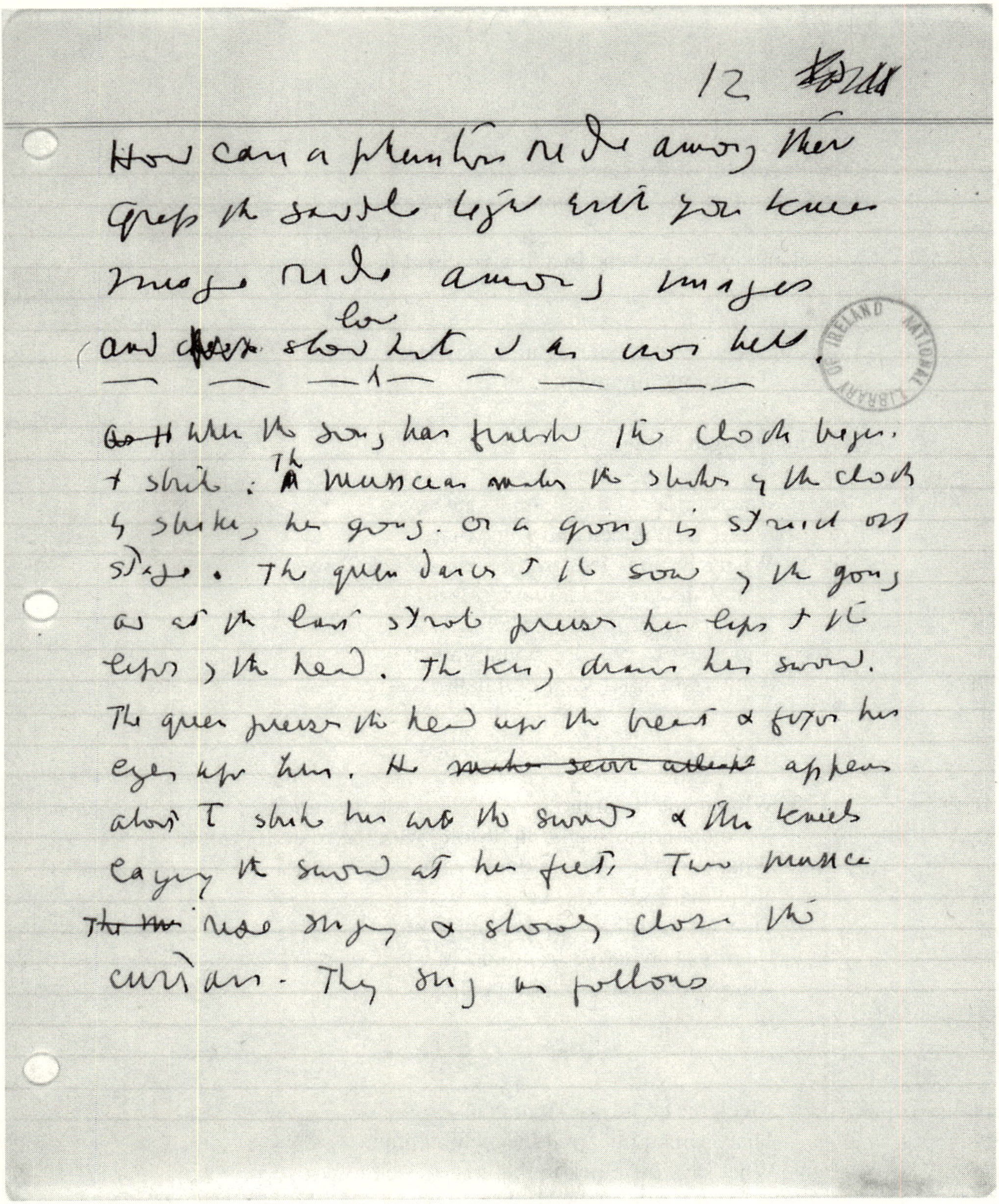

[NLI 8769(i), 12r]

[NLI 8769(i), 12r] [*VPl*, 161–164 and stage direction]

12 ~~10 11~~

How can a phantom ride among these
Grip the saddle tight with your knees
Image ride among images
low
And ~~deep~~ slow ^ note & an iron bell.

~~As th~~ When the song has finished the clock begins
The
to strike. ~~A~~ Musician makes the strokes of the clock by striking his gong. Or a gong is struck off stage. The queen dances to the sound of the gong and at the last stroke presses her lips to the lips of the head. The King draws his sword. The queen presses the head upon the breast & fixes her eyes upon him. He ~~makes sever attempt~~ appears about to strike her with the sword & then kneels laying the sword at her feet. Two musicians ~~The Mus~~ rise singing & slowly close the curtain. They sing as follows

1–3 Though most of the lyric as written here is close to its final form, these three lines posed a difficulty for Yeats, who continually revised them until the time of the play's publication in *Life and Letters* in November 1934.

[NLI 8769(i), 13r]

13

First Musician

O but I saw a solemn sight
Said the rambling, shambling travelling-man
Castle Dargan's ruin all lit
Lovely ladies dancing in it.

Second Musician

What things it danced! Those days are gone,
Said the wicked crooked hawthorn tree
Lovely lady, or gallant man
Are blown cold dust or a bit of bone.

First Musician

O what is life but a mouthful of air
Said the rambling, shambling, travelling-man
Yet all the lovely things that were
Live – for I saw them dancing there.

Second Musician

Nobody knows what may befall
Said the wicked crooked hawthorn tree
I have stood so long by a gap in the wall
Maybe I shall not die at all.

[NLI 8769(i), 13r] [*VPl*, 165–180]

~~10 12~~
13

First Musician
O but I saw a solemn sight
Said the rambling, shambling travelling-man
Castle Dargans ruin all lit
Lovely ladies dancing in it –

Second Musician
What though it danced! Those days are gone,
Said the wicked crooked hawthorn tree
Lovely lady, or gallant man
Are ~~bli~~ blown cold dust or a bit of bone.

First Musician
O what is life but a mouthful of air
Said the rambling, shambling travelling-man
Yet all the lovely things that were
Live – for I saw them dancing there.

Second Musician
Nobody knows what may befall
Said the wicked crooked hawthorn tree
I have stopped so long a gap in the wall
Maybe I shall not die at all.

Part I. *The King of the Great Clock Tower* (Prose)

B. The First Typescript: SIUC 76/1/7

The first typescript of the prose version of *The King of the Great Clock Tower* (SIUC 76/1/7)—the work of Yeats's secretary, Mrs. H. Lytton Wilson—incorporated the holograph revisions Yeats made to NLI 8769(i). In its turn this typescript was substantially revised before the text of the play was reproduced for the personnel at the Abbey Theatre involved in the production.

In Yeats's preparation of this initial full script of the play some uncertainties remain. He begins to envisage a potential design scheme for the play, but the possible venue for a production is still unsettled, as references to the Peacock Theatre are continually deleted and replaced with references to an "ordinary theatre" (namely the Abbey's main stage), where he could make use of the Abbey's set of Edward Gordon Craig's screens. (Yeats regularly used these in creating settings for his heroic plays after 1911.) The stage directions show cumulatively that he envisaged a formal, rather static staging for the first half of the play to contrast markedly with the dance and mime that are the focus of the concluding part of the action. On the level of character, continual changes to their speech prefixes reveal that Yeats is still unsure what vocal register each of the Musicians should ideally possess, a problem resolved only during rehearsals.

Yeats's sketches for the throne and cubes on 9^v are reproduced in appendix VI.

The numerals in dark pencil inserted in an unknown hand throughout the text (which have not been reproduced in the transcriptions) suggest that this typescript was at some point marked up as a copytext for typesetting and printing.

6. Copies

THE KING OF THE GREAT CLOCK TOWER 34

Characters:-

The King of the Great Clock Tower, (dressed in red)

The Queen (dressed in orange with details in black or red)

A Stranger (dressed in black with details in red)

First attendant (dressed in black. bass voice)

Second attendant (dressed in black. tenor voice.)

NOTE: The Queen should wear a beautiful inexpressive mask,

The Stranger a wild half-savage mask. It should cover the upper part of his face. The lower part being hidden by his red beard.

When the stage curtains rises it shows an inner curtain pale grey in colour, it may have a stencilled pattern of Dancers.

When the ordinary Theatre Orchestra is used only two musicians - one a singer, one both singer and speaker, are necessary.

The attendants stand one on either side of the Curtain, and after they have sung a few lines, slowly part it, singing:-

Second attendant: They dance all day that dance in Tir-na-nogue.

First attendant: There every lover is a happy rogue,
And should he speak, it is the speech of birds|| No thought has he, and therefore has no words,|| No thought because no clock, no clock because||
If I consider deeply, lad and lass,
Nerve touching nerve upon that happy ground||Are bobbins where all time is bound and wound.

[SIUC 76/1/7, 1r] [*VPl*, preliminaries, opening stage direction, 1–8]

6. Copies

34

THE KING OF THE GREAT CLOCK TOWER

(~~he is~~ dressed in red)
~~to be clothed in red~~
~~his clothes are red~~

Characters:-

The King of the Great Clock Tower, ~~his dress res dressed in~~ red

dressed in
The Queen (~~her dress~~ orange with details in black or red)

A Stranger (dressed in black with details in red

~~bass~~
First Attendant (~~tenor~~ dressed in black. ~~Tenor voice)~~ bass voice)
~~**Three or two Musicians**~~

Tenor
Second Attendant (~~bass)~~ dressed in black. ~~bass~~ voice.)

inexpressive
NOTE: The Queen should wear a beautiful ~~impassive~~ mask.

The Stranger ~~wears~~ a wild half-savage mask. It should cover the upper part of his face. The lower part being hidden by his ~~beard.~~ red beard.

~~**When the Play is performed in an ordinary Theatre**~~
When the stage curtain rises ~~it~~ shows an inner curtain pale ivory in colour,
~~**there mustbe an inner curtain which may have a pattern**~~
It may have a strencilled pattern of dancers
~~**representing Dancers. If played at the Peacock Theatre**~~
Where the Stage Curtain parts in the middle, no inner curtain is necessary.

6. Copies

THE KING OF THE GREAT CLOCK TOWER[34]

Characters:-

The King of the Great Clock Tower, (dressed in red)

The Queen (dressed in orange with details in black or red)

A Stranger (dressed in black with details in red

First attendant (dressed in black. bass voice)

Three or four Musicians

Second attendant (dressed in black. tenor voice.)

NOTE: The Queen should wear a beautiful ~~impassive~~ inexpressive mask,

The Stranger a wild half-savage mask. It should cover the upper part of his face. The lower part being hidden by his ~~beard~~ red beard.

~~When the Play is performed in an ordinary Theatre~~ when the stage curtain rises it shows an inner curtain pale orange in colour,

100 ~~there must be an inner curtain which may have a pattern~~ it may have a stencilled pattern of dancers

~~representing Dancers. If played at the Peacock Theatre where the Stage Curtain parts in the middle, no inner curtain is necessary.~~

~~When the ordinary Theatre Orchestra is used only two musicians - one a singer, one both singer and speaker, are necessary.~~

The attendants

~~A Musician~~ stands one on either side of ~~the~~ this Curtain, and after they have sung a few lines, slowly part ~~the curtain~~ it, singing:-

~~FIRST MUSICIAN~~ Second attendant: They dance all day that dance in Tir-na-nogue.

~~SECOND~~ First attendant: There every lover is a happy rogue,
And should he speak, it is the speech of birds|| No thought has he, and therefore has no words,|| No thought because no clock, no clock because||
If I consider deeply, lad and lass,
Nerve touching nerve upon that happy ground||Are bobbins where all time is bound and wound.

200

[SIUC 76/1/7, 1r, continued] [*VPl*, preliminaries, opening stage direction, 1–8]

When the ordinary Theatre Orchestra is used only two Musicians – one a singer, one both singer and speaker, are necessary.

The Attendants
~~**A Musici**~~**an stands one on either side of** ~~**the**~~ this
Curtain, a^nd after they have sung a few lines, slowly
it
part ~~**the curtain**~~**,** ~~**while**~~ **singing:-**

Second Attendant
~~**FIRST MUSICIAN**~~**: They dance all day that dance in Tir-na-nogue.**

First Attendant
~~**SECOND**~~ ~~//~~ **There every lover is a happy rogue,**
{A
{**and should he speak, it is the speech**
of birds.//**No thought has he, and**
{,
therefore has no words{**.**// **No thought**
because no clock, no clock because//
{I
{**if I consider deeply, lad and lass,**
Nerve touching nerve upon that happy
ground//**Are bobbins where all time is**
bound and wound.

2–10 The typist treated verse as prose. Yeats entered the double slashes to show line breaks.
6, 9 The first slash cancels the comma in each line.

7

2.

Second attendant
~~1st~~ ~~MUSICIAN~~ Oh never may that dismal thread run loose;

First attendant
~~2nd. MUSICIAN~~ For there the Hound that Oisin saw pursues/

The hornless deer that runs in such a fright;

And there the woman clasps an apple tight,

For all the clammer of a famished man;

They run ~~the~~ in foam, and there in foam they ran,

Nor can they stop to take a breath that still

Hear in the foam, the beating of a bell.

When the Curtains are parted one sees to left the King and Queen upon two Thrones, which may be two cubes. There should be two

300 cubes upon the opposite side to balance them. ~~If the ordinary~~ The background & the cubes are a peach blue. The background may be a curtain hung in a ~~semicircle~~ ~~orchestra is not used to create the music, a third musician~~ semi circle, or a semi circle of one foot Eras screens so painted that ~~sits upon the ground to right beside drum, gong, zither~~ the blue is darker below than above.

~~and flute. The TWO MUSICIANS sit down beside him. If the ordinary orchestra is used,~~ The TWO ~~MUSICIANS can~~ attendants remain standing, facing the audience ~~or sitting one~~ at either side of the Stage but a little in the shadow

THE KING A year ago this night, you walked into my house. I made you my Queen, yet neither I, not any other man, knows from what Country you came. And now before our friends and courtiers here assembled, I ask you, not for the first time, where that Country is, who

400 and what you were before you became my Queen. You have kept silence long enough, that silence has become unendurable to all here, and to me.

[SIUC 76/1/7, 2r] [*VPl*, 9–25]

2.

Second Attendant
~~**1st Musician**~~ **Oh never may that dismal thread run loose;**

First attendant
~~**2nd Musician**~~ **For there the Hound that Oisin saw pursues/** 7
The hornless deer that runs in such a fright;
And there the woman clasps an apple tight,
For all the clammer of a famished man;
in
They run ~~the~~ foam, and there in foam they ran,
Nor can they stop to take a breath that still
Hear in the foam, the beating of a bell.

<u>When the Curtains</u> are parted one sees to left the King and Queen upon two Thrones, which may be two cubes. There should be two
The background / & the
cubes upon the opposite side to balance them. ~~If the ordinary~~
cubes are a rich blue. The background may be a curtain hung in a ~~semi circ~~
~~**orchestra is not used to create the music, a third musician**~~
semi circle, or a semi circle of one foot <u>Craig</u> screnes so painted that
~~**sits upon the ground to xxxxx right beside drum, gong, zither**~~
the blue is darker below than above.
~~**and flute. The TWO MUSICIANS sit down beside him. If the**~~
Attendants
~~**ordinary orchestra is used**~~, **The TWO ~~MUSICIANS can~~ remain standing,**
facing the audience
~~**or sitting one**~~ ^ **at either side of the Stage.** but a little in the shadow

THE KING **A year ago this night, you walked into my house. I made you my Queen, yet neither I, not any other man, knows from what Country you came. And now before our friends and courtiers here assembled, I ask you, not for the first time, where that Country is, who and what you were before you became my Queen. You have kept silence long enough, that silence has become unendurable to all here, and to me.**

[SIUC 76/1/7, 3[r]]

3.

There is a pause. THE QUEEN neither speaks nor moves. ~~A MUSICIAN beats three times~~ upon the drum, ~~or the drum may be struck~~ off ~~stage~~. Three knocks, made by drum stroke off stage.

THE KING Captain of the Guard

First attendant
~~MUSICIAN~~ (Speaking as Capt. of the Guard ~~looking straight at the audience~~ and without turning his head) King, I am here.

KING Someone has struck three times upon the great door. Admit him !

(~~THE STRANGER~~)

First attendant
~~MUSICIAN~~ (Speaking as before) I will admit him.

(STRANGER ENTERS)

KING What is your name?

500 STRANGER It is enough that I am a/stroller and a fool, and that you are the King of the great Clock Tower.

KING I am that King. What do you want?

STRANGER A year ago somebody told me that you had married the most beautiful woman in the world, and from that moment I have had her image in my head, and month by month, it has grown more and more beautiful. I have made poems about her and sung them everywhere, but I have never seen her.

KING Have you no wife or sweetheart of your own?

STRANGER 600 I had a wife, but she was so much/uglier than the image in my head, that I left her. The other night I was eating my dinner in a Tavern; I am a man of

[SIUC 76/1/7, 3r] [*VPl*, 26–47]

3.

There is a pause. THE QUEEN neither speaks nor moves. A ~~MUSI~~CIAN ~~beats three times~~ upon the drum, ~~or the drum may be struck~~ off ~~stage.~~ Three knocks, made by drum stroke off stage.

THE KING **Captain of the Guard**

and without turning his head

First Attendant ~~& looking straight at the audience~~

~~MUSICIAN~~ (Speaking as Capt. of the Guard) King, I am here.

KING **Someone has struck three times upon the great door. Admit him!**

(~~THE STRANGER enters~~)

First Attendant

~~MUSICIAN~~ (Speaking as before) I will admit him.

(STRANGER ENTERS)

KING **What is your name?**

STRANGER **It is enough that I am a stroller and a fool, and that you are the King of the great Clock Tower.**

KING **I am that King. What do you want?**

STRANGER **A year ago somebody told me that you had married the most beautiful woman in the world, and from that moment I have had her image in my head, and month by month, it has grown more and more beautiful. I have made poems about her and sung them everywhere, but I have never seen her.**

KING **Have you no wife or sweetheart of your own?**

STRANGER **I have a wife, but she was so much uglier than the image in my head, that I left her. The other night I was eating my dinner in a Tavern; I am a man of**

4.

STRANGER — no account, and so must eat my meals amongst servants and boors; a man there said I was a fool, because I was in love with a woman I had never seen.

KING — But what have I to do with it?

STRANGER — I do not want to be called a fool. Send for the Queen that I may look at her.

KING 200 — You seem to me a brazen, audacious man, not / caring where you stand, nor of whom, nor to whom you speak.

STRANGER — I have never shown disrespect to the image in my head, yet ? must see the woman herself.

KING — She is at my side.

STRANGER — Is the this the Queen of the great Clock Tower?

KING — She is that Queen.

(THE STRANGER stands in front of ~~her~~ Queen. Pause)

STRANGER — She is not so tall as I had thought, not so white and red, but what does it matter, I shall proclaim everywhere that she is the most beautiful woman in the World.

800

KING — Then go; you have seen her.

STRANGER — Not yet. I was a little drunk that night when they mocked me, and I swore that not only would I see the Queen, but that - Oh, I must have been very drunk - that she would dance for me.

King. What!

The Stranger. When she has danced I ~~shall sing to her~~. I shall be grateful & I shall sing.

[SIUC 76/1/7, 4r] [*VPl*, 48–74]

4.

STRANGER **no account, and so must eat my meals amongst servants and boors; a man there said I was a fool, because I was in love with a woman I had never seen.**

KING **But what have I to do with it?**

STRANGER **I do not want to be called a fool. Send for the Queen that I may look at her.**

KING **You seem to me a brazen, audacious man, not caring where you stand, nor of whom, nor to whom you speak.**

STRANGER **I have never shown disrespect to the image in my head, yet** ∧I **must see the woman herself.**

KING **She is at my side.**

STRANGER **Is the this the Queen of the great Clock Tower?**

KING **She is that Queen.**

(THE <u>STRANGER</u> stands in front of ~~her~~ ∧Queen**. Pause)**

STRANGER **She is not so tall as I had thought, not so white and red, but what does it matter, I shall proclaim everywhere that she is the most beautiful woman in the World.**

KING **Then go; you have seen her.**

STRANGER **Not yet. I was a little drunk that night when they mocked me, and I swore that not only would I see the Queen, but that – Oh, I must have been very drunk – that she would dance for me.**

King. ~~What!~~ What!

The Stranger. When she has danced I ~~shall sing to her.~~ I shall be grateful & I shall sing.

5.

King   I ~~will~~ shall have you flogged.

STRANGER   Then you will flog a sacred man.

KING   How? A sacred man?

STRANGER   I will tell you a great secret. I went to the Boyne where the old Gods live. I lay there for a month
900 eating nothing. Then I saw Aengus and all the Gods. I told them of my oath and all the Gods shouted. After that there was silence and then Aengus spoke; and listen well for these were his very words:-

"Upon the last night of the Year, when the great Clock strikes the last note of midnight, the Queen shall kiss you upon the mouth."

KING   Captain of the Guard !

First attendant ~~MUSICIAN~~ (Speaking as Capt. and as before ~~of the Guard~~)   I am here !

KING   I give this man to you. He has said that the Queen
1000 will kiss him upon the mouth at the last stroke of the clock. Take him therefore and strike his head from his body.

First attendant ~~MUSICIAN~~ (Speaking as Capt. of the Guard)   I will strike his head from his body.

~~STRANGER   I am yet ... I have ... will happen. The Gods have shouted.~~

~~... Right~~

~~KING   Stop! That tale is all lies.~~ You knew the Queen before she came to this Country. You are somebody that she has made mad, as she has made me mad.

1100

[SIUC 76/1/7, 5[r]] [*VPl*, 75–101]

5.

King I [shall] ~~**will**~~ **have you flogged.**

STRANGER **Then you will flog a sacred man.**

KING **How? A sacred man?**

STRANGER **I will tell you a great secret. I went to the Boyne where the old Gods live. I lay there for a month eating nothing. Then I saw Aengus and all the Gods. I told them of my oath and all the Gods shouted. After that there was silence and then Aengus spoke; and listen well for these were his very words:-** ~~You shall sing to the Queen and~~ **"Upon the last night of the Year, when the great Clock strikes the last note of midnight, the Queen shall kiss you upon the mouth."**

KING **Captain of the Guard!**

First Attendant ~~**MUSICIAN**~~ **(Speaking as Capt.** [and as before] ~~**of the Guard**~~**)** **I am here!**

KING **I give this man to you. He has said that the Queen will kiss him upon the mouth at the last stroke of the clock. Take him therefore and strike his head from his body.**

First Attendant ~~**MUSICIAN**~~ **(Speaking as Capt. of the Guard)** **I will strike his head from his body.** ~~Stranger. No matter I shall sing~~

The Stranger I shall sing to her and then At the last stroke of the Clock she shall kiss me on

STRANGER ~~**I go yet all that I have said will happen. The Gods**~~ the mouth and I shall sing to her. ~~**have shouted.**~~

The King What sing when your head is off. (Stranger goes ~~out~~ R to R)

~~**(He goes to Right)**~~

The Stranger The gods have shouted. (He goes out)

~~**KING**~~ ~~**Stop! That tale is all lies.**~~ **You knew the Queen before she came to this Country. You are somebody that she has made mad, as she has made me mad.**

~~Stroller I shall be grateful and being grateful, I sing~~

I go but this is what will happen

Stranger ~~This is what will happen~~ First (counting on his fingers) the Queen will dance, second I shall sing –

The King. What with your head off.

Stranger When I am [grateful] ~~grateful~~ I sing. [Third] ~~Third~~ the Queen being grateful [will give me a kiss.] ~~will kiss me on the mouth~~ (goes R)

The King. Stop. You have told us nothing but lies.

6.

KING (To Queen) Speak! Who is this man? Perhaps if you will answer my question, I shall spare his life.

(THE QUEEN remains silent and immovable)

KING So be it. Whether his tale be true or not, it is plain that he wishes to sacrifice his life, to lay it down at your feet. Take him Capt. of the Guard.

First attendant ~~Capt~~ (as Captain of the Guard.) I take him.

(~~THE STRANGER goes out Right~~) (The King thrusts the Stranger out to R.)

King Bring me his head that I may know that he is dead.

(He has followed the ~~Stranger to the Back of Stage thrusting~~ him before him. (He now stands looking off Stage.))

1200

~~Head~~ If he was not your lover before you came into this Country, if he is nothing to you, if he is nothing but a stroller and fool, if he is nothing but a man who has insulted you, laugh or sing, I do not care which it is.

(THE QUEEN moves for the first time. Turning her head slowly and looking at the King)

KING Why do you fix your eyes upon me?

Second attendant ~~MUSICIAN~~ (Singing as Queen and in a low voice)

Oh what may come
Into my womb

KING 1300 Ah, that is better. But sing out loud/ that all here may know that you rejoice in his death.

[SIUC 76/1/7, 6r] [*VPl*, 102–119]

6.

KING (To Queen) **Speak! Who is this man? Perhaps if you will answer my question, I shall spare his life.**

(THE QUEEN remains silent and immoveable)

KING **So be it. Whether his tale be true or not, it is plain that he wishes to sacrifice his life, to lay it down at your feet. Take him Capt. of the Guard.**

First Attendant ~~Capt~~ ~~Musician~~ (as Captain of the Guard) I take ~~tike~~ him.

~~(THE STRANGER goes out Right~~) The King thrusts ~~forces~~ the Stranger out to R.)

King **Bring me his head that I may know that he is dead.**

(He has ~~followed the Stranger to the Right of Stage thrusting him before him.~~ He now stands looking off Stage.)

~~KING~~ **If he was not your lover before you came into this Country, if he is nothing to you, if he is nothing but a stroller and fool, if he is nothing but a man who has insulted you, laugh or sing, I do not care which it is.**

(THE QUEEN moves for the first time. Turning her head slowly and looking at the King)

KING **Why do you fix your eyes upon me?**

Second ~~First~~ Attendant **~~MUSICIAN~~ (Singing as Queen and in a low voice)**

Oh what may come
Into my womb

KING **Ah, that is better. But sing out loud that all here may know that you rejoice in his death.**

7.

MUSICIAN(Singing as Queen)

He longs to kill
My body, until
That sudden shudder
And limbs lie still.

Oh, what may come
Into my womb;
What caterpillar
My beauty consumes.

KING I do not know what those words mean, but they sound scornful.

(He goes out at right and returns with the head of THE STRANGER, and lays it upon one of the two cubicle thrones)

KING Now I shall know if those lips can sing. . You have our attention. Sing stroller and fool.

(The QUEEN rises) Why do you rise? (THE QUEEN begins to dance) That is a good fault; dance; turn him into mockery with a dance; Oh, a good thought. (He laughs), the QUEEN stands motionless before the head) Dance ; Dance : If you are nothing to him but a body or an image in his head, he is nothing to you but a head without a body. What is the good of a lover without a body? Dance.

1520 (THE QUEEN dances, then takes the head between her hands and raising it above her head, stands in the centre of the stage)

dance, display your beauty.)

[SIUC 76/1/7, 7r] [*VPl*, 120–139]

7.

MUSICIAN (singing as Queen)

He longs to kill
My body until
That sudden shudder
And limbs lie still.

Oh, what may come
Into my womb;
What caterpillar
My beauty consume~~s~~ ?

KING **I do not know what those words mean, but they sound scornful.**

(He goes out at right and returns with the head of THE
the cubical throne to R & nearest audience)
STRANGER, and lays it upon ~~one of the two cubicle thrones~~)

(He sits on the
KING **Now I shall know if those lips can sing. ~~I shall~~**
other ~~sid~~ cubical throne to R)
~~sit here beside the Quee~~n. You have our attention.
Sing stroller and fool.

(The QUEEN rises) Why do you rise? (THE QUEEN begins to dance). That is a good fault; dance; turn him into mockery with a dance; Oh a good thought. (He laughs), the
looking at
QUEEN stands motionless ~~before~~ the head) Dance! Dance! If you are nothing to him but a body or an image in his head, he is nothing to you but a head without a body. What is the good of a lover without a body?
~~He thought~~
Dance. ~~Dance!~~ ~~He you were not so fine as the image in his head, dance & display your beauty~~
(THE QUEEN dances, then takes the head between her hands and
dances then the head still raised.)
raising it above her head, stands in the centre of the stage)

(He thought you were not so fine as the image
not so tall, nor so ~~red~~ red & white
in his head, ~~not so tall, not so red & white~~,
dance, display your beauty.)

[SIUC 76/1/7, 8r]

8.

KING The lips are opening, the eyes are moving.

First attendant
~~MUSICIAN~~ (Singing as head in a low voice)

Images ride — I heard a man say.

KING Oh terror, it has begun to sing!

(He cowers down, covering his face)

MUSICIAN (Singing as head)

Images ride - I heard a man say -
Out of Benbulben and Knocknareagh.
What says the clock in the great Clock Tower?
1600 Out of the grave, saddle and ride
But turn from Rosses crawling tide,
The meet's upon the mountain side,
A slow low note and an iron bell .

What made them mount and what made them ~~ride~~ come,
Cuchulain that fought night long with the ~~sea~~ foam;
What says the clock in the great Clock Tower?
Niam that rode on it; lad and lass
That sat so still and played at the Chess —
Heart's deep, heroic, wantoness.
A slow low note and an iron bell.

Aileel his countess; Hannrahan ~~that seemed but a wild wenching~~
That seemed but a wild wenching man;
What says the clock in the great Clock Tower;
1700 How can a phantom ride among these;
Grip the saddle tight with your knees;
Image , ride among images.
A slow low note and an iron bell.

[SIUC 76/1/7, 8r] [*VPl*, 140–164]

8.

KING The lips are opening, the eyes are moving.
First Attendant
~~MUSICIAN~~ (Singing as head in a low voice)
Images ride — *I heard a man say.*

KING Oh terror, it has begun to sing!

(He cowers down, covering his face)

MUSICIAN (Singing as head)
Images ride – I heard a man say -
Out of Benbulbenn and Knocknareagh,
What says the clock in the great Clock Tower?
Out of the grave, saddle and ride
But turn from Rosses crawling tide,
The meet's upon the mountain side.
A slow low note and an iron bell.

come,
What made them mount and what made them ~~ride~~
foam;
Cuchulain that fought night long with the ~~foe;~~
What says the clock in the great Clock Tower?
Niam that rode on it; lad and lass
That sat so still and played at the Chess —
Heart's deep, heroic,wantoness.
A slow low note and an iron bell.

Alleel his countess; Hanrahan ~~that seemed but a wild wenching~~
That seemed but a wild wenching man;
says
What the clock in the great Clock Tower;
How can a phantom ride among these;
Grip the saddle tight with your knees;
Image, ride among images.
A slow low note and an iron bell.

(When the song has finished, the clock begins to strike. The strokes are represented by a gong, struck off stage. ~~A musician makes the strokes of the clock by striking his gong, or a gong is struck off stage.~~ THE QUEEN dances to the sound of the gong, and at the last stroke presses her lips to the lips of the head. THE KING has risen. and draws his sword. THE QUEEN lays the head upon her breast and fixes her eyes upon him. He appears about to strike, but kneels, laying the sword at her feet. The TWO ~~MUSICIANS~~ attendants rise singing, and slowly close the curtain. Their song is as follows)

1800

1st. attendant ~~Musician~~:
Oh, but I saw a solemn sight;
~~Said~~ said the rambling, shambling, travelling-man;
Castle Dargan's ruin all lit,
Lovely ladies dancing in it.

2nd. attendant ~~Musician~~
What tho' it danced ! Those days are gone;
Said the wicked crooked hawthorn tree;
Lovely lady or gallant man
Are blown cold dust or a bit of bone.

1st. attendant ~~Musician~~:
O, what is life but a mouthful of air;
Said the rambling, shambling travelling-man;
Yet all the lovely things that were
Live, for I saw them dancing there.

2nd. Musician:
Nobody knows what may befall;
Said the wicked crooked hawthorn tree;
I have stopped so long a gap in the wall
May be I shall not die at all.

1900

9.

(When the song has finished, the clock begins to strike.
The strokes are represented by a gong struck off stage.
~~**A musician makes the strokes of the clock by striking**~~
~~**his gong or a gong is struck off stag**~~**e. THE QUEEN**
dances to the sound of the gong, and at the last stroke
presses her lips to the lips of the head. THE KING *has risen*
and {*n*
draw{s his sword. THE QUEEN lays the head upon her breast
and fixes her eyes upon him. He appears about to strike,
The *Attendants*
but kneels, laying the sword at her feet. ^TWO ~~**MUSICIANS**~~
rise singing, and slowly close the curtain. Their song
is as follows)

Attendant
Lst ~~**Musician**~~**:** **Oh, but I saw a solemn sight***;*
~~**As**~~ **said the rambling, shambling, travelling-man***;*
Castle Dargan's ruin all lit,
Lovely ladies dancing in it.

Attendant
2nd. ~~**Musician**~~ **What tho' it danced! Those days are gone**
Said the wicked crooked hawthorn tree*;*
Lovely lady or gallant man
Are blown cold dust or a bit of bone.

Attendant
Lst. ~~**Musician**~~**:** **O, what is life but a mouthful of air***;*
Said the rambling, shambling travelling-man*;*
Yet all the lovely things that were
Live, for I saw them dancing there.

2nd. Musician: **Nobody knows what may befall***;*
Said the wicked crooked hawthorn tree*;*
I have stopped so long a gap in the wall
May be I shall not die at all.

Part I. *The King of the Great Clock Tower* (Prose)

C. Revised Typescript: SIUC 91/16/10

Two copies are extant of the six typescripts that Yeats asked to be created following his revisions to the first typescript, SIUC 76/1/7: SIUC 91/16/10 and NLI 29,550(1). The former, which is part of the Lennox Robinson Collection at Carbondale, has been chosen for transcription here, since it contains a substantial number of revisions in Yeats's holograph, while the cover carries the title in his hand together with the significant note, "Corrected April 1934." If five of the six copies were intended for the use of the actors rehearsing the Abbey's staging of the play, then SIUC 91/16/10, with its additional corrections, may in all likelihood have been the copy Lennox Robinson used as director; and it may also have been shared with Yeats when he attended rehearsals. The National Library's copy, NLI 29,550(1), also contains revisions and additional material, of which two are possibly in Yeats's holograph and the rest decidedly by one or more unidentified hands. But none of the revisions made to the Robinson text are to be found in the copy in the National Library. However, one revision possibly in Yeats's hand in the National Library copy, which is not recorded in the Robinson text, nonetheless occurs in the versions published in *Life and Letters* (November 1934) and the Cuala edition (December 1934) of the play.

A later typescript, NLI 29,550(2), gathers into its text all the revisions and additions made in SIUC 91/16/10 and one revision found in NLI 29,550(1). It seems likely to have been the version prepared for submission to both the Cuala Press and the editor of *Life and Letters*. It also includes two penciled revisions and some stage directions that clearly relate to staging in the Abbey's main theater, as, for example, in the opening directions on 1^{r}. All in Lennox Robinson's hand, they correct typographical errors, indicate movements for the actors at specific moments in the drama, and offer small diagrammatic illustrations of the disposition of the performers within the stage space, exactly in the manner that Robinson adopted with many of the plays that he was directing. Of the two revisions to the dialogue only one recurs in the published texts.

A penciled insertion in NLI 29,550(1), 9^{r}, "music begins PP / muted strings," in a neat, minute hand (not Yeats's), cues the music used in the Abbey production from a score composed for the purpose by Arthur Duff. Duff's score involved more than the prescription in Yeats's published texts for drum and gong (see appendix IV). That the orchestral entry was pianissimo ("PP") suggests that in production the desired effect was the Queen slowly moving, as though under the influence of music heard only by her in the depths of her being.

By far the most interesting addition to NLI 29,550(2) is the final one: "Insert 2 new verses" at the conclusion of the lyric, "Oh, but I saw a solemn sight," at the end of the play. This may be a first indication that in performance Yeats's newly composed lyric beginning "Why must those holy, haughty feet descend" was to be included at this point; but none of it is included in the NLI 29,550(2) typescript. Both published texts print the further sung lyric for the Musicians, the composition of which must have been concluded to Yeats's satisfaction before he left Rapallo for Dublin, where he attended the final week of rehearsals from July 25, 1934. These newly created stanzas were probably added to the performance at that date.

Included with the typescript NLI 29,550(2), between the list of characters and the first page of dialogue, is a floor plan of the stage for the Abbey production. The image is reproduced as appendix V and should be consulted to show the degree to which the final versions of the text are informed by Yeats's experience of the play in performance. Taken together, the three annotated typescripts offer insight into how the play was performed during its week-long run at the Abbey Theatre.

Collations of NLI 29,550(1) and NLI 29,550(2) with SIUC 91/16/10 are included here, with two exceptions: (1) pencil corrections to the new typescript of the typist's errors that do not alter the word or words themselves, and (2) differences in punctuation that do not appear to be authorial. Additional notes transcribe and comment on the holograph material that relates to Robinson's production.

[SIUC 91/16/10, ii[r]] [*VPl*, title and preliminaries]

THE KING OF THE GREAT CLOCK TOWER

CHARACTERS:

THE KING OF THE GREAT CLOCK TOWER: **(Dressed in red)**

THE QUEEN: **(Dressed in orange with details in black and red)**

A STRANGER: **(Dressed in black with details in red.)**

AN ATTENDANT: **(Dressed in black. Bass Voice)**

SECOND ATTENDANT: **(Dressed in black. Tenor Voice)**

~~NOTE~~: **THE QUEEN should wear a beautiful impassive mask.**

THE STRANGER: a wild half-savage mask. It should cover the upper part of his face. The lower part being hidden by his red beard.

Put in one sentence & paragraph

[1[r]] [*VPl*, initial stage directions, 1–6]

1.

<u>WHEN THE STAGE CURTAIN RISES</u> it shows an inner curtain, pale ivory in colour. It may have a stencilled pattern of dancers.
At the right and left sides near the Proscenium are a drum and gong.

by gong & drums. They
<u>THE ATTENDANTS</u> <u>stand</u> ~~one on either side of this Curtain, and after they have sung a few lines,~~
the curtain **slowly part ~~it~~, singing:-**

First
1 **~~SECOND~~ ATTENDANT:** **They dance all day that dance in Tir-na-nogue.**

Second
2 **~~FIRST~~ ATTENDANT:** **There every lover is a happy rogue.**
3 **And should he speak, it is the speech of birds.**
4 **No thought has he, and therefore** has ⋏ **⋏ no words,**
5 **No thought because no clock, no clock because**
6 **If I consider deeply, lad and lass**

---

4 *rev in pencil to* has no words, *NLI 29,550(1)*

---

4 The word "has" has been inserted in heavy pencil to match the lineation. The hand is not Yeats's.

[2r] [*VPl*, 7–16 and stage directions]

2.

Nerve touching nerve upon that happy ground,
Are bobbins where all time is bound and wound.

First
~~**SECOND**~~ **ATTENDANT:** **Oh never may that dismal thread run loose;** ⊙
Second Attendant: **For there the Hound that Oisin saw pursues**
The hornless deer that runs in such a fright;
And there the woman clasps an apple tight,
For all the clammer of a famished man;
They run in foam, and there in foam they ran,
Nor can they stop to take a breath that still
Hear in the foam, the beating of a bell.

When the Curtains are parted one sees to left the KING and Queen upon two Thrones, which may be two cubes. There should be two cubes upon the opposite side to balance them. The background and the cubes are a rich blue. The background may be a curtain hung in a semi-circle, or a semi-circle of one foot Craig Screens, so painted that the blue is darker below than above.

sit down by drum and gong, they remain
THE TWO ATTENDANTS ~~**remain standing,**~~ **facing the audience at either side of the Stage, but a little in the shadow.**

---

4 *rev in pencil to* First attendant For there the Hound that Oisin saw pursues *NLI 29,550(1)*

---

4 A speech prefix has been added in pencil, possibly in Yeats's hand, after the first line of the stanza, indicating that the First Attendant is to perform the remaining lines. While SIUC 91/16/10 also follows a pattern of dividing each stanza between the two Attendants, the speakers are reversed, suggesting that in performance a dominance of the tenor voice was preferred.

3.

<u>THE KING</u>: **A year ago this night, you walked into my house. I made you my Queen, yet neither I, nor any other man, knows from what Country you came. And now before our friends and courtiers here assembled, I ask you, not for the first time, where that Country is, who and what you were before you became my Queen. You have kept silence long enough** ^ [sat there an image of stone or wood.] **. That silence has become unendurable to all here, and to me.**

<u>There is a pause. THE QUEEN neither speaks nor moves.</u>
First Attendant strikes the drum three times.
~~**There are three knocks made by drum strokes off stage**~~.

<u>THE KING</u>: **Captain of the Guard.**

<u>FIRST ATTENDANT</u>: **(<u>Speaking as Captain of the Guaard, without turning his head.</u>) King, I am here.**

<u>KING:</u> **Someone has struck three times upon the great door. Admit him!**

4.

FIRST ATTENDANT: (speaking as before) I will admit him.

(THE STRANGER ENTERS)

THE KING: **What is your name?**

STRANGER: **It is enough that I am a stroller and a fool, and that you are the King of the Great Clock Tower.**

THE KING: **I am that King. What do you want?**

STRANGER: **A year ago somebody told me that you had married the most beautiful woman in the world, and from that moment I have had her image in my head, and month by month, it has grown more and more beautiful. I have made poems about her and sung them everywhere, but I have never seen her.**

THE KING: **Have you no wife or sweetheart of your own?**

---

3 *rev in pencil (by WBY?) to* STRANGER C. R. *NLI 28,550(2)*

---

3 The penciled note in NLI 28,550(2) indicates "center stage, to the right," referring to the position of the actor in relation to the King and Queen, seated to stage left.

[SIUC 91/16/10]

[5r] [*VPl*, 45–59]

5.

STRANGER: **I had a wife, but she was so much uglier than the image in my head, that I left her. The other night I was eating my dinner in a tavern; I am a man of no account, and so must eat my meals amongst servants and boors; a man there said I was a fool, because I was in love with a woman I had never seen.**

THE KING: **But what have I to do with it?**

STRANGER: **I do not want to be called a fool. Send for the Queen that I may look at her.**

THE KING: **You seem to me a brazen, audacious man, not caring where you stand, nor of whom, nor to whom you speak.**

STRANGER: **I have never shown disrespect to the image in my head, yet I must see the woman herself.**

THE KING: **She is at my side.**

[6r] [*VPl*, 60–74]

6.

STRANGER: **Is this the Queen of the great Clock Tower?**

THE KING: **She is that Queen.**

(THE STRANGER stands in front of THE QUEEN) – Pause.

STRANGER: **She is not so tall as I had thought, not so white and red, but what does it matter, I shall proclaim everywhere that she is the most beautiful woman in the world.**

THE KING: **Then go! You have seen her.**

STRANGER: **Not yet. I was a little drunk that night when they mocked me, and I swore that not only would I see the Queen, but that – Oh, I must have been very drunk – that she would dance for me.**

THE KING: **What!**

STRANGER: **When she has danced, I shall be grateful, and I shall sing.**

7.

THE KING: **I shall have you flogged.**

STRANGER: **Then you will flog a sacred man.**

THE KING: **How? A sacred man?**

STRANGER: **I will tell you a great secret. I went to the Boyne where the old Gods live. I lay there for a month eating nothing. Then I saw Aengus and all the Gods. I told them of my oath and all the Gods shouted. After that there was silence and then Aengus spoke; and listen well for these were his very words:-**

"Upon the last night of the Year, when the great Clock strikes the last note of midnight, the Queen shall kiss you upon the mouth."

THE KING: **Captain of the Guard!**

FIRST ATTENDANT: **(Speaking as Captain and as before) I am here!**

---

16 *sd* rise *inserted in pencil (by WBY?) after* THE KING *NLI 29,550(2)*

[8r] [*VPl*, 90–104]

8.

THE KING: I give this man to you. He has said that the Queen will kiss him upon the mouth at the last stroke of the clock. Take him therefore and strike his head from his body.

FIRST ATTENDANT: (Speaking as Captain of the Guard) I will strike his head.

STRANGER: I go, but this is what will happen. First (counting on his fingers) the Queen will dance; second, I shall sing --

THE KING: What with your head off?

STRANGER: When I am grateful, I sing. The Queen, being grateful, will give me a kiss.

(He goes Right)

THE KING: Stop! You have told us nothing but lies.

KING (To Queen) Speak! Who is this man? Perhaps if you will answer my question, I shall spare his life.

(THE QUEEN remains silent and immovable.)

---

6 *rev in pencil (by WBY?) to* strike his head from his body *NLI 29,550(1) and (2)*
11 *rev in pencil (by WBY?) to* sing. Third The Queen *NLI 29,550(2)*

---

6 The penciled revision in NLI 29,550(1) and (2) is lacking in SIUC 91/16/10. The revised reading appears, however, in both the *Life and Letters* text and in the Cuala proofs and edition.

[SIUC 91/16/10]

[9r] [*VPl*, 105–115]

9.

THE KING: **So be it. Whether his tale be true or not, it is plain that he wishes to sacrifice his life, to lay it down at your feet. Take him Captain of the Guard.**

FIRST ATTENDANT: (Speaking as Captain of the Guard) I take him.

(THE KING thrusts THE STRANGER out to Right.)

THE KING: **Bring me his head that I may know that he is dead. (He now stands looking off Stage.) If he was not your lover before you came into this Country. If he is nothing to you, if he is nothing but a stroller and fool, if he is nothing but a man who has insulted you, laugh or sing, I do not care which it is.**

(THE QUEEN moves for the first time. Turning her head showly and looking at THE KING.)

THE KING: **Why do you fix your eyes upon me?**

---

8 C— *sd inserted in pencil (by WBY?) in left margin NLI 29,550(2)*

10 ~~stranger~~ *rev to* stroller *NLI 29,550(2)*

13*sd* *inserted (not by WBY)* music begins PP / muted strings *NLI 29,550(1)*

---

8 WBY's prescription for the scenery indicates, as is further revealed in the diagram (see appendix V), that there was to be no exit at the rear of the stage where the semicircle of curtaining or screens was placed. As the First Attendant in the diagram is situated to stage right, then presumably he and the Stroller/Stranger made their exit to that side of the stage (indeed the diagram marks a pronounced exit with parallel heavy lines immediately upstage of the First Attendant's position). Therefore, the direction inserted in NLI 29,550(2) indicates that the King was to remain center stage while looking to offstage right at this moment.

10 The original reading "stranger" in NLI 29,550(2) raises the question whether the typist's error prompted Yeats to change the denomination of this character. "Stranger" carries none of the rich associations, social and psychological, that accrue to the term "stroller," which he subsequently deployed in both published texts.

13*sd* For comment on the addition to NLI 29,550(1), see p. 53 above.

[10r] [*VPl*, 116–129]

10.

SECOND ATTENDANT: (Singing as Queen in a low voice.)

Oh what may come
Into my womb

THE KING: **Ah, that is better. But sing out loud that all here may know that you rejoice in his death.**

SECOND ATTENDANT: (Singing as QUEEN)

He longs to kill
My body, until
That sudden shudder
And limbs lie still.

Oh, what may come
Into my womb;
What caterpillar
My beauty consume.

THE KING: **I do not know what those words mean, but they sound scornful.**

11.

(THE KING goes out Right and returns with the head of THE STRANGER, and lays it upon the cubical Throne to Right, nearest audience.)

THE KING: **Now I shall know if those lips can sing.
(He sits on the other cubical Throne to Right.)
You have our attention. Sing stroller and fool.
(THE QUEEN rises) Why do you rise?**

(THE QUEEN begins to dance)

THE KING: **That is a good ~~fault~~** thought**. Dance! Turn him into
mockery with a ^ dance. Oh, a good thought.
(He laughs. THE QUEEN stands motionless looking
at the head.) Dance! Dance! If you are
nothing to him but a body or an image in his head,
he is nothing to you but a head without a body.
What is the good of a lover without a body? Dance!
He thought you were not so fine as the image in his
head, nor so tall, nor so red and white. Dance!
Display your beauty!**

---

3 *line del and rev in pencil (by WBY?) to* (Drum and Gong) *NLI 29,550(2)*

---

3 The inserted direction in NLI 29,550(2) makes it unclear whether in performance the rhythmic music began after the Queen's first movements, as indicated here, or simultaneously with them as in NLI 29,550(1); see the note to 9r, 12–13*sd.*

6–12 Alongside these lines in NLI 29,550(2) there is a penciled diagram, most likely in Lennox Robinson's hand, which shows the disposition of the actors, props, and cubical thrones at this point in the action:

K *O*
v

H *Q*
v

H = head (mask of Stroller/Stranger); K = King; O = a rough representation of the empty throne; Q = Queen.

12.

(THE QUEEN dances, then takes the head between her hands and raising it above her head, dances. Then stands in the centre of the Stage, the head still raised.)

THE KING: **The lips are opening. The eyes are moving.**

FIRST ATTENDANT: (Singing as head in a low voice)

Images ride – I heard a man say.

THE KING: **Oh, terror, it has begun to sing!**
(He cowers down, covering his face.)

FIRST ATTENDANT: (Singing as head.)

Images ride – I heard a man say –
Out of Benbulben and Knockareagh,
What says the Clock in the Great Clock Tower?
Out of the grave, saddle and ride
But turn from Rosses crawling tide,
meet's
The ~~Meet's~~ upon the mountain side.
A slow low note and an iron bell.

---

2 say.] say – *NLI 29,550(2)*

13.

What made them mount and what made them come,
Cuchulain that fought night long with the foam;
What says the Clock in the great Clock Tower?
Niam that rode on it; lad and lass
That sat so still and played at the Chess -
What but
~~Heart's deep~~, heroic wantoness.
A slow low note and an iron bell.

Alleel his Countess; Hanrahan
That seemed but a wild wenching man;
What says the Clock in the great Clock Tower?
How can a phantom ride among these;
Grip the saddle tight with your knees;
Image, ride among images.
A slow low note and an iron bell.

Image, image, up & away;
Mountain to mountain travel they
That ~~trample~~ down the night & day,
trample

(When the song has finished, the Clock begins to strike. The strokes are represented by a gong struck off Stage. THE QUEEN dances to the sound

---

1 come *rev in pencil to* come; *NLI 29,550(1)*
6 Heart's deep, *rev in pencil to* O high, *NLI 29,550(1)*
11–13 Images, images, up and away;
Mountain to mountain travel they
That trample down the night and day. *NLI 29,550(2)*

---

6 The penciled revision in NLI 29,550(1), not in Yeats's hand, is another attempt at a line that continually missed the desired effect: one that focused an audience's attention on the paradoxical coupling of heroism and wantonness by placing maximum stress on the end of the line rather than its opening syllables. The revision here perhaps records a change made during rehearsal; the line was revised yet further in SIUC 91/16/10, where an expression is finally achieved that is reproduced in the published texts.

[14r] [*VPl*, stage direction, 152–172]

14.

of the gong, and at the last stroke presses her lips to the lips of the head. THE KING has risen and drawn his sword. THE QUEEN lays the head upon her breast and fixes her eyes upon him. He appears about to strike, but kneels, laying the sword at her feet. THE TWO ATTENDANTS rise singing, and slowly close the Curtain. Their song is as follows:-

FIRST ATTENDANT: **Oh, but I saw a solemn sight;**
Said the rambling, shambling travelling-man;
Castle Dargan's ruin all lit,
Lovely ladies dancing in it.

SECOND ATTENDANT: **What ~~the~~** though **it danced; those days are gone;**
Said the^wicked crooked hawthorn tree;
Lovely lady or gallant man
Are blown cold dust or a bit of bone.

[SIUC 91/16/10]

[15^{r}] [*VPl*, 173–180]

15.

<u>FIRST ATTENDANT</u>: **O, what is life but a mouthful of air;**
<u>Said the rambling, shambling travelling-man</u>;
Yet all the lovely things that were
Live, for I saw them dancing there.

<u>SECOND ATTENDANT</u>: **Nobody knows what may befall;**
<u>Said the wicked crooked hawthorn tree</u>;
I have stopped so long a gap in the wall
May be I shall not die at all.

<u>-------------------------------</u>

8*sd* *added in pencil (by Robinson?)* insert 2 new verses *and below the printed words* THE END *by same hand*

K Q
v v *NLI 29,550(2)*

---

8 In NLI 29,550(2) the diagram shows the relative disposition of the two actors at the final curtain. These diagrams are very similar to ones included in the manuscripts of several of T. C. Murray's plays, which were directed, as was *The King of the Great Clock Tower*, by Lennox Robinson. Perhaps the penciled insertions are largely his, suggesting that this particular text (rather than SIUC 91/16/10) may have been used either as director's copy or prompt copy during rehearsals.

Part I. *The King of the Great Clock Tower* (Prose)

D. The Rapallo Notebook: BC, 4^v

On 4^v of the Rapallo notebook, Yeats turns from his immediate concerns to attempt a rewriting of part of the first song for the severed head, "Images ride—I heard a man say." The conclusion of the final stanza had been much revised throughout the composition of *The King of the Great Clock Tower*, and, while Yeats finds at last in these lines a fitting figure from mythology in Mad King Sweeney to end his parade of heroic, passionately engaged figures, the exact ordering of the song still eludes him. This revision was not incorporated into the lines of the third stanza as set to music by Arthur Duff (see appendix VIII, pp. 347–372). It is likely, then, that Yeats worked on the passage between the date of the performance, July 30, 1934, and the preparation of a copy of the play for publication in *Life and Letters*, November 1934, which follows next in the sequence of materials relating to the prose version. This version was not the last in which Yeats polished the expression of particular lines: on BC, 40^r, there is a set of cryptic abbreviations for most of the lines in the first stanza (cf. ll. 13–20, p. 83, below) to indicate a wholly new reading for the fourth line, which gives a greater logic to the structure of the song, and the jottings end with a new opening line to the second stanza. The passage reads:

Correction in Clock Tower Song – p. 9
sadl & ride' – I heard a man say
Out of ~~Ben bul~~ Ben Bulben & Knocknarea
    those
All ~~the~~ tragic characters ride
But turn from Ros
        [?meet's]
What brought them there, so far from their home

These later changes were not incorporated into any published text of the play but were included when the lyric was printed, under the title "Alternative Song for the Severed Head in *The King of the Great Clock Tower*," among the poems in Macmillan's 1935 edition of *A Full Moon in March* (cf. p. 98 in *"Parnell's Funeral and Other Poems" from "A Full Moon in March": Manuscript Materials*, ed. David R. Clark, Ithaca: Cornell University Press, 2003).

This page is also presented with closely related materials in the Rapallo notebook on the development of the opening lyric on pp. 87–120 below.

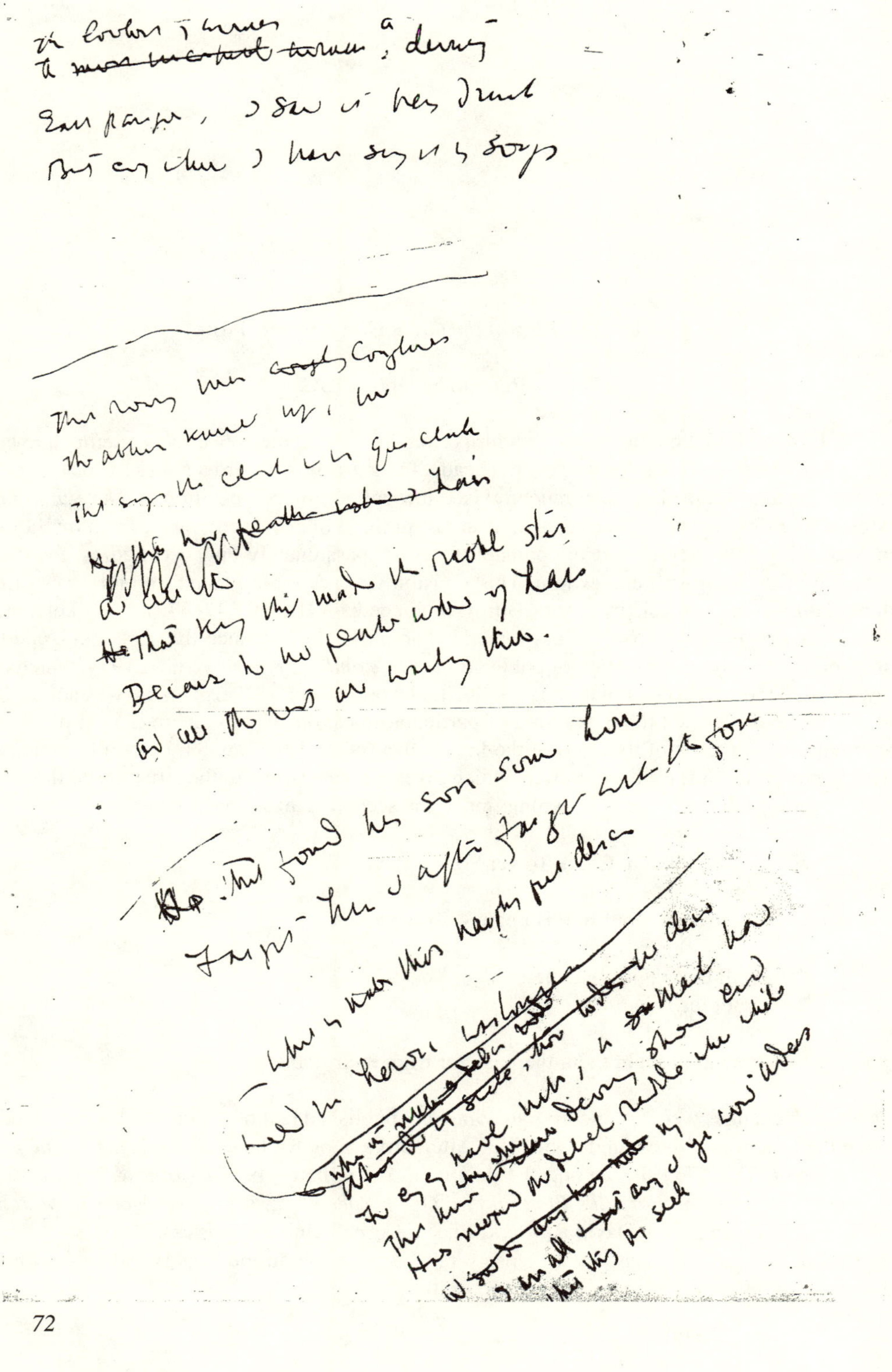

[BC, 4^{v}] [*VPl*, variously 152, 156, 161–164]

The loveliest of women
~~A more incomparable wo~~man: a divinity
[?Each] [?passion], I said it being drunk
But cry when I have sung it in songs

That roaring man ~~Congles~~ [?Conglures]
The ablest knight upon a time
That says the Clock in the Great Clock
~~He that has feathers instead of hair~~
And all the
~~He~~ That king that made the people stare
Because he had feathers instead of hair
And all the rest are waiting there

He that found his son some home
Fought him and after fought with the foam

It is difficult to estimate when these various sketches on 4^{v} were written, since they derive from more than one project. Yeats sets them off by leaving gaps between them and by marking off the first three with a dividing line after each of the first two sequences.

1–3 An attempt at some of the ideas that were later developed on BC, 43^{v}–44^{r}, leading finally to the version in *KGCT* (verse), *VPl*, ll. 38–53. Cf. transcriptions on pp. 271, 273, and 289, below.

4–5 Although neither of these lines found a place in the finished version of the song for the severed head, if this is a first reference to Congal, it may be the germ from which the later play, *The Herne's Egg* (1938), grew.

8–11 That king] Mad King Sweeney. Suibhne Geilt, or Sweeney, was cursed by St. Ronan so that, though he remained human, he took on the traits of a bird, leaping through the trees.

12–13 He] Cuchulain, who fought with the sea in despair after killing his son.

[BC, 4v]

[BC, 4v, continued] [*VPl*, variously 152, 156, 161–164]

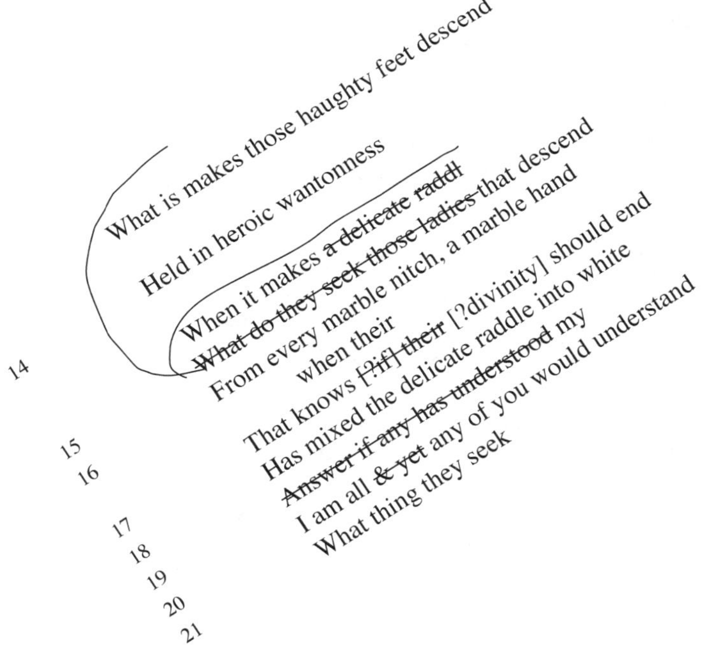
What is makes those haughty feet descend
14 Held in heroic wantonness
When it makes ~~a delicate raddl~~
15 ~~What do they seek those ladies~~ that descend
16 From every marble nitch, a marble hand
when their
17 That knows ~~[?if] their~~ [?divinity] should end
18 Has mixed the delicate raddle into white
19 ~~Answer if any has understood~~ my
20 I am all ~~& yet~~ any of you would understand
21 What thing they seek

14 A further redrafting of a troublesome line from the song for the severed head,
15–21 Early version of the opening stanza of the lyric, "Why must those holy, haughty feet descend."

Part I. *The King of the Great Clock Tower* (Prose)

E: The Text Published in *Life and Letters* (November 1934)

The first published text of the prose version of *The King of the Great Clock Tower* appeared in the journal, *Life and Letters*, in its November issue for 1934; Cuala published the play in *The King of the Great Clock Tower, Commentaries and Poems* a month later. No copy text or proof survives from the journal printing. Two sets of proofs survive relating to the Cuala edition, CDML and NLI 30,020. The typescript NLI 29,550(2) concludes with the penciled instruction, "Insert 2 new verses," which refers to Yeats's decision to include the recently finished lyric, "Why must those holy, haughty feet descend," as the Musicians' final song in the production (see the note on p. 70 above). The single page of holograph, NLI 30,800 (see pp. 116–117 below), would appear to cue these stanzas into a first set of proofs for the Cuala edition, which possibly preceded CDML.

The *Life and Letters* text is reproduced here as the earliest printed version. It seems to have been set from corrected proofs for the Cuala edition that were contemporary with CDML and NLI 30,020. However, it lacks both the final direction recounting Yeats's discomfort with the quantity of music and the song that ended the play as performed that are present in NLI 30,020. The *Life and Letters* text is collated with NLI 30,800, CDML, NLI 30,020—described on the cover as the "Final proof" of the Cuala edition—and that Cuala edition (*KGCT*). Yeats did not read proof for the New York edition, published by Macmillan in May 1935. The text was reset, with differences in styling, from the Cuala edition but is otherwise the same. The New York edition is not included in the collations.

The most significant differences between the typescript NLI 29,550(2) and the printed texts relate to the directions describing the movements of the Queen while holding the severed head. If, as seems likely, the stage directions of printed texts most closely describe Robinson's staging at the Abbey Theatre, then these changes probably reflect adaptations to Yeats's initial conception that were made in the interests of practicality and the dancer's stamina.

[p. 141] [*VPl*, preliminaries, opening stage direction, 1–16]

The King of the Great Clock Tower

by W. B. Yeats

THE PERSONS OF THE PLAY

The King	**(Dressed in red)**
The Queen	**(Dressed in orange with details in black or red)**
Stroller	**(Dressed in black with details in red)**
First Attendant	**(Dressed in black. Bass voice)**
Second Attendant	**(Dressed in black. Tenor voice)**

(The Queen *should wear a beautiful impassive mask.* The Stroller: *a wild half-savage mask. It should cover the upper part of his face. The lower part being hidden by his red beard.*

***When the stage curtain rises it shows an inner curtain, pale purple in colour. It may have a stencilled pattern of dancers. At the right and left side of the proscenium are a drum and gong.* The Attendants *stand by drum and gong; they slowly part the curtain, singing as follows:—*)**

Second Attendant. **They dance all day that dance in Tir-na-nogue.**

First Attendant. **There every lover is a happy rogue.**
And should he speak, it is the speech of birds.
No thought has he, and therefore has no words,
No thought because no clock, no clock because
If I consider deeply, lad and lass,
Nerve touching nerve upon that happy ground,
Are bobbins where all time is bound and wound.

P. 141

title THE KING OF THE GREAT CLOCK / TOWER: First performed at The Abbey Theatre on the thirtieth of June, nineteen thirty four. *NLI 30,020, KGCT*

persons *omitted CDML*

sd *CDML omits the first paragraph; NLI 30,020, KGCT reverse the two paragraphs* pale ivory *rev in pencil to* pale purple . . . curtains *CDML*

(When the stage curtain rises it shows an inner curtain, pale purple in colour. It may have a stencilled pattern of dancers. At the right and left sides of the proscenium are a drum and gong.)

(The Queen should wear a beautiful impassive mask, the Stranger, a wild half-savage mask. It should cover the upper part of his face, the lower part being hidden by his red beard.)

The Attendants stand by drum and gong; they slowly part the curtains, singing.) *NLI 30,020; KGCT as rev NLI 30,020*

1 Tir-nan-oge *NLI 30,020, KGCT*

2 rogue; *NLI 30,020, KGCT*

---

title, persons NLI 30,020 repeats this format but prints the material in red ink. Stage directions in CDML, NLI 30,020, and *KGCT* are set in italics throughout; none of these texts provides punctuation after the speaker name.

[*Life and Letters*]

[p. 141, continued] [*VPl*, preliminaries, opening stage direction, 1–16]

SECOND ATTENDANT. O never may that dismal thread run loose;

FIRST ATTENDANT. For there the Hound that Oisin saw pursues
The hornless deer that runs in such a fright;
And there the woman clasps an apple tight,
For all the clamour of a famished man;
They run in foam, and there in foam they ran,
Nor can they stop to take a breath that still
Hear in the foam, the beating of a bell.

[p. 142] [*VPl*, 17–53]

(When the curtains are parted one sees to the left the* KING *and* QUEEN *upon two thrones, which may be two cubes. There should be two cubes upon the opposite side to balance them. The background and the cubes are a rich blue. The background may be a curtain hung in a semi-circle, or a semi-circle of one foot Craig screens, so painted that the blue is darker below than above.

The* TWO ATTENDANTS *sit down by drum and gong, they remain facing the audience at either side of the stage, but a little in the shadow.)

THE KING. A year ago this night, you walked into my house. I made you my Queen, yet neither I, nor any other man, know from what country you came. And now before our friends and courtiers here assembled, I ask you, not for the first time, where that country is, who and what you were before you became my Queen? You have kept silence long enough. Sat there an image of stone or wood. That silence has become unendurable to these others, and to me.

(There is a pause.* THE QUEEN *neither speaks nor moves.* FIRST ATTENDANT *strikes the drum three times.)

THE KING. Captain of the Guard!

FIRST ATTENDANT. (*Speaking as Captain of the Guard, without turning his head.*) King, I am here.

THE KING. Someone has struck three times upon the great door. Admit him!

P. 142

sd two Attendants *CDML, NLI 30,020, KGCT*

2 knows *rev to* know *CDML* Country *CDML, NLI 30,020, KGCT*

4 Country *CDML, NLI 30,020, KGCT*

5 enough, sat *NLI 30,020, KGCT*

7 Guard. *CDML, NLI 30,020, KGCT*

FIRST ATTENDANT. (*Speaking as before.*) I will admit him.

(THE STROLLER *enters.*)

THE KING. What is your name?

STROLLER. It is enough that I am a stroller and a fool, and that you are the King of the Great Clock Tower.

THE KING. I am that King. What do you want?

STROLLER. A year ago somebody told me that you had married the most beautiful woman in the world, and from that moment I have had her image in my head, and month by month, it has grown more and more beautiful. I have made poems about her and sung them everywhere, but I have never seen her.

THE KING. Have you no wife or sweetheart of your own?

STROLLER. I had a wife, but she was so much uglier than the image in my head, that I left her. The other night I was eating my dinner in a tavern: I am a man of no account, and so must eat my meals amongst servants and boors; a man there said I was a fool, because I was in love with a woman I had never seen.

THE KING. But what have I to do with it?

STROLLER. I do not want to be called a fool. Send for the Queen that I may look at her.

[p. 143] [*VPl*, 54–97]

THE KING. You seem to me a brazen, audacious man, not caring where you stand, nor of whom, nor to whom you speak.

STROLLER. I have never shown disrespect to the image in my head, yet I must see the woman herself.

THE KING. She is at my side.

STROLLER. Is this the Queen of the Great Clock Tower?

THE KING. She is that Queen.

(THE STROLLER *stands in front of* THE QUEEN.)

P. 142

22 tavern; *KGCT*

P. 143

6 great *CDML, NLI 30,020, KGCT*

7*sd* (the Stroller . . . The Queen) *rev to* (The Stroller . . . the Queen) *CDML* (The Stroller . . . the Queen) *NLI 30,020, KGCT*

[p. 143, continued] [*VPl*, 54–97]

STROLLER. She is not so tall as I had thought, not so white and red, but what does it matter? I shall proclaim everywhere that she is the most beautiful woman in the world.

THE KING. Then go! You have seen her.

STROLLER. Not yet. I was a little drunk that night when they mocked me, and I swore that not only would I see the Queen, but that – O, I must have been very drunk – that she would dance for me.

THE KING. What!

STROLLER. When she has danced, I shall be grateful, and I shall sing.

THE KING. I shall have you flogged.

STROLLER. Then you will flog a sacred man.

THE KING. How! A sacred man?

STROLLER. I will tell you a great secret. I went to the Boyne where the old Gods live. I lay there for a month eating nothing. Then I saw Aengus and all the Gods. I told them of my oath, and all the Gods shouted. After that there was silence and then Aengus spoke; and listen well, for these were his very words: —
'Upon the last night of the year, when the Great Clock strikes the last note of midnight, the Queen shall kiss you upon the mouth.'

THE KING. Captain of the Guard!

FIRST ATTENDANT. (*Speaking as Captain and as before.*) I am here!

THE KING. I give this man to you. He has said that the Queen will kiss him upon the mouth at the last stroke of the clock. Take him therefore and strike his head from his body.

FIRST ATTENDANT. (*Speaking as Captain of the Guard.*) I will strike his head from his body.

STROLLER. I go, but this is what will happen. First (*Counting on his fingers.*)

P. 143

9 matter, *CDML, NLI 30,020, KGCT*
19 How? *CDML, NLI 30,020, KGCT*
23 well for *CDML, NLI 30,020, KGCT*
24 Year *rev to* year *CDML*
25 midnight. the *CDML, NLI 30,020, KGCT*
28 THE KING *omitted, inserted in ink CDML*
33 (counting . . . fingers) *CDML, NLI 30,020, KGCT*

the Queen will dance; second, I shall sing ——

[p. 144] [*VPl*, 98–129]

The King. What, with your head off?

Stroller. When I am grateful, I sing. The Queen, being grateful, will give me a kiss.

(*He goes right.*)

The King. Stop! You have told us nothing but lies.

The King. (*To Queen.*) Speak! Who is this man? Perhaps if you will answer my questions, I shall spare his life.

(The Queen *remains silent and immovable.*)

The King. So be it. Whether his tale be true or not, it is plain that he wishes to sacrifice his life, to lay it down at your feet. Take him, Captain of the Guard.

First Attendant. (*Speaking as Captain of the Guard.*) I take him.

(The King *thrusts* The Stroller *out to right.*)

The King. Bring me his head that I may know that he is dead. (*He now stands looking off stage.*) If he was not your lover before you came into this country. If he is nothing to you, if he is nothing but a stroller and a fool, if he is nothing but a man who has insulted you, laugh or sing, I do not care which it is.

(The Queen *moves for the first time. Turning her head slowly and looking at* The King.)

The King. Why do you fix your eyes upon me?

Second Attendant. (*Singing as Queen in a low voice.*)
O what may come
Into my womb!

The King. Ah, that is better. But sing out loud that all here may know

---

P. 144

1 KING.] QUEEN *rev to* KING *CDML* What with *CDML, NLI 30,020, KGCT*
8 him Captain *CDML, NLI 30,020, KGCT*
10*sd* the Stroller *CDML, NLI 30,020, KGCT*
13 country.] country *rev in pencil to* country. *CDML*
14*sd* the King. *CDML, NLI 30,020, KGCT*
17 womb. *rev in ink to* womb! *CDML*

[p. 144, continued] [*VPl*, 98–129]

that you rejoice in his death.

(The Queen *rises.*)

Second Attendant. (*Singing as Queen.*)

He longs to kill
My body, until
That sudden shudder
And limbs lie still.
O, what may come
Into my womb,
What caterpillar
My beauty consume!

The King. I do not know what those words mean, but they sound scornful.

(The King *goes out right and returns with the head of* The Stroller*, and lays it upon the cubical throne to right, nearest audience.*)

[p. 145] [*VPl*, 130–164]

The King. Now I shall know if those lips can sing. (*He sits on the other cubical throne to right.*) You have our attention. Sing, Stroller and fool.

(The Queen *begins to dance.*)

The King. That is a good thought. Dance! Turn him into mockery with a dance. O, a good thought. (*He laughs.* The Queen *lays head on the ground at the centre of the stage; stands motionless looking at the head.*) Dance! Dance! If you are nothing to him but an image, a body in his head, he is nothing to you but a head without a body. What is the good of a lover without a body? Dance! He thought you were not so fine as the image in his head, nor so tall, nor so red, nor

---

P. 144

19*sd* *omitted, inserted in ink CDML*

25 womb. *rev in ink to* womb, *CDML*

27 consume. *rev to* consume! *CDML*

28*sd* audience.)] audience, or continues to hold it, grasping it by the hair.) *rev in pencil to* audience.) *CDML* the Stroller, *CDML, NLI 30,020, KGCT*

P. 145

2 Sing Stroller *CDML, NLI 30,020, KGCT* (The QUEEN rises) Why do you rise? *del in ink CDML*

4*sd* The Queen stands motionless looking at the head. *rev in ink to* The Queen lays head on the ground at the center of the stage. stands motionless looking at the head *CDML* stage;] stage, *NLI 30,020, KGCT*

8 red,] red *CDML, NLI 30,020, KGCT*

P. 145

2 In CDML Yeats's transposition of the stage direction to follow the king's speech (l. 19 on p. 144) provides a more logical place in the action for the Queen to rise.

so white. Dance! Display your beauty!

(The Queen *dances. Then stands in the centre of the stage, facing audience, the head upon her shoulder.*)

The King. The lips are opening. The eyes are moving.

First Attendant. (*Singing as head in a low voice.*)
Images ride, I heard a man say

The King. O, terror, it has begun to sing!

(*He cowers down, covering his face.*)

First Attendant. (*Singing as head.*)
Images ride, I heard a man say,
Out of Benbulben and Knocknareagh,
What says the Clock in the Great Clock Tower?
Out of the grave. Saddle and ride
But turn from Rosses' crawling tide,
The meet's upon the mountain side.
A slow low note and an iron bell.

What made them mount and what made them come,
Cuchulain that fought night long with the foam;
What says the Clock in the Great Clock Tower?
Niam that rode on it; lad and lass
That sat so still and played at the chess—
What but heroic wantonness.
A slow low note and an iron bell.

Aleel, his Countess; Hanrahan
That seemed but a wild wenching man;
What says the Clock in the Great Clock Tower?
And all alone comes riding there
The King that could make his people stare,

P. 145

9*sd* (The QUEEN dances, then takes the head between her hands and raising it above her head, dances. Then stands in the centre of the stage, the head still raised.) *rev in pencil to* (The QUEEN dances, then . . . . stage, facing audience the head upon her shoulder.) *CDML; NLI 30,020, KGCT as revised CDML, but* dances. Then

11 ride— . . . say,— *rev in pencil to* ride, . . . say— *CDML*

13 ride— . . . say— *rev in pencil to* ride, . . . say, *CDML*

24 chess? *NLI 30,020, KGCT*

25 wantoness *rev in pencil to* wantonness *CDML*

27 Aleel *rev in ink to* Aleel, *CDML*

P. 145

11 In CDML the printer left a wide gap between the speaker name and the first verse of the song. In the top margin Yeats's penciled the query, "Why this space? W. B.Y.", and connected it by an arrow to the gap.

[p. 145, continued] [*VPl*, 130–164]

Because he had feathers instead of hair.
A slow low note and an iron bell.

(When the song has finished, the dance begins again, the clock strikes. The strokes are represented by a gong struck off stage.* THE QUEEN *dances to the sound of the gong,

[p. 146] [*VPl*, 165–198]

***and at the last stroke presses her lips to the lips of the head.* THE KING *has risen and drawn his sword.* THE QUEEN *lays the head upon her breast, and fixes her eyes upon him. He appears about to strike, but kneels, laying the sword at her feet. The* TWO ATTENDANTS *rise singing, and slowly close the inner curtain. Their song is as follows:—*)**

FIRST ATTENDANT. **O, but I saw a solemn sight;**
Said the rambling, shambling travelling-man;
Castle Dargan's ruin all lit,
Lovely ladies dancing in it.

SECOND ATTENDANT. **What though they danced; those days are gone;**
Said the wicked, crooked, hawthorn-tree;
Lovely lady or gallant man
Are blown cold dust or a bit of bone.

FIRST ATTENDANT. **O, what is life but a mouthful of air;**
***Said the rambling, shambling travelling-man*;**
Yet all the lovely things that were
Live, for I saw them dancing there.

(THE QUEEN *has come down stage and now stands framed in the half-closed curtains.*)

SECOND ATTENDANT. **Nobody knows what may befall;**
Said the wicked, crooked, hawthorn-tree.
I have stopped so long a gap in the wall

P. 145

33*sd* (When the song has finished, the Clock begins to strike. *rev in ink to* (When . . . finished the dance begins again, the Clock strikes. *CDML* the Clock . . . . represented by blows on a gong struck by second Attendant. . . . sound, and *NLI 30,020, KGCT*

P. 146

sd the Queen lays *rev to* The Queen lays *CDML* The Two Attendands] The two Attendants *CDML, NLI 30,020, KGCT* curtain. Their song is as follows:—)] curtain:) *NLI 30,020, KGCT*

12*sd* *omitted, inserted in pencil to read as LL but* half-closed] half closed *CDML, NLI 30,020, KGCT*

15 stood so long by *NLI 30,020, KGCT*

May be I shall not die at all.

(The inner curtain is closed; the* TWO ATTENDANTS *stand upon either side singing.)

SECOND ATTENDANT. **Why must those holy, haughty feet descend**
From emblematic niches and what hand
Ran such a delicate raddle through their white?
My heart is broken, yet must understand.

FIRST ATTENDANT. **For desecration and the lover's night.**

SECOND ATTENDANT. **I cannot face that emblem of the moon.**
Nor eyelids that the unmixed heavens dart,
Nor stand upon my feet, so great a fright
Descends upon my savage, sunlit heart.
What can she lack whose emblem is the moon?

FIRST ATTENDANT. **But desecration and the lover's night.**

SECOND ATTENDANT. **Delight my heart with sound; speak yet again;**

P. 146

16*sd* When the curtain is closed the attendants stand upon either side / singing, at the end of their song the folding ends or curtain falls *with* curtain *rev to* inner curtain *and* folding ends *rev to* stage *then all rev to* When . . . singing *NLI 30,800* When the inner curtain is closed the two Attendants . . . singing.) *rev to* (The inner . . . singing.) *CDML* two Attendants *NLI 30,020, KGCT*

17 haughty, holy *NLI 30,800*

18 nitches & *NLI 30,800* emblimatic *rev in ink to* emblematic *CDML*

19 Ran that *NLI 30,020, KGCT*

20/21 *line inserted in pencil* What do they seek for, why must they descend? *CDML*
~~What thing they seek and wherefore they~~
are they seeking?
What ~~do they seek &~~ why do they descend? *NLI 30,800*
What do they seek for? why must they descend? *NLI 30,020, KGCT*

22 moon *NLI 30,800* moon, *NLI 30,020, KGCT*

23 dart *NLI 30,800*

24 feet so *NLI 30,800*

P. 146

16*sd* In NLI 30,800 (see the collation above), "folding ends" refers to Yeats's ritual of the folding and unfolding of a cloth, which frames most of his dance plays.

But look and look with understanding eyes
Upon the pitchers that they carry; tight
Therein all time's completed treasure is:
What do they lack? O cry it out again.

FIRST ATTENDANT. Their desecration and the lover's night.

(The stage curtain descends.)

P. 146

31 times *NLI 30,800*

32 lack O
What do they ~~lack & look for~~, cry it out again. *NLI 30,800*

33*sd* descends] falls *NLI 30,800*

---

33 In place of this line the NLI 30,020 printed text concludes with a lengthy direction about performance, together with an additional lyric with which to end the play. Yeats added the marginal annotation in ink.

(I prefer the stanza in this form, but the musician may substitute the following as he may prefer something resembling a stop at the end of every line, nothing resembling a stop before the last word of any line, believing in spite of evidence that the words of the singer will be heard, even enjoyed, as words, if rythmn and punctuation be obvious. It might however be better to omit in performance this last song. I thought on the first night, though we left out one stanza that there was too much music between the end of the dance and the descent of the curtain.)

FIRST ATTENDANT Delight my heart with sound, speak it again;
I look on feet but not upon a face;
Cry it again but understand the sight,
All time's completed treasure in one place;
What do they lack O cry it all again.
SECOND ATTENDANT Their desecration and the lover's night.
(The stage curtain descends)

CDML prints most of the first sentence of the above only, but omits the final clause, "if rythmn and punctuation be obvious". The following is written in the bottom margin below the text in pencil in a hand other than Yeats's, then cued by an arrow to follow on from "even enjoyed, as words.)":

It might however be better to omit / in performance this last song. / It is not very singable, unless some Florence / Farr were the singer, and I thought / on the first night that there was too much / music between the end of the dance & / the fall of the curtain.)

The alternative stanza in CDML follows the wording of NLI 30,020, given above.

Arthur Duff set the first two stanzas of the main lyric and then the alternative stanza offered in NLI 30,020 for performance in the Abbey production (see appendix VIII). Although the *Life and Letters* text contains three stanzas with repeated refrain for the final lyric, Yeats's further direction at the close of the text in NLI 30,020 makes clear that only two stanzas were sung in the first production. Which of the stanzas was the one cut in the production, as the NLI 30,020 note intimates, is not clear from Duff's manuscripts. As each of the stanzas is introduced by a repetition of the initial musical opening to the song, it would be simple enough to cut a whole stanza without leaving an intrusive disjunction.

Part II. *A Full Moon in March*

A. The Evolution of the Lyric, "Why must those holy, haughty feet descend": BC, 1^{r}–7^{r}; NLI 30,336 a, 2^{r}; and NLI 30,800

Yeats began his Rapallo notebook by recording his evident anger at Pound's dismissal of *The King of the Great Clock Tower*. He immediately redrafted the opening of that play, attempting to give the King and Queen "character" in the way of more realist drama. Defining the Queen's look as one of "dread," for example (BC, 2^{r}, l. 11), introduces specific and limiting qualities into her characterization, where the prose version of the play gained its effects from the sheer ambiguity of a silent masked figure. Naming the King as O'Rourke and introducing Dervorgilla into the dialogue (1^{r}, l. 9) brings historical, emotional, and psychological connotations that Yeats had carefully pared away from the text of the prose version. He had already explored the consequences of Dervorgilla's adultery and the coming of the English into Ireland in *The Dreaming of the Bones*. But it is out of this specific context that Yeats next begins to focus on the antagonism between the sexes as a new theme. On 2^{r}, ll. 22–24, the imagery of masks and painted, expressionless faces on 1^{r} is transformed to suggest the idea of the statue, at once present yet aloof, and, as the draft continues, the constellation of images concerning mask, doll, and statue is developed alongside a new theme suggestive of a perverse, sadomasochistic eroticism. On 3^{r} he redrafted the King's opening speech to magnify these elements.

In his loose-leaf notebook, NLI 30,336, Yeats appears to have attempted a clean copy of the material that he had been working on until now in the Rapallo notebook. The loose-leaf notebook contains various materials relating to the transitional period between the completion of *The King of the Great Clock Tower* in prose and the drafting of the lyrics for *A Full Moon in March*. When Yeats made the copy (NLI 30,336 a, 2^{r}) is not certain; it is placed here in the sequence, however, because in it he gathered together many of the readings attempted on BC, 1^{r}–2^{v}, before moving into new subject matter on BC, 3^{r}.

In the draft of the lyric on BC, 6^{v}, Yeats assigned the refrain only to the Second Attendant, thereby endowing each attendant with a distinguishing character (unlike any of his previous choric figures). An astonished and questioning innocent sings the verse to a knowing and worldly respondent, a contrast Yeats built on when he created *A Full Moon in March*.

The version of the lyric in NLI 30,800 properly belongs with the materials relating to the prose play (see the apparatus on pp. 85–86) but is included here as well because it alone gathers together into a readable format the many revisions that occur on BC, 6^{v}–7^{r}. Here the lines assigned to the two attendants are reversed, a move perhaps dictated by the tonal ranges of the singers playing the two roles in the Abbey production; but the issue of how to assign the lines continued to tax Yeats (as his revisions to the proofs of *FMIM* show), although the published text of *FMIM(M)* assigns them as here.

Hovering between prose and verse, the various attempts suggest Yeats may have struggled to meet Pound's strictures while rendering the original play into verse. The materials included here, though closely related to the prose version of *The King of the Great Clock Tower*, are given in full, because out of all the wrestling to meet the new agenda steadily emerged the lyric, "Why must those holy, haughty feet descend," and with it the conception of a wholly new play.

Rapallo. June. 1934.

Gave "Clock Tower" to Ezra to read. He condemned it as "nobody's language". At first I took his condemnation as a confirmation of my fear that I am now too old. I have ~~[illegible]~~ written little verse for three years. But "nobody's language" is something I can remedy. I must write in verse, but first in prose & set structure.

I am [illegible]. At least what I mean, the [illegible] of [illegible]; [illegible] the [illegible] all other [illegible] has [illegible] the [illegible] of woman. ~~[illegible]~~ [illegible] generation will forget the name of Dervorgilla. Some great grandfather of mine gave to her some [illegible] must have [illegible] in some dark, empty [illegible] place. It is that [illegible] that tortures us, [illegible] those for whom they are masters. The more we think on things the more [illegible] out of words. ~~[illegible]~~ Why do our heart beats [illegible] longing, when they hold us at arm's length, when they [illegible] that their eyes [illegible] their [illegible] expression, as though we were the whole of life and they the whole of death; of the [illegible] of us [illegible] a thing we were [illegible] of some terrible dream, ~~[illegible]~~ [illegible] some unformed dream, [illegible] [illegible] the [illegible] of me. ~~[illegible]~~

Attendant ~~[illegible]~~ [illegible] some words [illegible] song

[BC, 1^{r}]

Rapallo. June, 1934
Gave
~~Read~~ "Clock Tower" to Ezra to read. He condemned it
"Nobody language". At first I took his condemnation
as a confirmation of my fear that I am now
too old. I have ~~hardly~~ written little verse for three
years. But 'nobody language" is something I can
remedy. I never write in verse, but first in prose
to get structure.

I am O'Rourke. All [?hear/?here] what it means to be
O'Rourke of Breffny: a race that before all other races
felt
has ~~[?not]~~ the curse of woman. ~~No generation~~ What
generation will forget the name, Dervorgilla, some
great grandfather of mine found in her [?some] that [?may /?many] [?find]
in some dark empty foolish place. It is their emptiness
that tortures us, they paint their faces make them like masks
The more [?they] speak our thoughts we [?surely] [?run] out of breath
or out of words. W~~hat is it that compels~~ Why do our
hands hold with longing, when they hold us as it were
at arms length, when they make their masks their eyes cold
their faces without expression, as though we were the whole of life
and they the whole of death; if they think of us it as though
we were a part of some terrible dream, ~~that they would~~ have us
~~drink the poison that [?they] [?lay] [?upon]~~ some unformed dream
some power that has made them what they are.
~~Attendant speaks~~
Attendant ~~sings some word~~ repeats some words from first song

---

found in BC, 1^{r}–7^{r} *transcribed above and below, pp. 89–95, 99–115*
NLI 30,336 a, 2^{r} *transcribed below, p. 97*
NLI 30,800 *transcribed below, p. 117*
published in *Life and Letters* (November 1934) *transcribed above, pp. 77–86*
KGCT
FMIM(M)

1–8 This account of the meeting with Pound differs markedly from that included in the Preface to the Cuala edition of *KGCT* (see introduction, pp. xlvi–xlviii above, and pp. 307–313 and 335–339 below).

[BC, 2r]

[BC, 2[r]]

A year ago this night. this woman walked into
my house. ~~I made her my queen. Neith~~
I did not ask what country she came from,
What gypsy troupe, what troupe of strolling players, what
troupe of outlaws she belonged belonged to. ~~She told~~ me
~~nothing.~~ no man's lands, some dark empty foolish place.
what did I care. She told me nothing. She tells me
nothing. And now since ~~she rose~~ we ~~rod~~ rose from
our bed ~~she~~ this morning, she has kept silent,
on this day as on many another day she looks at
me with dread or not at all. Am I ~~sho~~ so
hideous, some terrible, ~~so~~ monster.
Second Attendant sings some phrases from second song.
Then there is a ~~pore~~ pause etc as before.

~~Though I have~~
I am O'Rourke; all know the name; all know
~~Though I have nothing but~~
~~All know~~ What blood O'Rourke of Breffney inherits
~~If this~~ daughter my
~~All know my sister, all know [?her] [?for] [?a] [?] [?fatal]~~
~~That River [?for/?of] a woman [?as] [?for/?of] [?lightning]~~
All know that my grandfather had for wife
Accursed Devorgilla. Where did he find her?
~~He found her in some Noman's Land some dark~~
empty
In Noman's land, in some dark ~~forlorn~~ place
→ ~~In some dark empty place~~. ~~They torture us~~
They paint their faces but expression dies
They move or speak until they seem as statues
Made of
~~Fashioned~~ of marble or of hollow bronze
~~[? ? ? ? ? ?]~~

1–12 A wholly new attempt at the King's opening speech, traces of which are found in the versified format of the play. After l. 12 and the ensuing stage direction, Yeats draws a line across the width of the page and begins the speech yet again.

21 The arrow is drawn from a replacement on facing 1[v]: "They charm & torture us with their ~~emptimess~~ emptiness". But this, too, is canceled (see the reproduction of 1[v] and a transcription on pp. 254–255).

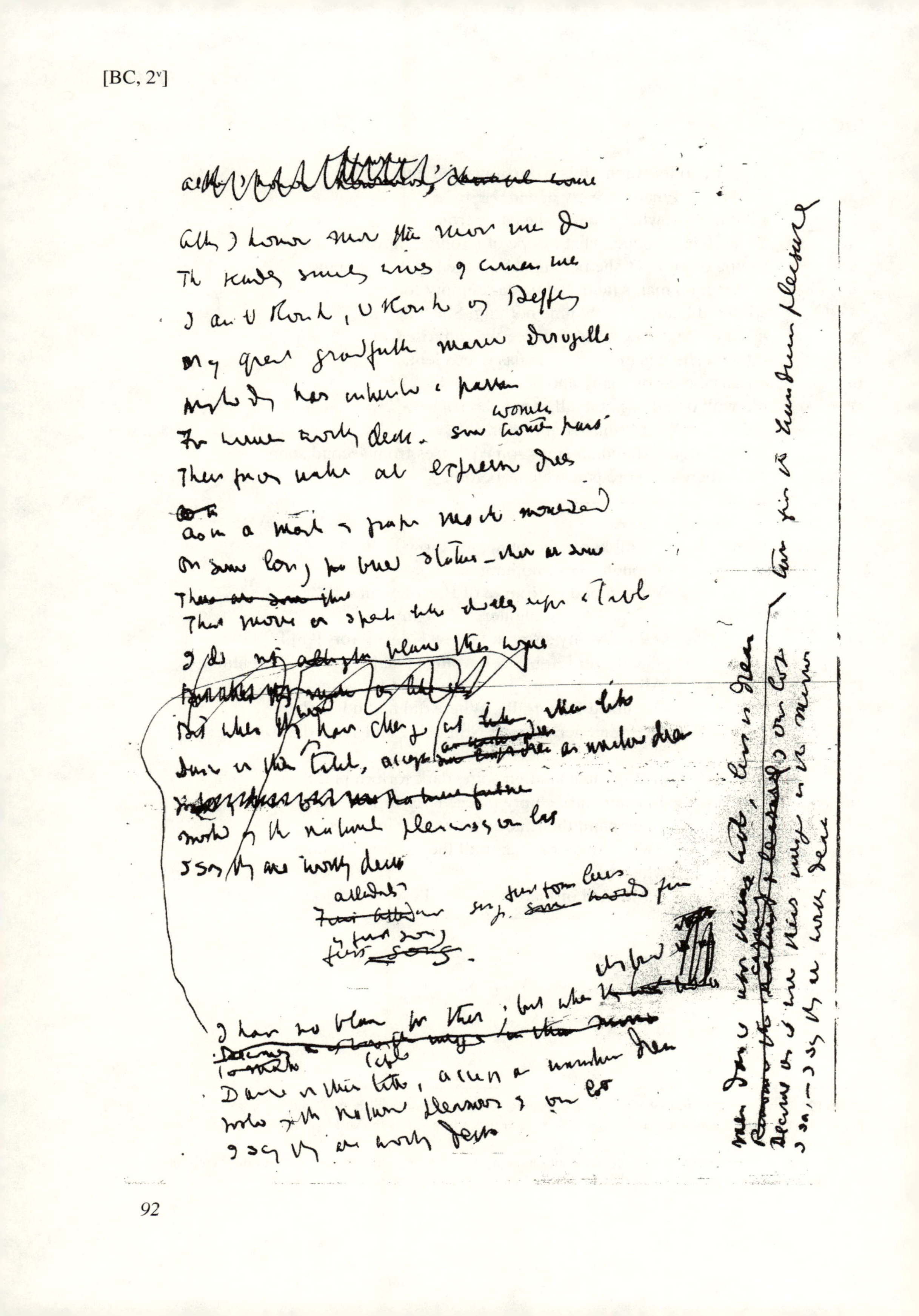

[BC, 2^{v}]

[BC, 2v]

(O Rourke)
Al~~though I honour [?housewives], dutiful women~~

1 Although I honour more than most men do
2 The kindly smiling wives of common men
3 I am O'Rourke, O'Rourke of Breffney
4 My great grandfather married Dervorgilla
5 My body has inherited a passion
women
6 For women worthy death. Some woman paint
7 Their faces until all expression dies
~~As in~~
8 As in a mask of paper machi moulded
9 On some long ~~po~~ [?buried /?blind] statue – there are some
~~There are some that~~
10 That move or speak like dolls upon a table
11 ~~I do not altogether blame these women~~
~~But when they mask or like us~~
would
12 But when they ^ have change not ~~like~~ when like
~~[?an] [?unnaturalness]~~
13 Dance on their table, accept ~~some laughable~~ an [?unnatural] dream
14 ~~[?] [?] [?] [?] that have fullness~~
15 Instead of the natural pleasures of our lot
16 I say they are worthy death
Attendants first four lines
~~First Attend~~ant sings ~~some words~~ from
of first song
first ~~song~~.

~~[?instead]~~
they find ~~it (?not)~~
17 I have no blame for them; but when ~~they [?] [?]~~

---

8 paper machi] Here and in a similar misspelling, "paper machis" (l. 6 on 2r of NLI 30,336, p. 97 below), Yeats refers to the common method of making theatrical masks and puppets out of papier-mâché.

16*sd* Presumably lines from the opening lyric, "They dance all day that dance in Tir-nan-oge."

17–20 These lines (transcription continues on p. 95) are clued to replace canceled ll. 11–16.

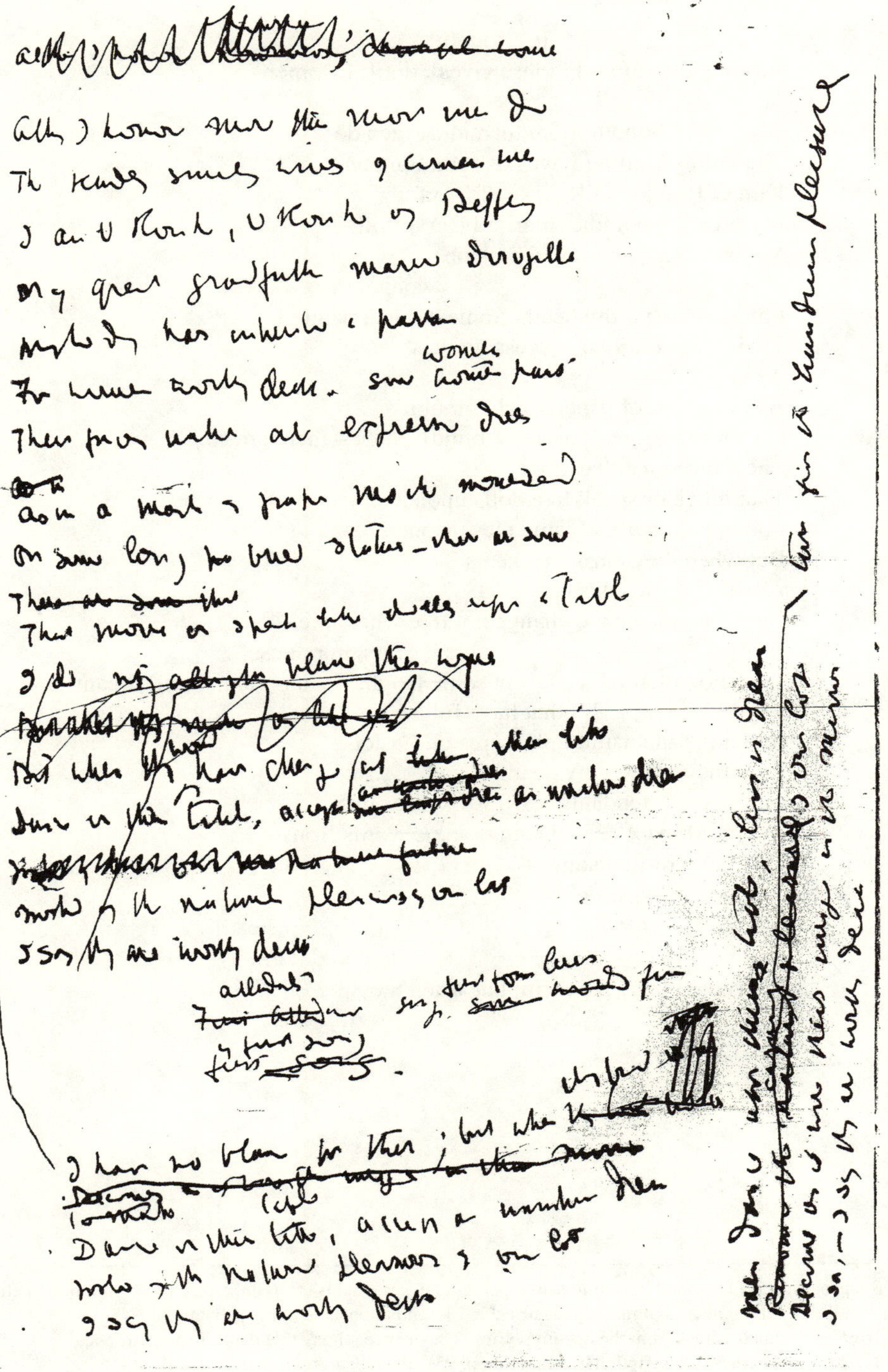

[BC, 2^{v}, continued]

~~Dreams of [?brutish] images in their minds~~
~~I make~~ table
18 Dance on this table, accept an [?unnatural /?monstrous] dream
19 Instead of the natural pleasures of our lot
20 I say they are worthy death

21 Men dance upon their [?table], lost in dream
~~casual~~
22 ~~Renounce the natural pleasures~~ of our lot Turn from the humdrum pleasure
23 Deceive as it were their image in the mirror
24 I say – I say they are worthy death

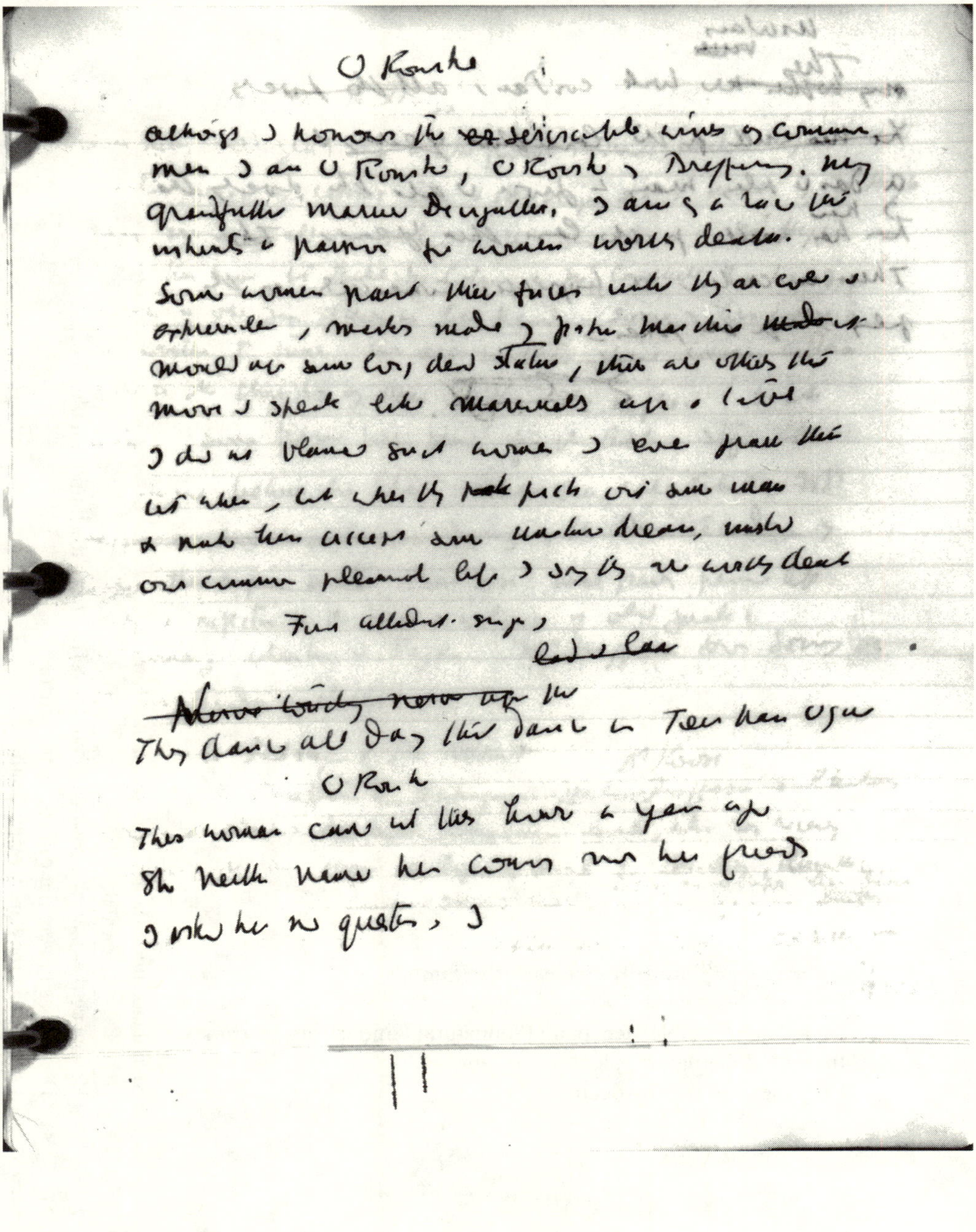

[NLI 30,336 a, 2^r]

O Rourke

Although I honour the ~~er~~ serviceable wives of common
men I am O Rourke, O Rourke of Breffney. My
grandfather married Dervorgaller. I am of a race that
inherits a passion for women worthy death.
Some women paint their faces until they are cold &
expressionless, masks made of paper marchis ~~made &~~
moulded over some long dead statue, there are others that
move & speak like marionettes upon a [?table]
I do not blame such women I even praise them
but when, but when they ~~pek~~ pick out some man
and make him accept some [?monstrous/unnatural] dream, instead
our common pleasant life I say they are worthy death

First Attendant sings)

~~lad & lass~~
~~Nerve touching nerve upon~~ that
They dance all day that dance in Teir Nan Ogue

O Rourke

This woman came into this house a year ago
She neither named her country nor her friends
I asked her no questions, I

---

11 If the queried word is "monstrous", WBY has actually written "mostrus"; if it is "unnatural", he has compressed it to "unatural" with the final "l" merely a slight upturn of the pen.

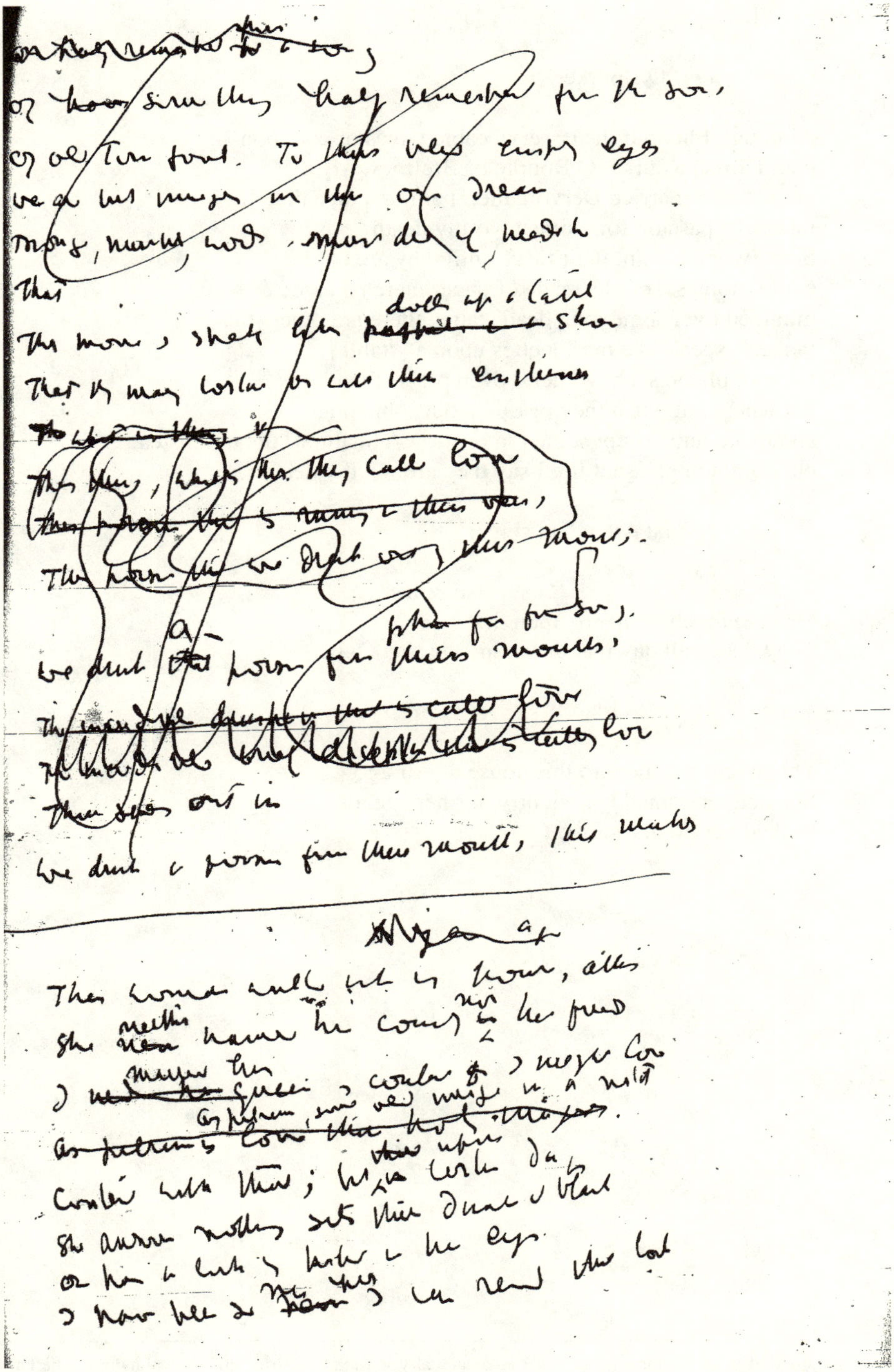

[BC, 3r]

~~this~~
~~or half remembered from a song~~
of ~~have~~ something half remembered from the song
of old Tom fool. To their blind empty eyes
We are but images in their [?own /?one] dream
Strong, [?hurtful] words, murder if needs be
That
dolls upon a table
They move & speak like ~~puppets in a~~ show
That they may torture us with their emptiness
~~The What is thing [?w]~~
This thing, what is this they call love
~~This poison that is running in their veins~~
This poison that we drink out of their mouths –
a – ~~phrase from first song~~
We drink ~~that~~ poison from their mouths
~~The incredible drunkeness that is called love~~
The incredible brief deception that is called love
Then sing out in
We drink a poison from their mouths, this makes
~~A year ago~~
This woman walked into my house, although
neither nor
She ~~never~~ named her country ~~or~~ ^ her friends
married her
I ~~made her queen~~, content if I might love
As palmers some old image in a nitch
~~As palmers love their holy images~~
~~that~~ upon
Content with that; but ^ [?on] [?certain] [?days]
She answers nothing sits there dumb and blank
Or has a look of hatred in her eyes.
near her
I have been so ~~near~~ I can read that look

3 Tom fool] Yeats's *The Herne's Egg* (1938), the next play he composed after *FMIM(M)*, features a character so named. Cf. BC, 4v, l. 5 where reference is made to "Congles" [Congal], the hero of that later play.

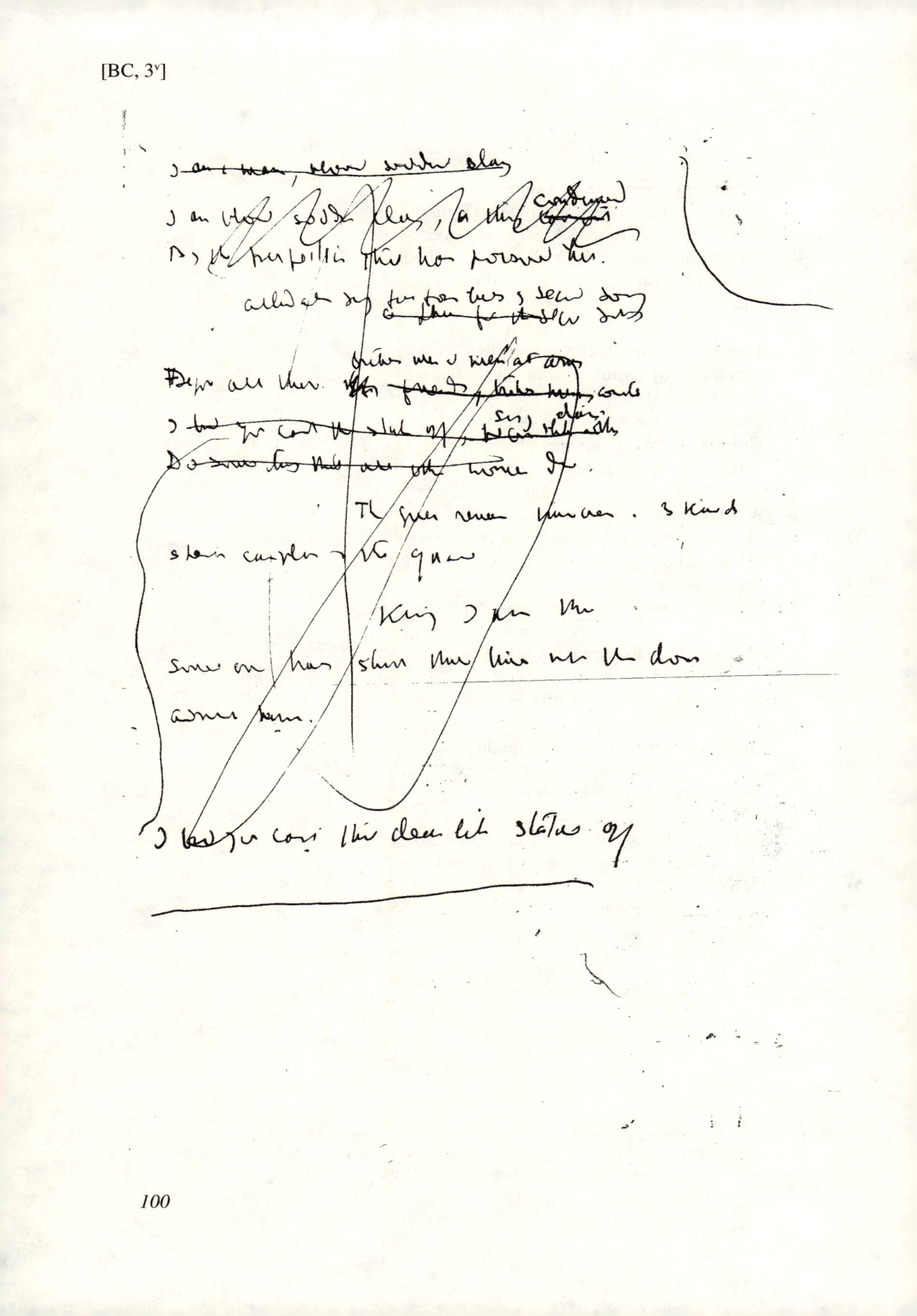

[BC, 3v]

[BC, 3v]

1 ~~I am a man, blood sodden clay~~

condemned

2 I am blood sodden clay, a thing [?~~corrupt~~]

3 By the [?perfection] that [?has] poisoned her

4 Attendants sing first four lines of second song

~~a phrase from the~~ second song

tribes men and men at arms

5 Before all here m~~y friends, tribes men, courtiers~~

sing, dance

6 I ~~bid you cast the statue off before this assembly~~

7 ~~Do some thing that all other women~~ do

8 The queen [?never] [?answers]. 3 knocks

9 Speak captain of the guard

10 King I am here

11 Someone has struck three times upon the door

12 Admit him.

13 I bid you cast this death like statue off.

1–3 The first three lines on facing 4r are encircled and clued in to replace these canceled lines.

4 second song] The song cannot be identified. Did Yeats envisage the stanzas of the opening lyric being interspersed at intervals throughout the dialogue in this version? As the stanzas (including the refrain) each number more than four lines, his intentions are not clear.

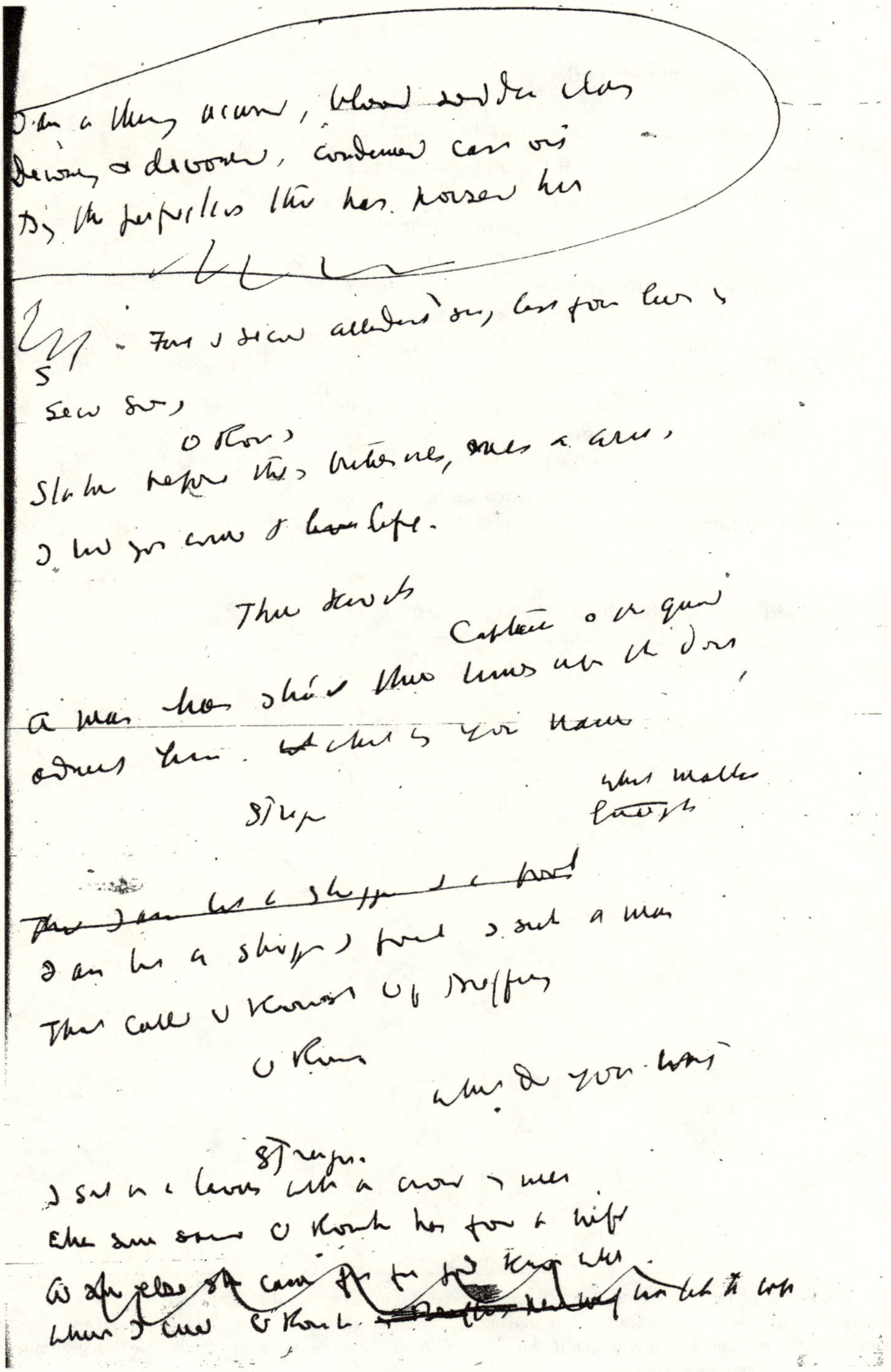

[BC, 4r]

1 I am a thing accursed, blood sodden clay
2 Devouring and devoured, condemned carrion
3 By the[?perfection] that has poisoned her

4 First & Second Attendant sing last four lines of
S
5 second song.

O'Rourke

6 Statue before these tribesmen, men at arms
7 I bid you come to ~~live~~ life

Three knocks

Captain of the guard

8 A man has struck three times upon the door
9 Admit him. ~~Wt~~ What is your name

Stranger What matter
~~Enough~~

10 ~~That I am but a stranger & a fool~~
11 I am but a stranger & fool I seek a man
12 That's called O'Rourke of Breffney

O'Rourke

What do you want

Stranger

13 I sat in a tavern with a crowd of men
14 When some said O'Rourke has for a wife
15 [?W] [?all] else she came from for god knows [?well /?where]
16 When I cried O'Rourke ~~of Breffney new wife~~ [?was] like to [?cry]

1–3 These lines clued to replace the first three lines on 3v (see pp. 101–102 above).

4–5 See note to 3v, l. 4. The last four lines of the second stanza of the opening lyric of *KGCT* (prose) would not make grammatical sense standing alone.

[BC, 4v]

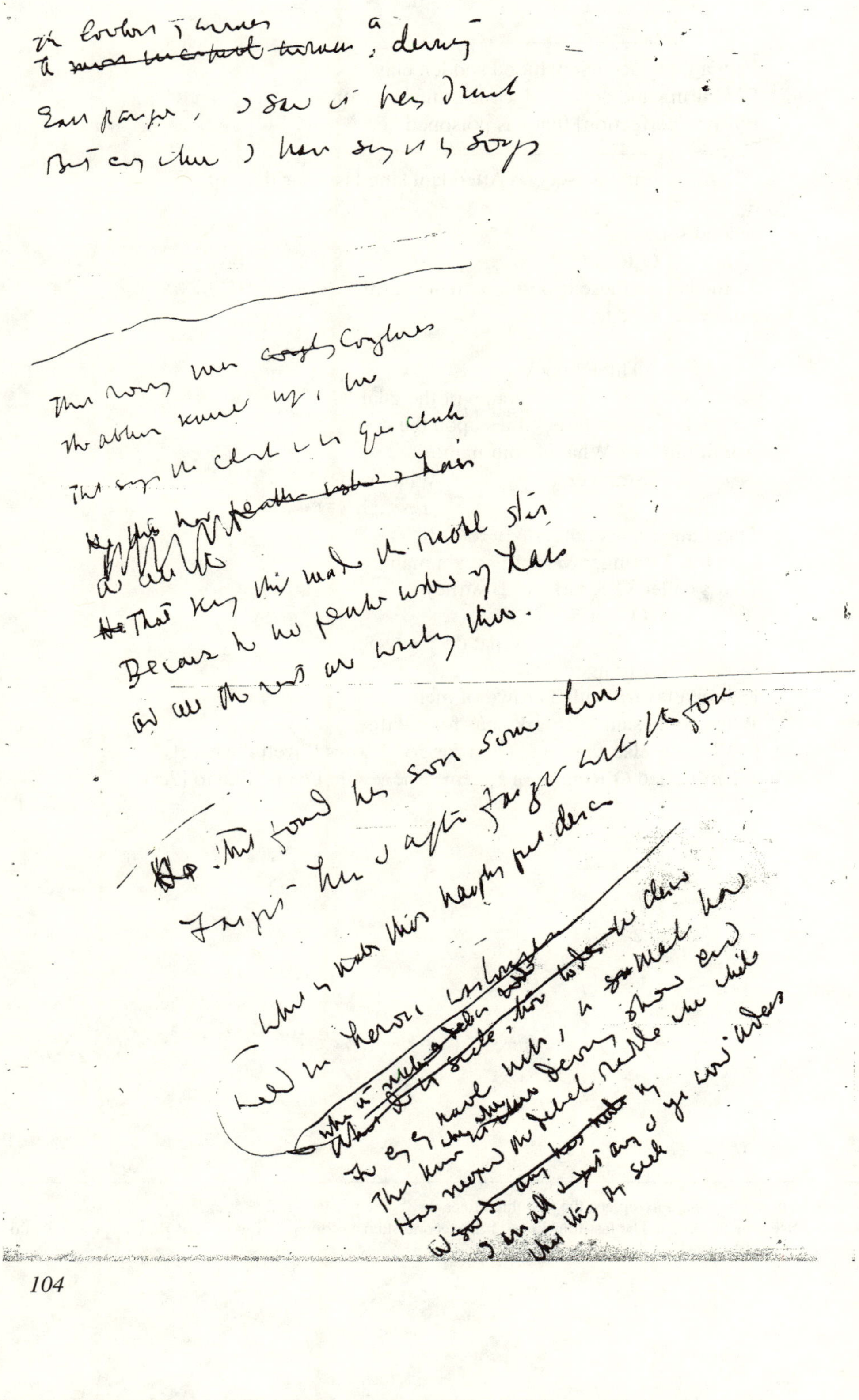

[BC, 4ᵛ]

The loveliest of women
A ~~more incomparable wo~~man: a divinity
[?Each] [?passion], I said it being drunk
But cry when I have sung it in songs

That roaring man ~~Congles~~ [?Conglures]
The ablest knight upon a time
That says the Clock in the Great Clock
~~He that has feathers instead of hair~~
And all the
~~He~~ That king that made the people stare
Because he had feathers instead of hair
And all the rest are waiting there

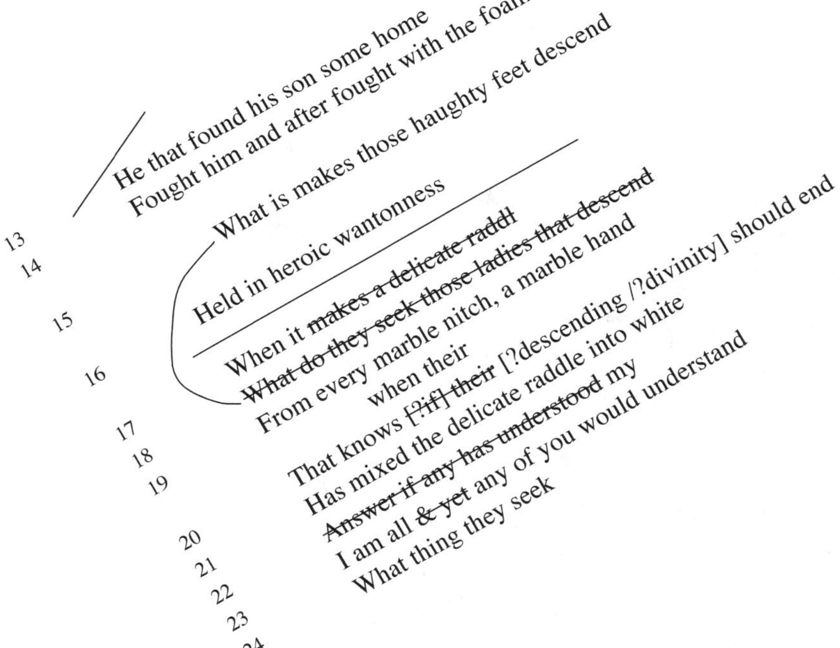

13 He that found his son some home
14 Fought him and after fought with the foam
15 What is makes those haughty feet descend
16 Held in heroic wantonness
17 When it ~~makes a delicate raddl~~
18 ~~What do they seek those ladies that descend~~
19 From every marble nitch, a marble hand
when their
20 That knows ~~[?if] their~~ [?descending /?divinity] should end
21 Has mixed the delicate raddle into white
22 ~~Answer if any has understood~~ my
23 I am all ~~& yet~~ any of you would understand
24 What thing they seek

Reproduced and transcribed above on pp. 72–75 in relation to Yeats's preparation of the *Life and Letters* text. See the notes on pp. 73, 75.

1–4 Cf. ll. 13–16 on 4ʳ and ll. 1–4 on 5ʳ.

5 For "~~Congles~~ [?Conglures]" see BC, 3ʳ, l. 3 and note.

another that her name was Dervorgilla
[illegible] the years; but I [illegible] [illegible]
Saw this [illegible] Rock [illegible] [illegible] [illegible]
but [illegible] [illegible] I have seen, the Passing.
~~[illegible]~~
But I have never seen [illegible]

O Rose

[illegible]

The sweet heart I gave over to [illegible], alas.

For desecration and the lovers' night.

~~[illegible]~~
[illegible] of some great [illegible]; ~~[illegible]~~ [illegible]
~~[illegible]~~
~~[illegible]~~
I woke
[illegible] I [illegible]
[illegible] [illegible] [illegible]
[illegible] [illegible] [illegible] [illegible].

sweet [illegible]
[illegible]
[illegible] [illegible] [illegible]
[illegible]

[BC, 5r]

1 Another that her name was Devorgilla
2 [?Who was] thy queen; but I being drunk cried out
3 Said that O'Rourke then found every [?passion]
that hour
4 But from ~~hour~~ I have sung the [?passion]
5 ~~And made its lady love suits~~
6 But I have never seen her

O'Rourke
Have you no wife
7 Nor sweet heart of your own to sing about

8 For desecration and the lover's night

9 Out of the marble nitches they descend
[?] [?]
~~[?could] [?that] [?hand] [?] [?]~~ [?]
10 Painted by some great masters; ~~[?in] [?fear] [?descend] [?again]~~
And
11 ~~[?Though] [?along] [?my] [?veins]~~ &
12 Although my heart had stopped in sudden [?frenzy]
I asked
13 [?Though] [?] [?] [?] [?] life and sudden fright
14 Had made the pulses of my body stop
15 I ask my heart what they intend
[?sweet /secret] [?artistry]
[?mystic /?master]
16 Some [?sacred] hand
17 Has mixed a delicate raddle with the white
18

1–7 Cf. ll. 13–16 on 4r.

9–18 This attempt at the first stanza of "Why must those holy, haughty feet descend" may have preceded that on 4v, but the chronological sequence underlying the compositions on these two pages is uncertain. Yeats also anticipates here some ideas that in time appear in the completed second stanza, with its account of a heart seized by fright.

[BC, 5v]

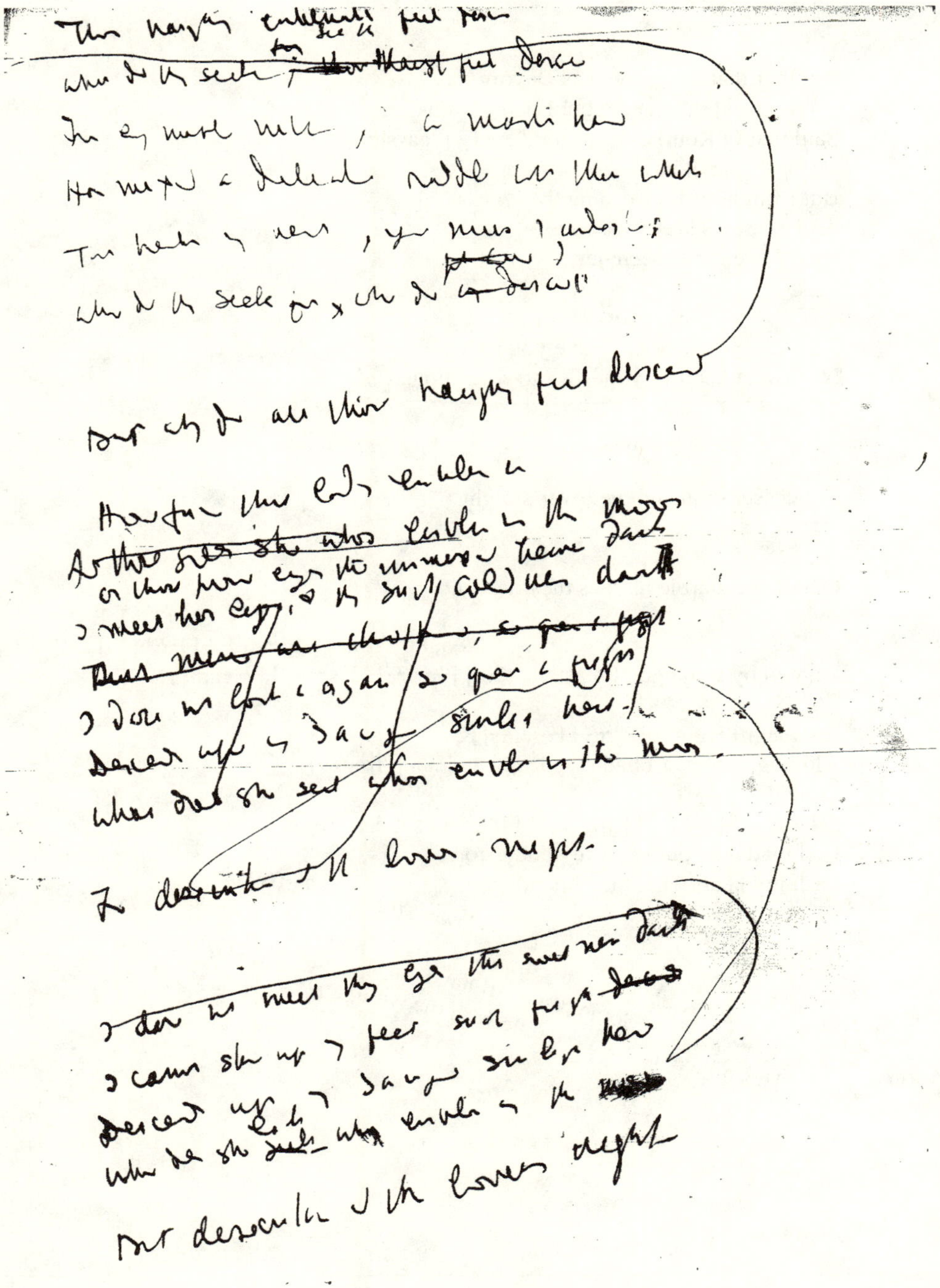

[BC, 5v] [*KGCT* (prose) 181–198; *FMIM* 180–197]

Those haughty emblematic feet descend
seek
~~for~~
What do they seek; ~~those~~ haughty feet descend
From every marble nitche, a master hand
Has mixed a delicate raddle with their white
This heart is vexed, yet must I understand
~~yet must~~ I
What do they seek for, why do ~~they~~ descend?

But why do all those haughty feet descend

How face this lady emblem is
~~And there goes she whose emblem~~ is the moon
Or those proud eyes the unmixed heaven darts
I meet her eyes & they such coldness dart
~~That men are [?chastened], so great a fright~~
I dare not look & again so great a fright
Descends upon my savage sunlit heart.
What does she seek whose emblem is the moon.

For desecration and the lovers night.

~~I dare not meet these eyes this sweetness darts~~
I cannot stand upon my feet such fright ~~descends~~
Descends upon my savage sunlit heart
lack
What does she ~~seek~~ whose emblem is the moon

But desecration and the lovers night

---

6 Clued for insertion between ll. 1 and 2, thus opening the lyric with a rhetorical question.
17–21 The lines are clued to replace the canceled four lines above.

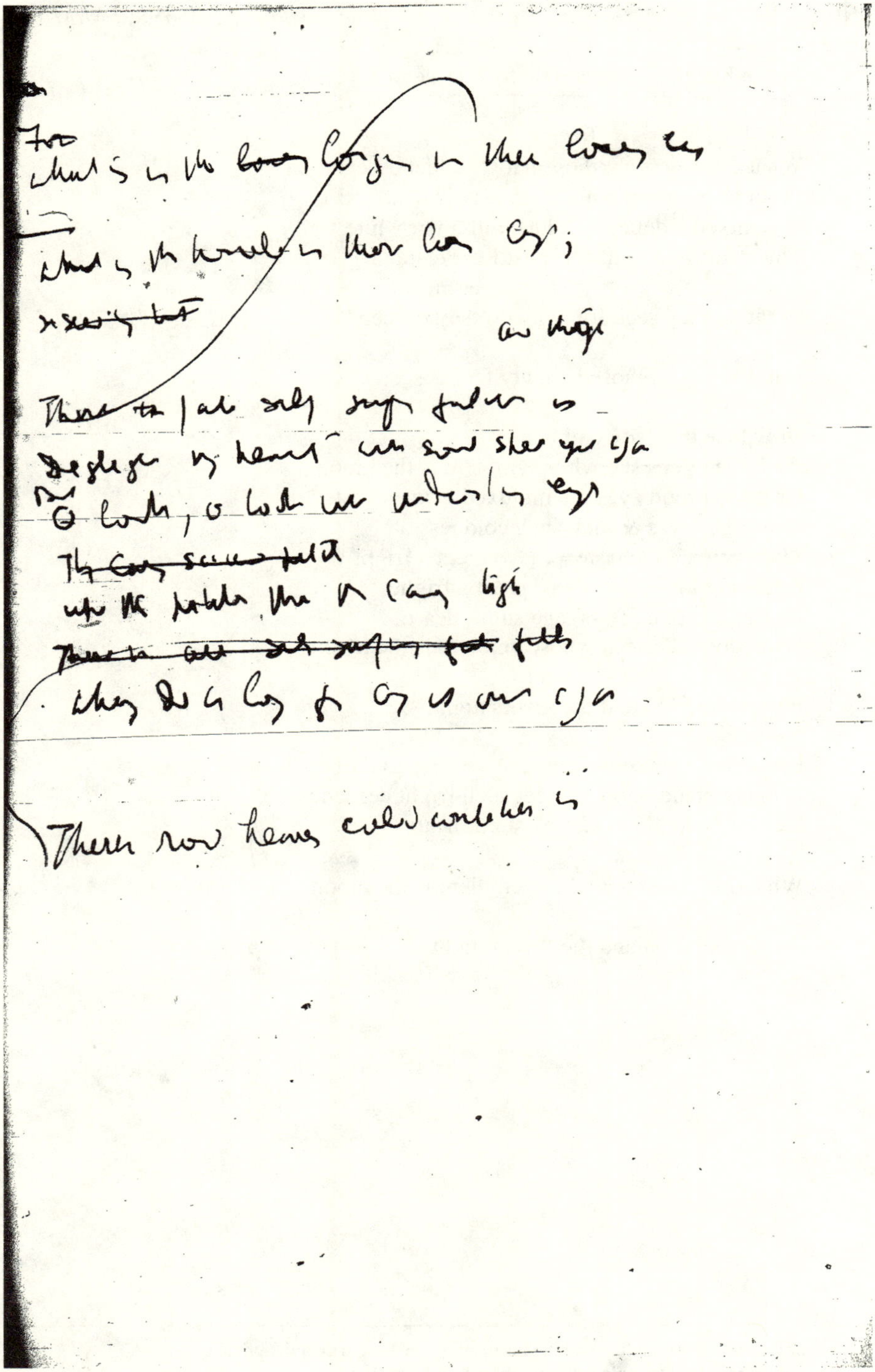

[BC, 6r] [*KGCT* (prose) 193–198; *FMIM* 192–197]

~~For~~

~~For~~

1 What is the ~~loving~~ longing in their [?loving] eyes

———

2 What is the knowledge in their loving eyes;

It [~~?] but~~ and {that / though}

3 There ~~in~~ [?if] all self sufficing fullness is

4 Delight my heart with sound speak yet again

But

5 ~~O~~ look, o look with understanding eyes

6 ~~They carry [?sacred] pitch~~

7 Upon the pitchers that they carry tight

8 ~~There in all self sufficing full fulns~~

9 What do they long for cry it out again

10 Therein round heavens cold [?contention] is

---

8 For "fuls" read "fulness".

[BC, 6^v]

First attendant

Those haughty ~~turbulence~~, feet descend
From any marble halls, a master's hand
Has wrought; never in a delicate wedded we that which
Pressed heaven, in heart, yet meant of undream
~~what are they seeking~~ ~~why do they seek~~ for, why do they descend

Second attendant

For desecration and the lovers night

First attendant

And these feet the whole ~~evil~~ begins the moon
~~I cannot stand with the feet such forgot~~
I cannot meet those eyes that sweetness dart
Nor stare at the feet so great a frequent
Innocent with long savage simplest heart
What ~~does~~ can she ~~seek~~ lack whose emblem is the moon

Second attendant

~~For~~ For desecration and the lovers night

First attendant

Delight of heart's shout yet no sound again
Dies, look, and look with understanding eyes
Upon the pitchers that they carry; light
~~Thereto all~~ Self suffering pitchers to
What do we bring but eyes and eyes

Second attendant

For desecration and the lovers night

[BC, 6[v]] [*KGCT* (prose) 181–198; *FMIM* 180–197]

First Attendant
haughty
Those emblematic feet descend
From every marble nitche, a master hand
Has ~~mingl~~ mixed a delicate raddle with their white
it
That breaks my heart, yet must ~~I~~ understand
What are they seeking
~~Why do they seek for~~, why do they descend

Second Attendant
For desecration and the lovers night

First Attendant
And then fear she whose emblem is the moon
I ~~cannot stand upon my feet such frig~~ht
I cannot meet those eyes that sweetness dart
Nor stand upon my feet so great a fright
Descends upon my savage sunlit heart
can lack
What ~~does~~ she ~~seek~~ whose emblem is the moon

Second Attendant
But
~~For~~ desecration and the lovers night

First Atten
with sound
Delight my heart ^ speak yet again
But look, O look with understanding eyes
Upon the pitchers that they carry; tight
~~There in all s~~elf sufficing fullness is
What do they long for cry it out again

~~F~~ Second Att
For desecration and the lovers night

13, 19 Yeats truncates the word "Attendant".

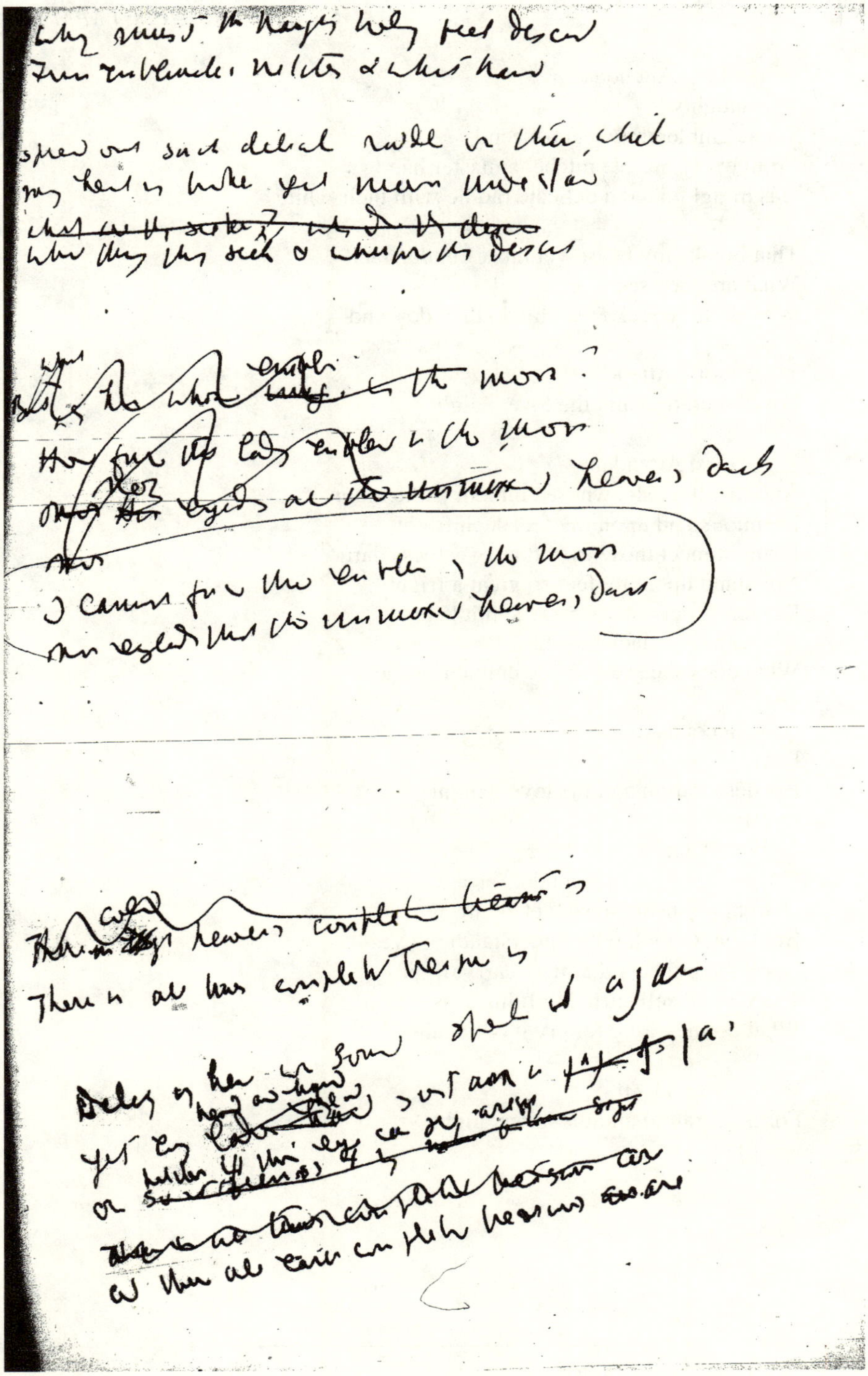

[BC, 7^r] [*KGCT* (prose) 181–198; *FMIM* 180–197]

Why must those haughty holy feet descend
From emblematic nitches and what hand

Spread out such delicate raddle in their white
My heart is broken yet must understand
~~What are they seeking? why do they descend~~
What they thus seek and wherefore they descend

what emblem
But ^ of her whose ~~image~~ is the moon?
How face this lady emblem in the moon
Nor
~~Over these~~ eyelids all the unmixed heavens dart
~~Nor~~
I cannot face that emblem of the moon
Nor eyelids that the unmixed heavens dart

~~cold~~
~~Therein high heavens complete treasure is~~
Therein all times completed treasure is

Delight my heart with sound speak it again
head and hand
~~hand~~
[?Let/Yet] every ~~[?ladys]~~ ~~hand~~ [?sustain] a ~~jug [?of]~~ jar
pitcher if this eye can see aright
Or ~~see its fullness to my natural astonished sight~~

~~There in all times completed treasures are~~
And there all earths completed treasures ~~are~~. are

1 Yeats rephrases the opening line in the form of a question, which remains his favored reading.
10–11 These lines are clued into page 6^v, where they are to replace canceled ll. 7–8.

[NLI 30,800]

(Continue on page 11 as follows)

When the [inner] curtain is closed the attendants stand on either side singing, ~~[illegible]~~ full

Second attendant. Why must those haughty, holy feet descend
From emblematic niches & what hand
Ran such a delicate raddle through their white
My heart is broken, yet must understand?
~~What they the seeking what for they.~~
What ~~[illegible]~~ [are they seeking?] why do they descend?

First attendant. For desecration and the lover's night.

Second attendant. I cannot face that emblem of the moon
Nor eyelids that the unmixed heavens dart
Nor stand upon my feet so great a fright
Descends upon my savage, sunlit heart.
What can she lack whose emblem is the moon?

First attendant. But desecration and the lover's night.

Second attendant. Delight my heart with sound; speak yet again;
But look & look with understanding eyes
Upon the pitchers that they carry; tight
~~[illegible]~~ [Therein] all times completed treasure is;
What do they ~~[illegible]~~ [lack] O, cry it out again.

First attendant. Their desecration and the lover's night.

The stage curtain falls.

[NLI 30,800] [*KGCT* (prose) 181–198; *FMIM* 180–197]

1 (continue on page 11 as follows)
inner
2 When the ^ curtain is closed the attendants stand upon either side
{ . ~~stage~~
3 singing { , ~~at the end of this song the proscenium curtain falls~~
4 Second Attendant. Why must those haughty, holy feet descend
5 From emblematic nitches & what hand
6 Ran such a delicate raddle through their white
{ . ~~?~~ ~~I~~
7 My heart is broken { ; yet must ^ understand?
8 ~~What thing they seek and wherefore they~~
are they seeking?
9 What ~~do they seek &~~ why do they descend?
10 First Attendant. For desecration and the lover's night.
11 Second Attendant. I cannot face that emblem of the moon
12 Nor eyelids that the unmixed heavens dart
13 Nor stand upon my feet so great a fright
14 Descends upon my savage, sunlit heart.
15 What can she lack whose emblem is the moon?
16 First Attendant. But desecration and the lover's night
17 Second Attendant. Delight my heart with sound; speak yet again;
18 But look & look with understanding eyes
19 Upon the pitchers that they carry; tight
Therein
20 ~~Therin~~ all times completed treasure is;
lack O
21 What do they ~~lack & look for~~, cry it out again.
22 First Attendant. Their desecration and the lover's night.
23 The stage curtain falls.

---

1 For a discussion of the significance of this line and of the entire manuscript, see the introduction, pp. xlii–xliii.

2–3 The similarity of this stage direction with that to be found at this point in the Cuala text of *KGCT* in prose further relates this manuscript to that play rather than to the printed texts of *FMIM*.

Part II. *A Full Moon in March*

B. The Evolution of the Lyric, "He had famished in a wilderness": BC, 8^{v}–12^{r}, and the Cuala Text (December 1934)

"He had famished in a wilderness," the lyric that divides the acted from the danced sections of *A Full Moon in March*, came very quickly into being; the structure of the opening two stanzas emerges on pages 8^{v}–9^{r} of the Rapallo notebook through Yeats's method of circling around an idea until it begins to satisfy him and allows him to move on. The lyric was first published in the Cuala edition of *The King of the Great Clock Tower* as a coda to the text of the "Commentary on 'The Great Clock Tower'" before finding its place in *A Full Moon in March*.

[BC, 8v]

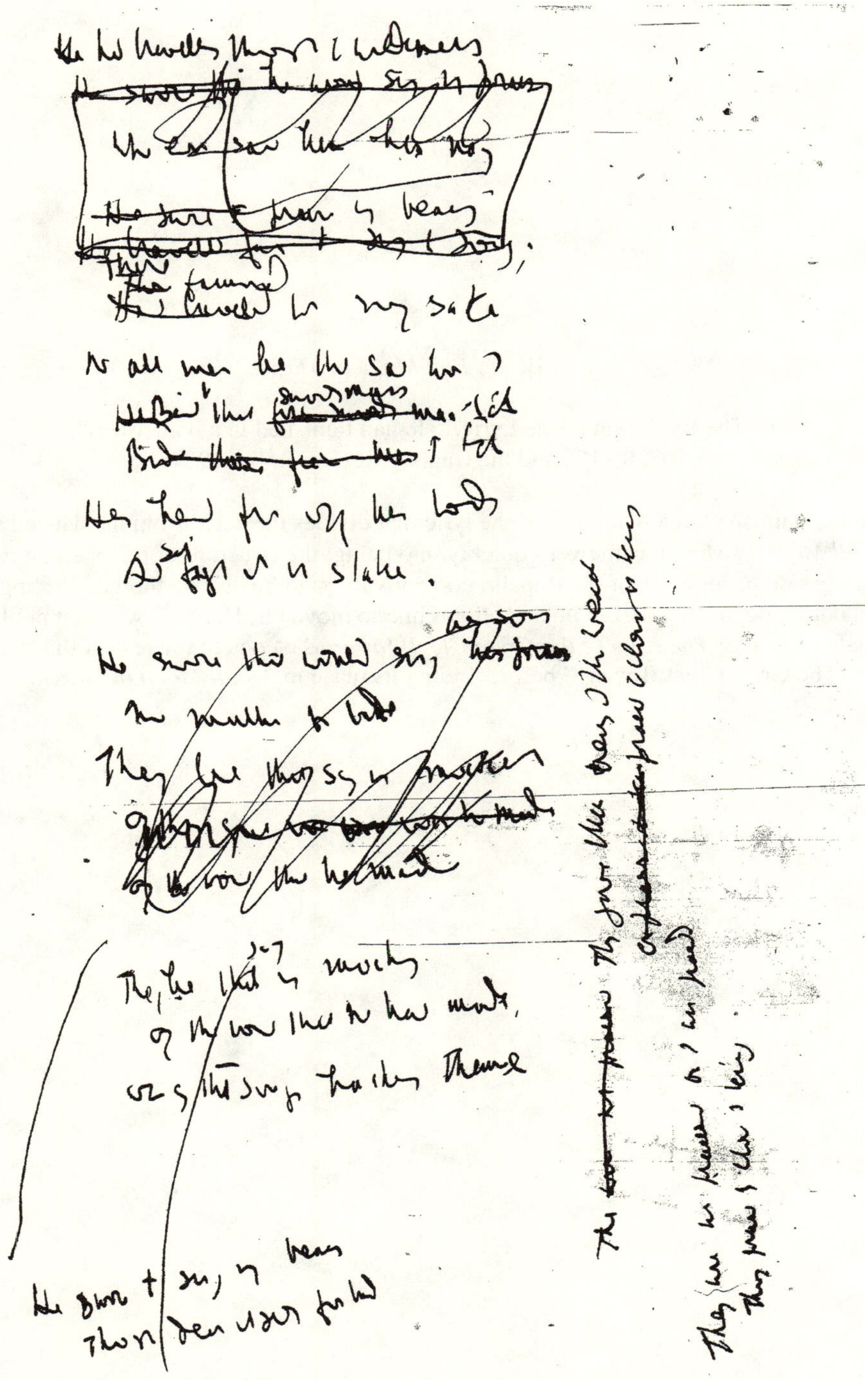

[BC, 8ᵛ] [*VPl*, 127–146]

1 He had travelled through a wilderness
2 He swore that he would sing in praise
3 Who ~~ever saw~~ his ~~head ro~~
4 ~~He swore to praise my beauty~~
5 ~~He travelled far to sing a song;~~
There
~~Thr~~ famished
6 ~~Had travelled~~ for my sake

7 Not all men lie that say that I
swordsman
8 ~~[?He]~~ Bid this ~~fierce swords~~ man strike
9 ~~Bid those fierce men~~ to strike
10 His head from off his body
set
11 And ~~fight~~ it on stake
his song
12 He swore this would sing ~~his praise~~
13 No matter for bade
14 They lie that say in mockery
~~Of the~~
15 ~~[?] [?] great vow [?fierce] vow he made~~
16 Of the vow that he made

say
17 They lie that in mockery
18 Of the vow that he had made
19 Only that songs hackney theme

20 He swore to sing my beauty
21 Though death itself forbade

22 ~~They were not praised~~ They gave their beauty & their wealth
23 In ~~praise to kin~~ praise to clown or king
24 They were not praised as I was praised
25 They praised by clown & king

found in BC, 8ᵛ, 9ʳ, 11ʳ–12ʳ *transcribed above and below, pp. 123–129*
published in *KGCT(C)* *transcribed below, p. 130*
FMIM(M)

2–5 Though these lines are canceled here, they form the substance of what was to become the second stanza.

12–16 Yeats redeployed the substance and much of the phrasing of these lines to achieve an almost finished version of the first three lines of the second stanza (ll. 17–19).

20–21 Clued to precede l. 17 and, despite cancellation when the stanza was redrafted on 9ʳ, remained unchanged as the opening verses of the second stanza.

22–25 These closely emended lines relate more to ll. 7–17 on 9ʳ than to the opening stanzas of the lyric, but they are not clued to any lines on the facing page. They are a first attempt at an opening to the fourth stanza.

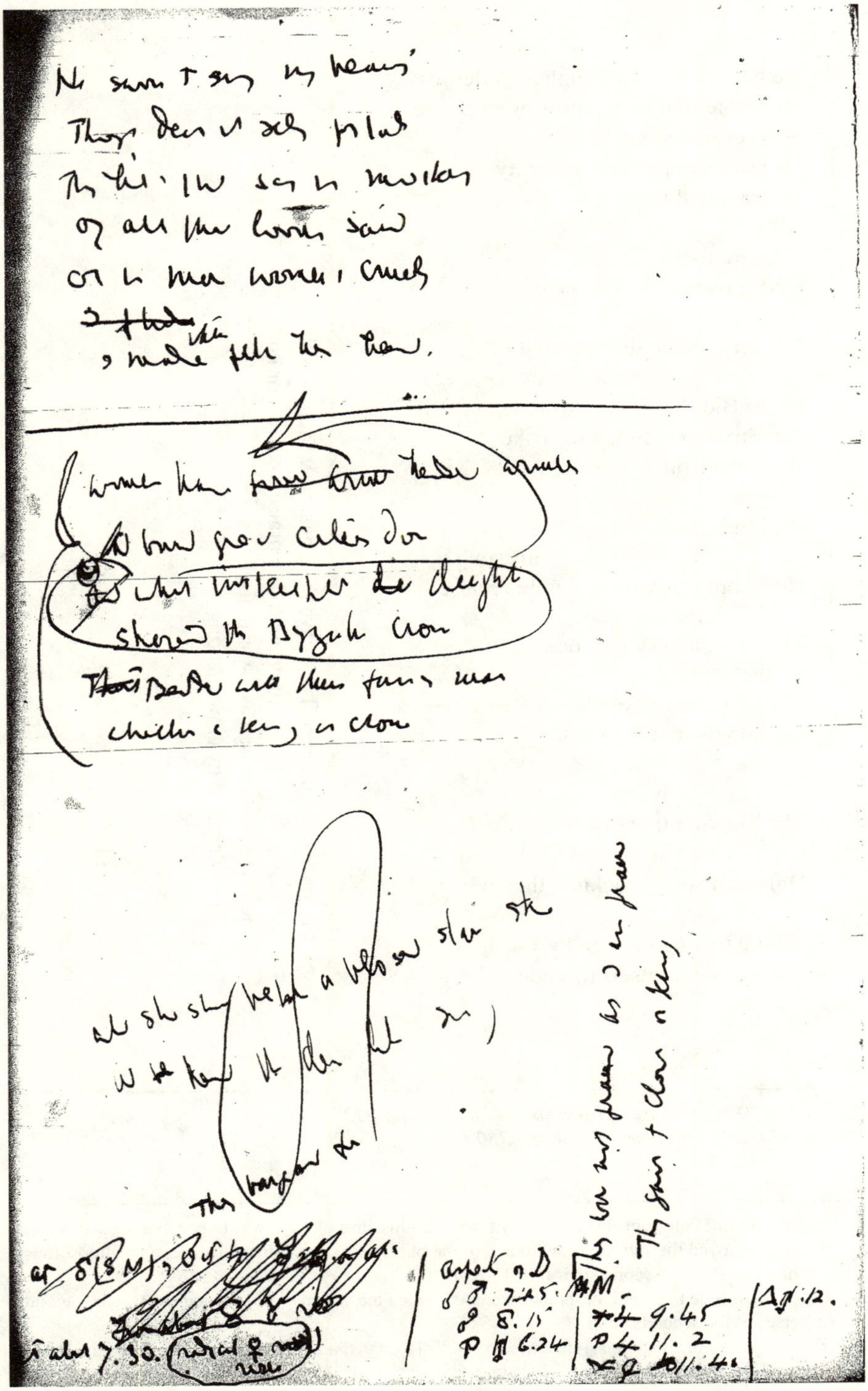

[BC, 9[r]] [*VPl*, 133–150]

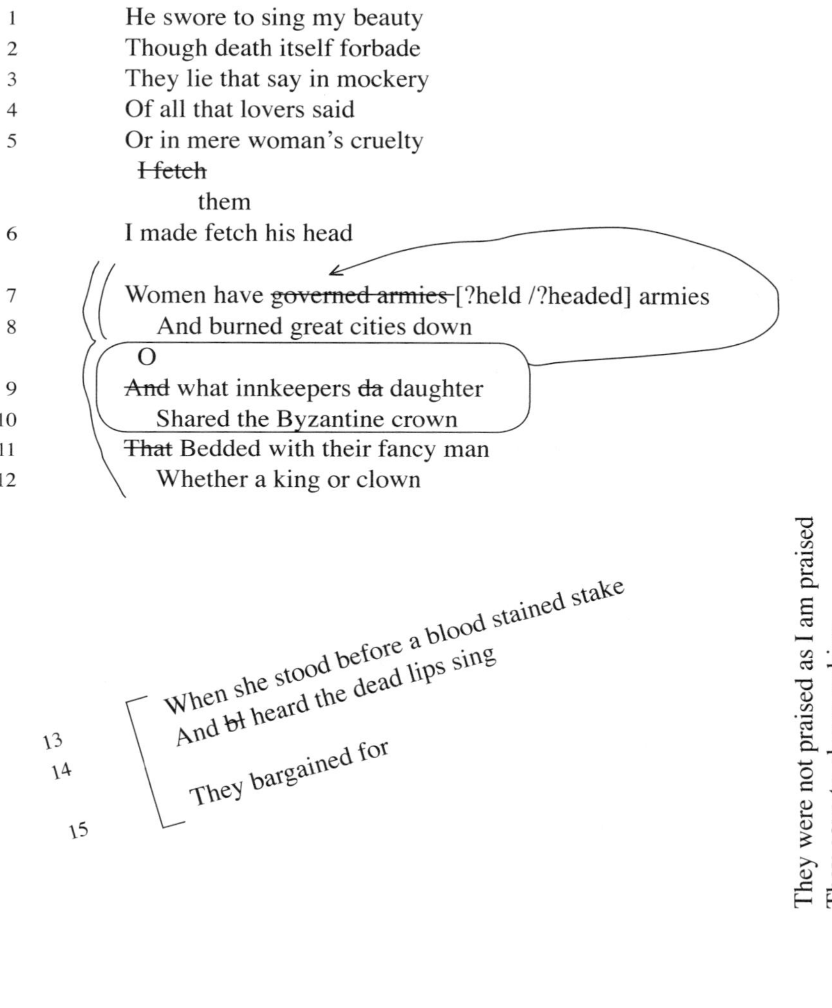

He swore to sing my beauty
Though death itself forbade
They lie that say in mockery
Of all that lovers said
Or in mere woman's cruelty
~~I fetch~~
them
I made fetch his head

Women have ~~governed armies~~ [?held /?headed] armies
And burned great cities down
O
~~And~~ what innkeepers ~~da~~ daughter
Shared the Byzantine crown
~~That~~ Bedded with their fancy man
Whether a king or clown

When she stood before a blood stained stake
And ~~bl~~ heard the dead lips sing

They bargained for

They were not praised as I am praised
They gave to clown or king

1–6 Apart from punctuation, these lines match the finished second stanza.

7 The word "held" seems the more likely reading, although when Yeats next attempts a version of this line on page 11[v], l. 15, the verb is clearly "headed".

9–10 With these lines clued to precede l. 7, the four lines (9–10, 7–8, 11–12) reach the final structure of the third stanza, if not the precise wording.

16–17 These lines are closely allied to ll. 22–25 on page 8[v].

17 After this line the remainder of the page is filled with astrological calculations. At this point composition of the lyric appears to have been disrupted by Yeats's need to draft the Preface to the Cuala edition of *KGCT*, which follows on pages 9[v]–10[v].

[BC, 11r]

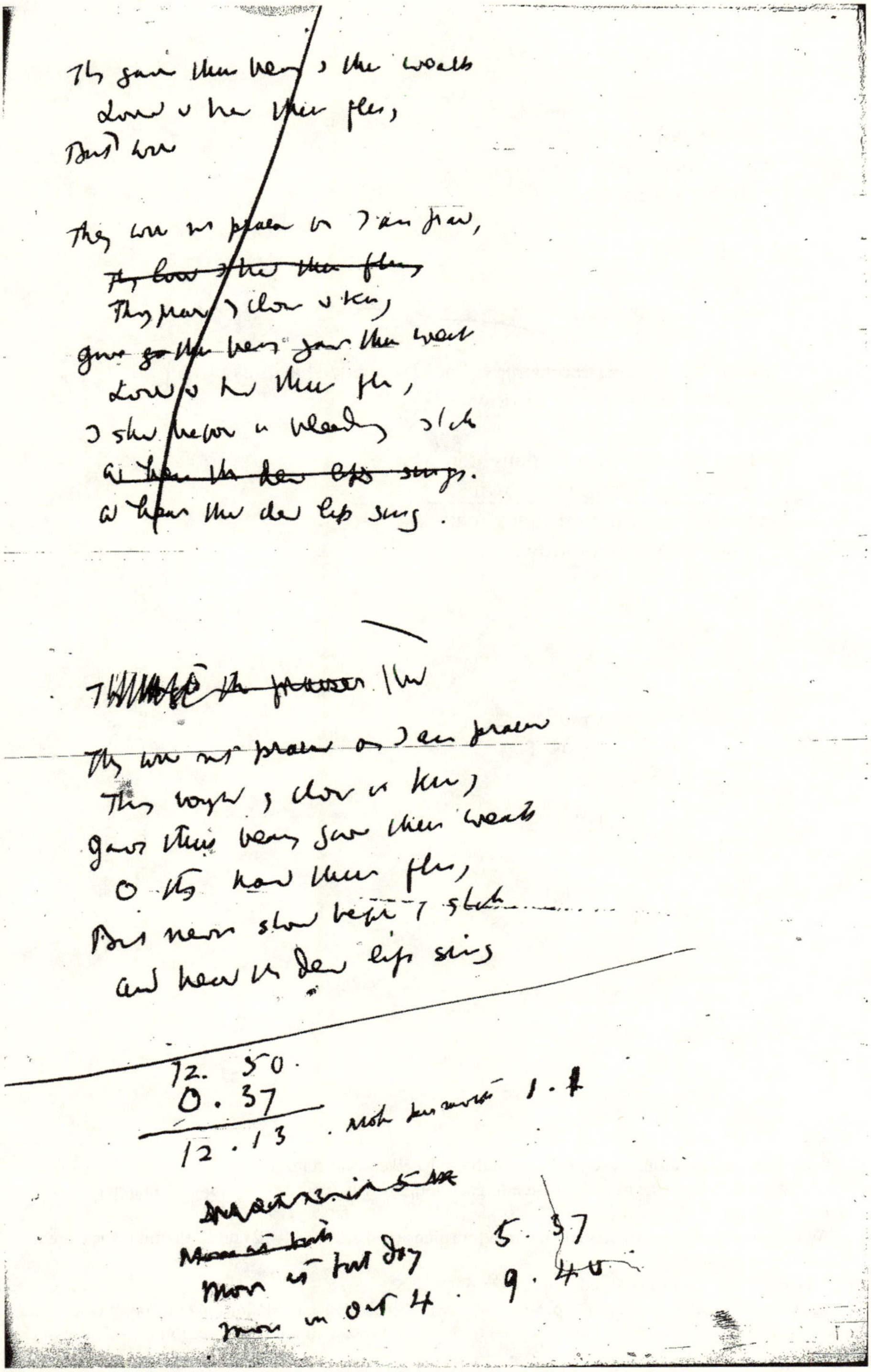

[BC, 11[r]]

[*VPl*, 145–150]

They gave their being & their wealth
    Loved and had their fling
But were

They were not praised as I am praised
    ~~They loved and had their fling~~
    They praised by clown and king
Give ~~ga~~ their being gave their wealth
    Loved and had their fling
I stand before a bleeding stake
    ~~And hear the dead lips sings~~
    And hear the dead lip sing.

~~They bought the praises~~ that

They were not praised as I am praised
    They bought of clown or king
Gave their beauty gave their wealth
    O they had their fling
But never stood before a stake
    And heard the dead lips sing

Composition of the lyric resumes with further drafting of the final stanza.

1–11 These at times heavily emended lines are finally canceled before a clean copy of their substance is attempted in ll. 13–18.

17–18 A thick line drawn across the page separates the drafts of the stanza from a short series of astrological calculations.

He had famished in a wilderness,
Braved lions for my sake,
And all men lie that say, that I
Bade that swordsman take
His head from off his body
And set it on a stake.

He swore to sing my beauty
Though death itself forbade.
They lie that say in mockery
Of all that lovers said
Or in mere woman's cruelty
I made them fetch his head

O what an inn-keeper's daughter
Shares the Byzantine crown;
Girls that have governed armies
[illegible] great cities down
[illegible] with their fancy man
Whether a king, or clown
But none were
[illegible] pleasure any sane person;
[illegible] a clown or a king
[illegible] dearly loved or money
[illegible]
But never stood before a stake
& heard the dead lips sing.

[BC, 11v] [*VPl*, 127–150]

~~fam~~ had famished in
He ~~had travelled through~~ a wilderness
Braved lions
~~Then famished~~ for my sake
And all men lie that say that I
Bade that swords man take
His head from off his body
set
And ~~fetch~~ it on a stake

He swore to sing my beauty
Though death itself forbade
They lie that say in mockery
Of all that lovers said
Or in mere woman's cruelty
I made them fetch his head

O what ~~ir~~ inn-keeper s daughter
Shared the Byzantine crown?
~~governed~~
~~O girls have headed armies~~ Girls that have governed armies
~~And~~ burned great cities down
Have bedded
~~Bedded~~ with their fancy man
Whether a king or clown

But none were
~~They were not~~ praised as I am praised
~~That gave to They gave~~ That give
~~They bought of king or clown~~ to clown or king
~~Gave their beauty, time and money~~ Beauty, love or money
O they had their fling
But never stood before a stake
And heard the dead lips sing

Yeats here attempts a clean copy of his composition to date. He later made only small changes in the first three stanzas, chiefly by adding punctuation.

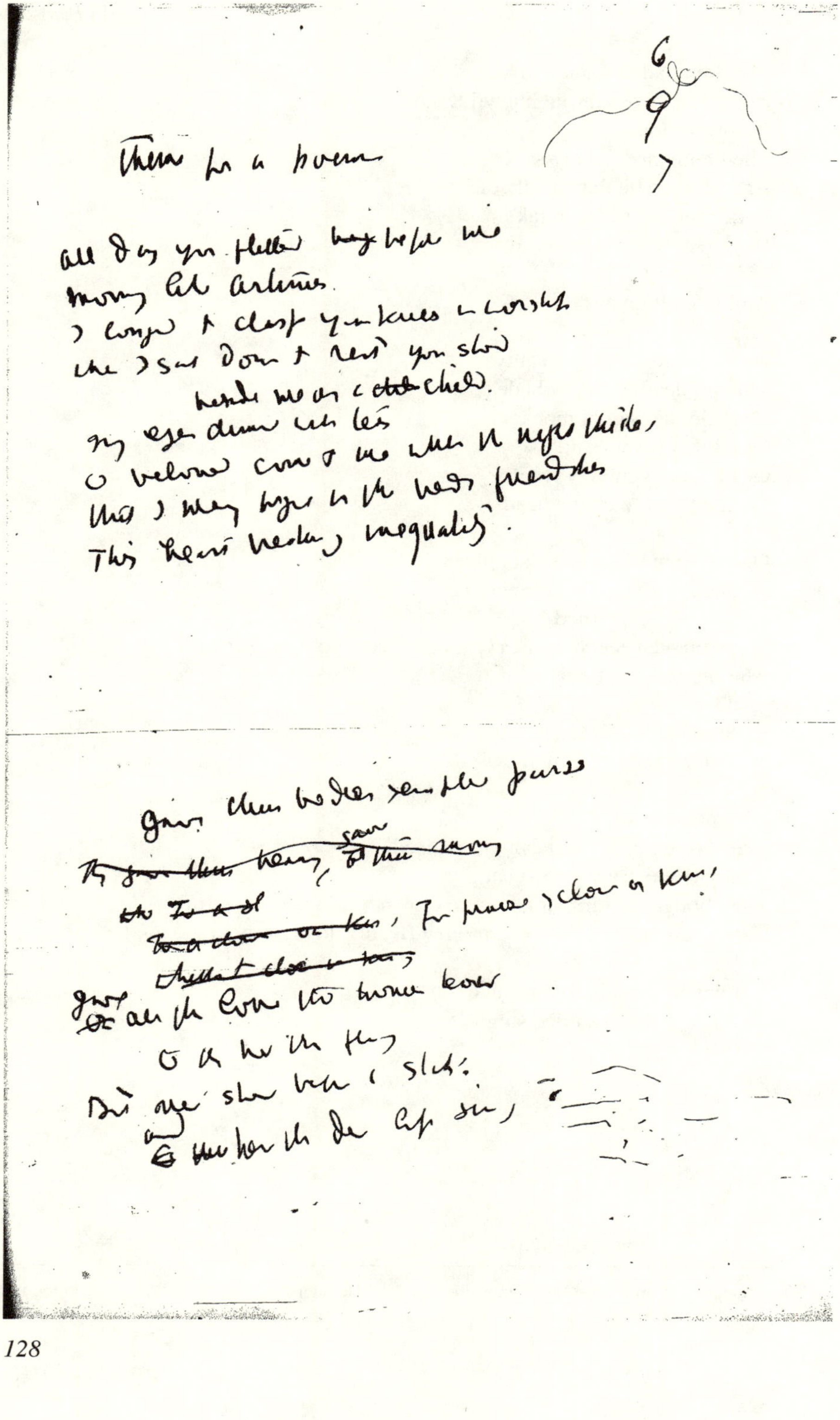

Gave their bodies, emptied purses
~~gave~~
1 ~~They gave their beauty, b their money~~
~~Wh For a sl~~
~~For a clown or king~~ For praise of clown or king
2 ~~Whether for clown or king~~
Gave
3 ~~Or~~ all the love that women know
4 O they had their fling
5 But never stood before a stake
And
6 ~~O tho~~ heard the dead lips sing

After revision, and apart from punctuation, Yeats has reached the finished version of the final stanza (see ll. 19–24 on p. 130 below). These lines are positioned directly opposite the canceled attempt at the final stanza on page 11^{v}. Above them are nine lines headed "Theme for a poem".

[*The King of the Great Clock Tower*, Cuala Press Edition]

[pp. 20–21] [*VPl*, 127–150]

He had famished in a wilderness,
Braved lions for my sake,
And all men lie that say that I
Bade that swordsman take
His head from off his body
And set it on a stake.

He swore to sing my beauty
Though death itself forbade,
They lie that say in mockery
Of all that lovers said,
Or in mere woman's cruelty
I bade them fetch his head.

O what innkeeper's daughter
Shared the Byzantine crown!
Girls that have governed cities,
Or burned great cities down,
Have bedded with their fancy-man
Whether a king or clown;

Gave their bodies, emptied purses
For praise or clown or king,
Gave all the love that women know!
O they had their fling
But never stood before a stake
And heard the dead lips sing.

---

8 forbade. *FMIM(M)*
9 say, *FMIM(M)*
14 crown? *FMIM(M)*
22 fling, *FMIM(M)*

The lyric was first published in the Cuala edition of *KGCT* as a conclusion to the "Commentary on 'The Great Clock Tower.'" It is given here in that form, as it is the first wholly clean copy of the four stanzas. The collations above give variant readings found in the lyric as published in Macmillan's *FMIM*.

Part II. *A Full Moon in March*

C. The Evolution of the Lyric, "Every loutish lad in love": BC, 25^{v}–26^{r}, 33^{r}, and NLI 30,336 e, 10^{r}, 10^{v}

The lyric "Every loutish lad in love," sung by the Second Attendant in *A Full Moon in March*, appears in draft first in the Rapallo notebook, BC, 25^{v}–26^{r}. Revised in the loose-leaf notebook, NLI 30,336 e, it was completed in fair copy on 33^{r} of the Rapallo notebook. This later version is separated from the initial group of drafts by Yeats's attempt at a prose scenario for *FMIM(M)* (26^{v}–27^{v} and 30^{v}–32^{v}); the two bursts of composition on the play are disrupted by several pages of astrological calculations for the period October to December 1934. Yeats seems next to have worked on both scenario and lyric in NLI 30,336 e; he expanded the former into dramatic dialogue through three linked and cumulative sketches for the opening acted section of the play, while his next draft of the lyric occurs between the second and third versions of the dialogue (the first stanza is preceded by two lines of prose, which have no bearing on the composition of the play: "scarcely by a story as miraculous & as beautiful as / one told of the childhood of some European saint"). In this version of the lyric Yeats begins systematically to rephrase the opening lines and he substantially reworks the third stanza. The further redrafting of the lyric in the Rapallo notebook (BC, 33^{r}) incorporates many of the revisions made in NLI 30,336 e or resolves uncertainties found in that version. Though the lyric has now come close to its final form, Yeats continued to work over certain details. The next draft occurs in NLI 8906, where for the first time Yeats assembles most of the separately composed elements of the play, and where, as a result of four notable revisions, the lyric is completed. That final version is found with the transcription of NLI 8906 (see pp. 208–211 below).

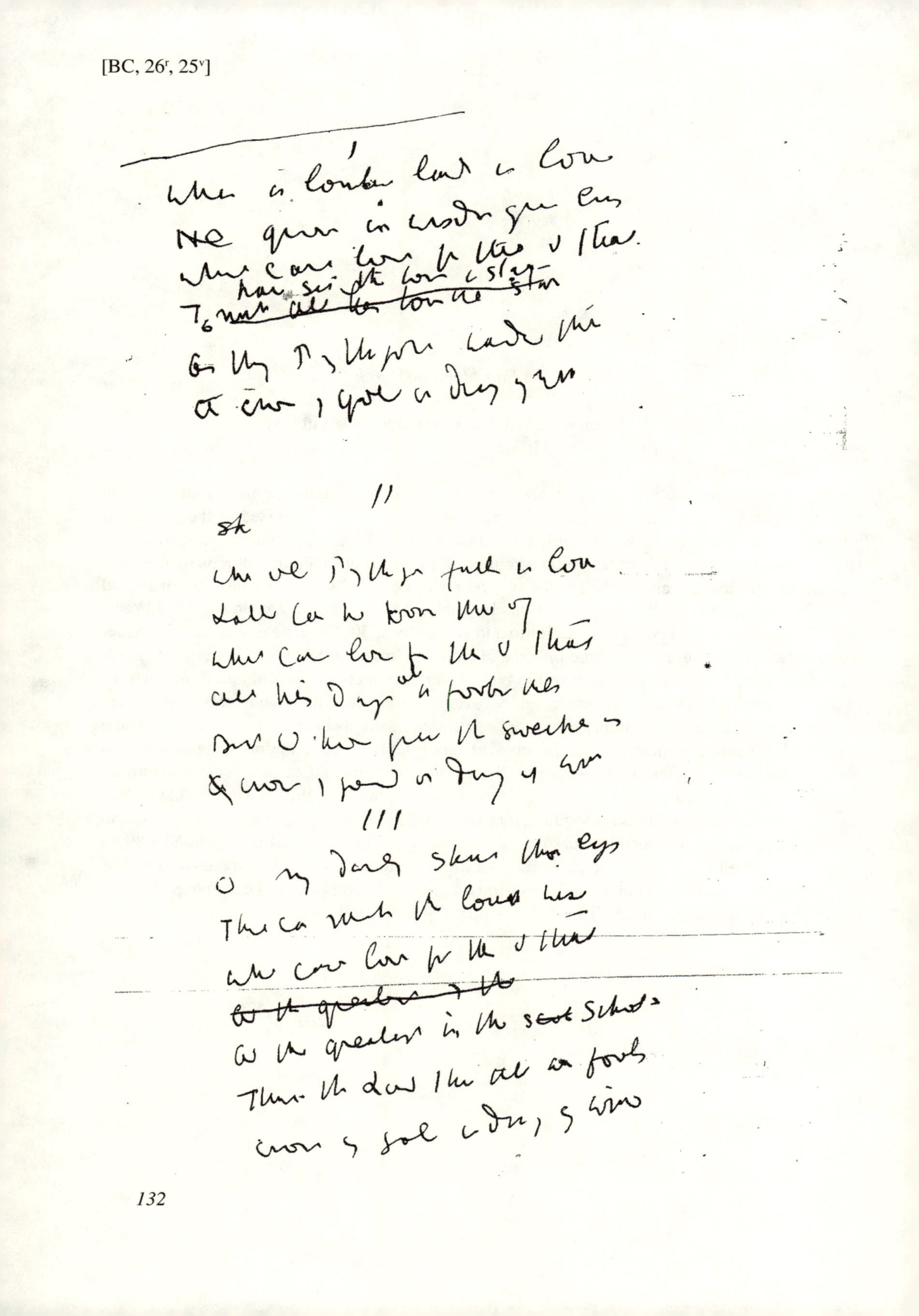

[BC, 26^{r}, 25^{v}]

[BC, 26^{r}] [*VPl*, 11–16]

I

1 When a loutish lad in love
2 ~~He~~ grows in wisdom great enough
3 What cares love for this and that
have set the town astare
4 To ~~make all his town then stare~~
5 As though Pythagoras wandered there
6 A crown of gold or dung of swine

[BC, 25^{v}] [*VPl*, 17–28]

II

~~Sh~~
1 When old Pythagoras falls in love
2 Little can he know thereof
3 What cares love for this and that
at
4 All his days in foolishness
5 But O how great the sweetness is
6 ~~A~~ crown of gold or dung of swine

III

7 O my darling shut those eyes
8 That can make the loutish wise
9 What cares love for this and that
~~All the greatest of the~~
10 All the greatest in the ~~scol~~ schools
11 Thank the Lord that all are fools
12 Crown of gold or dung of swine

---

found in BC, 25^{v}–26^{r}, 33^{r} *transcribed above and below, p. 139*
NLI 30,336 e, 10^{r}, 10^{v} *transcribed below, pp. 135–137*
published in *FMIM(M)*

26^{r} The first stanza of the lyric from *FMIM(M)* is preceded at the top of the page (not shown) by the poem ultimately titled "He and She," but here given the interim title of "Bride and Bridegroom." Yeats probably began this version of "Every loutish lad in love" on 26^{r} and completed it on the facing 25^{v}, numbering the stanzas in the order that he gave them on publication.

[NLI 30,336 e, 10r]

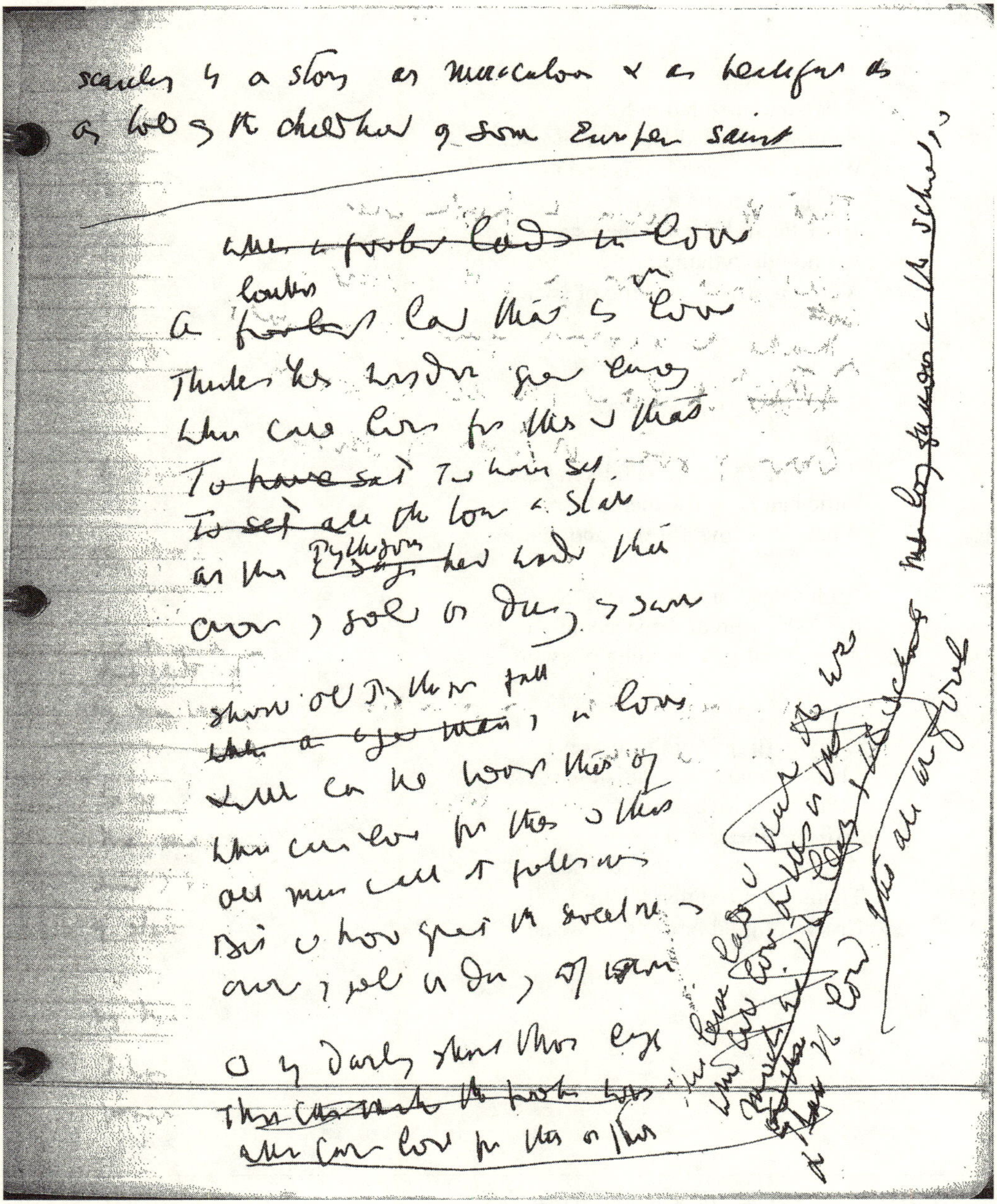

[NLI 30,336 e, 10r] [*VPl*, 11–28]

1 ~~When a foolish lads in love~~
loutish in
2 A ~~foolish~~ lad that is love
3 Thinks his wisdom great enough
4 What cares love for this and that
~~To have set~~ To have set
5 ~~To set all~~ the town a stare
Pythagoras
6 As tho ~~a sage~~ had wandered there
7 Crown of gold or dung of swine

Should old Pythagoras fall
8 ~~When an aged mans~~ in love
9 Little can he boast there of
10 What cares love for this and that
11 All men call it foolishness
12 But O how great the sweetness is
13 Crown of gold or dung of swine

14 O my darling shut those eyes
15 ~~That can make the foolish wise~~
16 <u>What cares love for this or that</u>

~~Men long famous in the schools~~
That [?please] lads & make them wise
What cares love for this or that
~~Made [?all] the leaders of the school~~
~~and tha~~
Thank the lord that all are fools

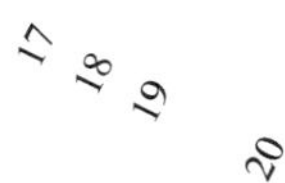

17 Whether an abbreviated form of "leisure" was intended or a misspelling of "please" (the offered reading here), it is difficult to gauge. The lighter touch of the pen in these marginalia suggests that they were a later addition to the main body of the text.

19 After experimenting with "masters," "famous" men, and "leaders," Yeats eventually opted for a variation on the line as given here: "Make a leader of the schools."

[NLI 30,336 e, 10^{v}]

[NLI 30,336 e, 10^{v}] [*VPl*, 24–28]

That ~~so~~ can make the foolish wise
What cares love for this and that
~~[?Even]~~
^Make the masters quit their schools
Thank
~~And tha~~ the lord that all are fools
Crown of gold or dung of swine

1 After canceling this line on the previous recto and attempting alternatives in the margin, Yeats returns here to his original phrasing.

5 Immediately after the lyric, are two lines relating to the opening page of the third draft of the dialogue, which are clued to a line on 11^{r} (see pp. 194–195 below).

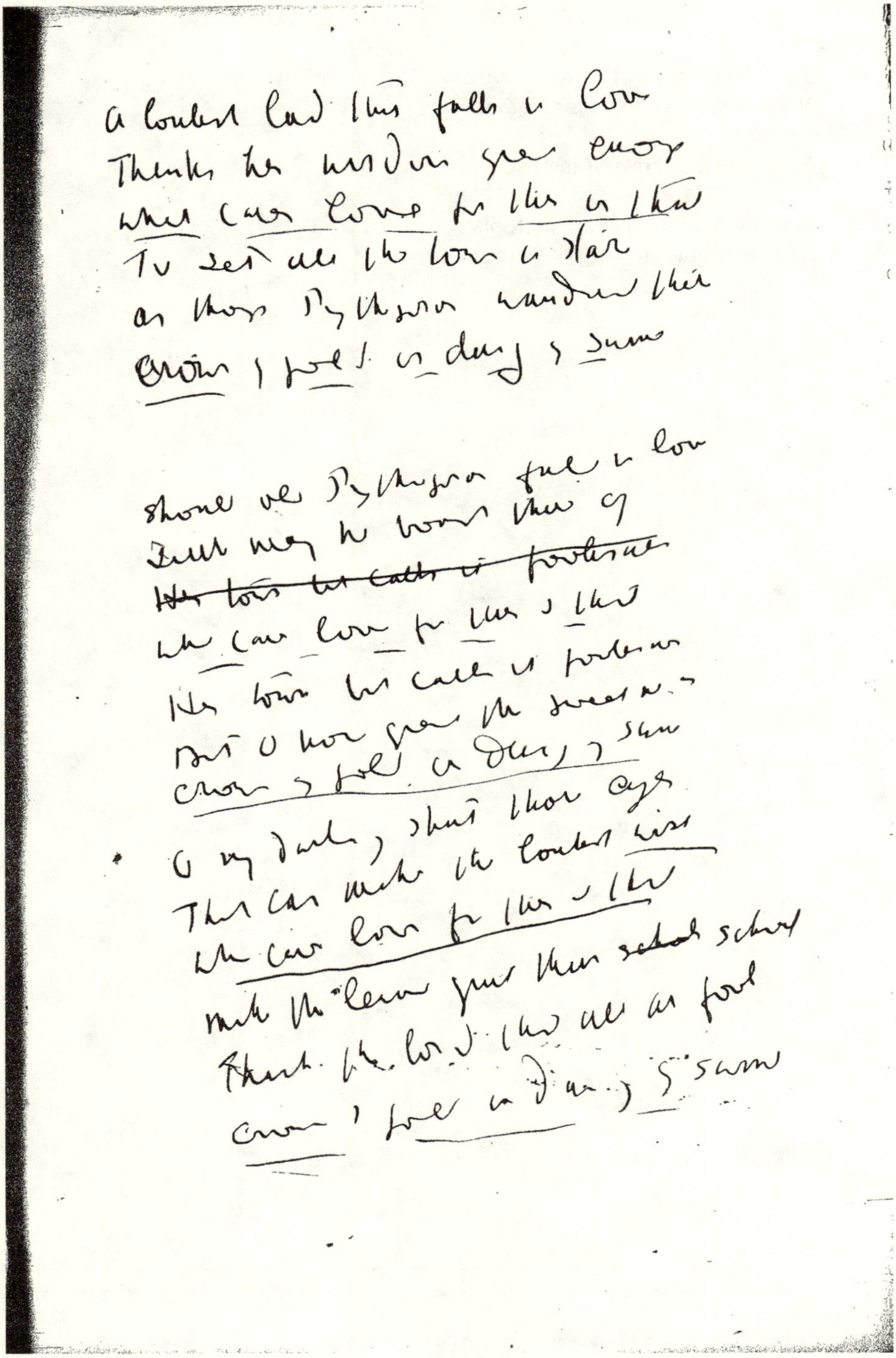

[BC, 33r] [*VPl*, 11–28]

A loutish lad that falls in love
Thinks his wisdom great enough
<u>What cares love for this or that</u>
To set all the town a stare
As though Pythagoras wandered there
<u>Crown of gold or dung of swine</u>

Should old Pythagoras fall in love
Little may he boast there of
~~His town but calls it foolishness~~
<u>What cares love for this and that</u>
His town but calls it foolishness
But O how great the sweetness is
<u>Crown of gold or dung of swine</u>

O my darling shut those eyes
That can make the loutish wise
<u>What cares love for this and that</u>
Make the learned quit their ~~schols~~ school
Thank the lord that all are fools
<u>Crown of gold or dung of swine</u>

---

9 The line is canceled because Yeats appeared to forget to include the refrain at this point.

14 This line was later revised to alter the verb and reverse the implication of the line, which in its finished state was to read: "Open wide those gleaming eyes".

Part II. *A Full Moon in March*

D. The First Prose Scenario: BC, 26^{v}–27^{v}

Yeats at first envisaged the new play as simply a redesign of the prose version of *The King of the Great Clock Tower* and clearly thought it would go by the same title. It was to be a chamber play intended, like those in *Four Plays for Dancers* (London: Macmillan, 1921) and *Wheels and Butterflies* (London: Macmillan, 1934), for performance in a small intimate space such as a drawing room. Initially the dialogue on 26^{v}–27^{v} of the Rapallo notebook is couched in reported speech, more like narrative than drama. The opening description of "unfolding" the curtain intimates that Yeats imagined a production following the principles of his Noh-inspired plays, which begin with a ceremonial folding and unfolding of a cloth. Here the term "curtain" carries overtones of a more conventional theatrical mode of presentation, but on 27^{v} the direction more clearly prescribes the ritual with the cloth to frame the main action, as it does in all the dance plays. Even though all three choral lyrics had been completed by the time of this scenario, there is no mention of one of them opening the play, but it is clear from the final direction that Yeats has already determined that the "desecration" lyric shall provide the fitting conclusion (27^{v}).

In this version, unlike the text of *KGCT* (prose), the events foretold are carefully timed in relation to the tolling of the clock (27^{v}, l. 7–10). The mystical union (l. 11) has yet to be imagined as a conception through blood, though the image of the woman bathing in the man's blood originates here (27^{r}, ll. 19–20). The line drawn across the page separates the scenario from a short series of diary-like entries referring to the week in October 1934, when Yeats entertained at L'Escargot restaurant (October 24), had meetings with personnel from the Group Theatre along with Margot Ruddock (26), and saw an hour-long exhibition of dancing at the Group Theatre's headquarters (27).

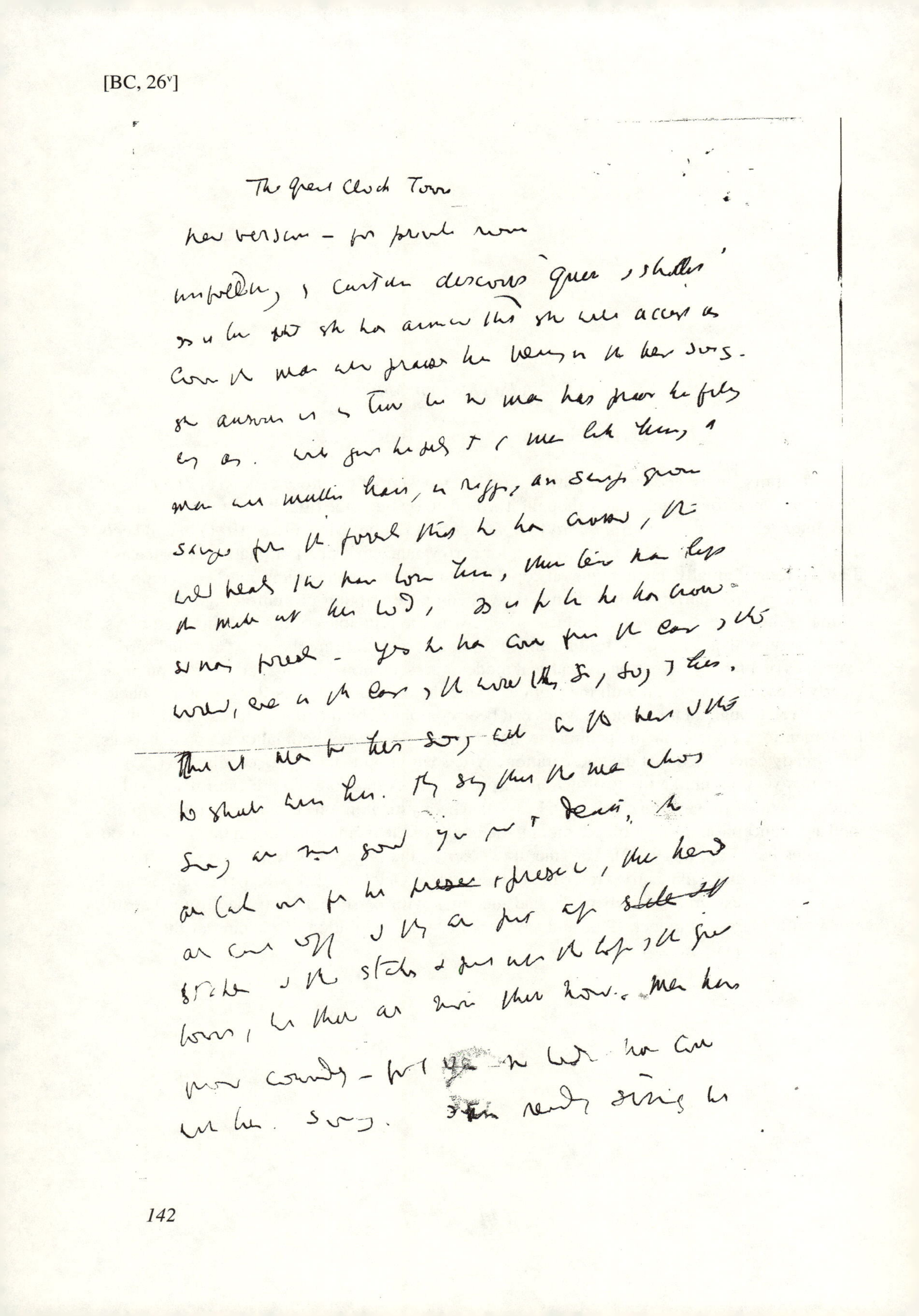

[BC, 26v]

The Great Clock Tower

New version — for prose notes

[illegible]

[BC, 26^{v}]

The Great Clock Tower
New version – for private room

Unfolding of curtain discovers 'Queen & Stroller'
Is it true what she has announced that she will accept as
lover the man who praises her beauty in the best song.
She answers it is true but no man has praised her fully
any one. Will give herself to a man like him, a
man with matted hair, in raggs, an savage, grown
savage from the forests that he has crossed, the
wild beasts that have torn him, [?their] [?tears] [?merciless]
[?they] made at his body Is it for her he has crossed
so many forests – yes he has come from the east of the
world, even in the east of the world they sing song of her.
That the man for his song will be the best and that
he shall win her. They sing that the men whose
songs are not good you put to death, they
are taken out from her ~~preser~~ presence, their heads
are cut off and they are put upon ~~stakes till~~
stakes & the stakes are put upon the top of the great
tower but there are [?none] there now. Men have
[?grown] [?cowardly] – but I from no lands have come
win her. Song. I [?am] ready Sing [?but]

---

found in BC, 26^{v}–27^{v} *transcribed above and below, pp. 145–147*

19–20 Made difficult by Yeats's elliptical grammar. He also begins to shift from reported speech into proper dramatic dialogue, with these lines occupying a midpoint between the two modes.

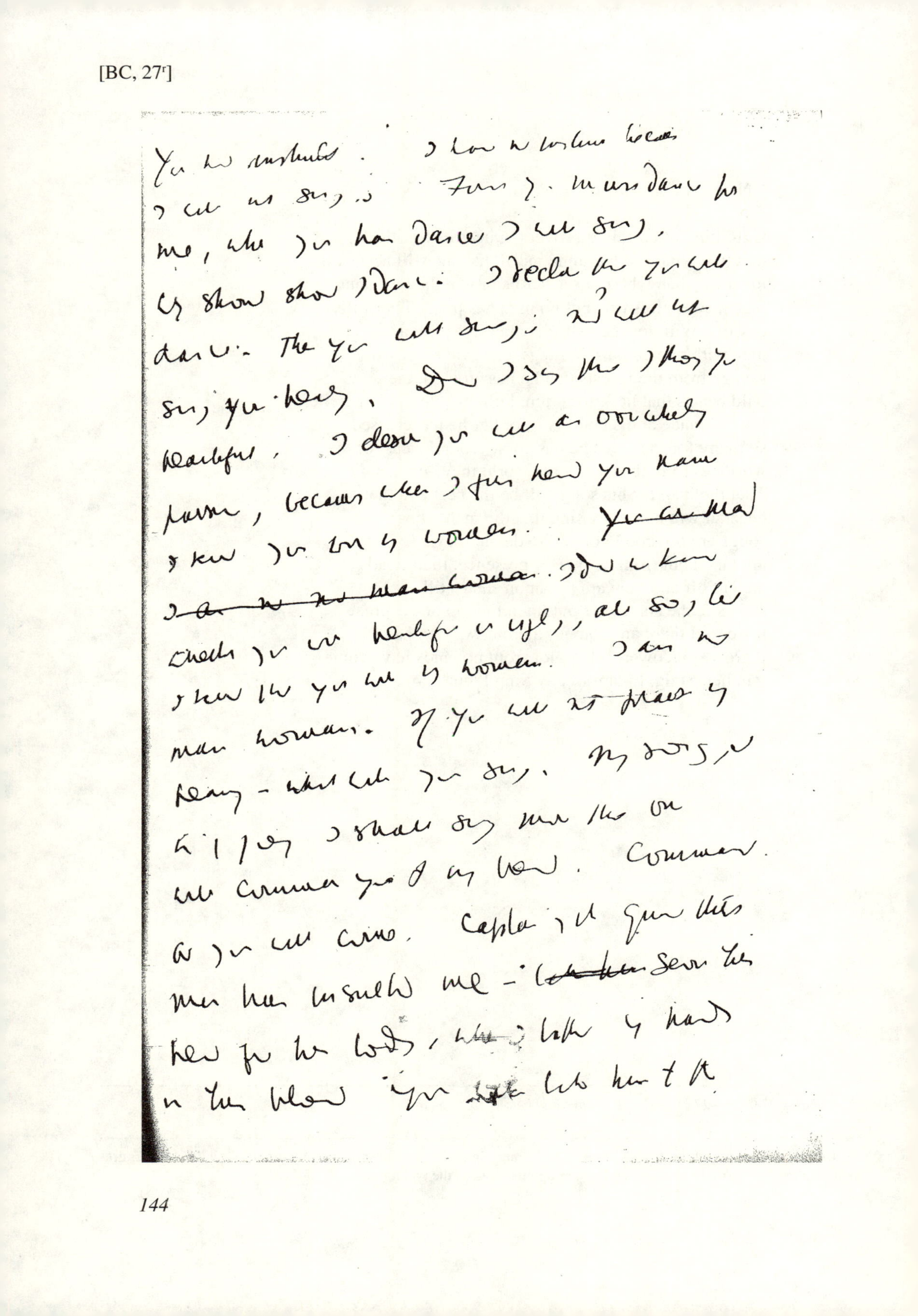

[BC, 27[r]]

You had instructions. I have no [?instructions] because
I will not sing. First you must dance for
me, when you have danced I will sing.
Why should should I dance. I declare that you will
I
dance. Then you will sing; [?but/?and] will not
sing your beauty. Dare I say that I thought you
beautiful. I desire you with an overwhelming
passion, because when I first heard your name
I knew you [?full [?of] wonders ~~You are mad~~
~~I am n no [?man] woman~~ I do not know
whether you are beautiful or ugly, all songs lie
I know that you are my woman. I am no
man woman. If you will not praise my
beauty – what will you sing. My song and
in my joy I shall sing more than one
will command you [?to/?for] my bed Command
and you will come. Captain of the Guard this
man has insulted me – ~~take him~~ sever his
head from his body – when I bathe my hands
in his blood you [~~?take~~] take him to the

10, 12–13 For "no man woman" read "no man's woman," to be spoken by the Queen.

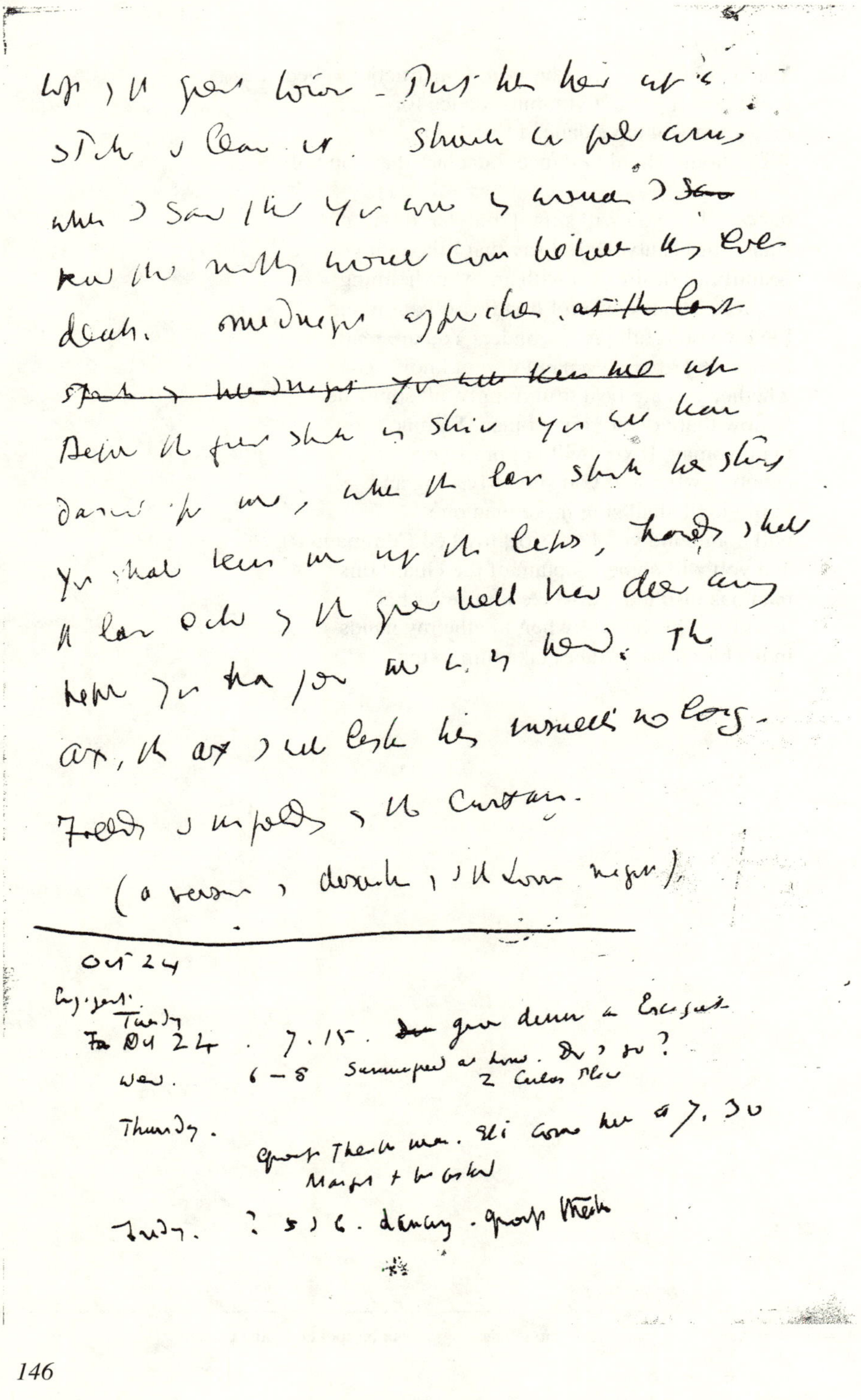

[BC, 27^{v}]

top of the great tower – Put his head upon a
stake & leave it. Stroller with folded arms
when I said that you were my woman I ~~saw~~
knew that nothing would come between us even
death. Midnight approaches. ~~At the last~~
~~stroke of midnight you will kiss me~~ upon
Before the first stroke is struck you will have
danced for me, when the last stroke has struck
you shall kiss me upon the lips, hardly shall
shall the last echo of the great bell have died away
before you shall [?join /?love] me in my [?bed]. The
ax, the ax, I will listen his insults no longer
Folding and unfolding of the curtain.
(a version of desecration & the lovers night).

Part II. *A Full Moon in March*

E. The Second Prose Scenario: BC, 30v–32v

Beginning on 30v of the Rapallo notebook, Yeats resumed the drafting of *A Full Moon in March* after some five sheets of astrological readings for the last three months of 1934, written for the most part in an intricate and miniscule hand. When he returned to the draft, he had a developed sense of the structure of the opening section of the play and so immediately began to compose in dialogue (by 31v, Yeats is confidently laying the material out on the page with spaces between the speakers to indicate its status as dramatic dialogue); to expand psychological and narrative detail; and to devise stage directions. For example, on 32r he indicates a change of performer in the role of the Queen ("dancer later place of speaker," l. 20) between the spoken section of the play and the final danced sequence; he instructs that the Queen's dress be symbolic rather than realistic in its depiction of bloodstains; and a mask, referred to as "it" (ll. 23–24), is used to represent the severed head of the Stroller. It is clear, however, that Yeats had not begun devising the Queen's song: the penultimate line of 32r indicates that the Attendant sings here "a song that is her song" (l. 26) while the final line ("I dread you no longer now that you are dead, O beloved") is encircled and then clued to a position toward the end of the preceding line, suggesting this might perhaps be a first attempt to give the words of the song that the Attendant is to sing in the Queen's place before she begins her dance; but this draft bears no relation to the finished text for that lyric. The first sketch of a song for the severed head ("What shall be born of us") offered on the final page is also unrelated to the final lyric. A draft of "I sing a song of Jack and Jill," however, follows immediately after the completion of this version of the play below a line drawn across the page (32v). The draft is treated below, pp. 161–163.

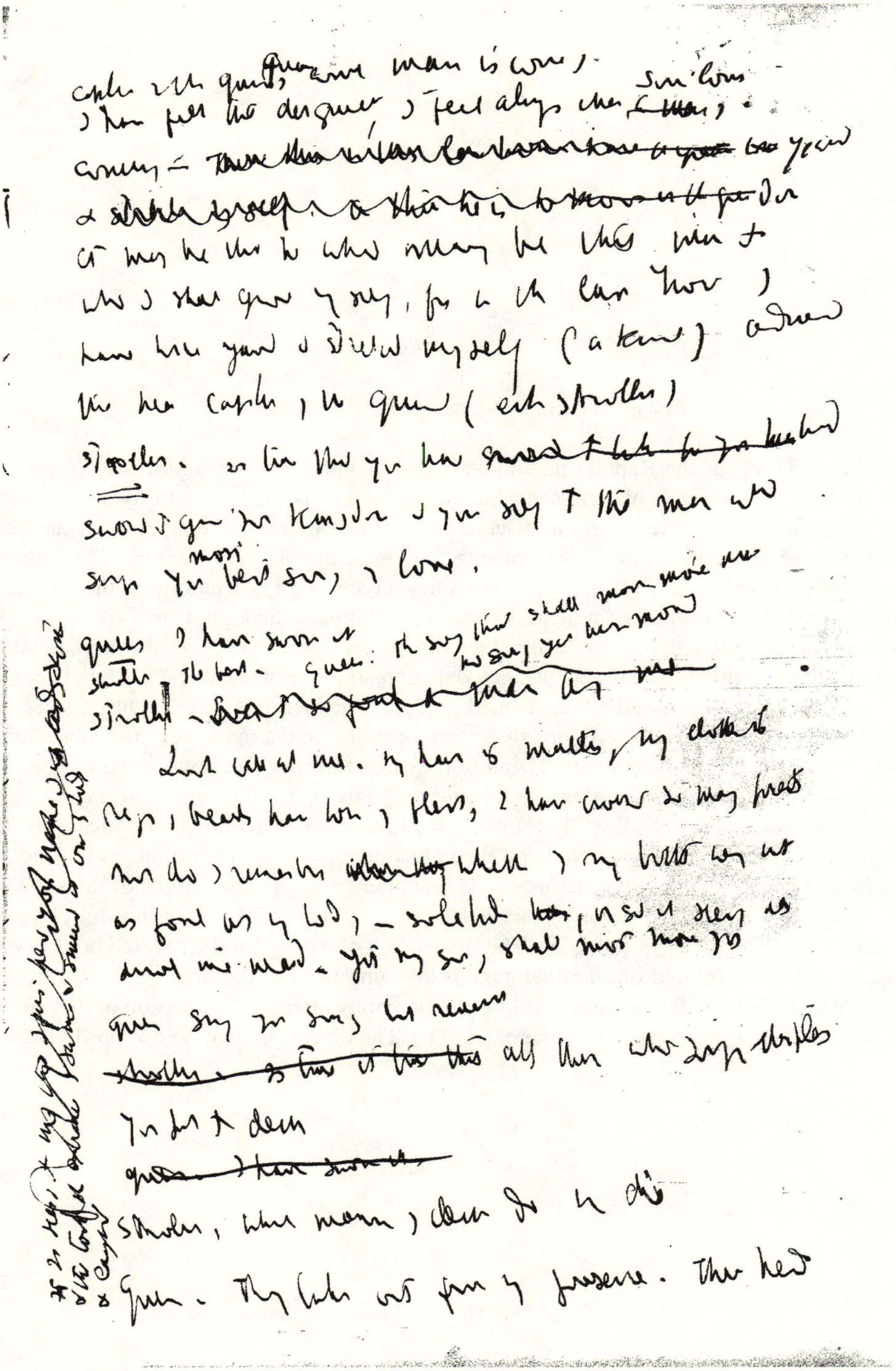

[BC, 30v]

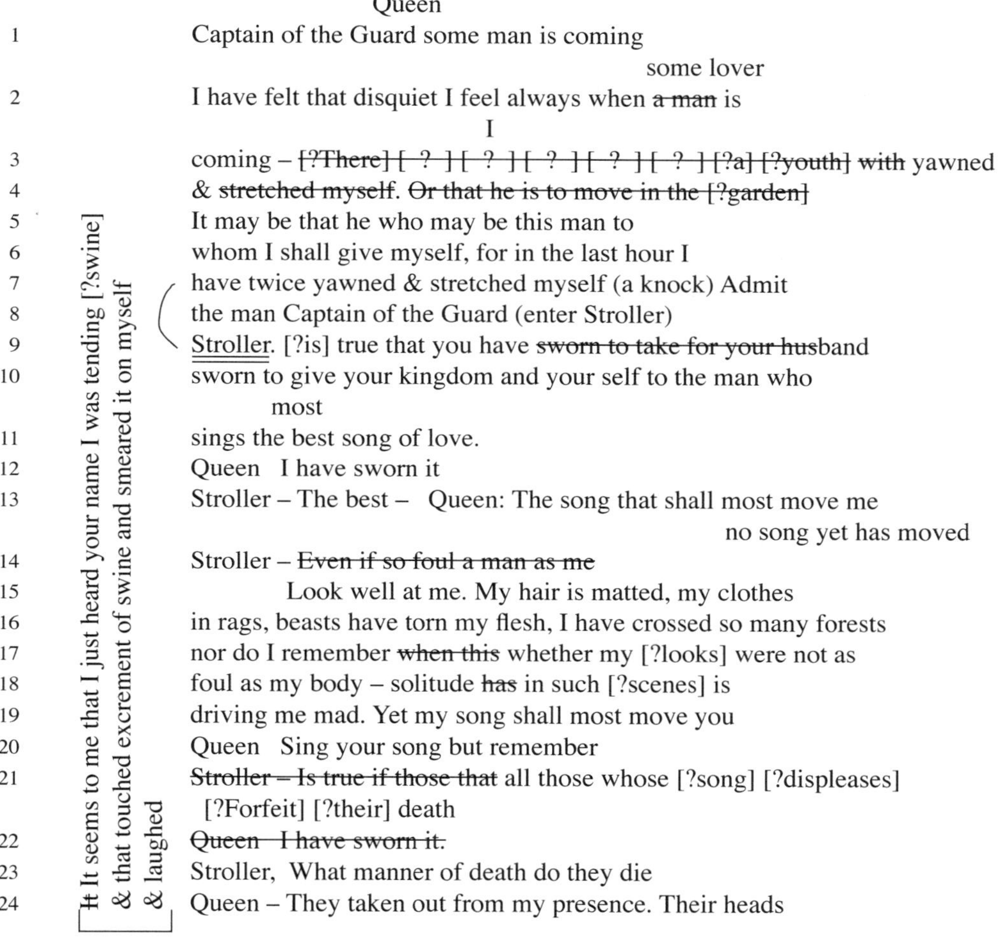

Queen

Captain of the Guard some man is coming

some lover

I have felt that disquiet I feel always when ~~a man~~ is

I

coming – ~~[?There] [?] [?] [?] [?] [?] [?a] [?youth] with~~ yawned

& ~~stretched myself~~. ~~Or that he is to move in the [?garden]~~

It may be that he who may be this man to

whom I shall give myself, for in the last hour I

have twice yawned & stretched myself (a knock) Admit

the man Captain of the Guard (enter Stroller)

Stroller. [?is] true that you have ~~sworn to take for your hus~~band

sworn to give your kingdom and your self to the man who

most

sings the best song of love.

Queen I have sworn it

Stroller – The best – Queen: The song that shall most move me

no song yet has moved

Stroller – ~~Even if so foul a man as me~~

Look well at me. My hair is matted, my clothes

in rags, beasts have torn my flesh, I have crossed so many forests

nor do I remember ~~when this~~ whether my [?looks] were not as

foul as my body – solitude ~~has~~ in such [?scenes] is

driving me mad. Yet my song shall most move you

Queen Sing your song but remember

~~Stroller – Is true if those that~~ all those whose [?song] [?displeases]

[?Forfeit] [?their] death

~~Queen I have sworn it.~~

Stroller, What manner of death do they die

Queen – They taken out from my presence. Their heads

~~It~~ It seems to me that I just heard your name I was tending [?swine]

& that touched excrement of swine and smeared it on myself

& laughed

---

found in BC, 30v–32v *transcribed above and below, pp. 153–159*

25–27 Possibly a revision or addition for the Stroller's speech at l. 14 and following; they explore a new idea that Yeats was not to incorporate into this text until 31v, ll. 3–4.

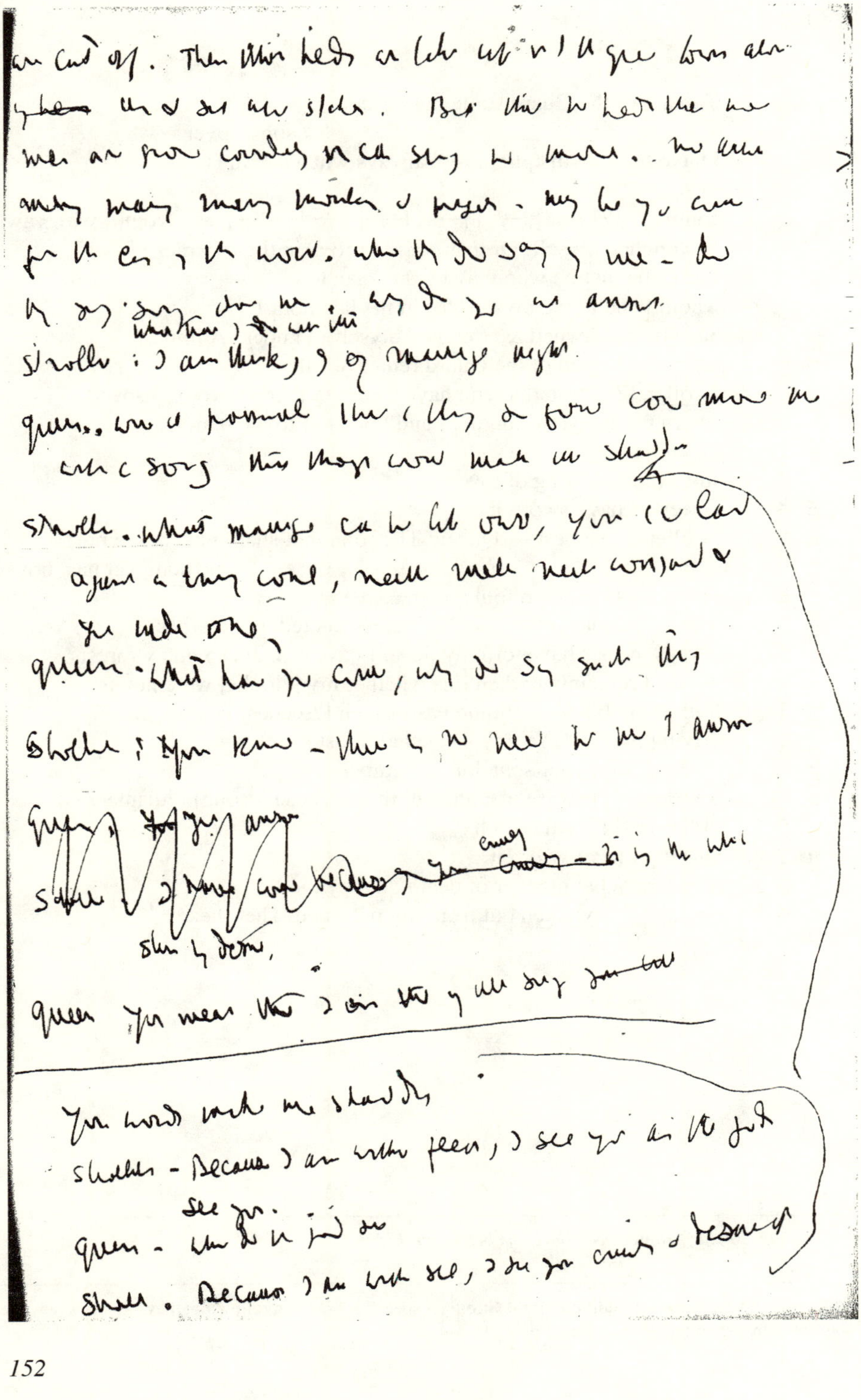

[BC, 31r]

are cut off. Then their heads are taken up into the great tower above
~~my [?hea]~~ [?there] & set upon stakes. But there no heads there now
men are grown cowardly or can sing no more. No [?]
[?make] [?many] [?men] [?drunken] and [?forget]. May be you come
from the east of the world. What do they say of me – do
they sing songs about me. Why do you not answer
What have I do with this
Stroller: I am thinking of our marriage night

Queen. Were it possible that a thing so foul could move me
with a song this thought would make me shudder

Stroller. What marriage can be like ours, you & I laid
[?against] a [?tiny] [?] neither [?mate] neither [?consort] &
yet made one

Queen – What have you come, why do say such things

Stroller: You know – there is no need for me to answer

Queen. ~~You~~ Yet answer

cruelty
Stroller. I have come ~~because of your cruelty~~ – it is the white
skin of desire

Queen You mean that [?for] [?this] that of all [?singers] ~~you will~~

Your words make me shudder

Stroller – Because I am without fear, I see you as the gods
see you

Queen – What do the gods see

Stroller. Because I am [?without fear], I see your cruelty and desire it

---

20–23 The phrasing of l. 10 was not adjusted to accommodate the insertion.

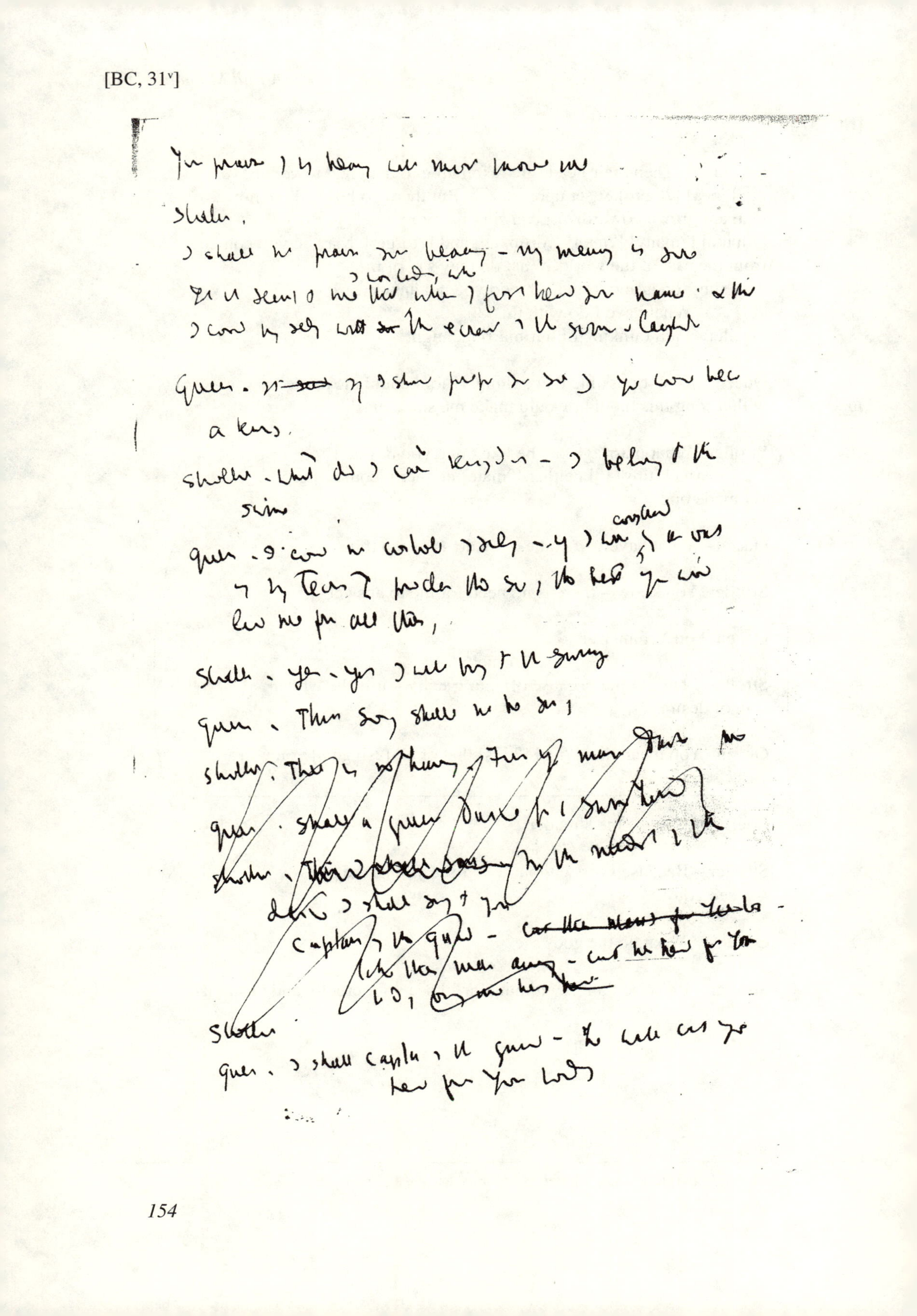

[BC, 31v]

[BC, 31v]

Your praise of my beauty will most move me

Stroller.
I shall not praise your beauty – my memory is gone
I was tending swine
Yet it seems to me that^when I first heard your name & that
I covered my self with ~~sw~~ the excrement of the swine & laughed

Queen – It ~~seems~~ If I should prefer your song you would become
a king.

Stroller – What do I care kingdoms – I belong to the
swine
[?constrained]
Queen – I [?could] not control myself – if I were^by the [?verse]
or by tears to proclaim the song the best you would
lead me from all this.

Stroller – Yes – yes I will bring to the swine

Queen – This song shall not be sung

Stroller. There is no hurry. First you must dance me

Queen. Shall a queen dance for a swineherd

Stroller – ~~Then I shall sing~~ In the midst of the
dance I shall sing to you

Captain of the Guard – ~~Cut this mans from his bo~~
Take this man away – cut his head from [?your]
Body bring me his head

~~Stroller~~

Queen. I shall Captain of the Guard – he will cut your
head from your body

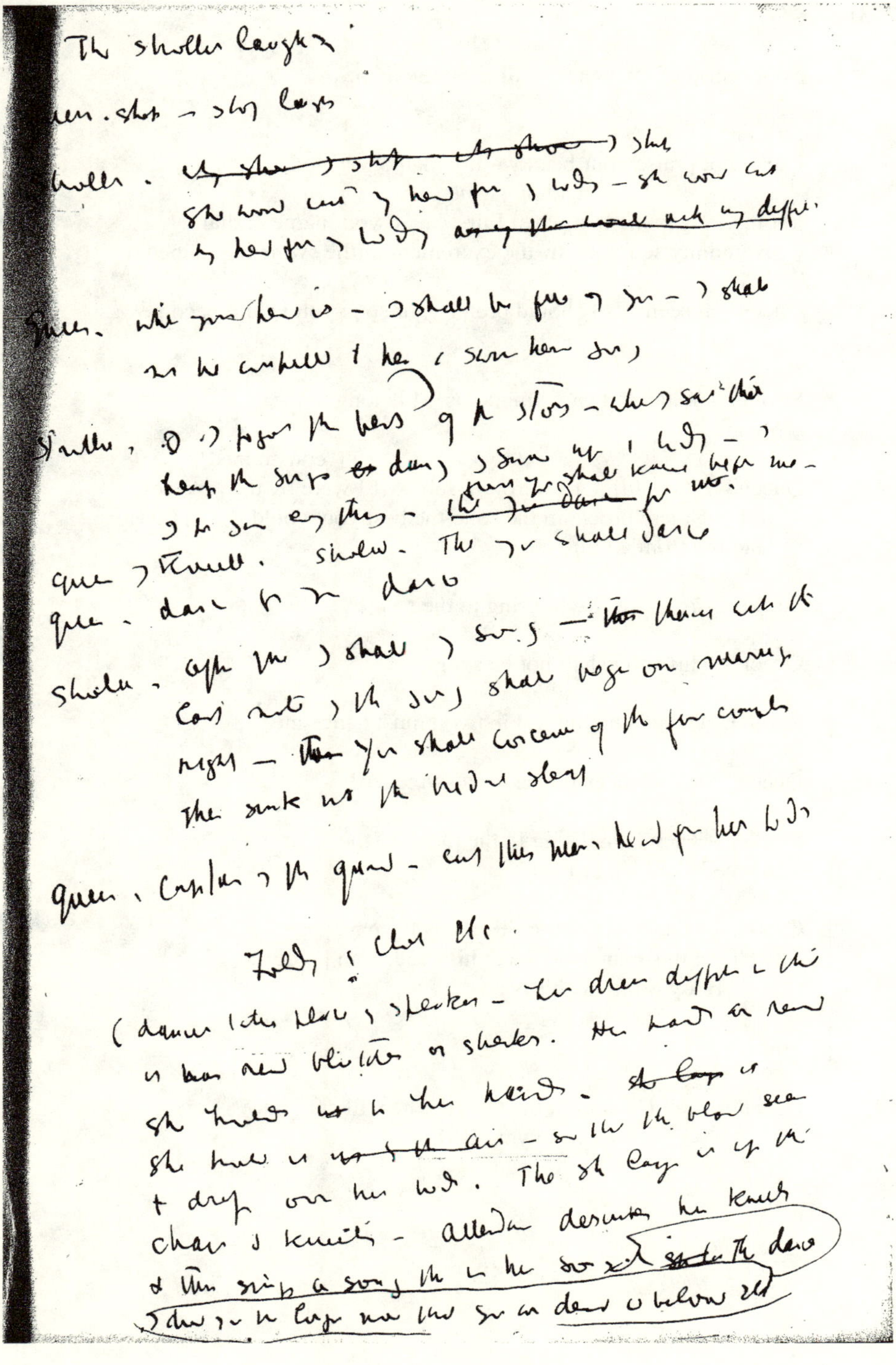

[BC, 32r]

The Stroller laughs
Queen. Stop – stop laughing

Stroller. ~~Why should I stop – why should~~ I stop
She would cut my head from my body – she would cut
my head from my body ~~as if that would make any difference~~

Queen. When your head is – I shall be free of you – I shall
not be compelled to hear a swineherd sing

Stroller. O I forgot the best of the story – when I said that
[?heap] the [?songs] ~~ex~~ dung of swine upon my body – I
first that you shall kneel before me
I foresaw every thing – ~~that you dance~~ for ~~me~~

Queen I Kneel. Stroller – Then you shall dance

Queen Dance for you dance

Stroller After that I shall my song – ~~this~~ thence with the
last note of the song shall begin our marriage
night – ~~then~~ you shall conceive of the first coupling
then sink into the bridal sleep

Queen Captain of the Guard – cut this man's head from his body

Folding of Cloth etc.

(dancer later place of speaker – her dress different in that
it has red blotches on shoulders. Her hands are red
she holds it in her hands. ~~She lays~~ it
She holds it ~~up in the air~~ – so that the blood seems
to drop over her body. Then she lays it upon the
chair and kneels – Attendant describes her kneeling
& then sings a song that is her song. ~~She has~~^The dance
I dread you no longer now that you are dead O beloved Etc

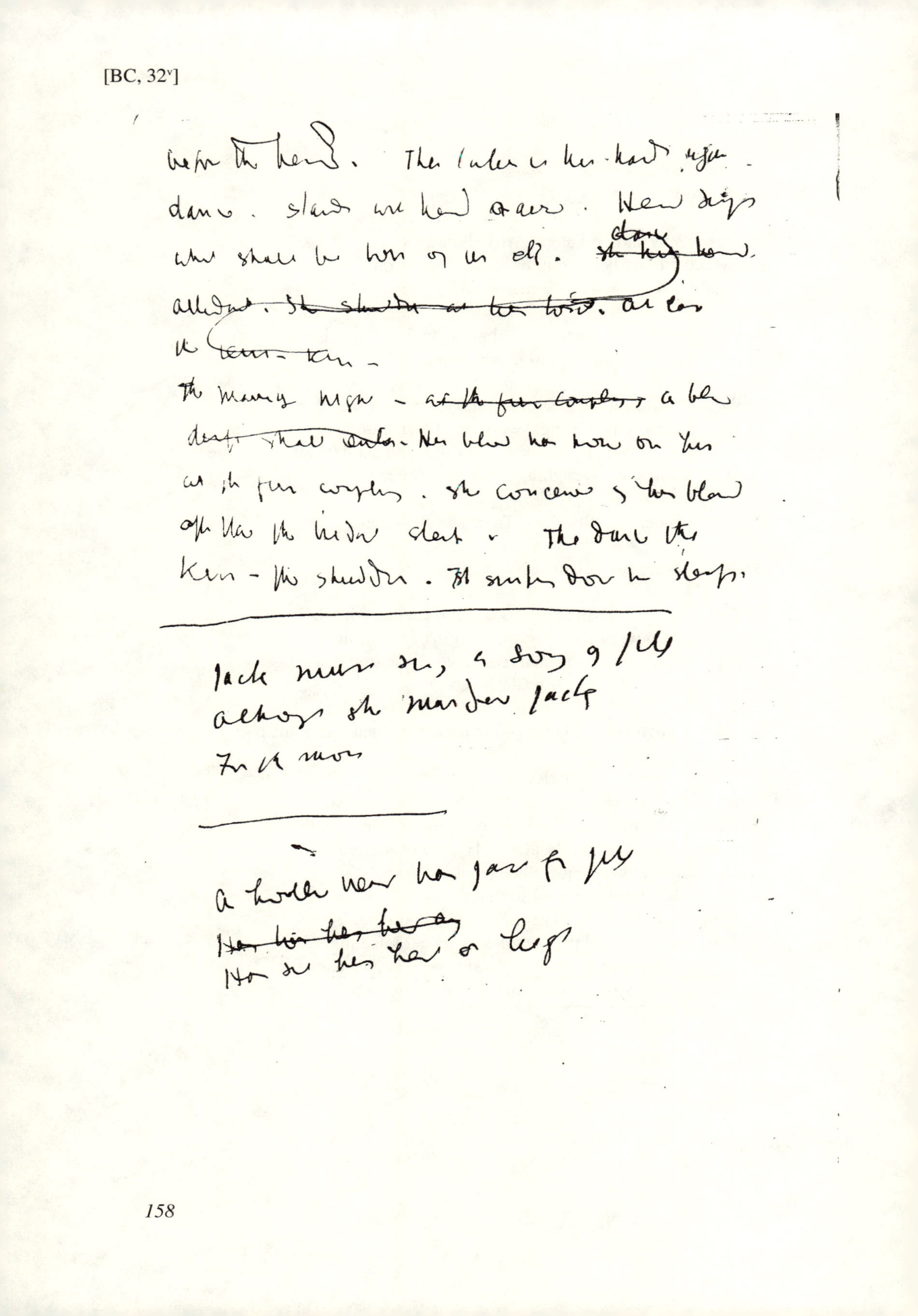

[BC, 32v]

[illegible]

[illegible]

[illegible]

[BC, 32^{v}]

before the head. Then later in her hands again
dance. Stands with head in air. Head sings
~~dance~~
What shall be born of us [?else]. ~~She has head~~
Attendant. ~~She shudders at her loins~~. At last
the terror – kiss –
The marriage night – ~~at the first coupling,~~ a blood
~~drop shall enter~~ – Her blood has flowed on his
at the first coupling. She conceives of his blood
after that the bridal sleep. The dance the
kiss – the shudder. She sinks down in sleep.

1 There is no grammatical link between the foot of 32^{r} and the opening words of 32^{v}.
3 For a transcription of the song, see pp. 162–163.

Part II. *A Full Moon in March*

F. Evolution of the "Song for the Severed Head": BC, 32^{v}, and NLI 30,336 c, 4^{v}, 5^{r}

There are two surviving holograph drafts of the "Song for the Severed Head": a rough outline in the Rapallo notebook (BC, 32^{v}), and an expansion of this to two stanzas and a refrain that comprises a nearly finished state in the loose-leaf notebook (NLI 30,336 c, 4^{v}, 5^{r}).

The second draft of the play concludes with a lengthy stage direction (see above pp. 156–159), after which Yeats draws a line across the width of the page and then attempts the outline of the song. It is not clear whether the one composition followed directly after the other. The ink throughout the song is darker, the letters more thickly scribed, and the hand generally firmer than is the case with the draft of the play. On the facing recto (BC, 33^{r}) is the second draft of the lyric "Every loutish lad in love," but from 33^{v} to 39^{v} Yeats worked at material that bears no relation to *FMIM* or *KGCT*. It is possible that he had a sudden inspiration for a lyric for the head and made these notes for random lines on the nearest available space in the album. What Yeats creates here is the opening for each of the two stanzas and a suggestion for a refrain.

The numerous materials related to *FMIM* in the loose-leaf notebook, NLI 30,336, are disparately arranged through the folder. The draft of the song for the severed head on 4^{v} and 5^{r} is one of the earliest in the current ordering of the contents of the notebook. The shape and main features of the two stanzas of the song as finally printed are visible, though Yeats continued to revise through typescripts and proofs of the play to achieve the sustained nursery-rhyme idiom and style.

[BC, 32^{v}] [*VPl*, 166–168 and 172–173]

Jack must sing a song of Jill
Although she murdered Jack
For the moon

A hollow heart has Jack for Jill
~~Has [?hung] his heart [?on]~~
Has set his heart on high

---

found in BC, 26^{v}–27^{v} *transcribed above*
NLI 30,336 c, 4^{v}–5^{r} *transcribed below, p. 165*

For the conclusion of the prose scenario, entered above the lyric, see above, pp. 158–159

[NLI 30,336 c, 5^{r}, 4^{v}]

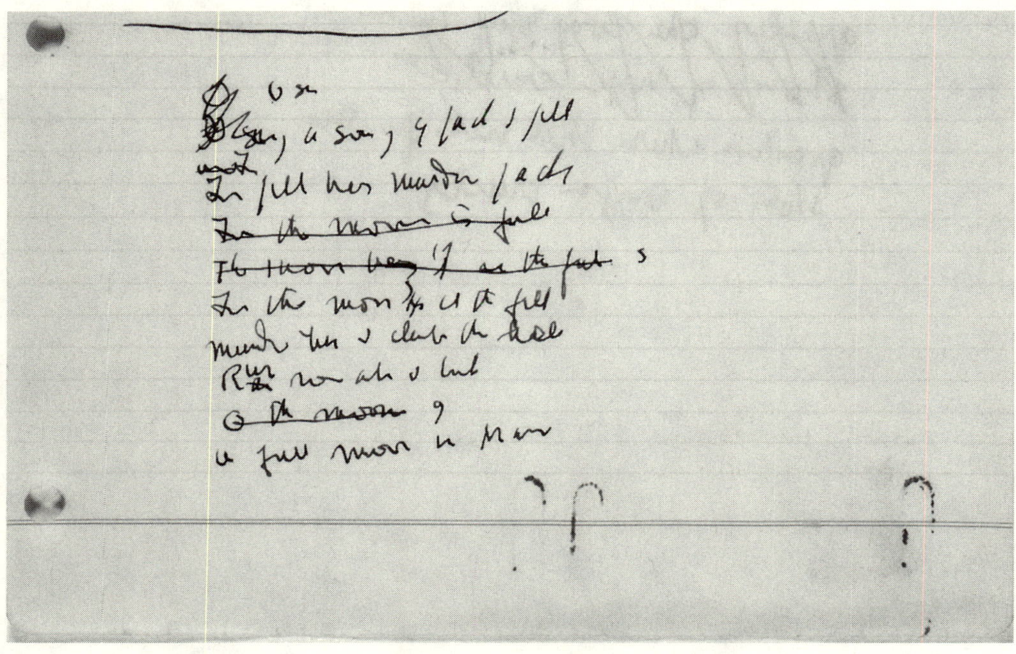

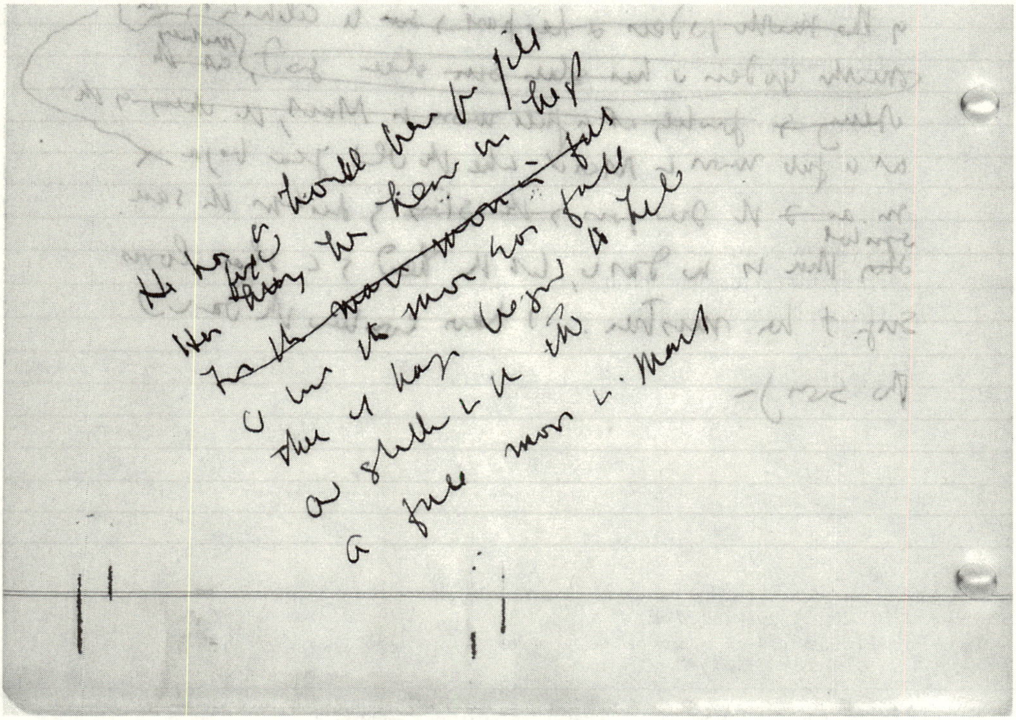

[NLI 30,336 c, 5^r] [*VPl*, 166–171]

~~O~~ I sing
1 ~~O sing~~ a song of Jack & Jill
2 For Jill has murdered Jack
3 ~~For the moon is full~~
4 ~~The moon being at the full~~
5 For the moon is at the full
6 Murdered him and climbed the hill
un
7 R~~an~~ round about and back
8 ~~O the moon~~
9 A full moon in March

[*VPl*, 172–177]

[NLI 30,336 c, 4^v]

1 He has a hollow heart for Jill
fixed
2 Has ~~hung~~ his heart on high
3 ~~For the March moon is full~~
4 O but the moon was full
5 There it hangs beyond the hill
6 And glitters in the sky
7 A full moon in March

Jottings unrelated to either play occupy the top half of 5^r. The top half of 4^v is blank.

Part II. *A Full Moon in March*

G. "The Severed Head," A Sequence of Three Drafts for the Dialogue Section of the Play: NLI 30,336 d, 1^{v}–12^{v}

Three drafts in NLI 30,336 d cumulatively build the dialogue sequences for the first section of *A Full Moon in March*. The first is found on 1^{v} through 7^{r}, the second on 8^{r} through 10^{v}, and the third on 10^{v} through 12^{v}. That they were entered shortly after the completion of the scenarios for the play in the Rapallo notebook is suggested by the entry on BC, 33^{r}, after the second version of the scenario in that notebook, of a full draft of the first lyric, "Every loutish lad," incorporating many of the revisions made to a draft of the lyric occurring in NLI 30,336 e, 10^{r} and 10^{v} (compare with NLI 30,336 e on pp. 134–137 and BC, 33^{r}, on pp. 138–139).

In the first draft Yeats attempts to create an uncertain mood through the Attendants' questioning about what they are to do to initiate the performance. To generate a sense of impending doom he cycles around the idea of the Ides of March, the date of the assassination of Julius Caesar, who reportedly died at the foot of the statue of his arch rival, Pompey. The date of the murder was momentous in classical history as initiating the imperial era and the end of the Roman republic. He also experiments with a conception of the Stroller as an elderly man (1^{v}, l. 14; see also 7^{r}, l. 4; the idea was subsequently dropped from the main action but remained as a theme running through the opening lyric, "Every loutish lad") and begins more confidently to conceive the character of the Stroller and to shape the rhythm of his dialogue to reflect his nature (6^{r}, ll. 2–3). In the second and third drafts Yeats continues to rework the main section of the play, refining the expression to achieve subtler psychological definition of the interaction between Queen and Stroller. He attempted no further draft of the opening sequence for the two attendants.

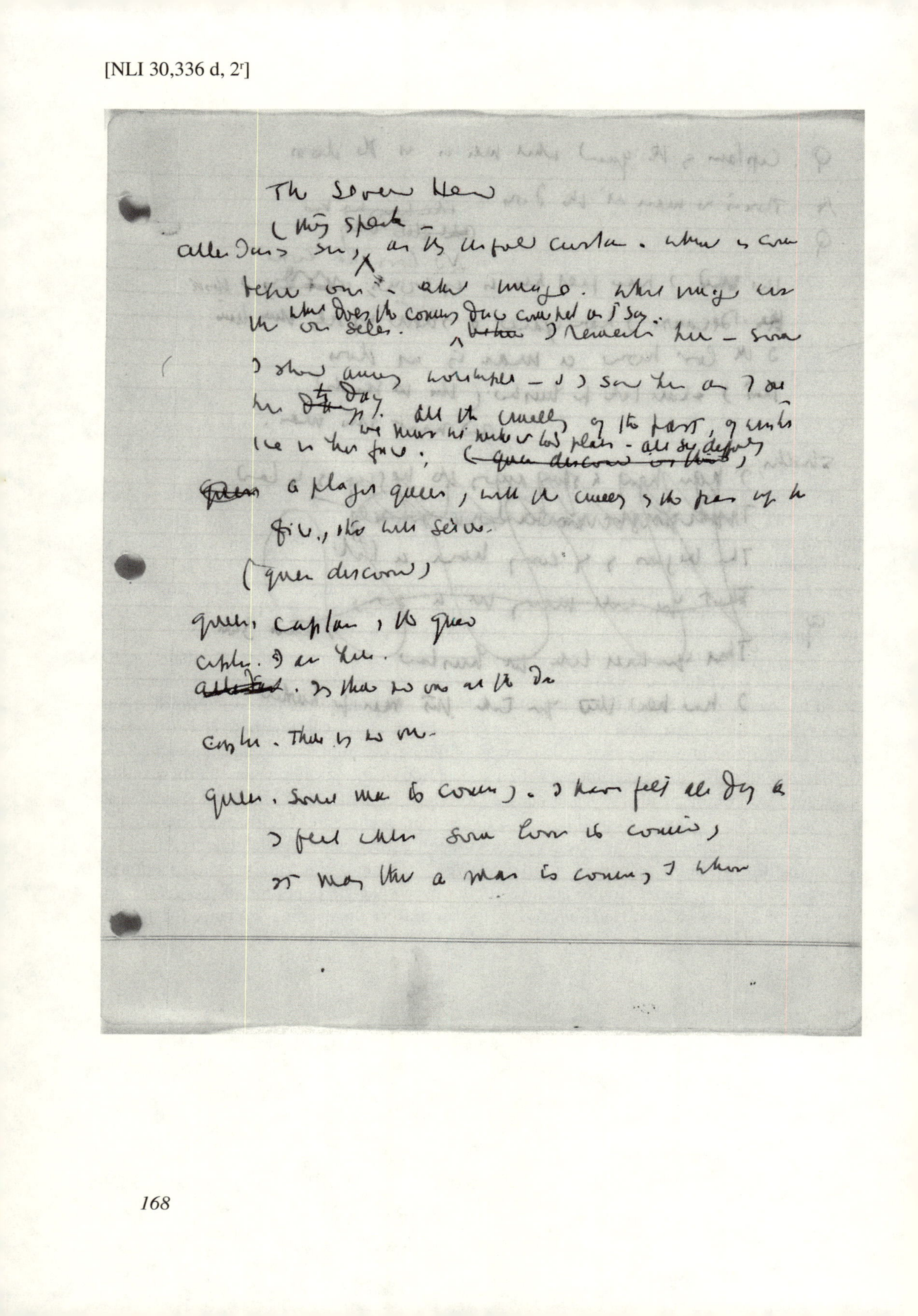

[NLI 30,336 d, 2r]

[NLI 30,336 d, 2^{r}] [*VPl*, 1–10 and 29–31]

The Severed Head

(they speak

1 Attendants sing^as they unfold curtain. [?Whence] is [?come]

2 Before one [?an] [?alien] image. What image was

What does the coming dance compel us to say

3 [?that] [?our] [?selves]. ^~~before~~ I remember her – since

4 I stood among worshippers – and I saw her as I see

today

5 her ~~days~~. All the cruelty of the past, of winter's

we [?hear] it make[?s] it loo[?k] [?plain] – all see differently

6 ice in her face; (~~queen discovered on throne~~)

7 ~~Queen~~ a player queen, with the cruelty of the past upon her

8 face., this will serve.

(Queen discovered)

9 Queen. Captain of the Guard

10 Captain. I am here.

11 ~~Attendant~~. Is there no one at the door

12 Captain. There is no one.

13 Queen. Some man is coming. I have felt all day as

14 I feel when some lover is coming

15 It may that a man is coming to whom

---

found in NLI 30,336 d, 1^{v}–12^{v} *transcribed above and below, pp. 171–201*
published in *FMIM(M)*

The first draft appears on 1^{v}–12^{v} of NLI 30,336 d. Given the brief indications of setting and an action for the attendants on 2^{r}, which take a form that roughly anticipates the opening stage direction in *FMIM(M)*, it is likely that the draft originally began here, rather than on the facing page, 1^{v}. After this sketch, Yeats then thought of developing the content of the attendants' exchange and composed the longer opening on the facing verso. On 2^{r}, he seems uncertain at what point the queen is to be revealed.

Yeats's pattern within this manuscript was to write chiefly on the recto of sheets in the loose-leaf file and to use the facing versos for corrections or redraftings: 1^{v} follows 2^{r}, for the reason given above, and 2^{v} follows 3^{r} because on the facing verso Yeats attempts a more succinct expression of the opening lines of 3^{r}. No marks clue the revision to any specific sections of the opposed recto.

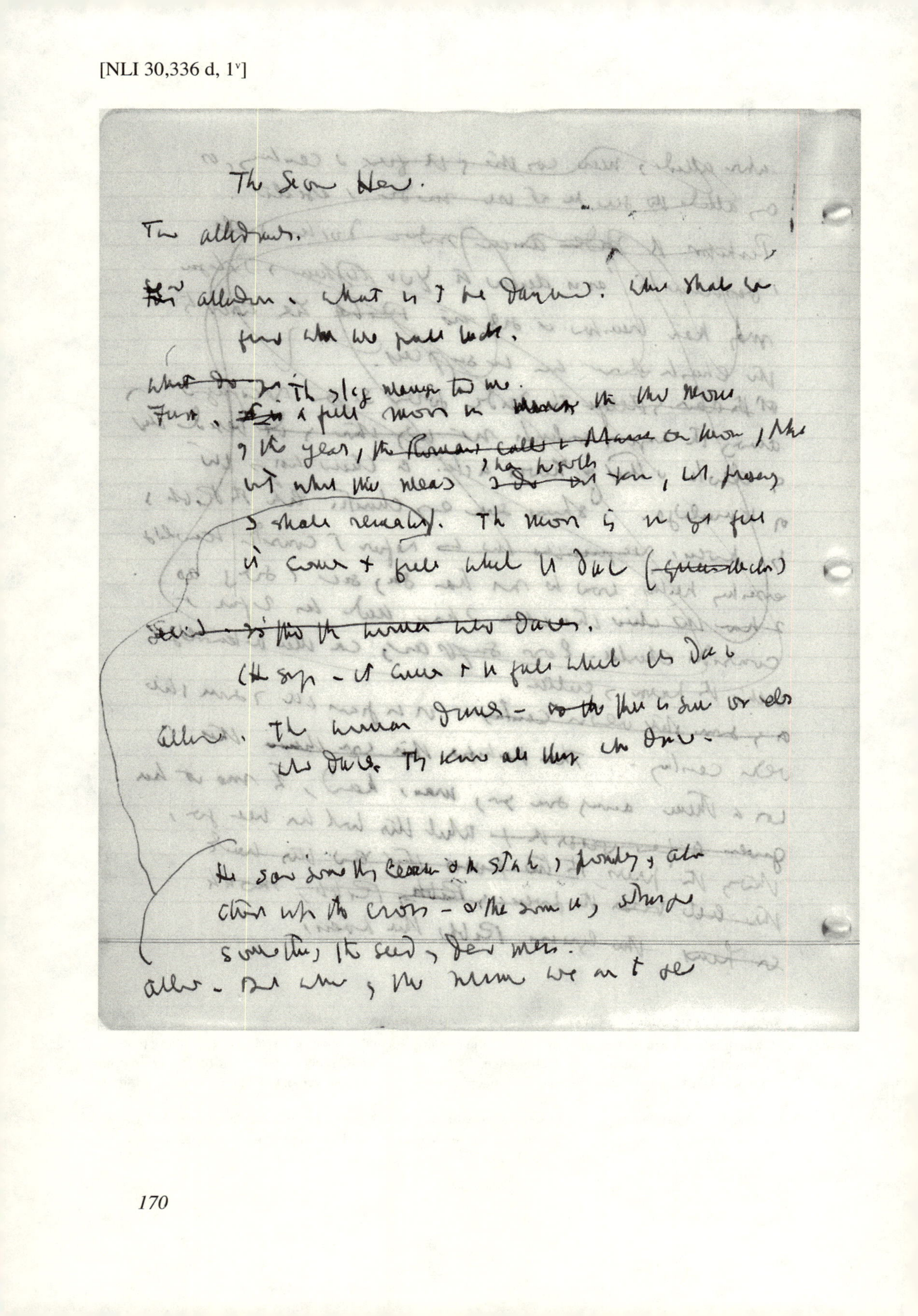

[NLI 30,336 d, 1v]

[NLI 30,336 d, 1v] [*VPl*, 1–10]

The Severed Head.

Two Attendants.

Second
~~First~~ Attendant. What is to be danced. What shall we
find when we pull back.

~~What do you~~ The stage manager told me
First. ~~It is~~ a full moon in ~~March~~, the third moon
of the year, ~~the Romans called it March~~ the moon of March
I have forgotten
but what that means ~~I do not~~ know, but presently
I shall remember.^The moon is not yet full
it comes to full while she dances (~~queen~~ disclosed)

~~Second. Is that the woman who dances~~.
(He says – it comes to the full while she dances

Attendant. The woman dances – ~~is there~~ there is some one else
who dances. They know all things who dance.

He said some thing Caesar & the statue of Pompey, also
Christ upon the cross – & then something strange
Something the seed of old men

Attendant. But who is the man we are to see

15 After this speech, presumably, the dialogue picks up with the Queen's entrance at l. 8 on 2r.

[NLI 30,336 d, 3r]

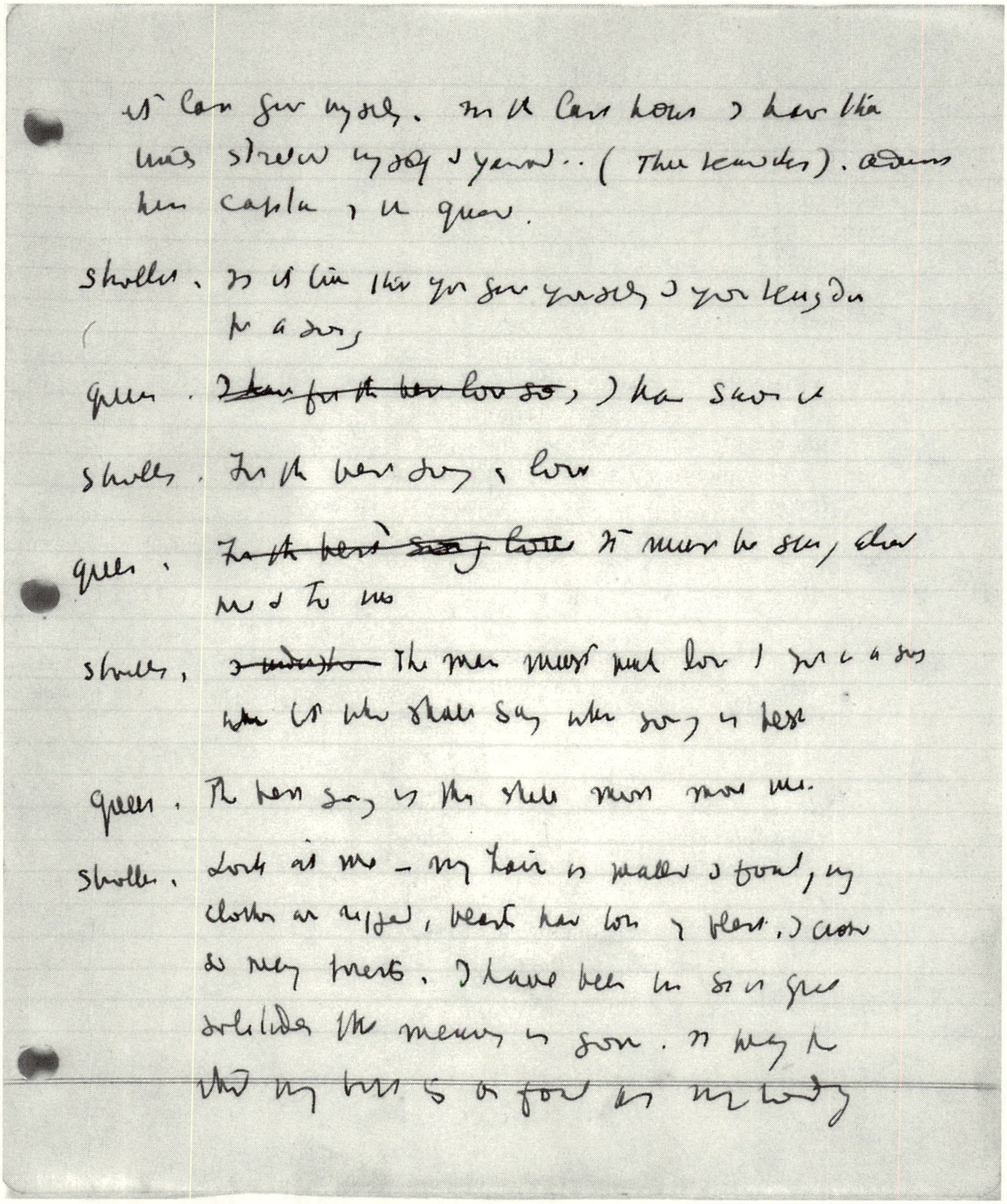

[NLI 30,336 d, 3^{r}] [*VPl*, 31–49]

at last give myself. In the last hour I have three times stretched myself and yawned.. (Three knocks) Admit him Captain of the Guard.

Stroller. Is it true that you give yourself & your kingdom for a song

Queen. ~~I have for the best love song~~ I have sworn it.

Stroller. For the best song of love

Queen. ~~For the best song of love~~ It must be sung about me and to me

Stroller. ~~I understand~~ The man must make love to you in a song ~~When~~ but who shall say which song is best

Queen. The best song is that shall most move me.

Stroller. Look at me – my hair is matted and foul, my clothes are ragged, beasts have torn my flesh, I crossed so many forests. I have been in such great solitudes that memory is gone. It may be that my birth is as foul as my body

[NLI 30,336 d, 2v]

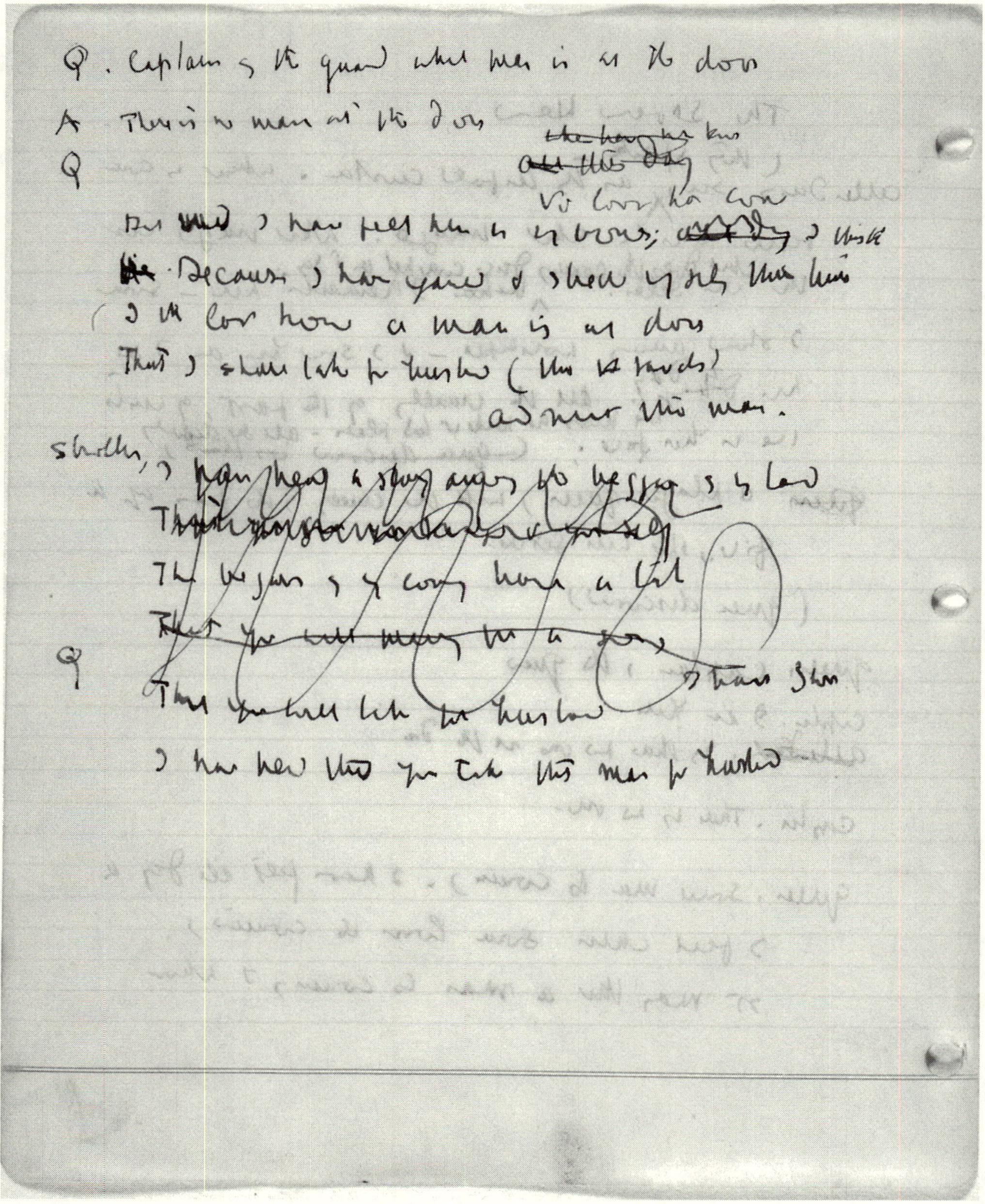

[NLI 30,336 d, 2[v]] [*VPl*, 29–35]

Q. Captain of the Guard what man is at the door

A. There is no man at the door

Q. When have we [?known]
~~All this day~~
No lover has come
But ~~now~~ I have felt him in my bones; ~~all day~~ I think
~~He~~ Because I have yawned & stretched myself three times
I in love know a man is at door
That I shall take for husband (three ~~k~~ knocks)
Admit this man.

Stroller. I have heard a story among the beggars of my land
~~That you [?vowed] you [?would] give your self~~
The beggars of my country have a tale
~~That you will marry for a song~~

Q. I have sworn
That you will take for husband
I have heard that you take that man for husband

Though this offers a tighter reading of the material than is found on 2[r] and 3[r], there is no attempt to clue it to the opposed recto, suggesting Yeats was not wholly satisfied with the draft.

[NLI 30,336 d, 4r]

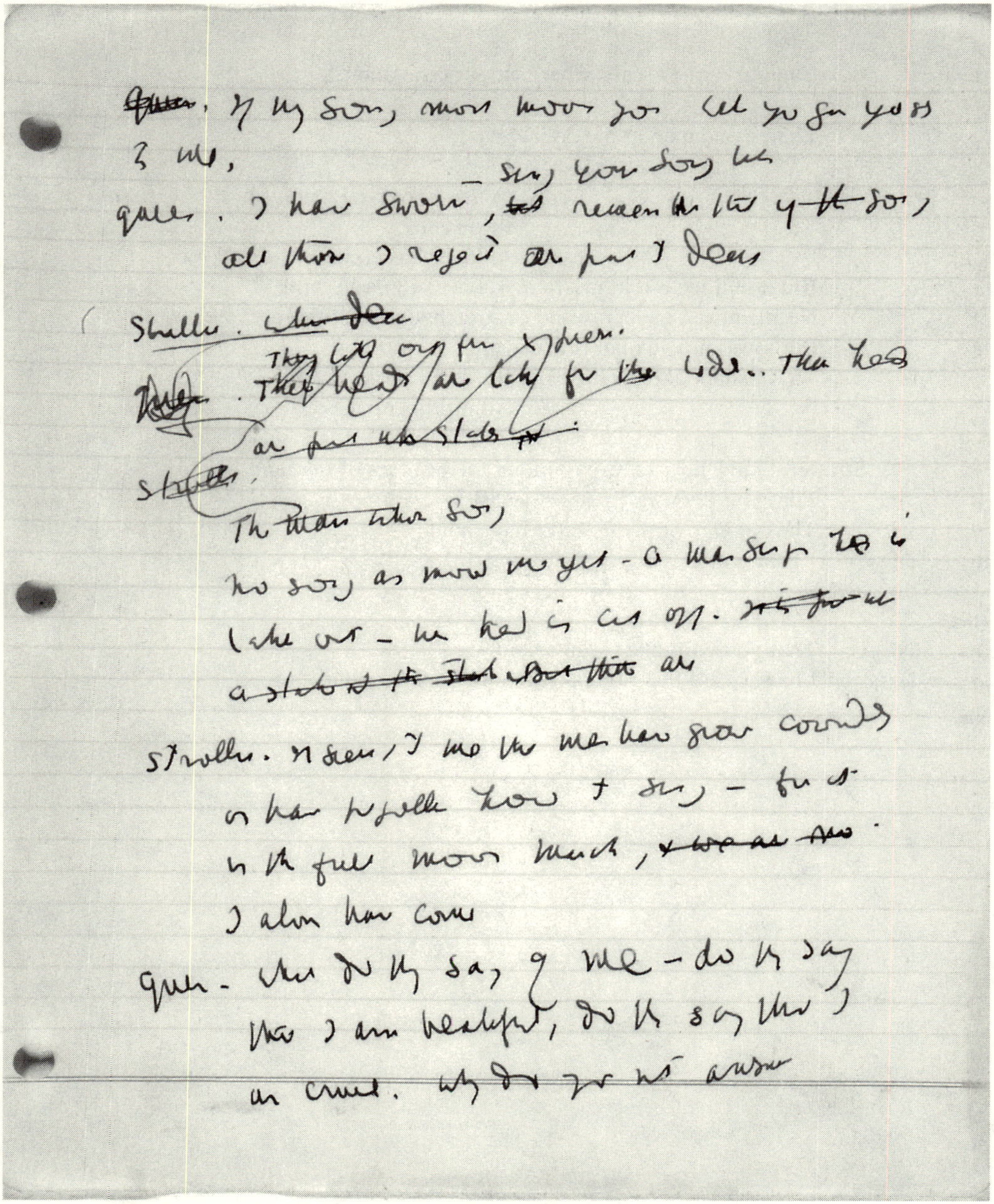

[NLI 30,336 d, 4r] [*VPl*, 52–58]

~~Queen~~. If my song most move you will you give yourself
[?Q] to me.

– sing your song but
Queen. I have sworn, ~~but~~ remember that ~~if the song~~
all those I reject are put to death

~~Stroller. What death~~
They taken out from the queen.
~~Queen~~. ~~Their heads~~ are taken from their bodies. Their heads
~~are put upon stakes~~

~~Stroller~~.
The man whose song
No song has moved me yet – a man sings he is
taken out – his head is cut off. ~~It is put upon~~
~~a stake and the stake is But there~~ are

Stroller. It seems to me that men have grown cowardly
or have forgotten how to sing – for it
is the full moon march, ~~& we are [?now]~~
I alone have come

Queen. What do they say of me – do they say
that I am beautiful, do they say that I
am cruel. Why do you not answer

[NLI 30,336 d, 5r]

Stroller: I am thinking of our marriage night

Queen: How could a thing so foul move us (so),
as it the thought of your approaching death, or the
thought of your foulness [illegible] make me
shudder

Stroller. Because I am [illegible] I can see you
as the gods can see you.

Queen. What do the gods see ~~gods~~

Stroller. Your cruelty, ~~[illegible]~~.
When I shall touch your body I shall love
this cruelty, & my desire for one is as my desire
for the other

Queen – ~~Silence, silence~~ Why do you come, what makes
you say such things

Stroller. You know there is no need for me to
answer

Queen. You mean that your ~~[illegible]~~ song
shall move me more than any other words

~~Stroller. [illegible]~~

[NLI 30,336 d, 5r] [*VPl*, 70–87]

Stroller. I am thinking of our marriage night

Queen. How could a thing so foul move with a song,
Is it the thought of your approaching death, is it
thought of your foulness that makes me
shudder

Stroller. Because I am with fear I can see you
as the gods can see you.

the gods see
Queen. What do ~~you see~~

Stroller. Your cruelty, ~~can be seen they say, I desire~~ it.
When I shall touch your body I shall touch
this cruelty, & my desire for one is as my desire
for the other

Queen – ~~Silence, silence~~ Why do you come, what makes
you say such things

Stroller. You know there is no need for me to
answer

song
Queen. You mean that your ~~praise of my beauty~~
shall move me more than any other man's

~~Stroller.~~ ~~What have I to do with beauty. My memory~~ is

---

6 Only in the final draft of the play did Yeats change "with fear" to "without fear," a more apt comparison with the gods.

9 The conjectured "say" may have been written "sae" or even "see" in a back-formation from the word "seen."

[NLI 30,336 d, 6r]

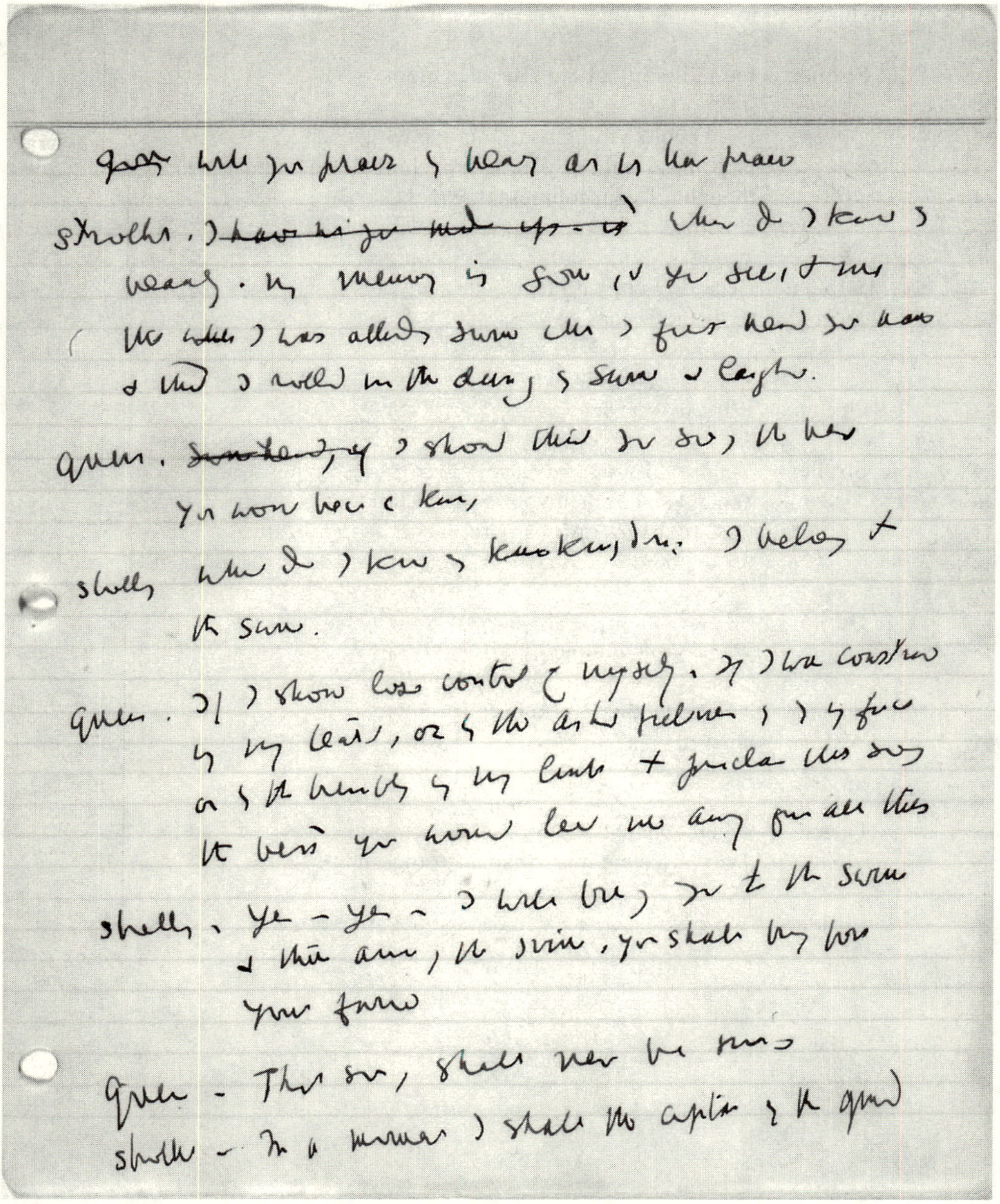

[NLI 30,336 d, 6r] [*VPl*, 80–101]

~~Queen~~ Will you praise my beauty or is that praise

Stroller. ~~I have not yet made up – it~~ What do I know of
beauty. My memory is gone, and yet seems to me
that ~~when~~ I was attending swine when I first heard your name
& that I rolled in the dung of swine & laughed.

Queen. ~~Swineherd~~, if I should think your song the best
You would become a king

Stroller What do I know of ~~kind~~ kingdoms. I belong to
the swine.

Queen. If I should lose control of myself. If I was constrained
by my tears, or by the [?ashen] fulness of my face
or by the trembling of my limbs to proclaim this song
the best you would lead me away from all this

Stroller. Yes – yes – I would bring you to the swine
& there among the swine, you should bring forth
your farrow

Queen. That song shall never be sung

Stroller. In a moment I shall the Captain of the Guard

18 The speech assignment of the line to the Stroller is clearly wrong, as the words are more appropriate for the Queen, but there is no cancellation.

[NLI 30,336 d, 7r]

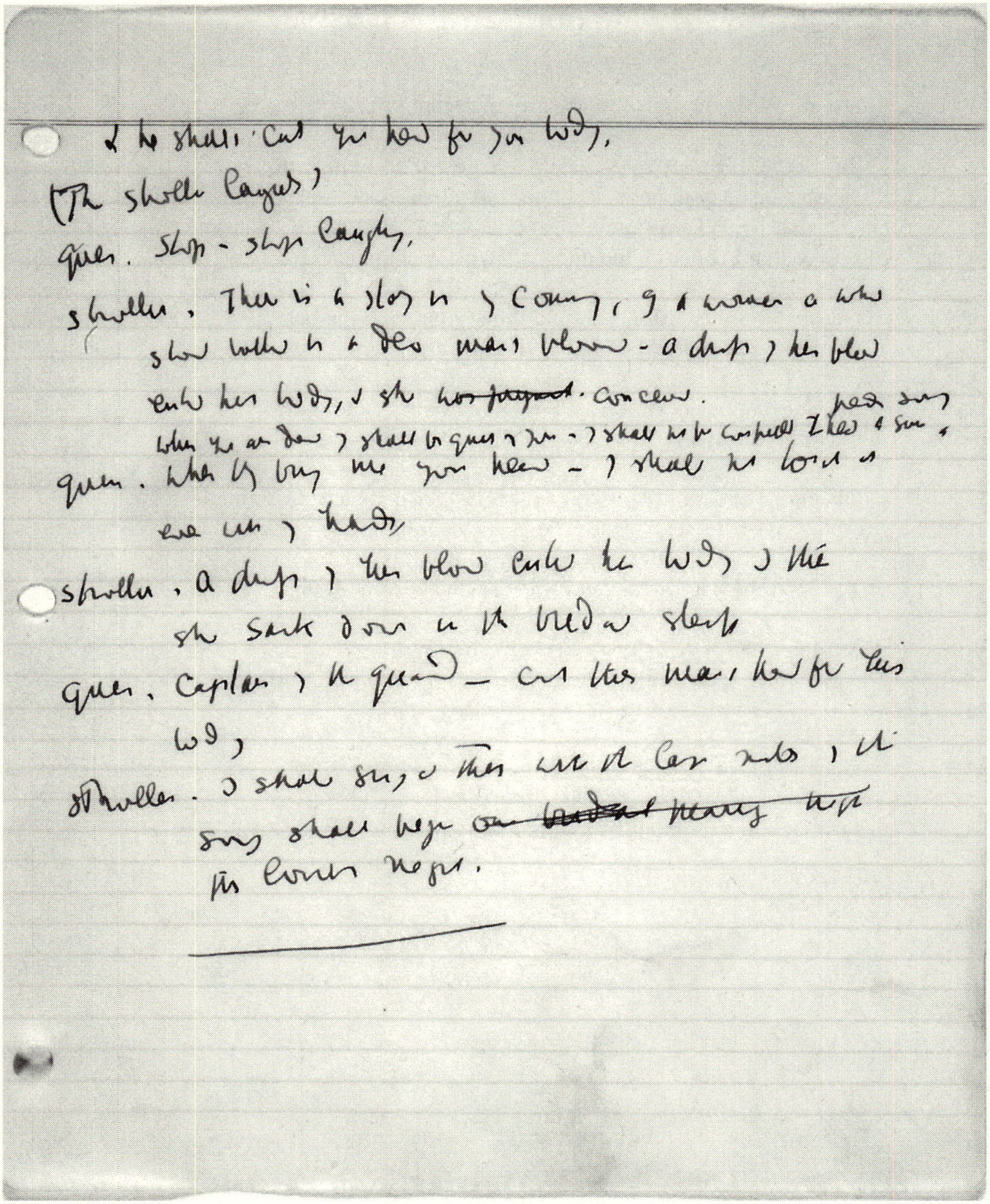

[NLI 30,336 d, 7[r]] [*VPl*, 114–121]

1 & he shall cut your head from your body

(The Stroller laughs)

2 Queen. Stop – stop laughing.

3 Stroller. There is a story in my country of a woman [?once] who
4 stood bathed in an old man's blood – a drop of his blood
5 entered her body, & she ~~was pregnant~~ conceived.

heed song
6 When you are dead I shall be quit of you – I shall not be compelled to hed & give a
7 Queen. When they bring me your head – I shall not touch it
8 even with my hands.

9 Stroller. A drop of his blood entered her body and then
10 she sank down in the bridal sleep

11 Queen. Captain of the Guard – cut this man's head from his
12 body

13 Stroller. I shall sing & then with the last notes of the
14 the song shall begin ~~our bridal marriage night~~
16 the lovers night.

---

16 With the short line across the page Yeats indicates the completion of this draft. "The Lovers' Night" was the title Yeats assigned the play in the HRC typescript, where it was quickly revised in favor of "A Full Moon in March."

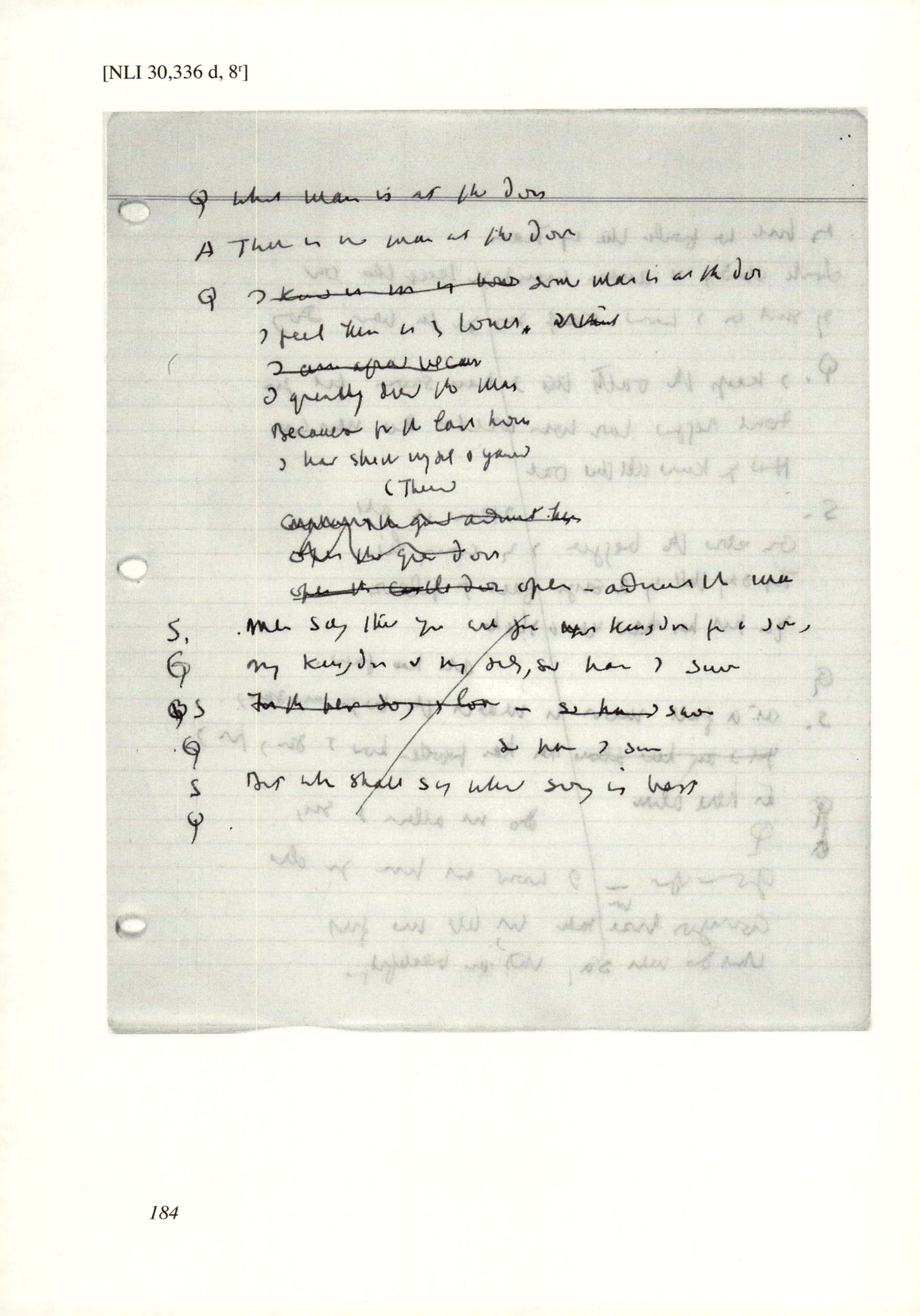

[NLI 30,336 d, 8r]

[NLI 30,336 d, 8^{r}] [*VPl*, 29–53]

Q What man is at the door

A There is no man at the door

Q ~~I know it in my bones~~ some man is at the door
I feel him in my bones. ~~I think~~
~~I am afraid because~~
I greatly dread the man
Because for the last hour
I have stretched myself & yawned

(Three)
~~Captain of the Guard admit him~~
~~Open the great door~~
~~Open the castle door~~ open – admit the man

S. Men say that you will give your kingdom for a song

Q. My kingdom & my self, so have I sworn

~~Q~~ S ~~For the best song of love~~ – ~~so have I~~ sworn

Q So have I sworn

S But who shall say which song is best

Q.

The second draft occupies 8^{r}–9^{v}. The sequencing of this draft of the dialogue is irregular. Yeats appeared at first to follow the pattern he had established with most of the first draft and so began this version on 8^{r} and then decided to rework that material on 7^{v}. However, he next continued the dialogue from 7^{v} to 8^{v}, concluding it first on 9^{r} and then on 9^{v}. Having completed the draft, he canceled all but 8^{r} with a single diagonal ink stroke across each sheet of holograph. This is the first draft to structure the dialogue in verse. Yeats pays scant attention to appropriate punctuation at this stage of composition.

[NLI 30,336 d, 7v]

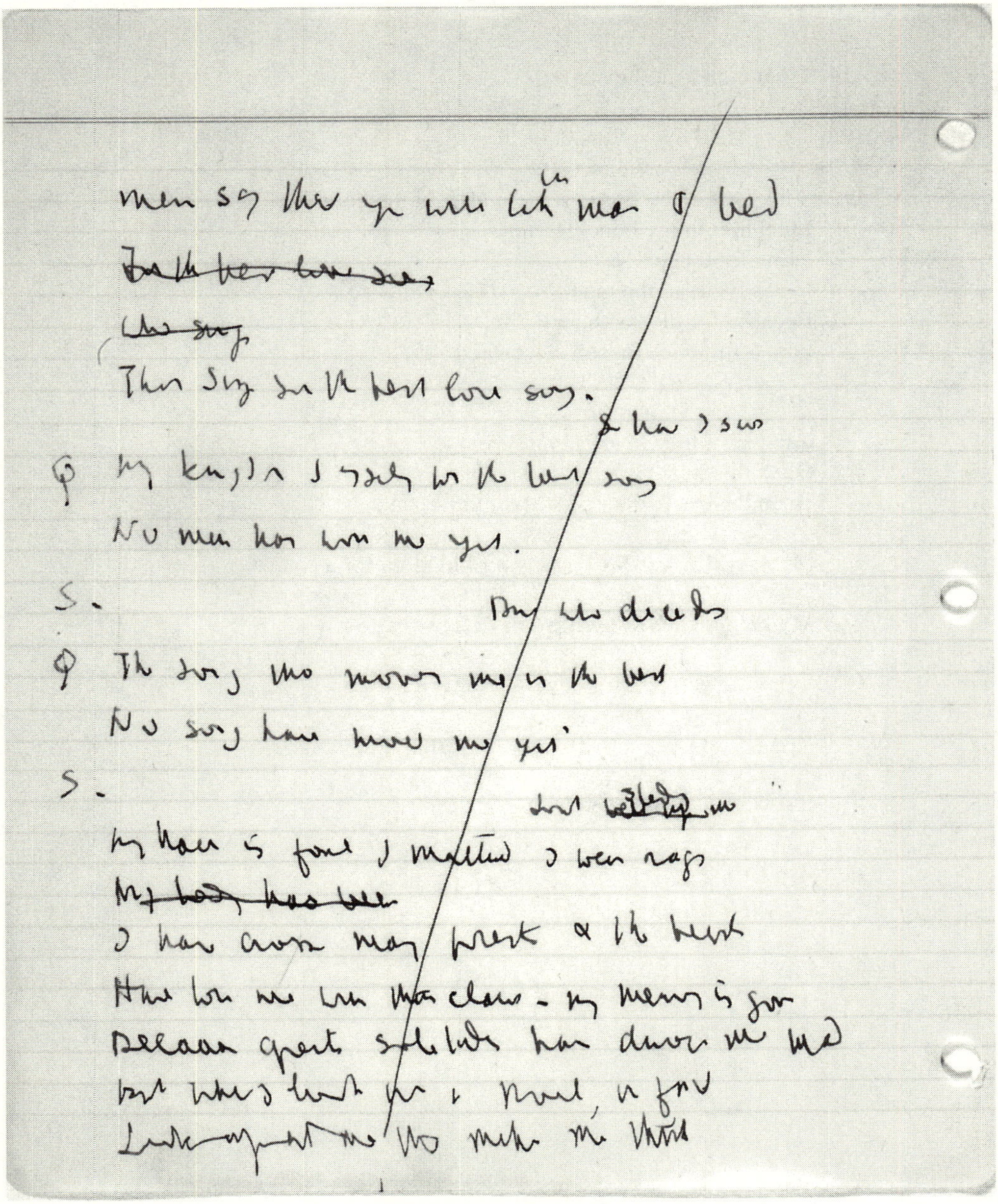

[NLI 30,336 d, 7[v]] [*VPl*, 33–48]

a
1 men say that you will take man to bed
2 ~~For the best love song~~
3 ~~Who sings~~
4 That sings you the best love song

So have I sworn
5 Q My kingdom & myself for the best song
6 No man has won me yet.

S. But who decides

7 Q The song that moves me is the best
8 No song has moved me yet
study
S. Look ~~well upon~~ me
9 My hair is foul & matted I wear rags
10 ~~My body has been~~
11 I have crossed many forests & the beasts
12 Have torn me with their claws – my memory is gone
13 Because great solitude has driven me mad
14 But when I look in a river, a face
15 Looks up at me that makes me think

[NLI 30,336 d, 8v]

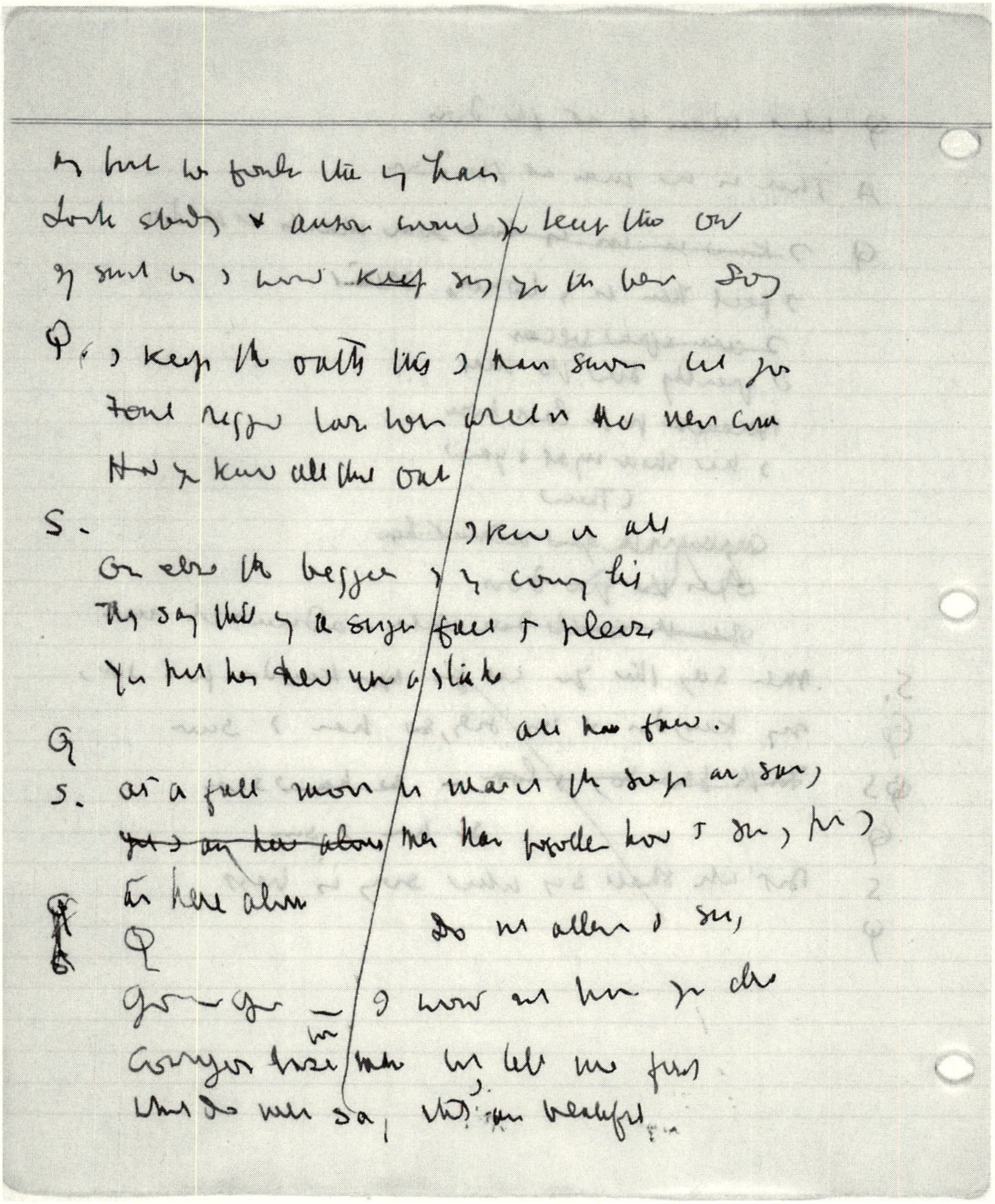

[NLI 30,336 d, 8v] [*VPl*, 49–68]

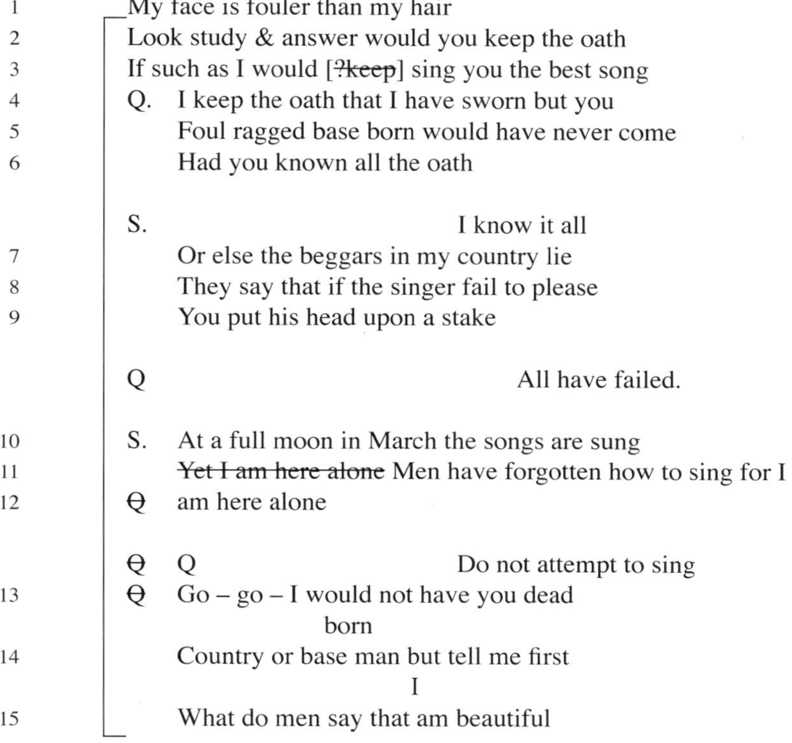

My face is fouler than my hair
Look study & answer would you keep the oath
If such as I would [~~?keep~~] sing you the best song
Q. I keep the oath that I have sworn but you
Foul ragged base born would have never come
Had you known all the oath

S. I know it all
Or else the beggars in my country lie
They say that if the singer fail to please
You put his head upon a stake

Q All have failed.

S. At a full moon in March the songs are sung
~~Yet I am here alone~~ Men have forgotten how to sing for I
~~Q~~ am here alone

~~Q~~ Q Do not attempt to sing
~~Q~~ Go – go – I would not have you dead
born
Country or base man but tell me first
I
What do men say that am beautiful

[NLI 30,336 d, 9r]

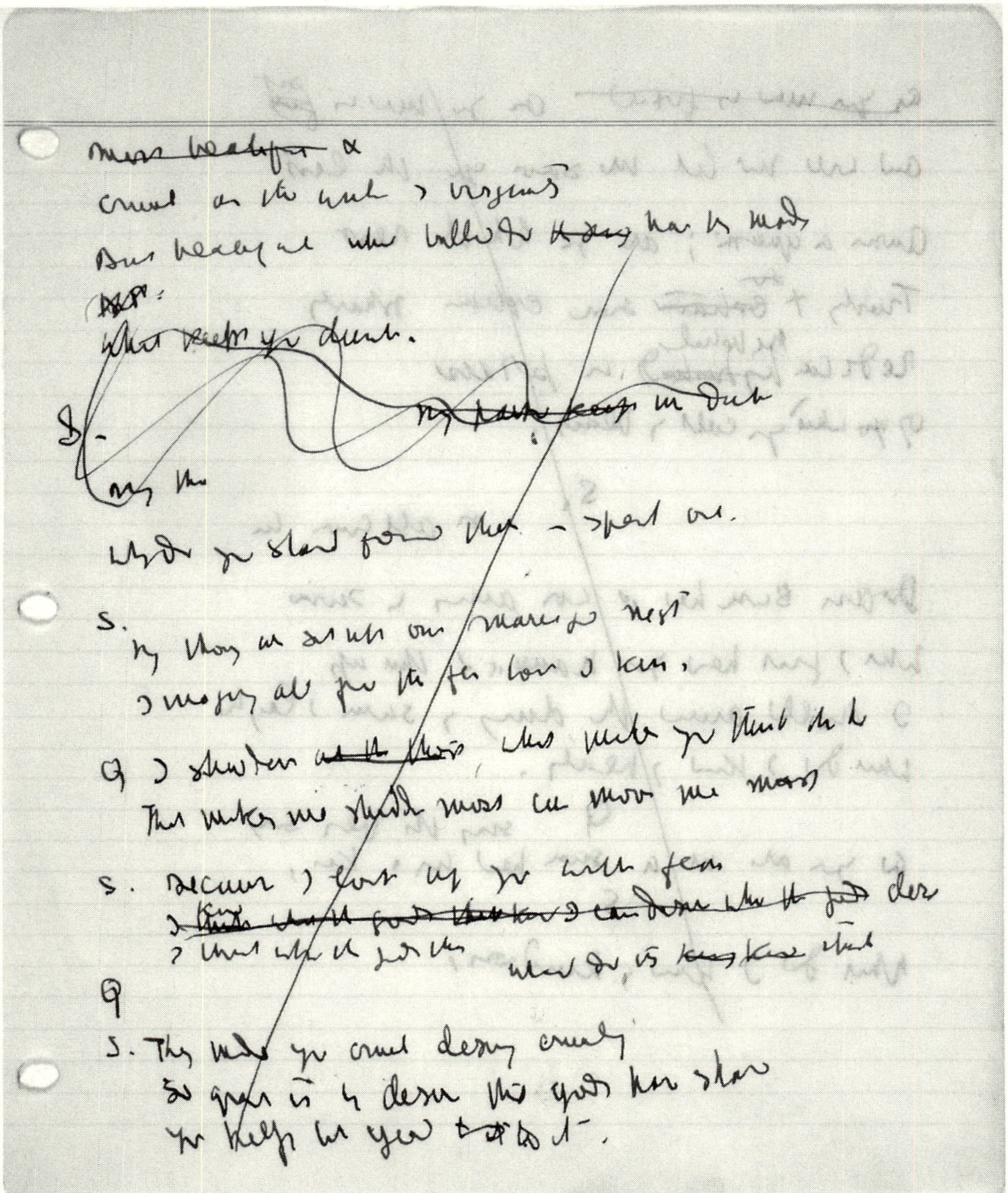

[NLI 30,336 d, 9r] [*VPl*, 64–79]

1 ~~Most beautiful~~ &
2 Cruel as the winter of virginity
3 But beautiful when ballad or ~~the song~~ has been made
4 ~~[?Most]~~
5 ~~What keeps you dumb~~.
S. ~~My passion keeps me dumb~~
6 May the
7 Why do you stand [?formal] there – speak out.

8 S. My thoughts are set upon our marriage night
9 Imagining all from the first touch and kiss.

10 Q I shudder ~~at these things~~, what makes you think that he
11 That makes me shudder most can move me most

12 S. Because I look upon you with fear
know
13 ~~I think what the gods think know I can desire what the gods~~ desire
14 I think what the gods think
Q What do they ~~kng know~~ think

15 S. They made you cruel desiring cruelty
16 So great is my desire the gods have shown
17 You help but yield ~~to it~~ to it.

17 For "You help" read "You cannot help".

[NLI 30,336 d, 9v]

[NLI 30,336 d, 9[v]] [*VPl*, 80–87]

set
~~As your mind is fixed~~ As your mind is ~~fix~~
And will not let me save you the last
Answer a question; are you like the rest
~~som~~
Trusting to ~~extrava~~ some extrava phrases
hyperboles
Rediculous ~~hyperbols~~ in praise
Of ~~you~~ what you call my beauty

S.
or all were lie[?s]
{I
{~~On~~ am swineherd, I was among the swine
When I first heard your name, & thereupon
I rolled amid the dung of swine & laughed
What do I know of beauty.

Q
Sing the best song
And you are not a swineherd but a king

S
What do I know of kingdoms

---

4 The incomplete "extrava" could be "exhaus" in both places, but Yeats's final choice, "wild hyperbole," suggests "extravagant phrases" is probably his intention here. Cf. *HRC*, 4[r], l. 23, p. 243 below.

Third draft occupies 10[v]–12[v]. Before Yeats began this draft of the dialogue on 11[r], he had attempted a version of the opening lyric "Every loutish lad" on 10[r], 10[v] (see pp. 134–137). It is possible that the lyric was incorporated here from another initial situation, since the opening stanza is preceded by two lines of prose, which have no bearing on the composition of the play (see p. 131 and the note on p. 137 above). The entry at the base of 10[v] shows that this sheet was incorporated before Yeats began the third version of the dialogue ("B" also heads the remaining pages devoted to this draft of the dialogue). To make the sequence clear for this draft headed "B", Yeats numbered the sheets 1 to 4. As with the other two drafts in this sequence, Yeats did not punctuate his text.

[NLI 30,336 d, 11[r]] [*VPl*, 33–45]

1

B

They say that man shall you for a wife
That sings the best.

~~That sings me the be~~st
~~That won me best in~~ a song
~~My kind was~~ ~~But he~~
That sings his passion best

He

And that the kindom is added to the gift

She

The kindom & my self this have I sworn

He

~~What if a blind old man sing~~ best
But what if some blind aged crippled man
Or some base beggar ~~[?for] the [?woman]~~ sing the best

She

~~Some I reject – no base born man can sing~~
No man abhorrent to these eyes can sing –
Some I have punished for their impudence
In standing there & looking at my my face

He

My hair is foul & matted I wear rags
I have crossed many forests & the beasts
Have torn me with their claws – my memory gone

[NLI 30,336 e, 10[v]] [*VPl*, 27–38]

B

Or some base beggar out of her favour sing
Better than full men
Some I reject

10[v], 1–2 Tagged to replace ll. 11–12 on 11[r]. For the facsimile of the full page, see p. 136 above.

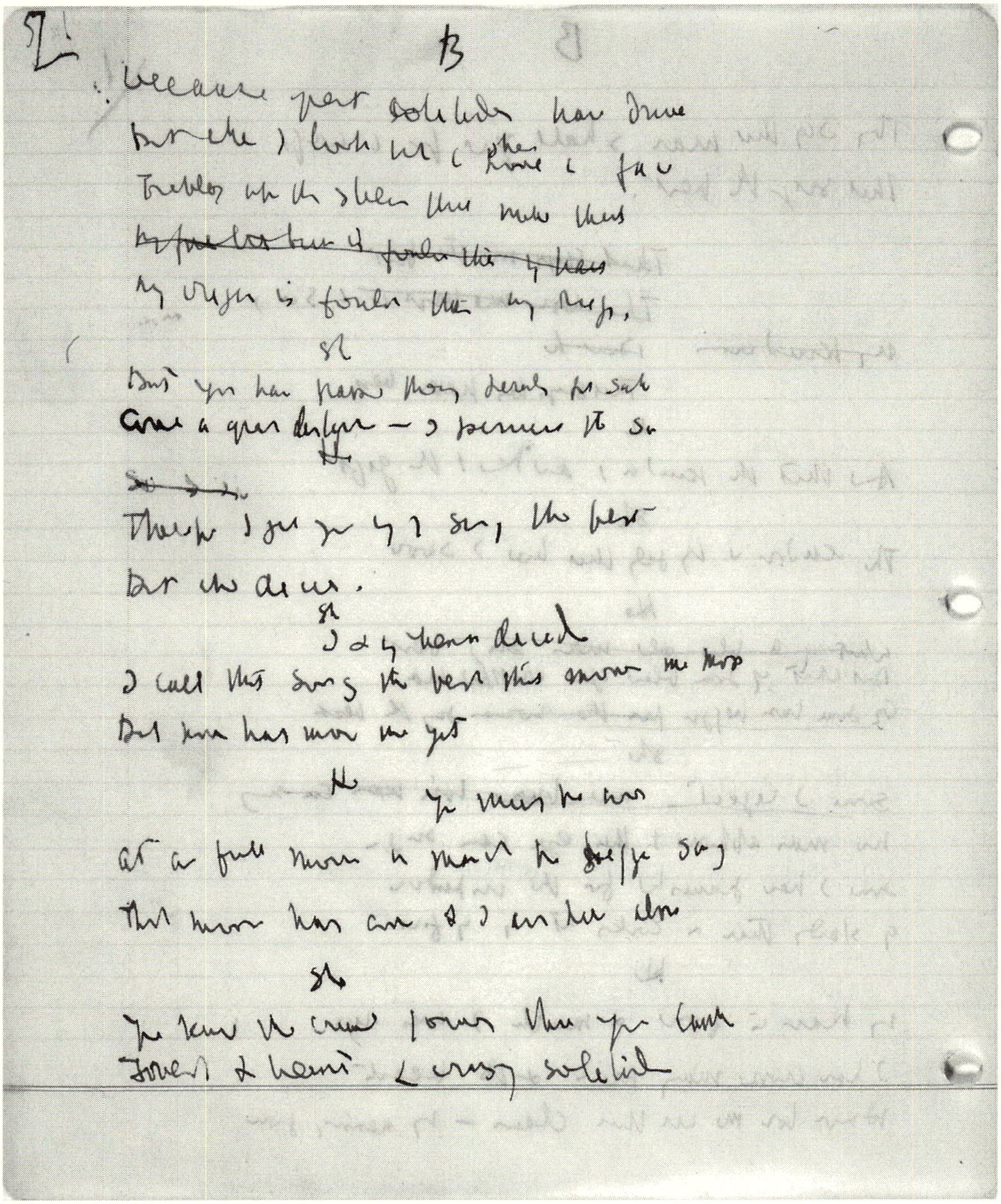

[NLI 30,336 d, 11v] [*VPl*, 46–61]

2

B

Because great solitudes have driven
stream
But when I look into a river a face
Trembles upon the stream that makes think
~~My face [?has] [?been] is fouler than my hair~~
My origin is fouler than my rags.

She

But you have passed through perils for sake
Come a great distance – I permit the song

He

~~So I sin~~
Therefore I get you if I sing the best
But who decides.

She

I & my heart decide
I call that song the best that moves me most
But none has moved me yet

He

You must be won
At a full moon in March the beggar sang
That moon has come & I am here alone

She

You know the cruel journey that you came
Forest & beast & crazy solitude

[NLI 30,336 d, 12r]

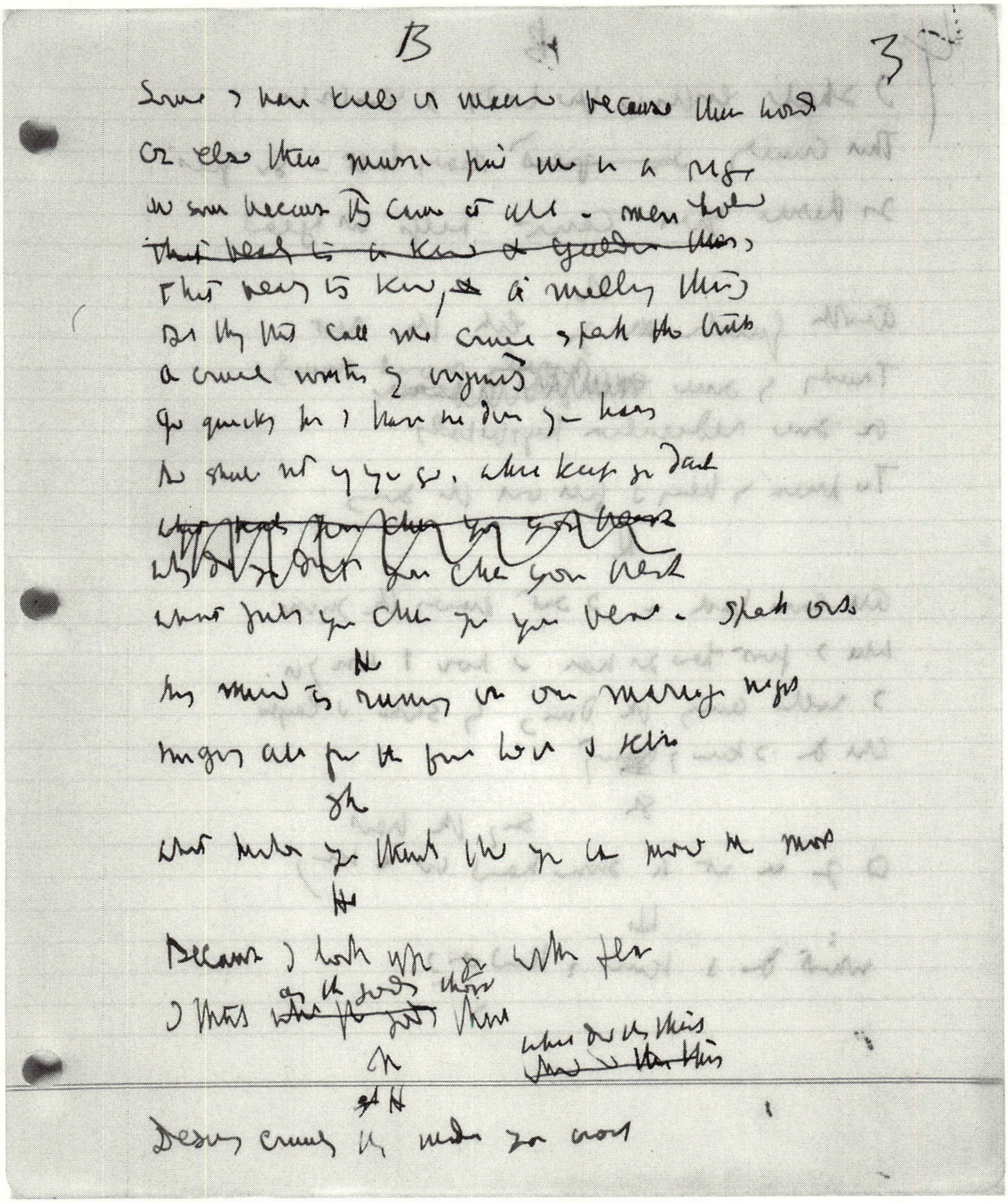

[NLI 30,336 d, 12^{r}] [*VPl*, 61–77]

3

B

Some I have killed or maimed because their howl
Or else their music put me in a rage
And some because they came at all – men hold
~~That beauty is a kind & yielding thing~~
That beauty is kind, & a melting thing
But they that call me cruel speak the truth
A cruel winter of virginity
Go quickly for I have no desire you harm
And shall not if you go. What keeps you dumb
~~What pulls your chin upon your breast~~
Why do you drop your chin upon breast
What pulls your chin upon your breast – Speak out

He

My mind is running on our marriage night
Imagining all from the first touch and kiss

She

What makes you think that you can move me most

He

Because I look upon you with fear
as the gods think
I think ~~what the gods think~~

She

What do they think
~~What do they think~~

~~Sh~~ He

Desiring cruelty they made you cruel

10–11 Yeats first cancels l. 10 with a single line through the text, then deciding not to incorporate the alternative he cancels both lines with a strong wavy flourish of the pen.

[NLI 30,336 d, 12v]

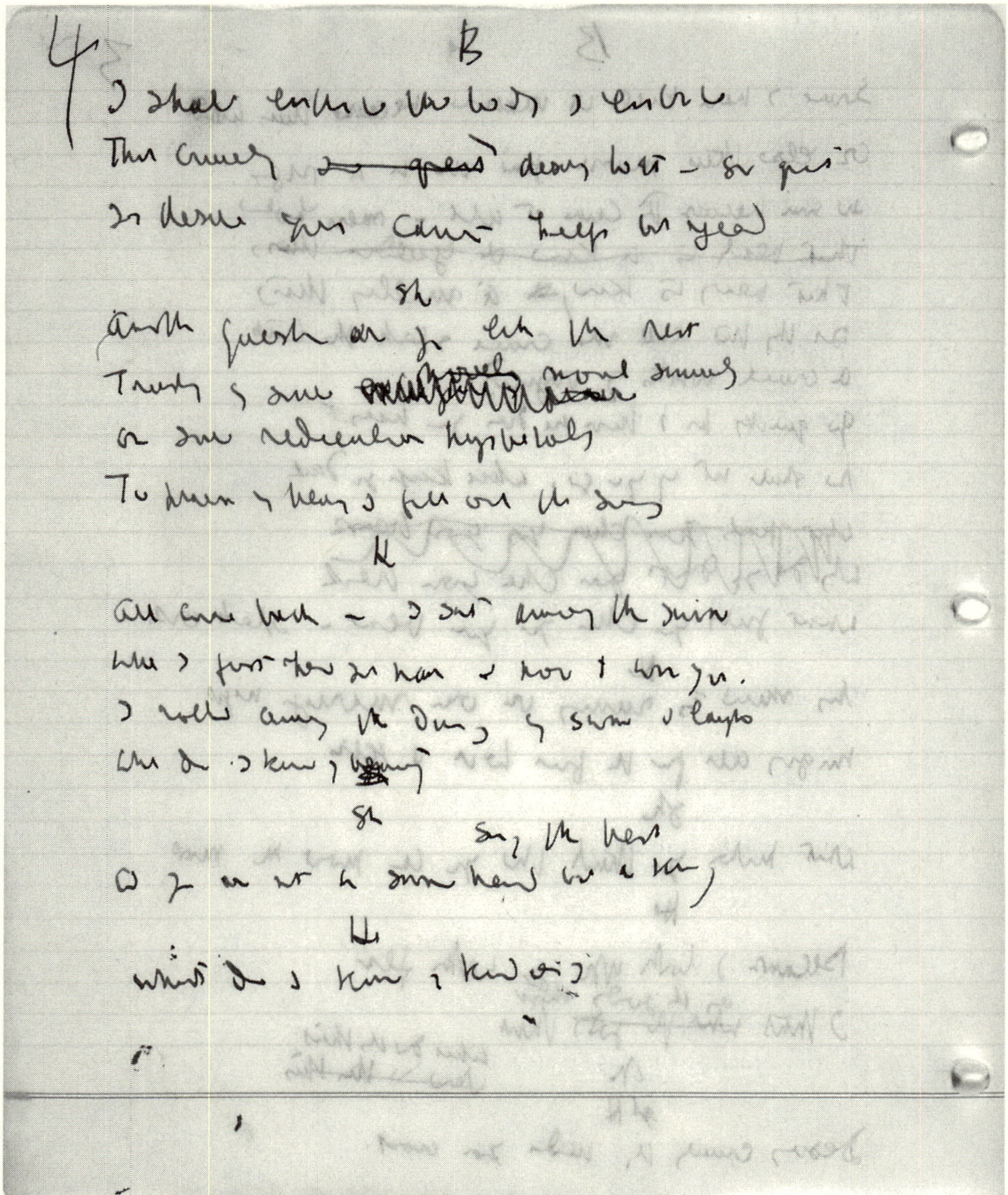

[NLI 30,336 d, 12v] [*VPl*, 78–87]

4

B

1 I shall embrace that body & embrace
2 That cruelty ~~so great~~ desiring both – so great
3 Is desire you cannot help but yeald

She

4 Another question are you like the rest
~~novel~~ novel simily
5 Trusting in some ~~[?extravagance] of phrase~~
6 Or some ridiculous hyperbole
7 To praise my beauty and fill out the song

He

8 All comes back – I sat among the swine
9 When I first heard your name and how to win you.
10 I rolled among the dung of swine and laughed
11 What do I know of beauty

~~She~~
She

Sing the best
12 And you are not a swineherd but a king

He

13 What do I know of kingdoms

Part II. *A Full Moon in March*

H. First Draft for the Queen's Song: NLI 30,336 c, 5v

If the version of the Queen's song found in NLI 30,336 c is the only draft, then its finished form was achieved almost without revision. It is a remarkably frank self-appraisal and confession, which explains the Queen's strange behavior throughout the opening section of the play culminating in the unexpected revelation of her face. In rewriting the final two lines of the lyric (ll. 7–10), Yeats found "virgin cruelty" the phrase with which to conclude the first stanza, thus bringing an organic and thematic coherence to the whole. An intricate psychological state is defined succinctly in some eight lines. The lines were next incorporated with few emendations into the text of the version of the play Yeats called "The Swine-herd" (see pp. 207–235).

[NLI 30,336 c, 5[v]]

[NLI 30,336 c, 5v] [*VPl*, 154-161]

Child & darling hear song
cry
Never say I did you wrong
~~*Say*~~
Cry this wrong came not from me
But my [?*revenging*] *cruelty*

Great my love before you came
Greater when I loved in shame
Greatest when love stirred in me
Storms of virgin cruelty
Greatest when there broke from me
Storm of virgin cruelty

---

found in NLI 30,336 c, 5v *transcribed above*
published in *FMIM(M)*

Part II. *A Full Moon in March*

I. "The Swine-herd": NLI 8906

NLI 8906 contains the first draft of the finished work, here called "The Swine-herd." The manuscript overall is fairly clean, since Yeats is in large measure finalizing the versification of the dialogue that he had worked on now through several drafts. This is the first such draft to bring together most of the elements that until now Yeats had been working on independently so that the structure and organization of the play is clear, even though the central and final lyrics ("He had famished in a wilderness" and "Why must those holy, haughty feet descend") are not included in full but merely referred to. The lines of the play that here display heavy revision tend to be those (such as the opening exchange for the attendants, the sequence leading up to the Queen dropping her veil, and the words for the attendants observing the consequences of the beheading) that Yeats either has drafted only once to date or is sketching in for the first time. At this point in its development he is still envisaging the play as being staged in the manner of his Noh-inspired plays for dancers. Dialogue characterizing the Queen concentrates on images suggestive of her wealth and influence, not yet moving, as in later versions, to language more suggestive of her heritage, fame, and history. In this version, in rendering the moment when the Queen responds to the Swineherd's story of the mystic conception, Yeats explored ways of defining her disgust; at a later stage he interpreted her response as embodying a profound awe.

[NLI 8906, 1r]

MS8906

1

The Swine-herd

First attendant

Did you ask ~~[illegible]~~ him what the play was about?

Second attendant.

~~He~~ I died [illegible] ~~[illegible]~~ ~~[illegible]~~

~~[illegible]~~

but all I could get out of ~~him~~ he said something about a full moon in March, ~~[illegible]~~, about up the crown, Caesar dead at the foot of Pompey's statue, but that is nonsense.

~~First~~ First attendant

did he say what we are to sing,

Second attendant

~~He said first that we might sing~~ at first he said any love song you ~~too~~ could remember, ~~then~~ he said ~~not this~~ then this you must sing this song with the line "crown of gold, dung of swine."

Song of the unfolding, & feeding of the cloth

Second attendant

~~a [illegible] lad that falls~~

Every loveless lad in love

Thinks his wisdom great enough

What cares love for this or that?

To set all the lovers a stare

as though Pythagoras wandered there

crown of gold or dung of swine

[NLI 8906, 1r] [*VPl*, 1–16]

The Swine-herd

1

First Attendant

him
Did you ask ~~the author~~ what the play was about?

Second Attendant

Yes ~~I~~ did & ~~all~~ I ~~got~~ for ~~my~~ ~~[?pla]~~ ~~pains was some~~
~~unintelligible symbolism & [?aims]~~
He said
~~but all I could get out of him~~ ~~was~~ something about a full
moon in March, ~~swine herd~~, Christ upon the cross, Caesar dead
at the foot of Pompey's statue, but that is nonsense.

First Attendant I am to
~~But~~ did he say what ~~we are~~ sing

Second Attendant

At first he said
~~He said first that we might sing~~ any love sing you
then that you
~~we~~ could remember, ~~then~~ ~~he said no that you~~ must
sing this song with the line "Crown of gold, dung of swine."

Song of the unfolding & folding of the cloth

Second Attendant

~~A far loutish lad that falls~~
Every loutish lad in love
Thinks his wisdom great enough
What cares love for this or that?
To set all the town a stare
As though Pythagoras wandered there
Crown of gold or dung of swine

---

found in NLI 8906, 1r–14r *transcribed above and below, pp. 211–235*
published in *FMIM(M)*

Yeats began entering copy on the verso of this leaf, with the sheet rotated 180 degrees, getting only as far as the title, "The Swine Heard", before turning the sheet over, reversing it, and beginning again. Note that the following three sheets were used in the original orientation, with the double bar at the foot.

Shall old Pythagoras fall in love
Little may he boast thereof
What cares love for this or that?
Days go by in foolishness
O how great their sweetness is.
Crown of gold, or dung of swine.

Open wide those gleaming eyes
That can make the loveliest wise
What cares love for this or that?
Make a leader of the schools
Thank the Lord all men are fools
Crown of gold or dung of swine

The first attendant may join in singing the burden at the end of the first and second verses.
When the cloth has been folded up by the three attendants, as the [illegible] will go[?] sit at one side or at both sides of the stage, where at their entrance they may have placed [illegible], [illegible] place of sitting.
The queen is discovered seated. She is veiled. cloak
The queen
What man is at the door. (she stretches her self yawns)
Attendant.
Nobody queen.
Queen
Some man has come
Some man has come, some terrifying man
Some man that I shall lift for hastier comes

[NLI 8906, 2r] [*VPl*, 17–31]

2

Should old Pythagoras fall in love
Little may he boast thereof
What cares love for this or that?
Days go by in foolishness
O how great the sweetness is.
Crown of gold, or dung of swine.

Open wide those gleaming eyes
That can make the loutish wise
What cares love for this or that?
a leader
Make ~~the greatest~~ of the schools
Thank the Lord all men are fools
Crown of gold or dung of swine

The First Attendant may join in singing the burden at the end of the first or second verse.
When the cloth has been folded up ~~as~~ by the three Attendants as the Hawks Well they sit at one side or at both sides of the stage, where at their entrance they may have placed gong, ~~flu~~ drum flute & zither.
She is veiled.
The Queen is discovered seated. ~~Her face is vei she wears~~ cloak ~~and veil~~.

The Queen
What man is at the door. (She stretches her self yawns)

Attendant
Nobody Queen.

Queen
a
~~Some man is there, some terrifying man~~
~~Some~~ ~~is~~
~~A man standing there at, a terrifying man some man has come~~
Some man has come, some terrifying man
Some man that I shall take for husband comes

9

For I have yawned & stretched myself three times
Admit him chamberlain, the Queen
attendant.
He comes

(enter the swineherd.)

Swineherd.
say that he
The beggars of my country ~~learned that~~
~~That sings you best shall take you for a wife~~
~~That the [illegible] [illegible] [illegible] you [illegible] a wife~~
~~That he who sings the best~~ shall be your husband

Queen.
best sings his passion
He that ~~can sing his passion~~

Swineherd ~~He~~
And they say
The kingdom is added to the gift

Queen
I have so sworn.

Swineherd.
~~[illegible] [illegible] some blind old cripple man sing~~ best
But what if some blind aged cripple sings
Or some lack-wit beggar on the famine roads,
Better than ~~[illegible]~~ [illegible] some man.

Queen
Some I reject.
No man admires that eyes can see,
Some I have punished for their impudence

Swineherd
So that's the case

[NLI 8906, 3^{r}] [*VPl*, 31–40]

3

1 For I have yawned & stretched my self three times
2 Admit him Captain of the Queen

Attendant

He comes

(Enter the Swineheard.

Swineherd,

say that he
3 The beggars of my country ~~have a tale~~
4 That sings you best shall take you for a wife
5 ~~That the best singer takes you a for a wife~~
6 ~~That he who sings the best shall be your husband~~

Queen. best sings his passion
7 He that ~~can sing his pass~~ion

Swine herd ~~He~~

And they say
8 The kingdom is added to the gift

Queen So have I sworn.

Swineherd.
9 ~~So what if some blind old crippled man sin~~g best
10 But what if some blind aged crippled man
11 Or some base beggar in his famine sing
12 Better than ~~[?shall a]~~ whole some men.

Queen Some I reject
13 No man abhorrent to these eyes can sing
14 Some I have punished for their impudence

Swineherd
15 So that's the catch

---

2 "Queen" is a slip for "Guard".

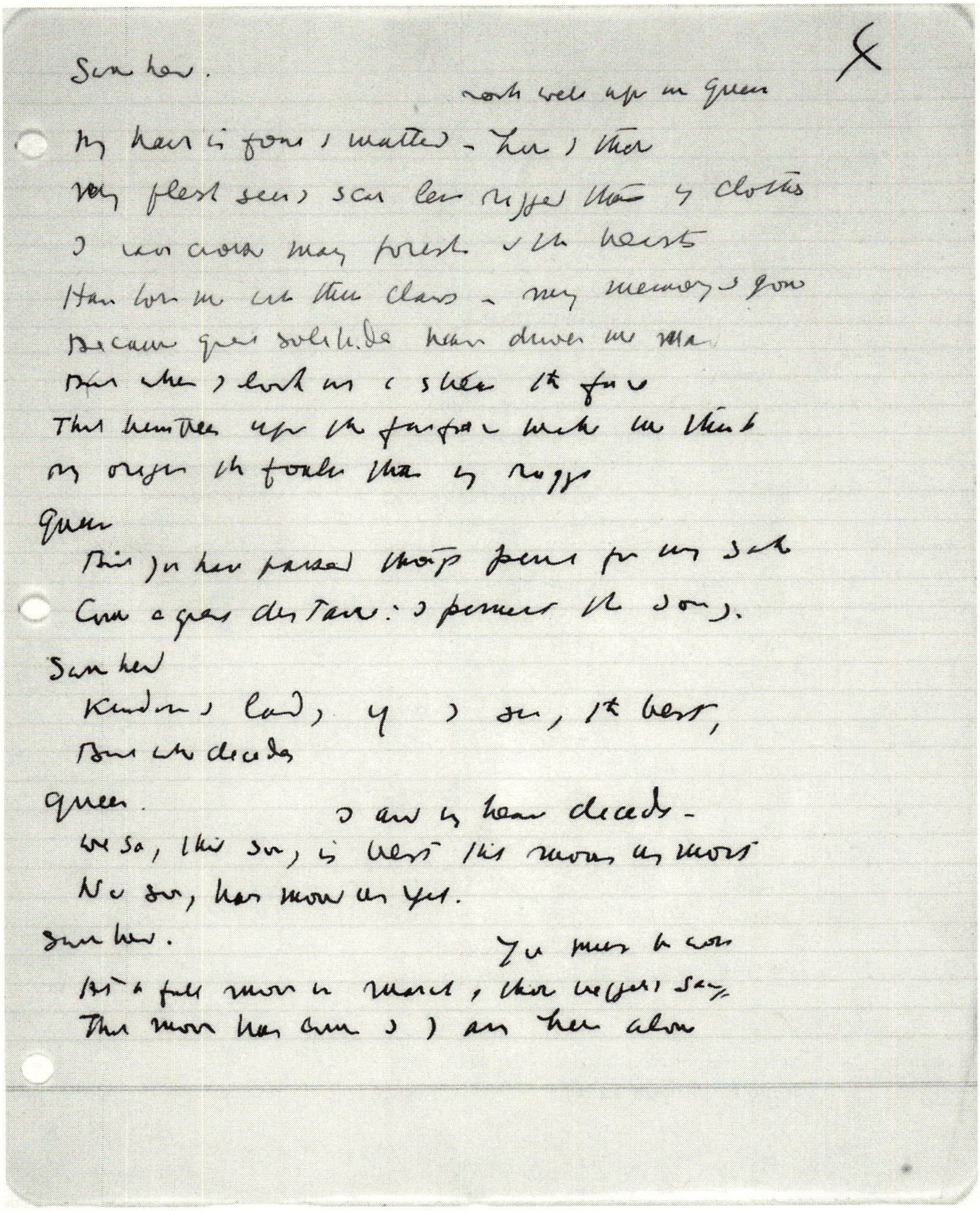

[NLI 8906, 4^{r}] [*VPl*, 41–57]

4

Swineherd.

Look well upon me queen
My hair is foul & matted –here & there
My flesh seems scarce less ragged than my clothes
I have crossed many forests and the beasts
Have torn me with their claws – my memory is gone
Because great solitudes have driven me mad
But when I look into a stream the face
That trembles upon the furface makes me think
My origin the fouler than my raggs

Queen

But you have passed through perils for my sake
Come a great distance: I permit the song.

Swineherd

Kingdom & lady if I sing the best,
But who decides

Queen

I and my heart decide.
We say that song is best that moves us most
No song has moved us yet.

Swineherd.

You must be won
At a full moon in March, those beggars say.
That moon has come and I am here alone

[NLI 8906, 5r] [*VPl*, 59–77]

5

Queen
Remember through what perils you come
But I am crueller than solitude
Forest or beast. Some I have killed or maimed
Because their singing put me in a rage
Or some because they came at all. Men hold
That woman's beauty is a melting thing
But they call me cruel speak the truth
A cruel winter of virginity
But for a reason that I cannot guess
I would not harm you; go before I change
What do you stand for chin upon breast

Swineherd
My mind is running on our marriage night
Imaging all from the first touch & kiss

Queen
~~What makes you think you think that you can si~~ng your self
~~Into my heart & me~~.
What gives you strange confidence, what makes
you
You think that can move my heart and me.

Swineherd
Because I look upon you without fear
I know the thought of god.

Queen
What is this thought

Swineherd
Desiring cruelty he made you cruel

[NLI 8906, 6r]

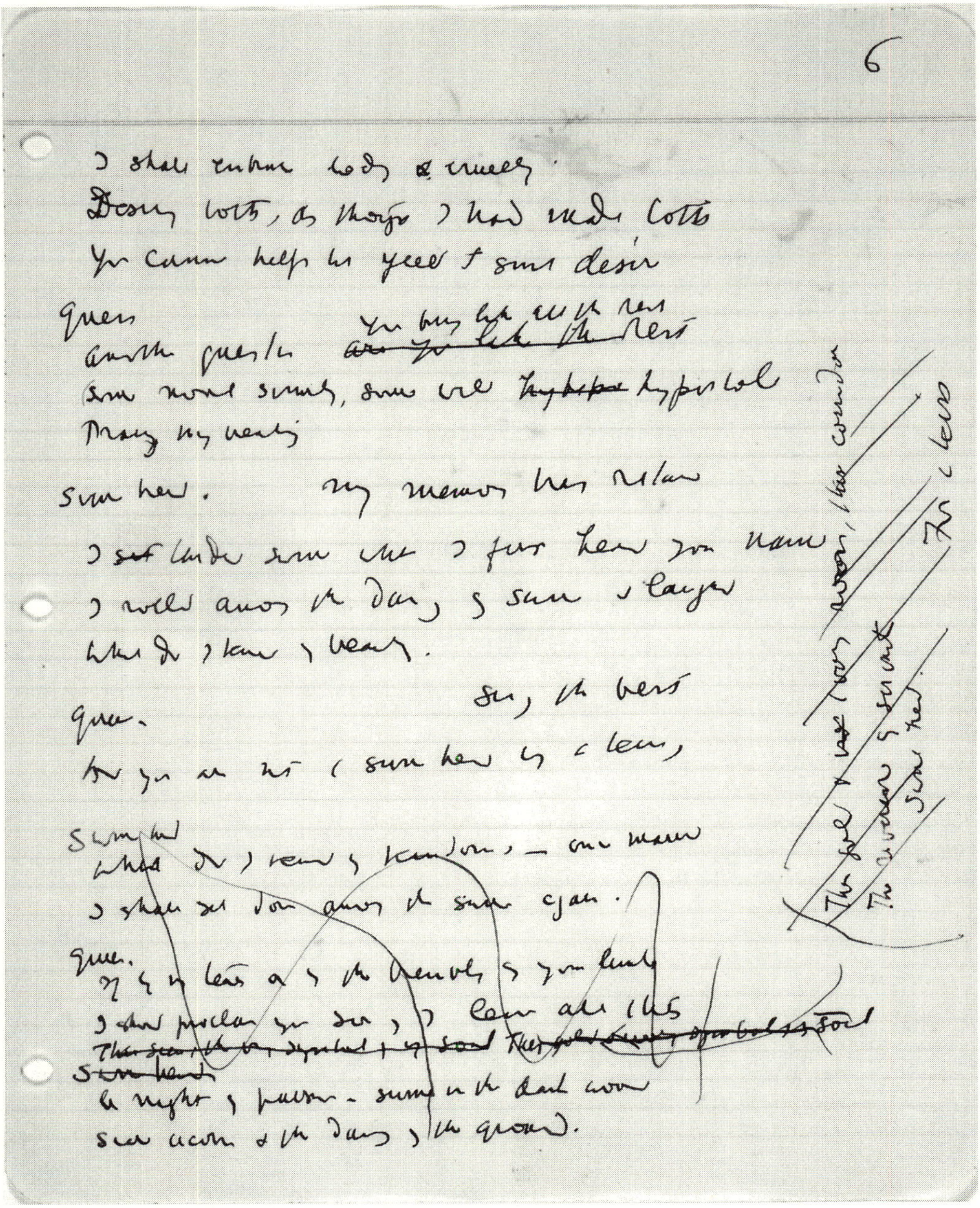

[NLI 8906, 6[r]] [*VPl*, 78–93]

6

I shall embrace body & cruelty
Desiring both, as though I had made both
You cannot help but yield to such desire

Queen You bring like all the rest
Another question. ~~Are you like the~~ rest
Some novel simily, some wild ~~hybeper~~ hyperbole
Praising my beauty

Swineherd. My memory has returned
I ~~sat~~ tended swine when I first heard your name
I rolled among the dung of swine and laughed
What do I know of beauty.

Queen. Sing the best
And you are not a swineherd but a king

Swineherd
What do I know of kingdoms – once married
I shall sit down among the swine again.

Queen.
If by my tears or by the trembling of your limbs
I shall proclaim your song, I leave all this
~~That seems the very symbol of my soul This gold & ivory symbol of my soul~~

~~Swineherd~~
A night of passion – swine in the dark wood
Such acorns & the dung upon the ground

This gold & ~~[ivo]~~ & ivory room, this corridor
The reverence of servants
Swine herd.
For a kiss

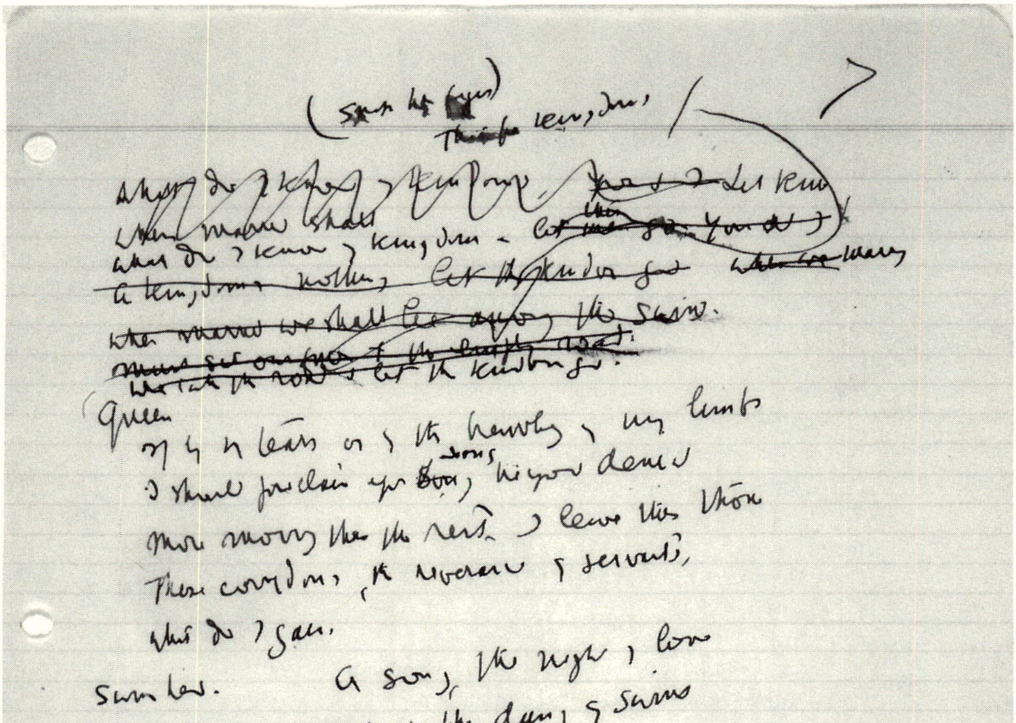

[NLI 8906, 7r]

[NLI 8906, 7r] [*VPl*, 87–93]

7

(snaps his fingers)
That for kingdoms

What do I know of kingdoms ~~You & I~~ Let kin
When married shall ~~this~~
What do I know of kingdoms – ~~let men go You and I~~
~~A kingdoms nothing Let this kindom go When we~~ marry
~~When married we shall lie among the swine~~.
~~Must set our faces to the empty road~~.
~~We take the road & let the kindom go.~~

Queen
If by my tears or by the trembling of my limbs
song
I shall proclaim your ~~song~~ beyond denial
More moving than the rest, I leave this throne
These corridors, the reverence of servants,
What do I gain.

Swineherd. A song, the night of love
An ignorant forest and the dung of swine

[NLI 8906, 8r]

[NLI 8906, 8r] [*VPl*, 94–107]

8

sh /
1 ~~All here have heard him, all~~ & have
Queen
2 All here have heard the man and all have judged
led
3 I led him, that I might not seem unjust,
4 From point to point, established in all eyes
5 ~~That he has come to insult not to woo~~
6 That he has brought an insult not his love

Swineherd.
7 She shall bring forth her farrow in the dung
8 But first my song – what nonsense shall I sing?

Queen
9 ~~Send for the heads man captain of the~~
10 ~~O foul in origin~~,
11 ~~Foul in your rags, in origin in speech~~
12 Send for the heads man captain of the guard

Attendant
13 I have sent already queen

Queen
his his his
14 Foul in ~~your~~ rags, ~~in~~ origin ~~in~~ speech
15 ~~[?] [?] [?] [?] [?] he shall, &~~ yet
~~I than~~ to god this
16 I owe my thanks that foul ~~wretch~~ wretch
origin
17 Foul in his rags, his ~~origin~~ his speech
In spite of all dared, has not dared
18 ~~That came to sing his passion has not [?dared]~~
19 Ask me to drop my veil – insulted ears
but face
20 Have heard & shuddered ~~[?by]~~ my ~~face~~ is pure

1 The purpose of Yeats's penciled "sh" and the vertical deletion mark is not clear. There are four further penciled corrections or marginalia of his on 10r, 11r, and 12r.

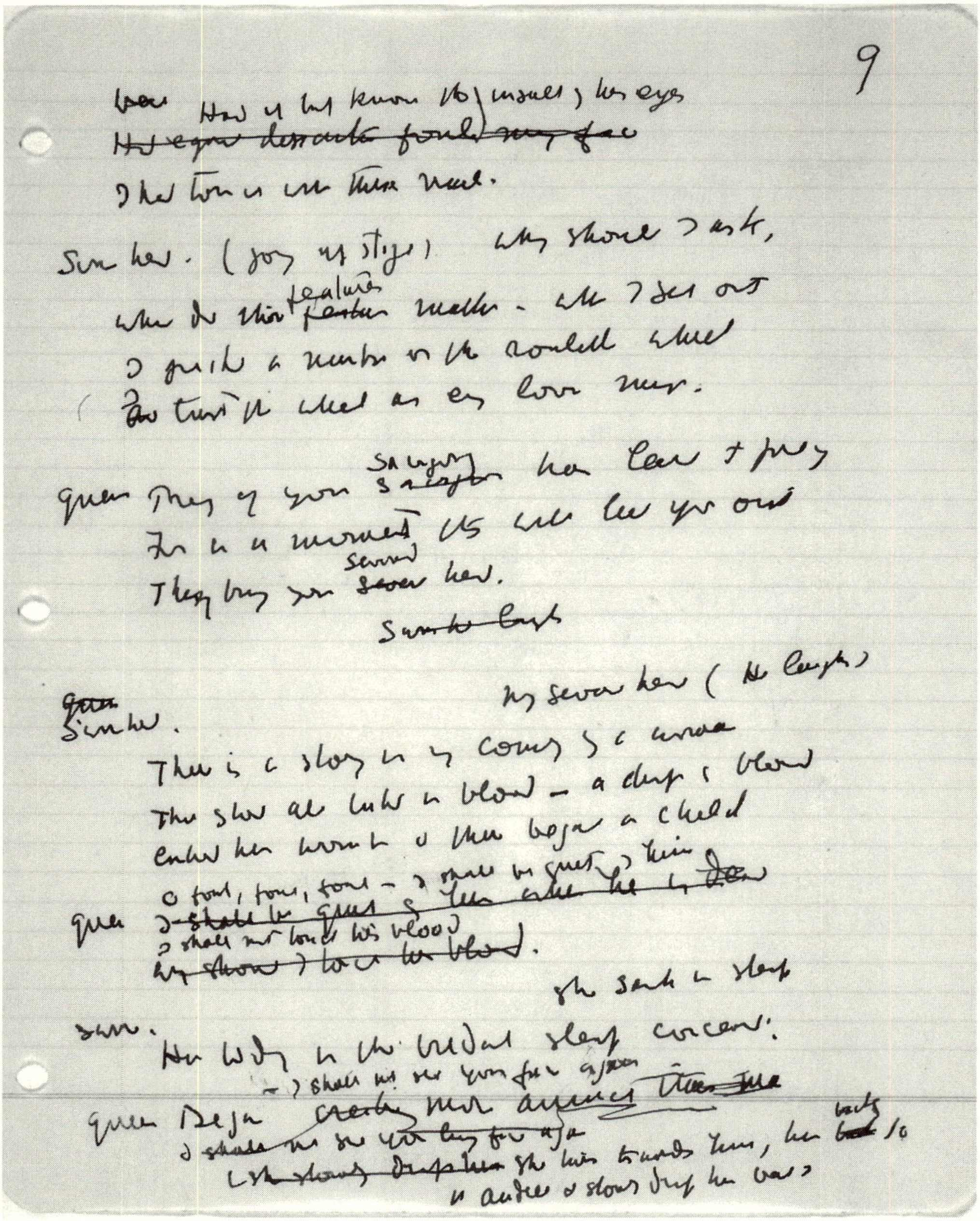

[NLI 8906, 9r] [*VPl*, 108–123]

9

~~Were~~

1 Had it but known the insult of his eyes
2 ~~Had [?equal] desecration fouled my face~~
3 I had torn it with these nails.

Swineherd. (going up stage) Why should I ask,
features
4 What do those ~~ferturs~~ matter – when I set out
5 I picked a number on the roulette wheel
I
6 ~~And~~ trust the wheel as every lover must.

Queen savagery
7 Pray if your ~~savrger~~ has learnt to pray
8 For in a moment they will lead you out
severed
9 Then bring your ~~sever~~ head.

~~Swineherd lau~~ghs

~~Queen~~
Swineherd. My severed head (He laughs)
10 There is a story in my country of a woman
11 That stood all bathed in blood – a drop of blood
12 Entered her womb and there begat a child

O foul, foul, foul – I shall be quit of him
13 Queen ~~I shall be quit of him when he is dead~~
I shall not touch his blood
14 ~~Why should I touch his blood~~.

Swine. She sank in sleep
15 Her body in the bridal sleep conceived.

– I shall not see your face again
16 Queen Begone ~~creature~~ more ~~animal~~ ~~than man~~
17 ~~I shall~~ not see ~~your living~~ face ~~again~~
back
(~~She slowly drops her~~ She turns towards him, her ~~bak~~ to
the audience & slowly drops her veil)

7/8

10

Queen.
Stop singing stop — stop — pray if you can pray

Swineherd.
There is a story in my country of a woman
That stood all bathed in blood — a drop of blood
Entered her womb & there begat a child

Queen
I shall be queen of you when you are dead
Though they shall bury you, you hear I shall not look on
all [illegible] I [illegible] your blood.

Swineherd
She sinks in sleep
Her body in the [illegible] sleep conceived.

~~She [illegible] toward him. Her head is [illegible] the audience. She drops her veil.~~

The attendants begin the ~~folding of~~ unfolding of the ~~curtain~~ cloth, or close draw
close the stage curtain

First attendant. What are you to sing.

Second attendant. The song ~~[illegible]~~ by that
ancient [illegible] queen, who had five her
Cover them up & stitch.

First attendant. But this has nothing, to do with this place,
this was quite a different queen.

Second attendant. I must do what he told me to do

[NLI 8906, 10r] [*VPl*, 116–126]

~~7~~ ~~8~~
10

Queen
Stop laughing stop – stop – pray if you can pray

Swineherd.
There is a story in my country of a woman
That stood all bathed in blood – a drop of blood
Entered her womb and there begat a child

Queen
I shall be quit of you when you are dead
Though they shall bring your head I shall not touch it
Why should I touch your blood.

Swineherd
She sank in sleep
Her body in that sleep conceived.

She turns towards him. Her back is to the audience. She drops the veil.

cloth
The attendants begin the ~~folding &~~ unfolding of the ~~curtain~~, or else ~~draw~~ close the stage curtain

First attendant.
you
What are ~~we~~ to sing.

Second Attendant.
The
~~That~~ song ~~men supposed to be sung by~~ that ancient Irish queen, who had put her lovers head upon a stake.

First Attendant. But that has nothing to do with this place, ⨁ that was quite a different queen.

Second Attendant. I must do what he told me to do

At some stage Yeats's numbering of the individual sheets in the manuscript got out of order.

10–12 A reference to Yeats's story "The Binding of the Hair" from *The Secret Rose* (London: Lawrence & Bullen, 1897).

11

Second attendant sings the song,
~~Flas[?]~~ of the severed head from the lute in King of the Great Clock
Tower. When the curtain is parted or the cloth folded up again.
The queen is seen standing exactly as before the dropped veil
at her side, but she holds above her the severed head, the
same head. Her hands are red, there are small red blotches
on her, there must be no realism — red gloves, red
cloth masks, seem [?] of harmony or pollen stone
suggests the blood. She ~~[illegible]~~

Second
~~First attendant: she is drenched with blood, & [illegible]~~ (?) ([illegible])

First
~~Second attend. she has begun to sing (He sings)~~

Second attendant. ~~You drown her head & her breast~~ Her lips are moving,

First attendant. she has begun to sing. ~~(attendant sings as queen)~~

Second atten. What is she singing? Come near that. So
that I can hear.

First attendant. (singing, as queen)
Child & darling, hear my song
Never cry I did you wrong
Cry that wrong came not from me
But my virgin cruelty.

Great my love before you came
~~Greater in~~
Greater when I loved in shame
Greatest when there broke from me
Storm of virgin cruelty

[NLI 8906, 11[r]] [*VPl*, stage direction and 151–161]

~~9~~ 11

Second Attendant sings the song
~~The song~~ of the severed head from the note in King of the Great Clock
Tower. When the curtain is parted or the cloth folded up again,
The Queen is seen standing exactly as before the dropped veil
at her side, but she holds above her severed head of the
swine heard. Her hands are red, there are ~~read~~ red blotches
on her, these must not be realistic – red gloves, red
cloth making some kind of harmony or pattern should
~~in a dance lays the head upon the ground~~
suggest the blood. She ~~in a dance lays the head upon~~ the throne
& ~~kneels before it~~.

Second
~~First Attendant~~ ~~She is drenc[?h]ed by his blood, and yet~~

First
~~Second Attendant~~ ~~Listen she has begun to sing. (he sings)~~
~~Yet draws her head to her breast~~

Second Attendant. Her lips are moving

First Attendant She has begun to sing. ~~(He sings as queen)~~

Second Attendant. What is she singing I cannot hear ~~her~~. Ah
now I can hear.

First Attendant. (singing as queen)
Child and darling hear my song
Never cry I did you wrong
Cry that wrong came not from me
But my virgin cruelty.

Great my love before you came
~~Greatest w~~
Greater when I loved in shame
Greatest when there broke from me
Storm of virgin cruelty.

---

sd The "song" the Attendant is to sing is "He had famished in a wilderness," printed with no introduction or explanation at the conclusion to the "Commentary on 'The Great Clock Tower'" in the Cuala edition of *KGCT*.

8–15 The Queen's song has been copied with few emendations from NLI 30,336 c, 5[v].

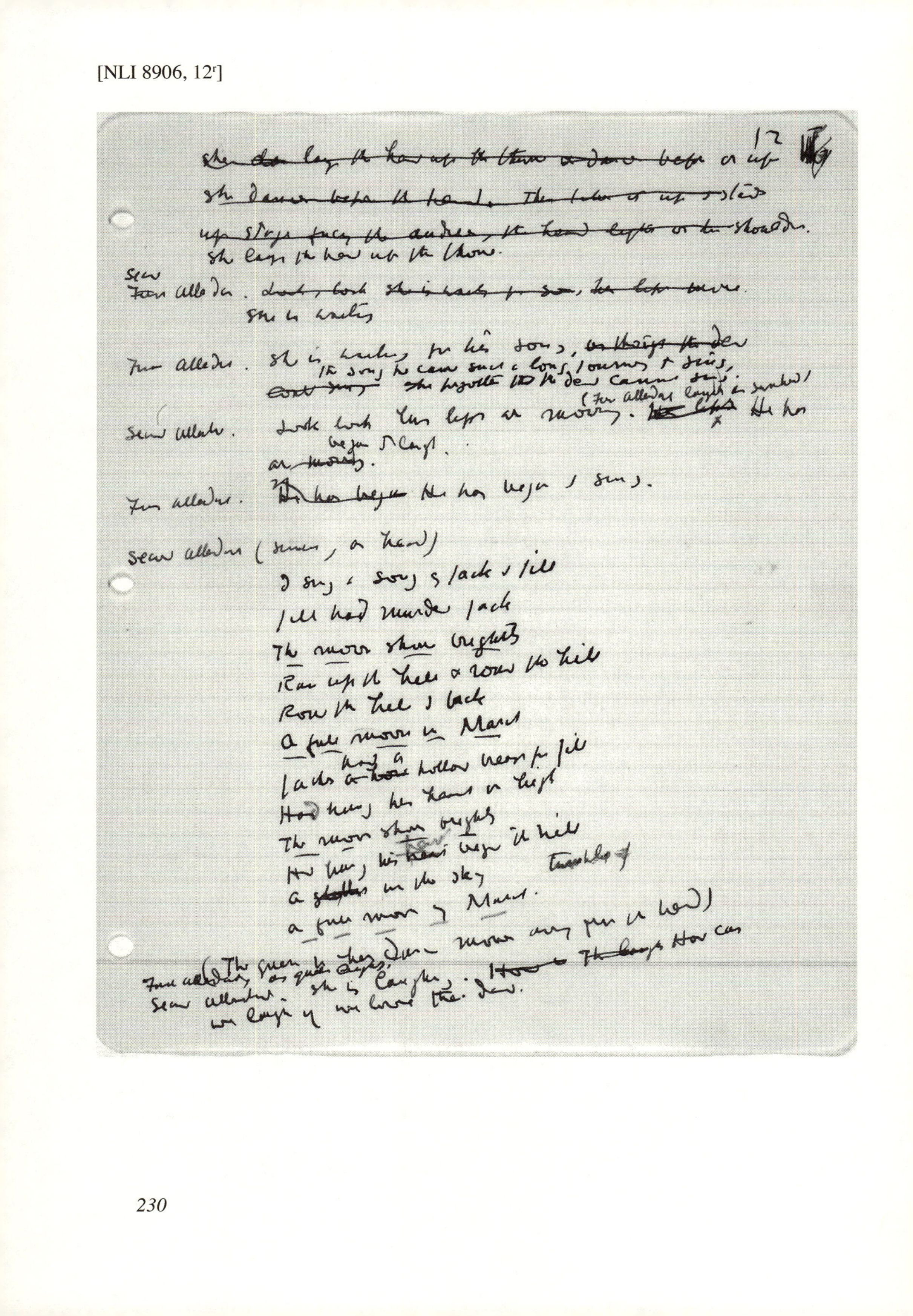

[NLI 8906, 12r]

[NLI 8906, 12r] [*VPl*, stage direction and 162–165]

12
~~11~~

~~she dan lays the head upon the throne & dances before~~ or upon
she~~ dances before the head. Then takes it up and~~ stands
~~up stage facing the audience, the head lifted on her~~ shoulder.
She lays the head upon the throne.

Second
~~First~~ Attendant ~~Look, look she is waiting for song, his lips m~~ove.
She is waiting.

First Attendant. She is waiting for his song, ~~as though the dead~~
the song he came such a long journey to sing,
~~could sing~~ She forgotten that the dead cannot sing.

(First Attendant laughs as swineherd)

Second Attendant Look look his lips are moving. ~~His lips~~ He has
begun to laugh. ^
~~are moving~~.

~~It~~
First Attendant ~~He has begun~~ He has begun to sing.

[NLI 8906, 12r]

[NLI 8906, 12^{r}, continued] [*VPl*, 166–178]

Second Attendant (singing as head)

I sing a song of Jack and Jill
Jill had murdered Jack
The moon shone brightly
Ran up the hill & round the hill
Round the hill and back
A full moon in March
had a
Jacks ~~a hor~~ hollow breast for Jill
Ha*d* hung his heart on high
The moon shone brightly
heart
Had hung his ~~hart~~ beyond the hill
A ~~glitter~~ in the sky twinkle /
A full moon in March.

(The queen in her dance moves away from the head)

First Attendant as queen laughs

Second Attendant. She is laughing. ~~How c The laughs~~ How can we laugh if we love the dead.

20 Underlining is in pencil.

[NLI 8906, 13r]

For Alden.

She is crazy, that is why she is laughing. (He laughs again) TR

(The dance expresses ~~allurement~~ refusal. She takes up the head & lays it upon the ground. She dances B before it. Her dance is a dance of simulation. She takes up head & dances with the head to drum taps, which grow quicker & quicker. Her dance expresses the sexual act. She kisses the head ~~& sinks slowly down holding it to~~ Her body shivers. She sinks slowly down — holding the head against her breast.

Song of the closing of the curtain or of the unfolding & folding of the cloth. The song at the end of Clock Tower with the tune — then description of the lovers' night.

[NLI 8906, 13r] [*VPl*, 179 and ensuing stage direction]

~~12~~
13

First Attendant

1 She is crazy, that is why she is laughing. (He laughs again)

(The dance expresses ~~alluring~~ refusal. She takes up the
head and lays it upon the ground. She dances
before it. Her dance is a dance of invitation. She
takes up head & dances with the head
to drum taps, which grow quicker and quicker. Her
dance expresses the sexual act. She kisses the head
& ~~sinks slowly down holding the he~~ Her body shivers.
She sinks slowly down – holding the head against her breast.

Song of the closing of the curtain or of the unfolding and folding
of the cloth. The song at the end of Clock Tower
with the line 'Their desecration and the lovers night.

sd The reference in the last two lines to "the song at the end of Clock Tower" instructs the typist to copy the verses from the Cuala edition of *KGCT*.

Part II. *A Full Moon in March*

J. The First Typescript: HRC

HRC is the original top copy of which NLI 30,186 and JRL1 are carbon copies. JRL1 is the actual copy text used for setting the play in *Poetry* (Chicago, March 1935). HRC was corrected and revised by Yeats in black ink; the other two copies were subsequently emended to incorporate most of the changes. The typist simply erased the original text on the carbon copy (not always fully) and typed the emendations in or near the erased text. Some revisions, however, appear in holograph in all three copies. The typescript that served as copy text (JRL1) has been heavily worked over with annotations in pencil (dated "March 1935") as it was prepared by the editors for typesetting and publication. As these markings are not by Yeats and do not affect the text of the play in any way, they are not recorded here. JRL2 comprises the galley proofs of the play for publication in *Poetry*, which Yeats corrected. Although the proofs arrived too late for the publication date for his revisions to be incorporated into the text printed in *Poetry*, they are recorded here, since several involve redraftings of the play that were not included in the text in the first edition of *A Full Moon in March*, published by Macmillan in 1935.

Two aspects of the revisions to HRC merit comment. The stage directions as originally typed offer a choice of settings: within a conventional proscenium theater with curtains (as in the Abbey production of *The King of the Great Clock Tower*), or with use of the more stylized ritual folding and unfolding of a cloth (as envisaged for productions of his *Four Plays for Dancers*). Yeats systematically cut all reference to the first option in HRC, leaving the second method as prescriptive. This change was followed through to the first printed version of the play in *Poetry*. However, Macmillan's edition of the play eliminates references to a ritualized presentation, revising the directions to leave a conventional staging as prescriptive. When that significant change occurred is not revealed by any extant materials, but it may have been when Yeats prepared a copy of the play for a possible production by Nancy Price and made a number of small but important revisions. Yeats's continuing indecision about how to assign lines between the two attendants relates to his initial expectation that the roles would be played by two men, as in *The King of the Great Clock Tower* (the directions in *Poetry* specify one tenor, one bass). Over the process of fine-tuning, perhaps again in response to Price's desire to direct the play, the vocal registers were changed to soprano and bass, and, unusually amongst his dance plays, the roles were further characterized in the Macmillan text as "an elderly woman and a young man." The potential for that change was latent within his earliest drafts for the final lyric (see p. 87).

[HRC]

[1r] [*VPl*, 1–22]

A Full Moon in March

"~~THE LOVER'S NIGHT~~"

~~Enter the Three Attendants necessary for the unfolding & folding of the cloth as in The~~

Enter Three Attendants.

FIRST ATTENDANT: **What are we to do? What part do we take in the Play? Did he tell you that?**

SECOND ATTENDANT: **He said we were to join in wherever we thought it necessary, singing or speaking.**

FIRST ATTENDANT: **But what are we to do ~~now~~ before the Play begins?**

---

found in HRC, 1r–10r *transcribed above and below, pp. 239–252*
JRL1
NLI 30,186
JRL2
published in *P, FMIM(M)*

---

persons *lacking JRL1, NLI 30,186, JRL2, P* CHARACTERS / FIRST ATTENDANT / SECOND ATTENDANT / THE QUEEN / THE SWINEHERD *FMIM(M)*

sd *lacking JRL1, NLI 30,186, JRL2, P* The Swineherd wears a half-savage mask covering the upper part of his face. He is bearded. When the inner curtain rises for the second time the player who has hitherto taken the part of the Queen is replaced by a dancer. *FMIM(M)*

title *JRL1, NLI 30,186, JRL2, FMIM(M), P as rev HRC*

1*sd* *JRL1, NLI 30,186, JRL2, P as rev HRC*

When the stage curtain rises, two Attendants, an elderly woman and a young man, are discovered standing before an inner curtain. *FMIM(M)*

1–11 *JRL1, NLI 30,186; JRL2 as rev HRC*

FIRST ATTENDANT What do we do?
What part do we take?
What did he say?
SECOND ATTENDANT Join when we like,
Singing or speaking.
FIRST ATTENDANT Before the curtain rises on the play?
SECOND ATTENDANT Before it rises.
FIRST ATTENDANT What do we sing?
SECOND ATTENDANT 'Sing anything, sing any old thing,' said he.
FIRST ATTENDANT Come then and sing about the dung of swine. *FMIM(M)*

2 play *JRL2*

5 play *JRL2*

The typist's occasionally uneven left margins in HRC have been regularized in the transcription. The annotations to the text of HRC collate that typescript with the two carbon copies (NLI 30,186 and JRL1), the corrected proofs (JRL2), *P*, and *FMIM(M)*. In *VPl*, R. K. Alspach collates *FMIM(M)* with *P* and the texts published in *The Herne's Egg and Other Plays* (New York, 1938) and *Collected Plays* (London, 1952; New York, 1953).

Stage directions in all the proofs and printed texts are in italics. Yeats's revisions are in black ink.

title Yeats had at various stages tried "The Severed Head," "The Swine Herd," and "The Lovers' Night" before settling here on *A Full Moon in March*.

SECOND ATTENDANT: **We are to sing, of course.**

FIRST ATTENDANT: **But what?**

SECOND ATTENDANT: **At first he said any love song ~~you~~** I **could**
remember. And then he said that ~~you~~ I **must**
sing that song with the line:
"Crown of gold, dung of Swine"

SECOND ATTENDANT sings, unfolding/ and folding a cloth as in the Hawk's well, ~~or parting the curtains as in the "King of The Great Clock Tower~~. THE FIRST ATTENDANT may join in singing the burden at the end of the first or second verse.) The FIRST ATTENDANT has a tenor voice; the SECOND ATTENDANT a bass voice.

SECOND ATTENDANT: **Every loutish lad in love**
Thinks his wisdom great enough,
What cares love for this and that?
To make all his parish stare,
As though Pythagoras wandered there
Crown of gold or dung of swine

Should old Pythagoras fall in love
Little may be boast thereof.
What cares love for this and that?
Days go by in foolishness.
Oh, how great their sweetness is
Crown of gold or dung of swine

11*sd* They slowly part the inner curtain. The Second Attendant sings—the First Attendant may join in the singing at the end of the first or second verse. The First Attendant has a soprano, the Second a bass voice. *FMIM(M)*

16 wandered there. *JRL1, NLI 30,186, JRL2, P*

---

23 Holograph underlining by Yeats.

[HRC]

[2r] [*VPl*, 23–36]

2.

Second Attendant: **Open wide those gleaming eyes,**
That can make the loutish wise.
What cares love for this and that?
Make a leader of the schools
Thank the Lord, all men are fools.
Crown of gold or dung of swine.

When the cloth has been folded ~~or the Curtain has been parted~~, the THREE ATTENDANTS ~~necessary for the first, or the TWO ATTENDANTS necessary for the second~~, sit at one or both sides of the stage, where it is nearest to the Stage. They may find there, or have placed there at their first entrance, gong, drum, flute and zither. ~~Whatever the Play requires may be their work~~.

THE QUEEN is discovered seated and veiled.

THE QUEEN: **(Stretching and yawning)**

What man is at the door?

First Attendant: **Nobody, Queen.**

QUEEN: **Some man has come, some terrifying man**
For I have yawned and stretched myself three times.
,Admit him, Captain of the Guard . . . .

First Attendant: **He comes.**

(Enter THE SWINEHERD)

THE SWINEHERD: **The beggars of my country say that he**
That sings you best, shall take you for a wife.

2r, 6*sd* *JRL1, NLI 30,186 rev by typist as HRC; JRL2 prints rev JRL1 but* nearest to the Stage *rev to* nearest to the audience *JRL2* They sit at one side of stage near audience. If they are musicians, they have beside them drum, flute and zither. The Queen is discovered seated and veiled. *FMIM(M)*

7 First] Second *FMIM(M)*

10 ,Admit *rev to* Admit *JRL1* Admit *JRL2, P, FMIM(M)*
Second Attendant (speaking as Captain of the Guard) He comes. *FMIM(M)*

~~QUEEN~~: **~~He that si~~**

QUEEN: **He that best sings his passion**

THE SWINEHERD: **And they say**
The kingdom is added to the gift.

[3r] [*VPl*, 36–57]

3.

Queen: **So have I sworn.**

Swineherd: **But what if some blind aged crippled man,**
Or some base beggar in his famine sing
Better than wholesome men.

Queen: **Some I reject.**
No man abhorrent to these eyes can sing
Some I have punished for their impudence.

Swineherd: **So that's the catch.**
Look well upon me Queen
My hair is foul and matted – here and there
My flesh seems scarce less ragged than my ~~clothes~~ rags ^
I have crossed many forests and the beasts
Have torn me with their claws – my memory's gone

3r, 1 *JRL1, NLI 30,186 rev as HRC; JRL2, P, FMIM(M) as rev JRL1*

4 men. *rev to* men? *JRL1* men? *JRL2, P, FMIM(M)*

5–6 Some I have punished for their impudence.
None I abhor can sing. *FMIM(M)*

7–8 *JRL1, NLI 30,186 rev as first HRC rev but not cancellation of marks in l. 7; JRL2, P as rev JRL1 but two lines marked to* "print as one line" *in JRL2*

8–12 Queen, look at me, look long at these foul rags,
At hair more foul and ragged than my rags;
Look on my scratched foul flesh. Have I not come
Through dust and mire? There in the dust and mire
Beasts scratched my flesh; my memory too is gone, *FMIM(M)*

9 matted *rev to* ragged *JRL2* *entire line rev to* At hair more foul and ragged than my rags *FMIM(M)*

10 clothes *rev to* rags. *JRL1, NLI 30,186* rags. *JRL2, P*

2r, 13 The false start above the line was canceled by the typist.

3r, 1 The graphic directs the printer to set as a half line of verse, completing the verse line on 2r, 14.

10 The revision of "clothes" to "rags" establishes a pattern of repetitions (with "foul") in describing the Swineherd. It is made in ink in Yeats's holograph on all three copies, not by the typist, suggesting a late alteration.

[3r, continued] [*VPl*, 36–57]

Because great solititudes have driven me mad
But when I look into a stream, the face
That trembles upon the surface makes me think
My origin was fouler than my rags.

Queen: **But you have passed through perils for my sake;**
Come a great distance. I permit the song.

Swineherd: **Kingdom and lady, if I sing the best?**
But who decides?

Queen: **I and my heart decide**
We say that song is best that moves us most
No song has moved us yet.

Swineherd: **You must be won**
At a full Moon in March, those beggars say,
That Moon has come but I am here alone.

[4r] [*VPl*, 59–84]

4.

Queen: **Remember ~~what~~ through what perils you have come.**
But I am crueller than solititude,
Forest or beast. Some I have killed or maimed
Because their singing put me in a rage
And some because they came at all. Men hold
kindly
That woman's beauty is a ~~melting~~ thing
^

3r, 13 mad *rev to* mad, *JRL1* mad, *JRL2, P* mad. *FMIM(M)*
14 stream, *rev to* stream *JRL1* stream *JRL2, P* stream, *FMIM(M)*
16 My origin more foul than rag or flesh. *FMIM(M)*
20 decide *rev to* decide. *JRL2* decide. *FMIM(M)*
21 most *rev to* most. *JRL2* most. *FMIM(M)*
23 full Moon *rev to* Full Moon *JRL2* full moon *FMIM(M)* March . . . say *rev to* March, . . . say, *JRL1, NLI 30,186* March, . . . say, *JRL2, P* March, . . . say. *FMIM(M)*
24 moon . . . come, *FMIM(M)*
24/ THE QUEEN No other man has come.
THE SWINEHERD The moon is full. *FMIM(M)*
4r, 4 rage, *FMIM(M)*
6 *NLI 30,186 rev as HRC* melting thing *rev to* kindly thing, *JRL1* kindly thing. *JRL2, P* kindly thing, *FMIM(M)*

But they that call me cruel, speak the truth
Cruel as the winter of virginity.
But for a reason that I cannot guess
I would not harm you. Go before I change
Why do you stand, your chin upon your breast?

Swineheard: **My mind is running on our marriage night**
Imagining all from the first touch and kiss.

Queen: **What gives you that strange confidence. What makes**
You think that you can move my heart and me?

Swineheard: **Because I look upon you without fear**
~~**God shares with me**~~
I know the thought of God

Queen: **What is that thought?**

Swineheard: **Desiring cruelty, he made you cruel.**
I shall embrace body and cruelty
Desiring both as though I had made both.
You cannot help but yield to such desire.

Queen: **Another question. You bring like all the rest**
Some novel simile some wild hyperbole
Praising my beauty ?

Swineheard: **My memory has returned.** ——————
I tended swine, when I first heard your name.
I rolled among the dung of swine and laughed

4^{r}, 7 cruel, . . . truth *rev to* cruel . . . truth, *JRL1* cruel . . . truth, *JRL2, P, FMIM(M)*
16–17 THE SWINEHERD Because I look upon you without fear.
THE QUEEN A lover in railing or in flattery said
God only looks upon me without fear. *FMIM(M)*
21–22 THE QUEEN You cannot help but yield to such desire.
Another question. You . . . *P*
21 *omitted FMIM(M)*
22 THE QUEEN One question more. You bring like all the rest *FMIM(M)*
24 beauty *rev to* beauty? *JRL1* beauty? *JRL2, P, FMIM(M)*
27 laughed. *FMIM(M)*

4^{r}, 16–17 For an interim revision of these lines see BC, 41^{v}, ll. 1–5 and the accompanying note on p. 265 below.
25 Marks to indicate a half line also appear in JRL1 and NLI 30,186.

[5r] [*VPl*, 85–107]

5.

1 **Swineherd:** **What do I know of beauty?**

2 **Queen:** **Sing the best** ——————
3 **And you are not a Swineherd, but a king.**

4 **Swineherd:** **What do I know of kingdoms. (snapping his fingers) That for kingdoms!**

5 **Queen:** **If by the trembling of my limbs or sudden tears**
6 **I should proclaim your song beyond denial**
7 **More moving than the rest, I leave this throne**
8 **These corridors, the reverence of servants.**
9 **What do I gain?**

10 **Swineherd:** **A song – the night of love** ——————
11 **An ignorant forest and the dung of swine**

(QUEEN leaves throne and comes down stage.)

12 **Queen:** **All here have heard the man and all have judged**
13 **I led him, that I might not seem unjust,**
14 **From point to point established in all eyes**
He has brought hither insult & not love.
15 ~~**But he came here to insult not to love**~~
~~That~~
16 ~~**But he has brought an insult not his love**~~**.**

5r, 3 swineherd *FMIM(M)*
4 kingdoms. *rev to* kingdoms? *JRL1* kingdoms? *JRL2*, *P*, *FMIM(M)*
5–8 If trembling of my limbs or sudden tears
Proclaim your song beyond denial best
I leave these corridors, this ancient house,
A famous throne, the reverence of servants— *FMIM(M)*
8 servants *rev to* servants, *JRL1* servants, *JRL2, P*
10 love *rev to* love, *JRL1* love, *JRL2*, *P*, *FMIM(M)*
11 swine. *FMIM(M)*
12 judged *rev to* judged. *JRL1* judged. *JRL2, P, FMIM(M)*
14 point to point, *FMIM(M)*
15–16 That he came hither not to sing but to heap
Complexities of insult upon my head. *FMIM(M)*

5r, 2, 10 Marks to set as a half line appear also in JRL1 and NLI 30,186.

Swineherd: **She shall bring forth her farrow in the dung**
But first my song – what nonsense shall I sing?

Queen: **Send ~~ofr~~ for the headsman Captain of the Guard.**

First Attendant: **I have sent already, Q[ueen. ——————**
He stands without.

Queen: **I owe my thanks to God that this foul wretch**
Foul in his rags, his origin, his speech
Inspite of all his daring has not dared
Asked me to drop my veil. Insulted ears
Have heard and shuddered, but my face is pure

[6r] [*VPl*, 108–126]

6.

~~Queen~~: **Had it but known the insult of his eyes**
I had torn it with these nails

Swineherd: (Going up Stage)
Why should I ask?
What do those features matter. When I set out
I picked a number on the roulette wheel
I trust the wheel, as every lover must.

Queen: **Pray if your savagery has learnt to pray**
For in a moment they will lead you out
Then bring your severed head.

5r, 17 dung. *FMIM(M)*
19 headsman, *JRL2, P, FMIM(M)*
20 First Attendant (speaking as Captain of the Guard) I have already sent. *FMIM(M)*
20–21 *JRL1, NLI 30,186 rev as HRC; set as one line JRL2, P, FMIM(M)*
22 wretch, *FMIM(M)*
23 speech *rev to* speech, *JRL1* speech, *JRL2, P, FMIM(M)*
25 Asked *rev to* Ask *JRL2* Ask *P, FMIM(M)*
26 pure *rev to* pure. *JRL1* pure. *JRL2, P, FMIM(M)*
6r, 2 nails. *FMIM(M)*
2*sd* Stage *rev to* stage *JRL2* stage *P, FMIM(M)*
3 matter? *FMIM(M)*
4 wheel, *JRL2, P* wheel. *FMIM(M)*
6 Pray, *FMIM(M)*

5r, 20 Marks to set as a half line appear also in JRL1 and NLI 30,186.

[6r, continued] [*VPl*, 108–126]

Swineherd: **My severed head. (<u>laughs</u>)**
9 **There is a story in my country of a woman**
10 **That stood all bathed in blood – a drop of blood**
11 **Entered her womb and there begat a child.**

, foul
12 **Queen:** **Oh, foul, foul^– I shall be quit of him.**
13 **I shall not touch his blood.**

Swineherd: **She sank in sleep,**
14 **Her body in the bridal sleep, conceived.**

15 **Queen:** **Begone! I shall not see your face again.**
(She <u>turns towards him, her back to the</u> a<u>udience, and slowly drops her vei</u>l)
unfold
<u>**ATTENDANTS ~~fold~~ the cloth, ~~or close the stage curtains~~.**</u>

Second
16 **~~First~~ Attendant:** **What are you to sing?**
First
17 **~~Second~~ Attendant:** **The song of that ancient Irish Queen**
18 **Who put her lover's head upon a stake.**
Second
19 **~~First~~ Attendant:** **But that has nothing to do with this Play.**

6r, 8 Laughs. *FMIM(M)*
12 THE QUEEN A severed head! She took it in her hands;
She stood all bathed in blood; the blood begat.
O foul, foul, foul! *FMIM(M)*
12 foul, foul *rev to* foul, foul, foul *JRL1, NLI 30,186* foul, foul, foul— *JRL2, P*
13 *final sentence lacking FMIM(M)*
13–15 SWINEHERD She sank in bridal sleep.
THE QUEEN Her body in that sleep conceived a child.
Begone! . . . . *FMIM(M)*
15*sd* *JRL1 (ink and type), NLI 30,186 (ink) rev as HRC; JRL2, P as rev HRC* veil. / The Attendants close the inner curtain. *FMIM(M)*
16–19 *JRL1, NLI 30,186 rev as HRC; JRL2, P as rev HRC but l. 18* Who *rev to* who *JRL2, and l. 19* Play. *rev to* play; *with the instruction* Print as prose
SECOND ATTENDANT What do we sing?
FIRST ATTENDANT An ancient Irish Queen
That stuck a head upon a stake.
SECOND ATTENDANT Her lover's head;
But that's a different queen,
A different story. *FMIM(M)*

6r, 15*sd* The word "fold" was revised in ink to "unfold" also in JRL1 and NLI 30,186, suggesting a late revision.

[7r] [*VPl*, 126–153]

7.

~~Second~~
~~First~~ Attendant: **That was quite a different Queen.**
First
~~Second~~ Attendant: **~~I must sing what he told me to sing~~.**

He had famished in a wilderness,
Braved lions for my sake,
And all men lie that say that I
Bade that swordsman take
His head from off his body
And set ~~on a stake~~ it on a stake.

He swore to sing my beauty
~~Through death itse~~
Though death itself forbade,
They lie that say in mockery
Of all that lovers said,
Or in mere woman's cruelty
I bade them fetch his head

O what innkeeper's daughter
Shared the Byzantine crown!
Girls that have governed cities,
Or burned great cities down,
Have bedded with their fancy-man
Whether a king or clown;

Gave their bodies, emptied purses
For praise of clown or king
Gave all the love that women know!
O they had their fling
But never stood before a stake
And heard the dead lips sing.

7r, 1 That *rev to* that *JRL2*
2 *sd added* (singing) *JRL2*
11 say, *FMIM(M)*
14 head. *JRL2, P, FMIM(M)* *sd inserted* (They begin to part the inner curtain.) *FMIM(M)*
16 crown? *FMIM(M)*
22 king *rev to* king. *JRL1* king. *JRL2, P* king, *FMIM(M)*
24 fling, *FMIM(M)*

[7^r, continued] [*VPl*, 126–153]

has been again

(When the ~~curtain has been parted or~~ the cloth folded up ^ the QUEEN is discovered standing exactly as before, ^ the dropped veil at her side, but she holds above her head the severed head of the SWINEHERD. Her hands are red. There are red blotches upon her dress, not realistically represented ; red gloves, some pattern of red cloth are sufficient.

2nd
~~**First**~~
~~**Second**~~ **Attendant:** **Her lips are moving.**

First
~~**Second**~~
~~**First**~~ **Attendant:** **She has begun to sing.**

Second
~~**First**~~ **Attendant:** **I cannot hear what she is singing.**
Ah, now I can hear.

7[r], 26*sd* *JRL1, NLI 30,186 rev by typist as HRC* represented; . . . cloth are sufficient.] represented: . . . cloth. *FMIM(M)* sufficient. *rev to* sufficient. The part is now played by a dancer *JRL2*

27 Second *rev to* First *rev to* Second *JRL1, NLI 30,186* Second *JRL2, P* First *FMIM(M)*

28 First *rev to* Second *rev to* First *JRL1, NLI 30,186* First *JRL2, P* Second *FMIM(M)*

29 First *rev to* Second *JRL1, NLI 30,186* Second *JRL2, P* First *FMIM(M)*

7[r], 26*sd* The additions to the directions about the "cloth" make that mode of staging more emphatically prescriptive. The additional underlining was entered by the typist to JRL1 and NLI 30,186. In *FMIM(M)* Yeats's addition to JRL2, "The part is now played by a dancer," was incorporated in the prefatory comments after the list of characters and not repeated here.

27–29 The revisions to the speech prefixes suggest Yeats was thinking of the First Attendant as female, since on 8[r] this Attendant is required to sing "as Queen," while later the Second Attendant is directed to sing "as Head." The revisions smooth the transition into the song.

[8^{r}] [*VPl*, 154–171]

8.

First Attendant (Singing as Queen)

1 **Child and darling, hear my song**
2 **Never cry I did you wrong**
3 **Cry that wrong came not from me**
4 **But my virgin cruelty**

5 **Great my love before you came,**
6 **Greater when I loved in shame,**
7 **Greatest when there broke from me**
8 **Storm of virgin cruelty.**

(THE QUEEN dances and in the dance lays the head upon the throne)

~~1st.~~ 2nd.
9 **~~Second~~/ Attendant:** **She is waiting.**

~~2nd.~~ 1st.
10 **~~First~~ Attendant:** **She is waiting for his song.**
11 **The song he has come such a long way to sing.**
12 **She has forgotten that the dead cannot sing.**

2nd. **head**
~~First~~ Attendant. (Laughs softly as ~~Swineher~~d)
13 **He has begun to laugh.**

14 **1st. Attendant:** **He has begun to sing.**

8^{r}, 1*sd* singing *FMIM(M)*
1 song *rev to* song, *JRL1* song, *JRL2, P, FMIM(M)*
2 wrong *rev to* wrong, *JRL1* wrong, *JRL2, P* wrong; *FMIM(M)*
4 cruelty *rev to* cruelty. *JRL2* cruelty. *FMIM(M)*
5 came *rev to* came, *JRL1* came, *JRL2, P, FMIM(M)*
6 shame *rev to* shame, *JRL1* shame, *JRL2, P, FMIM(M)*
8*sd* dances and . . . throne] dances to drum-taps and . . . throne. *FMIM(M)*
9 Second *rev to* First *rev to* Second *JRL1, NLI 30,186* Second *JRL2, P, FMIM(M)*
9–13 *marked to* print as prose *JRL2*
10 First *rev to* Second *rev to* First *JRL1, NLI 30,186* First *JRL2, P, FMIM(M)* song. *rev to* song, *JRL2*
11 The . . . sing. *rev to* the . . . sing; *JRL2* such . . . way] so many miles *FMIM(M)*
12 She *rev to* she *JRL2* the dead cannot sing] no dead man sings *FMIM(M)*
13*sd* *JRL1, NLI 30,186 rev as HRC* laughs . . . Head *FMIM(M)*
13 First *rev to* Second *JRL1, NLI 30,186* Second *JRL2, P, FMIM(M)*
14 He] No; he *FMIM(M)*

8^{r}, 1–8 Though here and in the manuscripts the song is divided into two stanzas, it was eventually printed in *FMIM(M)* as one.

9–14 The revised prefixes lead more smoothly into the Second Attendant's singing "as Head."

[8^{r}, continued] [*VPl*, 154–171]

2nd. Attendant: **(Singing as head)**

I sing a song of Jack and Jill
Jill had murdered Jack
The moon shone brightly
Ran up the hill, and round the hill,
Round the hill and back.
A full moon in March.

[9^{r}] [*VPl*, 172–182]

9.

2nd. Attendant:

heart
Jack had a hollow/ for Jill
Had hung his heart on high
The moon shone brightly.
Had hung his heart beyond the hill.
A-
lc/ ^ **~~T~~winkle in the sky**
A full Moon in March.

(THE QUEEN in her dance moves away from the head. Alluring and refusing.)

1st. Attendant: **(Laughs as Queen)**

8^{r}, 15*sd* 2nd. *rev to* Second *JRL1* Second *JRL2, P, FMIM(M)* Head *FMIM(M)*
15 Jill *rev to* Jill, *JRL1* Jill, *JRL2, P* Jill. *FMIM(M)*
16 Jack *rev to* Jack, *JRL1* Jack, *JRL2, P* Jack; *FMIM(M)*
17 brightly *rev to* brightly, *JRL1* brightly, *JRL2, P* brightly; *FMIM(M)*
9^{r}, 1 2nd. *rev to* Second *JRL1* Second *JRL2, P, FMIM(M)* heart *rev to* heart, *JRL2* heart, *FMIM(M)* Jill *rev to* Jill, *JRL1* Jill, *JRL2, P*
2 high *rev to* high, *JRL1* high, *JRL2, P* high; *FMIM(M)*
3 brightly, *JRL2, P* brightly; *FMIM(M)*
4 hill. *rev to* hill, *JRL1* hill, *JRL2, P* hill. *FMIM(M)*
5 Twinkle *rev by typist to* A twinkle *JRL1, NLI 30,186* A twinkle *JRL2, P, FMIM(M)* sky *rev to* sky, *JRL1* sky, *JRL2, P* sky. *FMIM(M)*
6 moon *FMIM(M)*
7*sd* 1st. *rev to* First *JRL1* First *JRL2, P, FMIM(M)* laughs *FMIM(M)*

9^{r}, 5 The HRC reading, "A-twinkle," reappears in *The Collected Plays of W. B. Yeats* (London: Macmillan, 1934).

she

2nd. Attendant: **She is laughing. How can ~~we~~ laugh**

she s

if ~~we~~ love^ the dead?

1st. Attendant: **She is crazy. That is why she is laughing.**

(He laughs again as QUEEN)

(QUEEN takes up the head and lays it upon the ground. She dances before it – a dance of adoration. She takes the head up and dances with it to drum taps, which grow quicker and quicker. As the drum taps approach their climax, she presses her lips to the head. Her body shivers~~. The drum taps increase~~ to very rapid drum taps. The drum taps cease. She sinks slowly down, holding the head to her breast.

Song of ~~the closing of the Curtain~~
~~or of~~
the
~~The~~ Folding and Unfolding of the Cloth.

2nd. Attendant:
Why must those holy, haughty feet descend
From emblematic niches and what hand
Ran that delicate raddle through their white?

9ʳ, 7, 10 2nd. *rev to* Second *JRL1* Second *JRL2, P, FMIM(M)*
7–8 *JRL1, NLI 30,186 rev as HRC* How can she laugh if she loves the dead? *JRL2, P* She . . . laugh, / Loving the dead? *FMIM(M)*
9 1st. *rev to* First *JRL1* First *JRL2, P, FMIM(M)*
9*sd, l. 1* He laughs . . . Queen] Laughs . . . Queen. *FMIM(M)*
l. 4 takes the head up *rev in pencil to* takes up the head *JRL2*
ll. 5, 6, 9 drum-taps *FMIM(M)*
l. 7 lips to the lips of the head *FMIM(M)*
l. 8 shivers. The drum taps increase to *rev in pencil to* shivers to *JRL1, NLI 30,186* shivers to *JRL2, P, FMIM(M)*
ll. 11–13 Song of . . . / or of / The *rev in type to* Song / The *JRL1* Song of . . . or of *rev in type to* Song of / The *NLI 30,186* Song. The *JRL2, P* The Attendants close the inner curtain, singing, and then stand one on either side while the stage curtain descends. *FMIM(M)*
10 2nd. *rev to* Second *JRL1* Second *JRL2, P, FMIM(M)*
11 niches, *FMIM(M)*

9ʳ, 7–8 Yeats's holograph revisions HRC, JRL1, and NLI 30,186 suggest a late change.

[HRC]

[10^r^] [*VPl*, 183–197]

10.

~~2nd. Attendant:~~ **My heart is broken, yet must understand.**
What do they seek for? Why must they descend?

1st. Attendant: **For descration and the lover's night.**

2nd. Attendant: **I cannot face that emblem of the moon**
Nor eyelids that the unmixed heavens dart,
Nor stand upon my feet, so great a fright
Descends upon my savage, sunlit heart.
What can she lack whose emblem is the moon?

First Attendant: **But descration and the lover's night.**

2nd. Attendant: **Delight my heart with sound; speak yet again.**
But look and look with understanding eyes
Upon the pitchers that they carry; tight
Therein all time's completed treasure is:
What do they lack? O cry it out again.

First Attendant: **Their descration and the lover's night.**

10r, 2 *rev to* What are they seeking? Why do they descend? *JRL2*
3 1st. *rev to* First *JRL1* First *JRL2, P, FMIM(M)*
4, 10 2nd. *rev to* Second *JRL1* Second *JRL2, P, FMIM(M)*
15/ *inserted* William Butler Yeats *JRL1; JRL2, P print signature*

Part III. *The King of the Great Clock Tower* (Verse)

A. Drafts for a New Song for the Severed Head: BC, 1^v; BC, 40^v–42^r

Yeats's holograph drafts in the Rapallo notebook for a new song for the severed head suggest that the lyric was completed in two creative stages. On 1^v he appears to be jotting down ideas and possible phrasings for a lyric, probably his initial entries for the new song. Despite their fragmentary character, a theme is steadily established that at first discriminates between love among the living and the more charged but platonic nature of love among the dead, and then moves into musing on the possibility of a union between the dead and the living, elements that form the substance of the final version. From the beginning, particularly in the repeated refrains, there is a mounting tension concerning the passage of time and the imminence of midnight, when all the suppositions defined in the lyric will be put to the test. Dissatisfied with the song for the severed head in the prose version of *The King of the Great Clock Tower*, Yeats may have begun this alternative while drafting the material on surrounding pages, BC, 1^r and 2^r, about O'Rourke and his tortured relations with women, material with which this new lyric has some thematic resonance (the quality of the ink and the holograph are similar on this sequence of pages, 1^r, 1^v, 2^r). But it is equally possible that he returned to a blank 1^v at some later date to sketch out an idea that he then returned to in earnest on 40^v through 42^r. What is clear, as was the case with *A Full Moon in March*, is that he completed the new lyrical material for the song before versifying *The King of the Great Clock Tower*, the drafts for which begin directly after the fullest version in the notebook of "Clip and lip and long for more," on 42^r. An account of the development of the lyric through these notebook pages may help in understanding the relationships among the several drafts.

Some time after sketching the material on 1^v, Yeats turned to 40^v to redraft the song. If the order of material within the bound pages of the Rapallo notebook is roughly chronological, then between the first and second drafts of this song he probably worked on the lyrics and dialogue of *A Full Moon in March*, many of the poems and "Supernatural Songs" that he included in either the Cuala edition of *The King of the Great Clock Tower* (1934) or the Macmillan edition of *A Full Moon in March* (1935), and several unpublished poems addressed to Margot Ruddock.

On 41^r are the poet's reworkings of sequences of lines from the full lyric on the facing verso. Each fragment is roughly paired opposite the portion of the individual stanza to which it relates. All but the concluding lines come near to final form. Yeats continues on 42^r, where he starts what looks like an attempt at a clean copy of the song but soon engages in a flurry of corrections, notably the ominous "and it tolls midnight" as the concluding line to each stanza. The final two stanzas are eventually heavily crossed through, and a cleaner copy of these is next attempted on 41^v. To give a clear sense of how these sequences evolved, therefore, 42^r is transcribed first. On 41^v, four lines of verse unrelated to either play give way to redrafting of the second and third stanzas of the song.

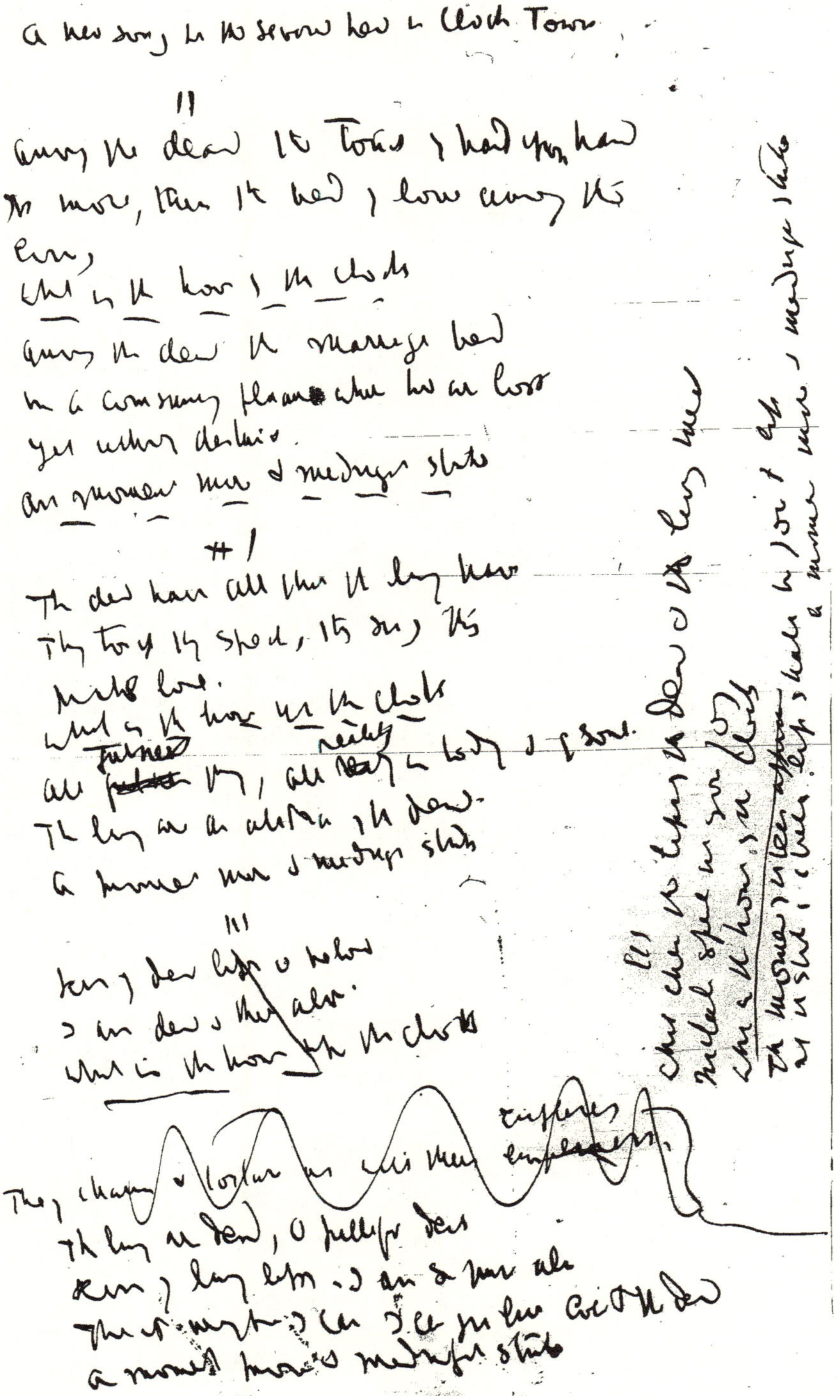

[BC, 1[v]] [*VPl*, 131–151]

A new song for the severed head in Clock Tower

II

1 Among the dead the touch of hand upon hand
2 Is more, than the bed of love among the living,
3 What is the hour of the clock
4 Among the dead the marriage bed
5 Is a consuming flame where [?all /?lives] are lost
6 Yet without [?destruction]
7 A moment more & midnight strikes

~~II~~ I

8 The dead have all that the living have
9 They touch, they speak, they sing they make love
10 What is the hour upon the clock
fullness reality
11 All ~~fullness~~ [?there /?they], all ~~realy~~ in looking at the soul
12 The living are the abstracts of the dead.
13 A moment more & midnight strikes

III

14 Kiss of dead lips is [?beloved /?below]
15 I am dead & [?they/ ?then /?thou] alive
16 What is the hour upon the clock
[?emptiness/influences]
17 They charm and torture us with their ~~emptiness~~

18 The living are dead, O [?pitiful] dead
19 [?Kiss] of living before. I am [?so] [?much] [?alive]
20 Then it may be I can [?I] [?can] [?feel] [?love] [?even] for the dead
21 A moment more & midnight strikes

III

22 What when the lips of the dead & the living meet
23 [?] speak in your joy
24 What is the hour upon the clock
25 The moment of intense [?affinity]
26 At instant I speak lip shall be joined to lip
27 A moment more & midnight strikes

---

found in BC, 1[v], 40[v]–42[r] *transcribed above and below, pp. 257–265*

1–7 After reordering, the new second stanza states what will be the theme of the finished lyric but without that version's poetic evocation of an imaginary and mystical experience.

8–13 Only the conception of the living as the "abstracts" of the dead survives in later revision.

17 This isolated line is canceled but also clued by an arrow to replace canceled wording from the sketch concerning O'Rourke on 2[r]. The presence of this line may indicate that this first attempt at the "new song" was undertaken after the material that faces it.

22–27 The alternative version comes closer than the first attempt in ll. 14–17 to evoking the "marvel" that can occur in relations between dead and living.

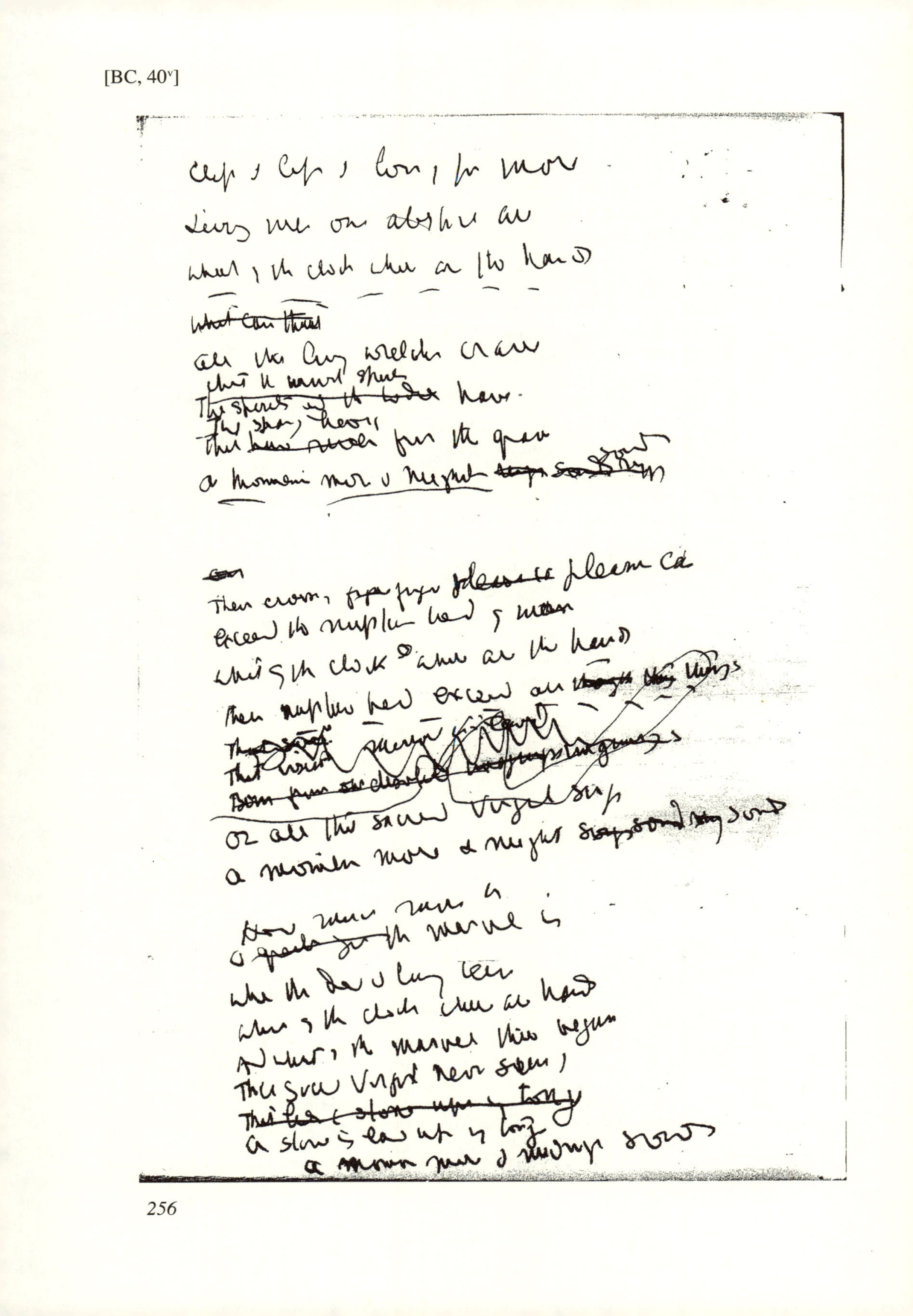

[BC, 40v]

[BC, 40v] [*VPl*, 131–151]

1 Clip & lip & long for more
2 Living men our abstracts are
3 What of the clock where are the hands?
~~What can threat~~
4 All those living wretches crave
What the [?immortal] spirits
5 ~~The spirits and the bodies~~ have
That sprang heroic
6 That ~~have risen~~ from the grave
sounds
7 A moment more & mi[?dni]ght ~~rings sounds rings~~

~~Our~~
8 Teir crossed ~~figne~~ fingers ~~pleasure ca~~ pleasure can
9 Exceed the nuptial bed of man
10 What of the clock? Where are the hands
11 Their nuptial bed exceed all ~~thought thing~~ things
~~That [?since]~~
That ~~vision mirror in lewd~~
12 ~~Born from our desolate imaginings imaginings~~
13 Or all that sacred Virgil sings
14 A moment more & midnight ~~sings sound ring~~ sounds

How much more the
15 ~~O greater far~~ the marvel is
16 When the dead and living kiss
17 What of the clock where are hands
18 And what of the marvel there begun
19 That sacred Virgil never sung
~~That lies a stone upon my tongue~~
20 A stone is laid upon my tongue
21 A moment more & midnight sounds

11 Broken underlining indicates the words are to remain despite the overlapping cancellation from l. 12

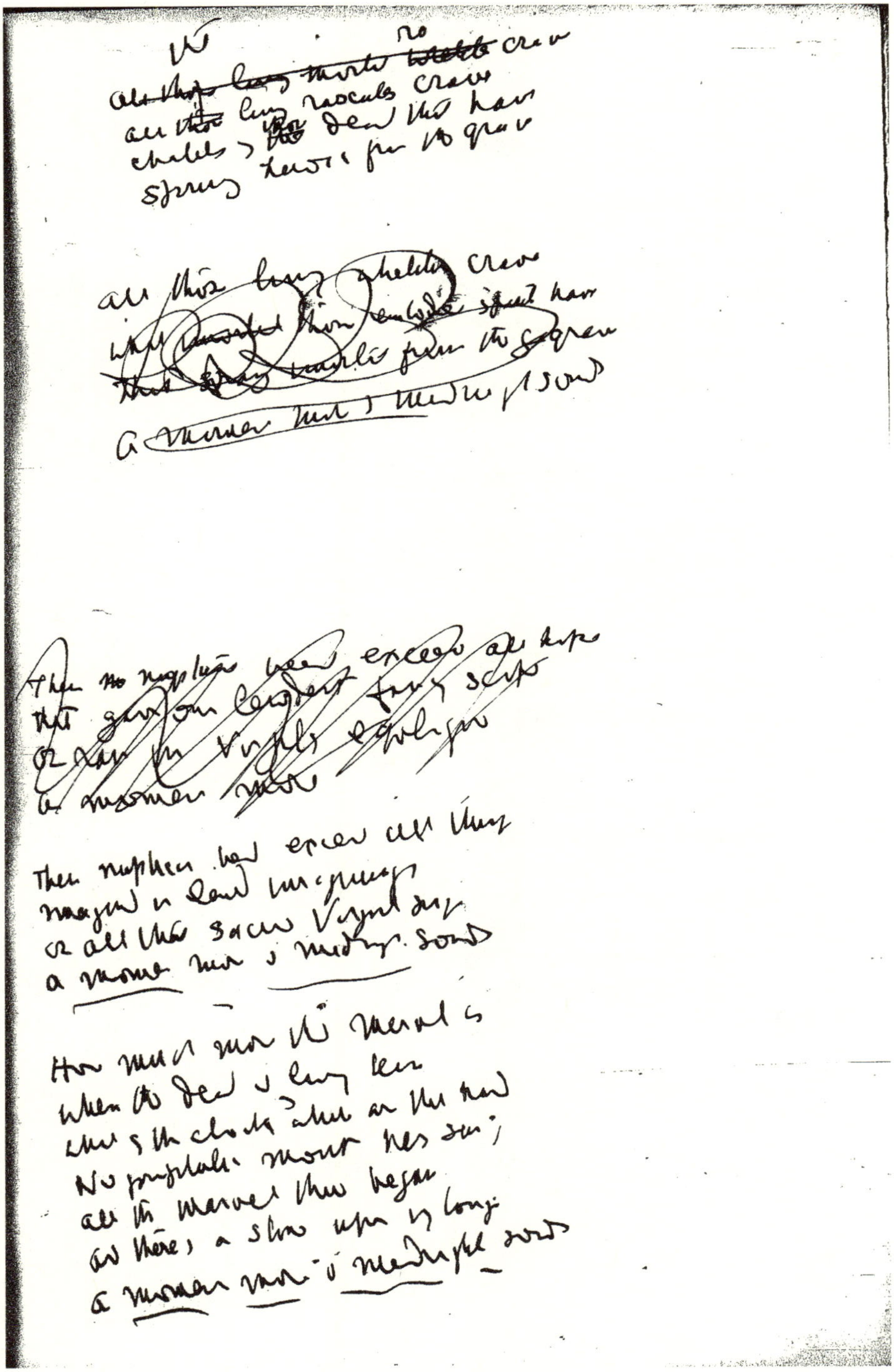

[BC, 41[r]] [*VPl*, 134-151]

that no
~~All those living mortal wretches~~ crave
All ~~those~~ living rascals crave
those
[?Ability] of the dead that have
Sprung heroic from the grave

All those living wretches crave
What ~~immortal~~ those embodied spirits have
That sprang immortal from the ~~g~~ grave
<u>A moment more &</u> midnight sounds

Their ~~ni~~ nuptial bed exceed all hope
That gave our lewdest fancy scope
Or ran in Virgil's eclogue
A moment more

Their nuptial bed exceed all things
Imagined in lewd imaginings
Or all that sacred Virgil sings
A <u>moment</u> m<u>or</u>e <u>& midnight</u> sounds

How much more the marvel is
When the dead and living kiss
What of the clock? where are the hands
No prophetic mouth has sung
All the marvel there begun
And there s a stone upon my tongue
A <u>moment more & midnight so</u>unds

20 The image of prophecy first enters the lyric at this juncture, later transformed to the commanding rhetorical question that eventually opens this stanza.

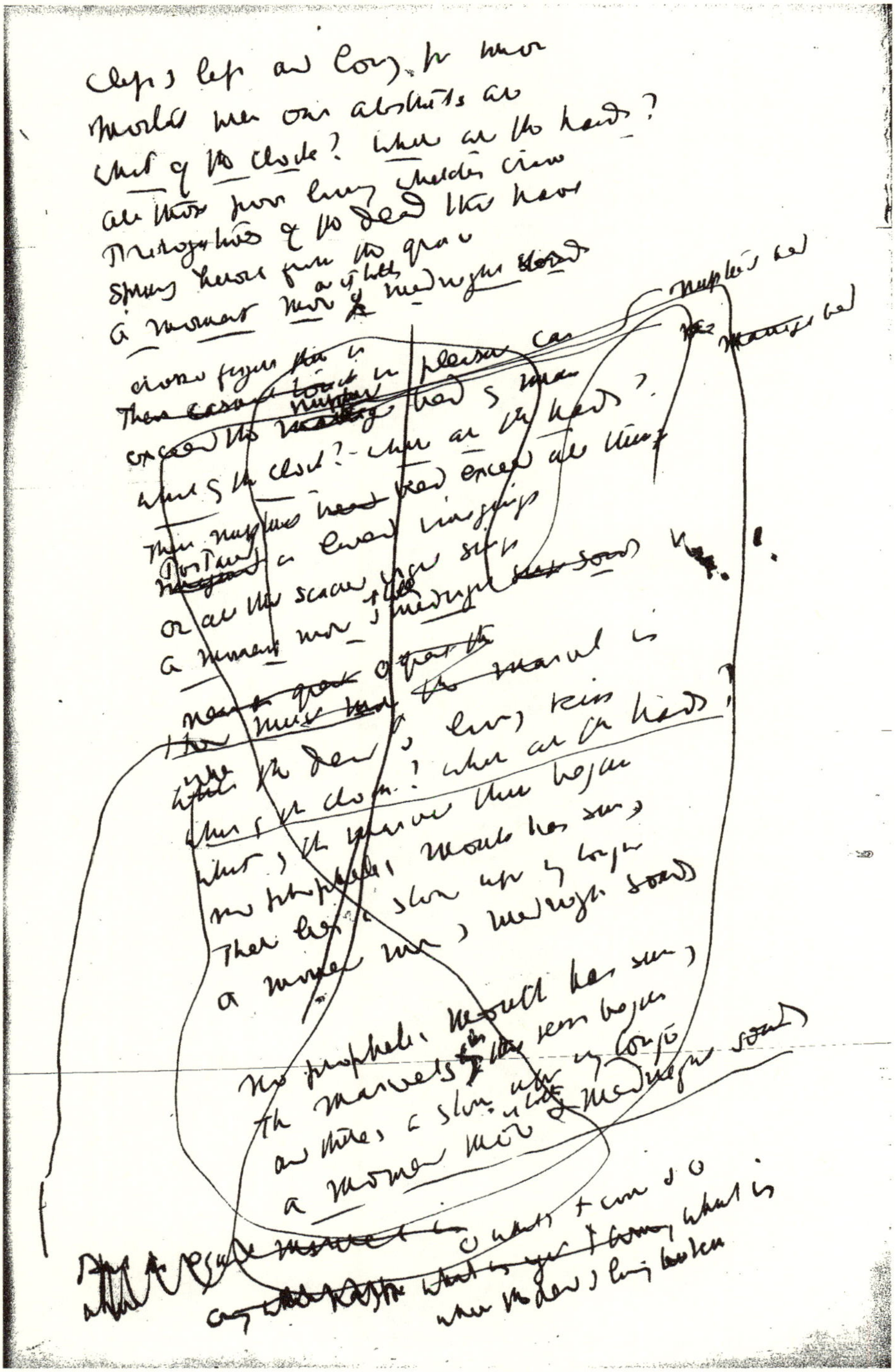

[BC, 42r] [*VPl*, 131-151]

Clip & lip and long for more
Mortal men our abstracts are
What of the clock? Where are the hands?
All those poor living wretches crave
Prerogatives of the dead that have
Sprung heroic from the grave
and it tolls
A moment more & midnight ~~sounds~~

Crossed fingers there in
~~There casual touch~~ in pleasure can nuptial bed
nuptial
Exceed the ~~marriage~~ bed of man ~~marriage~~ bed
What of the clock? – Where are the hands?
Their nuptial ~~bead~~ bed exceed all things
Portaining
~~Imagined~~ in lewd imaginings
Or all that sacred Virgil sings
it tolls
A moment more & midnight ~~sings~~ ~~sounds~~
~~Never as great~~ O ~~great the~~
~~How~~ mu~~ch more the ma~~rvel is
Where
~~When~~ the dead & living kiss
What of the clock? Where are the hands?
What of the marvel there begun
No prophetic mouth has sung
There lies a stone upon my tongue
A moment more & midnight sounds

16–23 The replacement arrow reaches from l. 17 down to l. 28 at the foot; see p. 263.

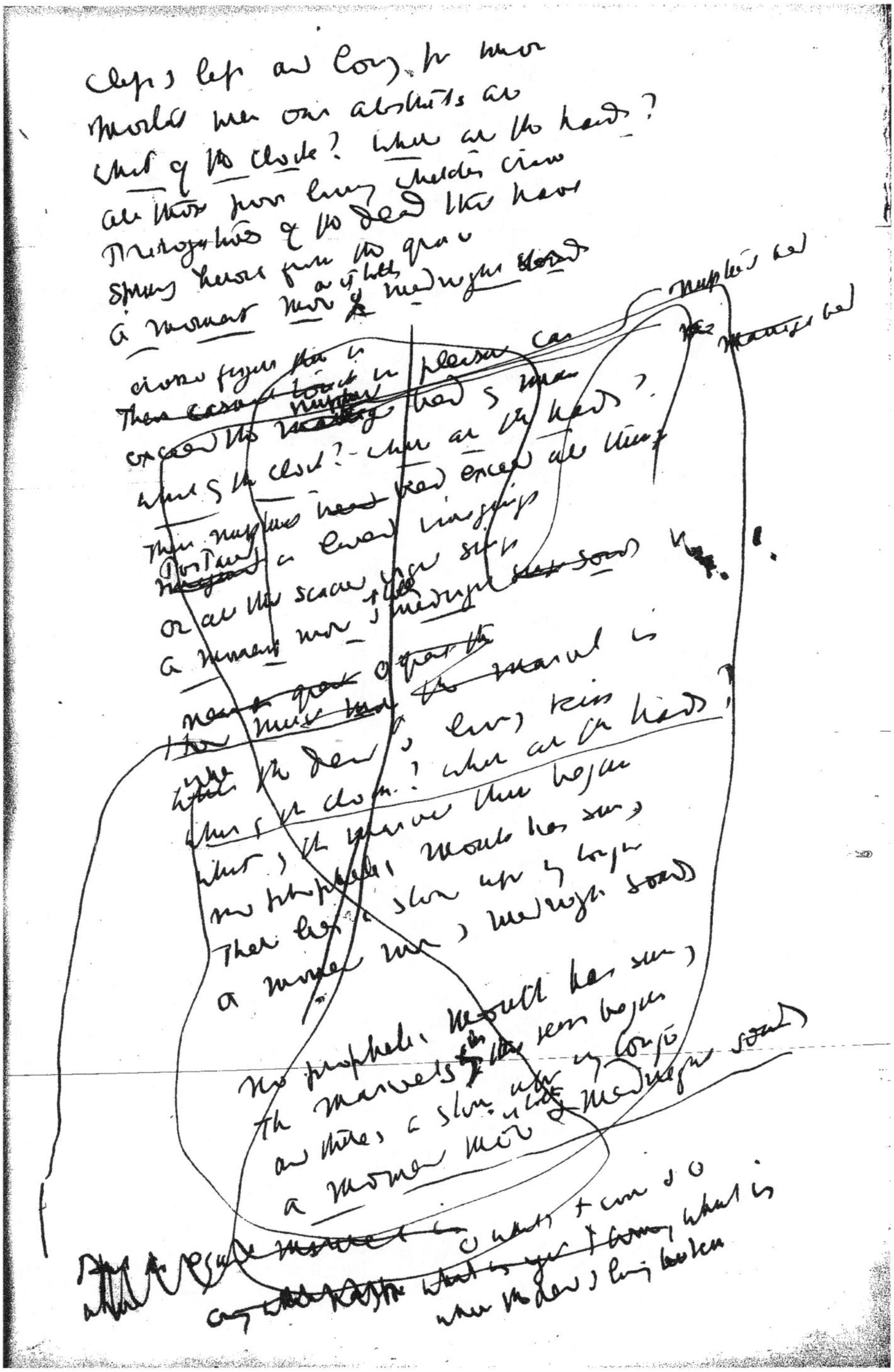

[BC, 42r, continued] [*VPl*, 131-151]

No prophetic mouth has sung
                    in
The marvels [?~~by~~] this sense begun
And there's a stone upon my tongue
                    <u>i</u>t tolls
<u>A moment more & midnight</u> <u>~~sounds~~</u>

~~But how great marvel is~~
~~When~~
                                        O what's to come & O
                        C~~ry with passion~~ w~~hat is yet to come~~, what is
                                        When the dead & living ~~bi~~ kiss

29–30 These two lines are partially run through with the marks that cancel ll. 8–28; Yeats probably meant to cancel them as well.

[BC, 41ᵛ]

Yet I know how *bodily loves* say
This yes loves I *seek* in in t flatter say
Those *of of* too too *lit its* lither *flow*
That my *could too* that.

This meeting fingers
Hands then *closer* Heaven can
ever the *rapture* between
that is the hand on th great clock for
Oh then *rapture beds* exceed all this
Boys or puberty have things
or Sibyls in them in a freshness sages
a moment more *at* both *mednight*

What is *jupiter*, what is
when the dew is long seen?
where is th hand on the great clock for
sacred sage never *stay* *son suns*
are th *minuet* their *bejus*.
And this, a shoe upon my *loin*
a moment more at th both mednight

[BC, 41[v]] [*VPl*, 75–76, 138–151]

Yet I have heard reviling lovers say
~~That~~
Yet lovers to revile me or to flatter say
~~That only God can look upon me without fear~~
That only God does that.

Their meeting fingers'
~~Hands there clasped in~~ pleasure can
Exceed the nuptial bed [~~?~~]‸man of ⁄
What of the hands on the great clock face
~~A~~ Their
[?~~Man~~] nuptial beds ~~en~~ exceed all that
Boys at puberty have thought
sibyls
Or ~~sybells~~ ~~in their~~ in a ~~frez~~ frenzy sought
A moment more and it tolls midnight

What is prophesied, what is
Where the dead & living kiss
What of the hands on the great clock face
Sacred Virgil never ~~sung sin~~ sung
All the marvel there begun
And there's a stone upon my tongue
A moment more and it tolls midnight

1–5 These trial lines are unrelated to the "Song for the Severed Head" or to *FMIM(K)*. They comprise an interim revision of the exchange between Queen and Swineherd that chronologically must have been attempted between HRC (see above, p. 243, ll. 16–20 and note) and the text as printed in *FMIM(M)*, which reads: "A lover in railing or in flattery said / God only looks upon me without fear" (*VPl.* ll. 75–76).

5 Random marks appear to cancel part of this line.

Part III. *The King of the Great Clock Tower* (Verse)

B. First Draft in the Rapallo Notebook: BC, 42v–46v

The Rapallo notebook contains the first draft in verse of the *The King of the Great Clock Tower*. It is throughout in the same black ink as the drafts for the new song of the severed head, which are closely associated with it. Composition follows a characteristic Yeatsian pattern: immediate reworkings are attempted to lines or short passages when they fail to satisfy on the first try. Progress is therefore somewhat halting and fragmentary, as Yeats relies on earlier versions to supply speech prefixes, stage directions, and lyrical passages.

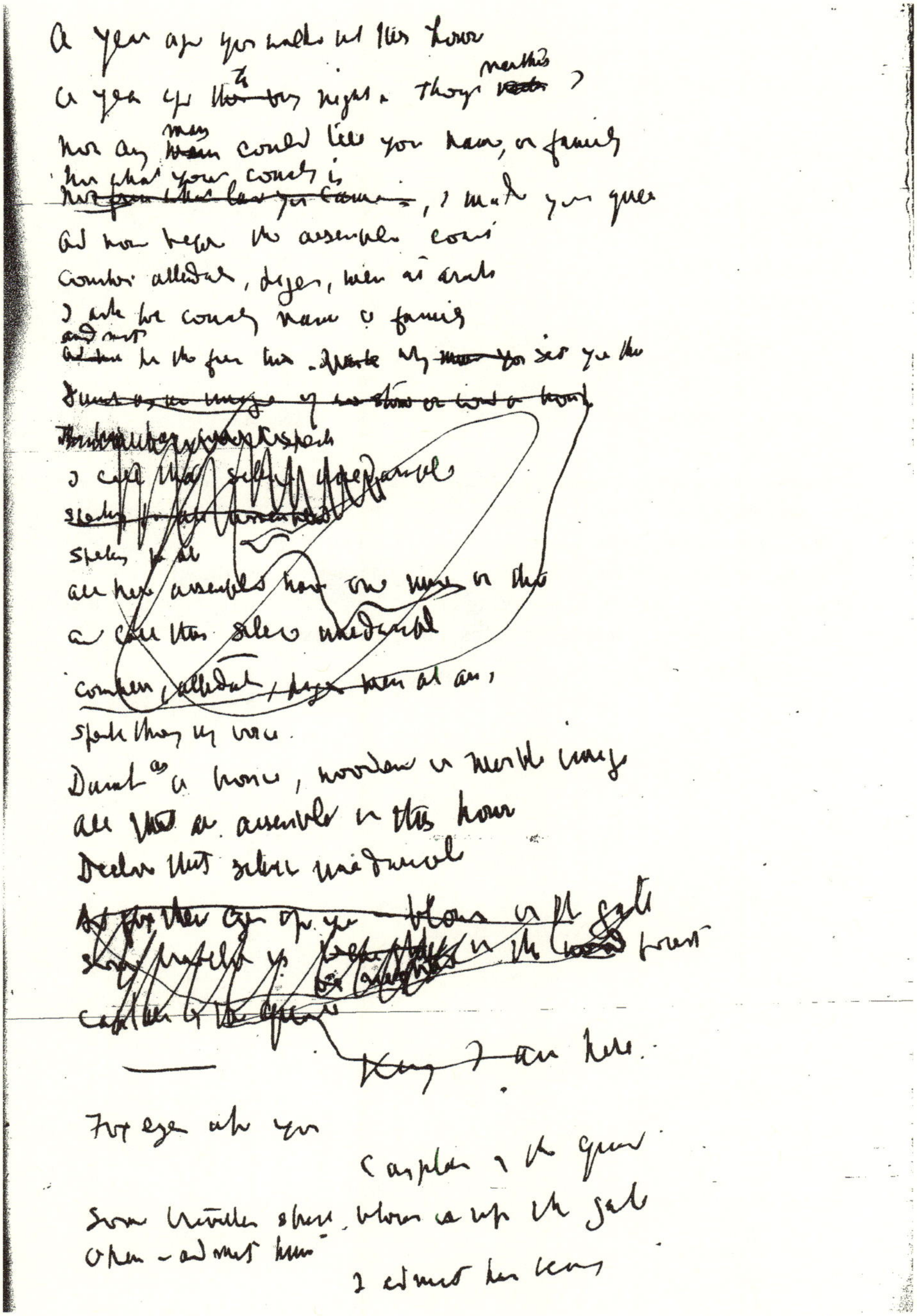

[BC, 43^{r}] [*VPl*, 17–31]

A year ago you walked into this house
to neither
A year ago ~~this very~~ night. Though ~~neiter~~ I
man
Nor any main could tell your name, or family
Nor what your country is
~~Nor from what land you came –~~ , I made you queen
And now before the assembled court
Courtiers, attendants, pages, men at arms
I ask for country name & family
And not
~~And firs~~ for the first time. ~~I ask~~ why ~~must you~~ sit you there
~~Dumb as an image~~ of ~~woo~~ stone or wood or bronze
~~That long has [?withheld] speech~~
I call that silence unendurable
~~Speaking for all assembled~~
Speaking for all
All here assembled have one view in this
And call this silence unendurable
Courtiers, attendants, pages men at arms
Speak through my voice
as
Dumb a bronze, wooden or marble image
All that are assembled in this house
Declare this silence unendurable
~~And fix their eyes upon you – blows on the gate~~
Some traveller is [~~– ? – ? –~~] in the ~~wood~~ forest
benighted
Captain of ~~the Guard~~
——— ~~King I a~~m here
Fix eyes upon you
Captain of the Guard
Some traveller strikes blows ~~on~~ upon the gate
Open – admit him
I admit him king

---

found in BC, 42^{v}–46^{v} *transcribed above and below, pp. 271–283*
NLI 8769(ii) a *transcribed below, pp. 287–299*
published in *FMIM(K)*

---

18 Two lines on 42^{v}, directly opposite this line, expand upon it but lack any marks to show placement: "Dumb as an image made of wood or metal / A sort of screen between the dead & living". The published text reads: "Dumb as an image made of wood or metal, / A screen between the living and the dead".

21–23 In l. 25, Yeats has the King speak what seems in l. 21 to be a stage direction.

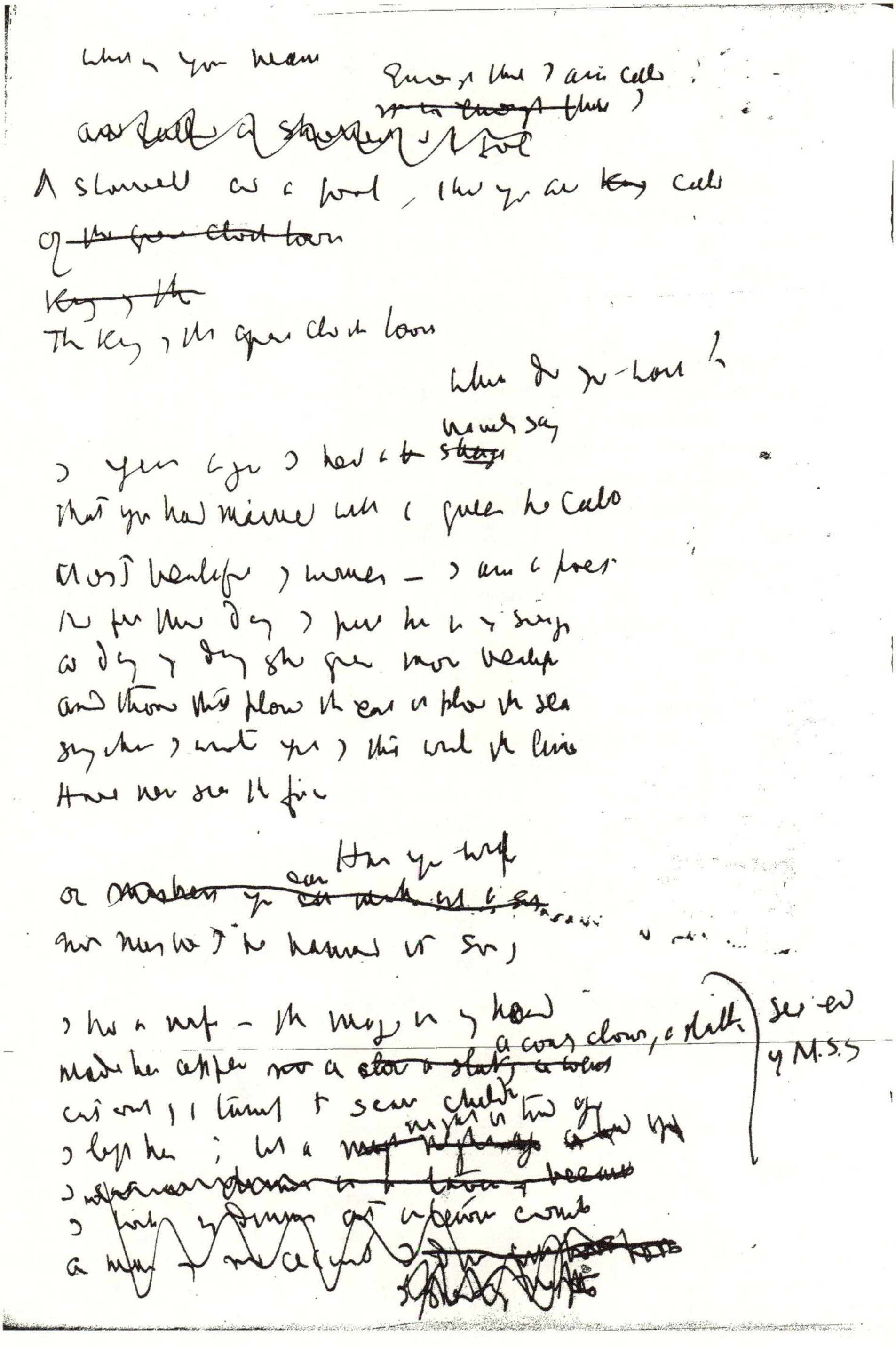

[BC, 43^{v}] [*VPl*, 32–50]

1 What is your name
Enough that I am called
~~It is enough t~~hat I
2 ~~Am called a stroller and a fool~~
3 A stroller and a fool that you are ~~king~~ called
Of ~~the Great Clock tower~~
~~King of the~~
4 The King of the Great Clock tower
What do you want?
brawler say
5 A year ago I heard a ~~br~~ ~~stranger~~
6 That you had married with a queen he called
7 Most beautiful of women – I am a poet
8 And from that day I put her in my songs
9 And day by day she grew more beautiful
10 And those that plow the earth or plow the sea
11 Sing what I wrote yet I that wrote the lines
12 Have never seen the face
Have you wife
can
13 Or ~~mistress you cn make into a song~~
14 Nor mistress to be honoured in song

15 I had a wife – the image in my head
a country clown, a slattern
16 Made her appear but a ~~clown, a slut, a we~~nch
17 Caterwal, a turnip to scare children
night or two ago
18 I left her; but a ~~migt~~ ~~night ago or two ago,~~
19 I ~~ate my dinner in a tavern & because~~
20 I took my dinner at a tavern counter
21 A man of no account ~~I dine with boor bors~~
I shared my thoughts

see end of M.S.S

12–14 In revision Yeats introduced a negative but failed to insert "no" before "wife" to complete the sense.

15–18 The bracket and note in the right-hand margin refer the reader to 46^{v} (the end of this particular manuscript in the notebook), where there is a detailed redrafting (some twelve lines in length) of not only ll. 16–21 on 43^{v} but also ll. 1–16 on 44^{r}.

[illegible]

[BC, 44r] [*VPl*, 50–62]

With knaves & cutthroats that [?] [?] [?]
The knaves and cutthroats mocked said that I
~~[?] [?away] [?turned] [?upon]~~
No [?work /words] left & turned to skin & bone
Because of a woman that I had never seen
lavished my
Run out of fat & ~~that I spent all my~~ breath in sighs
Because of a woman that I had never seen
Ran out of fat, squandered my breath in sighs
Because of a woman I had never seen

I took my dinner at a tavern table
A stroller and a man of no account
I eat among the turnips, a turnip scoffed
Cried for the other turnips that I

I dine among the turnips, a turnip scoffed
Said that I cried & drank myself to sleep
Because of a woman that I had never seen

———

But what have I to do with it

———

Send for the queen
They cannot scoff at me when I have seen her

———

He seems a most audacious brazen man
Not caring what he speaks of nor to whom
Nor where he stands

———

Never have I ~~thought~~ spoken
~~Nor spoken a disrespectful word of that~~
A brazen audacious disrespectful word
Of the image in my head; but let me look
On the original.

———

She is at my side

———

1–16 For discussion of this passage, see the introduction, p. lxiv.

16–17 From this point on, Yeats draws a short line after the conclusion of each character's speech to indicate a change of speaker.

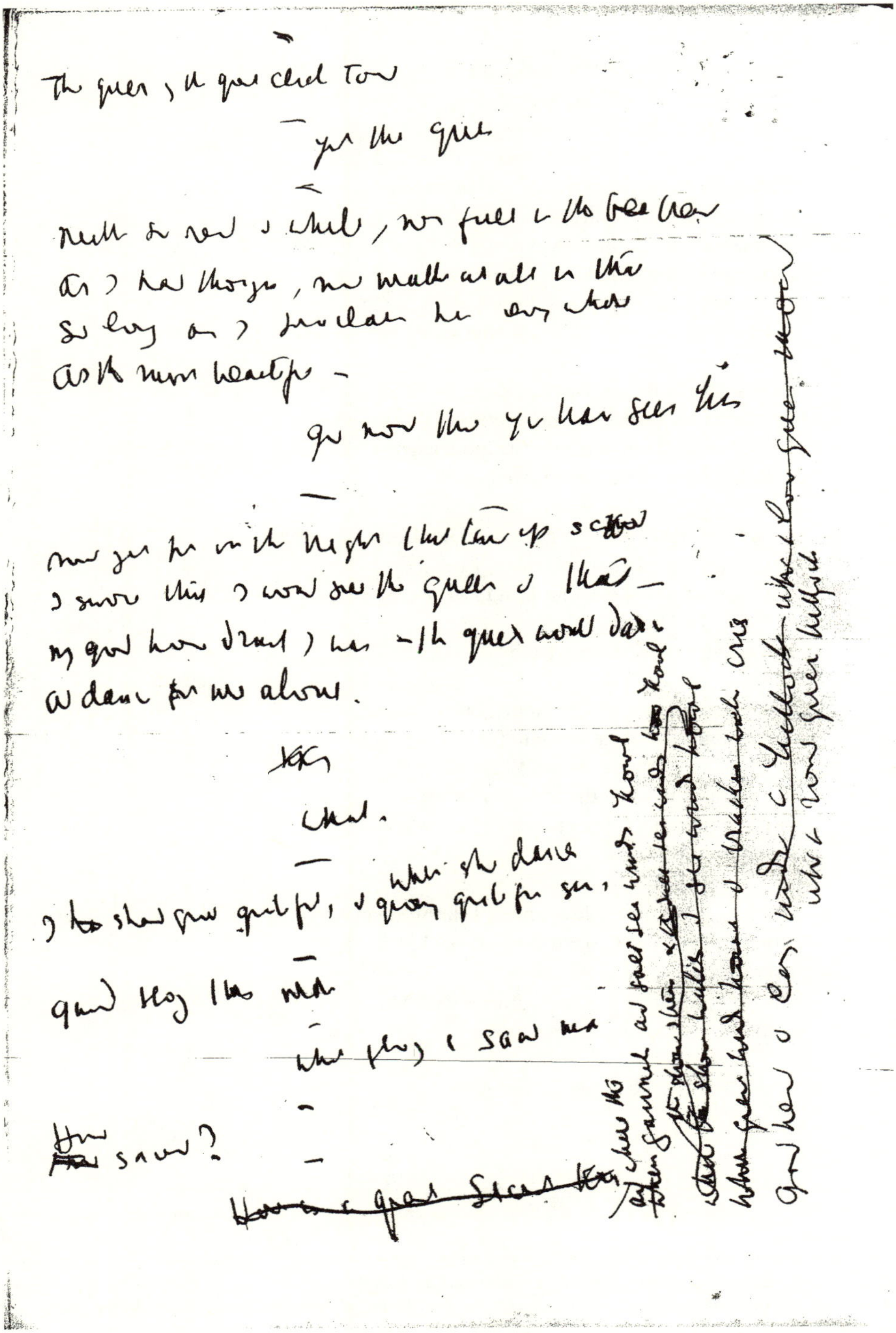

[BC, 44v] [*VPl*, 62–77]

1 The queen of the great Clock Tower

———

Yes the queen

———

2 Neither so red and white nor full in the ~~bea~~ breast
3 As I had thought, no matter at all in that
4 So long as I proclaim her every where
5 As the most beautiful

———

Go now that you have seen her

———

6 Not yet for on the night that turnip scoffed
7 I swore that I would see the queen & that –
8 My god how drunk I was – the queen would dance
9 And dance for me alone.

~~K~~King
What

———

When she dances
10 I ~~ha~~ shall grow grateful, & grown grateful sing

———

11 Guard flog this man

———

What flog a sacred man

———

How
12 ~~How~~ sacred?

———

~~Here is a great secret King~~

And where the
13 ~~Where~~ gannets and salt sea winds howl
14 ~~the slow stream & the salt sea wind how~~ howls
15 ~~Where the slow waters & sea winds howl~~
16 ~~Where great winds howl & bracken [?wails]~~ cries
17 God head & lay ~~under a hillock upon a low green mound~~
upon a round green hillock

---

9 Yeats writes a speech prefix for the King then deletes it as inconsistent with his current way of indicating a change of speaker.

13–17 These lines relate more closely to the speech developed at the top of 45r than to the text evolved on 44v, though they are not clued to show placement. The passage marks a significant tonal change from the Stroller's previous satirical stance to a degree of awe, and the lines posed some difficulty in terms of the dramatic pacing of this effect, undergoing much revision. In the final version, vivid details of the landscape effect the transition smoothly.

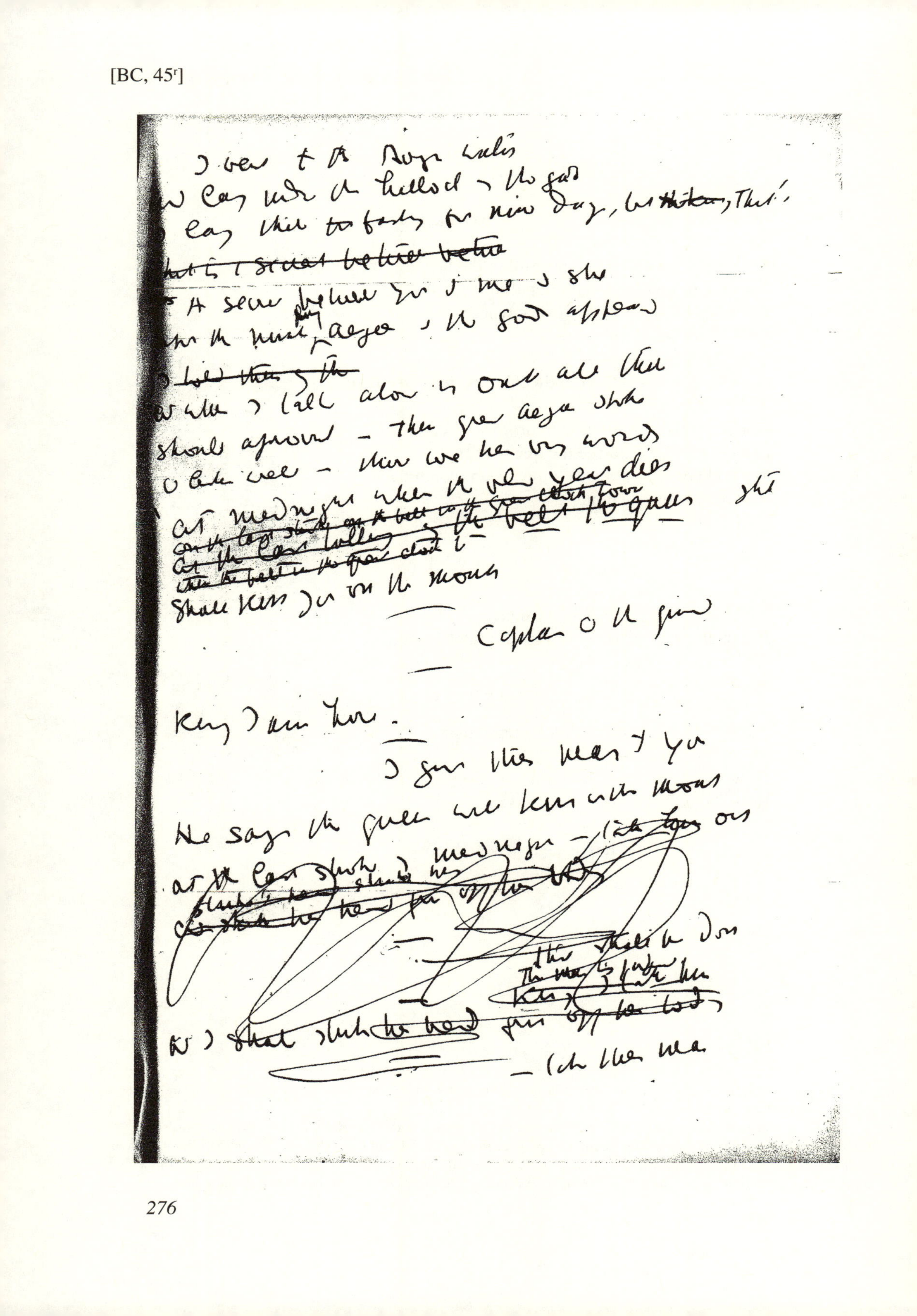

[BC, 45r]

[BC, 45r] [*VPl*, 75–89]

I went to the Boyne Water
And lay under a hillock in the field
I lay there ~~[?]~~ fasting for nine days, but ~~thinking~~ that's
~~That is a secret between betwe~~
~~It's~~ A secret between you & me & she
day
Upon the ninth ^ Aengus & the gods appeared
~~I told them of the~~
And when I called aloud my oath all there
Shouted approval – Then great Aengus spoke
O listen well – these were his very words
'At midnight when the old year dies
~~On the last stroke of the bell in the Great Clock Tower~~
~~At the last tolling of the bell the queen~~ stet
~~When the bell in the great clock t~~
Shall kiss you on the mouth

Captain of the Guard

King I am here

I give this man to you
He says the queen will kiss on the mouth
At the last stroke of midnight – take him out
~~Strike's head strike his~~
~~And strike his head from off his body~~

This shall be done
This man is judged
King I take him
And I shall strike his head from off his body

Take this man

1–15 For discussion of the revisions to these lines, see the introduction, pp. lxiv–lxv.

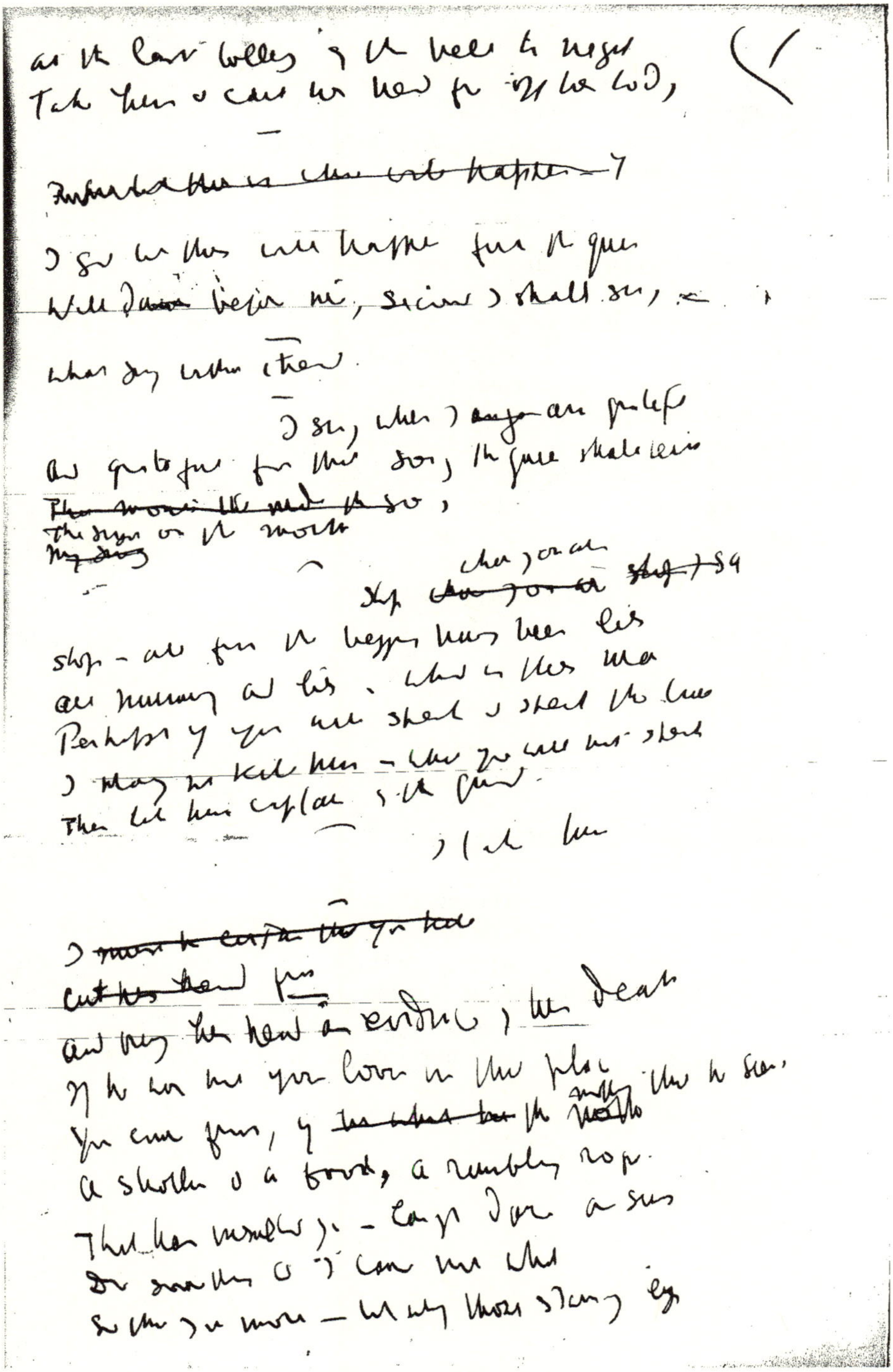

[BC, 46[r]] [*VPl*, 89–106]

(1

At the last tolling of the bell to night
Take him & cut his head from off his body

———

~~I go but this is what will happen~~ – F
I go but this will happen first the queen
Will dance before me, second I shall sing –

———

What sing without a head

———

I sing when I ~~am ga~~ am grateful
And grateful for that song the queen shall kiss
~~The mouth that made the song~~
The singer on the mouth
~~My song~~

———

where you are
Stop ~~where you are Stand I~~ say
Stop – all from the beginning has been lies
All mummery and lies. Who is this man
Perhaps if you will speak and speak the truth
I may not kill him – What you will not speak
Then take him Captain of the Guard.

———

I take him

———

~~I must be certain that you kill~~
~~Cut his head~~ from
And bring his head as evidence of his death
If he was not your lover in that place
nothing that he seems
You come from, if ~~he what but~~ the ~~noth~~
A stroller & a fool, a rambling rogue
That has insulted you – laugh, dance or sing
Do something O I care not what
So that you move – but why those staring eyes

1–24 Having continued his text from 45[r] directly to 46[r], not his usual practice with bound notebooks, Yeats avoided confusion by numbering 46[r] as "1" and 45[v] as "2" to indicate where the text continues.

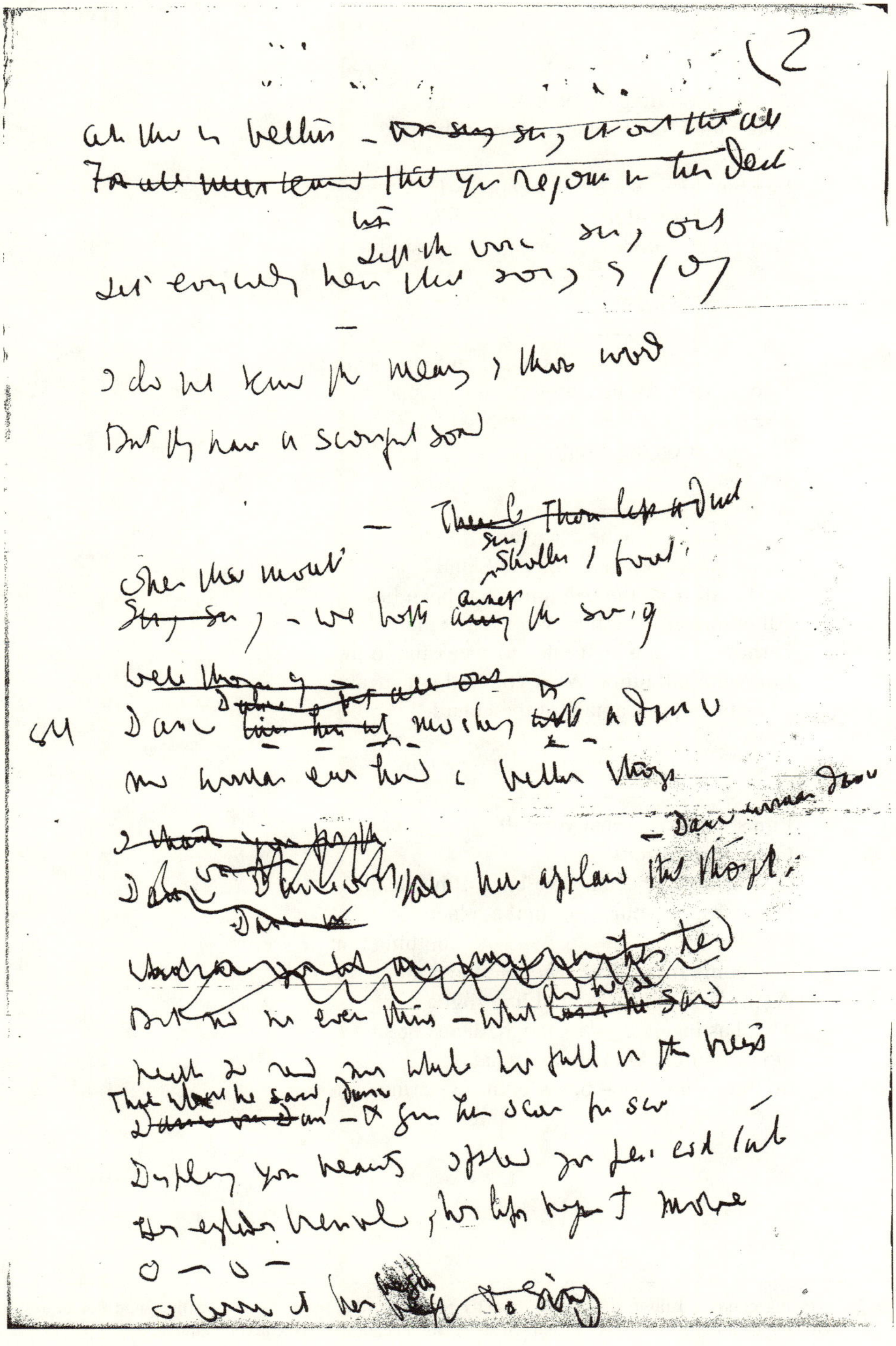

[BC, 45[v]] [*VPl*, 109–130]

(2

1 Ah that is better – ~~but sing sing it out that~~ all
2 ~~For all men know that you rejoice in his~~ death
~~but~~
3 Lift the voice sing out
4 Let everybody hear that song of joy

---

5 I do not know the meaning of those words
6 But they have a scornful sound

~~Then li Then lip a d~~uet
sing
Stroller & fool
Open that mouth await
7 ~~Sing si~~ng – we both ~~away~~ the song

8 ~~Well thought of~~
~~Dance put all our~~ ~~in~~
9 Stet Dance ~~turn him into~~ mockery ~~with~~ a dance
10 No woman ever had a better thought
11 ~~I thank you for the~~
12 ~~On~~ – Dance, woman dance
13 ~~Dance Dance on~~, All here applaud that thought;
~~Dance on.~~
14 ~~What are you but an image in his head~~
did he say
15 But now not even this – What ~~was it he s~~aid
16 Neither so red nor white nor full in the breast
That's what he said, dance
17 ~~Dance on, dance~~ - & give him scorn for scorn
18 Display your beauty spread your peacock tail
19 His eyelids tremble, his lips begin to move
20 O – O –
begun
21 O terror it has ~~begun~~ to sing

1–4 Yeats left the lyrical material to be inserted: Second Attendant sings the first two lines of the Queen's song before l. 1, and the full song after l. 4.

6–7 Omitted stage direction: the King is to fetch the severed head and lay it upon the throne nearest the audience after l. 6, and the Queen begins to dance after l. 7.

9–17 Yeats condenses ten lines to six; later, l. 15 was dropped.

18 For a discussion of the image of the "peacock tail," see the introduction, p. lxv.
Omitted stage direction: the Queen now lifts the severed head to her shoulder.

19 Omitted stage direction: the First Attendant sings the opening line of the "new song for the severed head".

21 The draft ends at this point. What remain are the song (completed elsewhere in the Rapallo notebook), stage directions for a mime and tableau, and the final choric lyric for the attendants (both to be picked up from the prose version of the play but without "Why must those holy, haughty feet descend," now sited in *A Full Moon in March*).

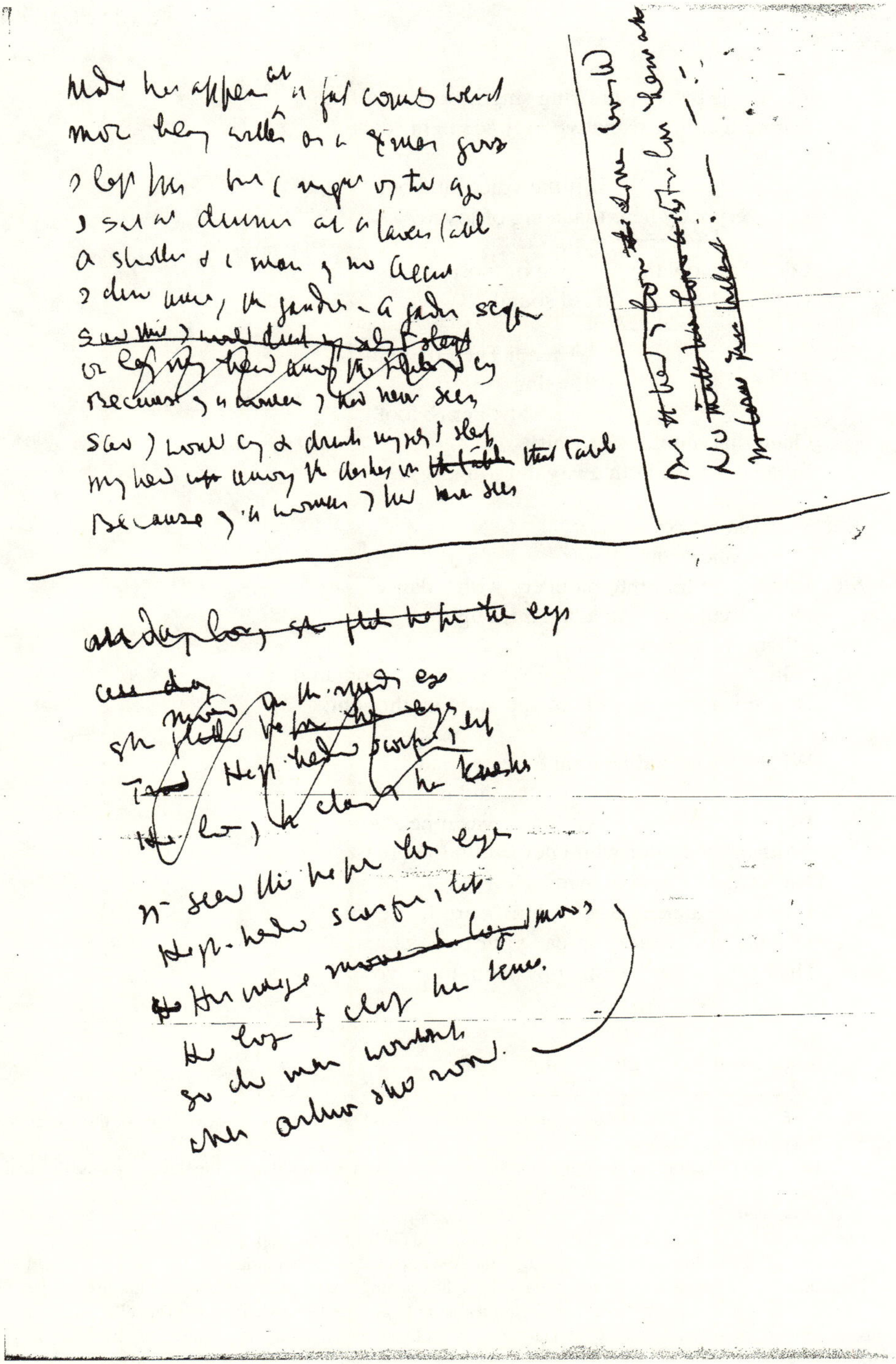

[BC, 46^{v}] [*VPl*, 45–53]

but
Made her appear^a fat country wench
More heavy [?wether /?walker] or a Xmas goose
I left her but a night or two ago
I sat at dinner at a tavern table
A stroller & a man of no account
I dine among the ganders – a gander scoffed
~~Said that I would drink myself to sleep~~
~~Or lay my head among the plates & cry~~
Because of a woman I had never seen
Said I would cry & drink myself to sleep
My head ~~upon~~ among the dishes on ~~the table~~ that table
Because of a woman I had never seen

These lines comprise the revision Yeats refers to in the marginal note on 43^{v} (see p. 271). For a discussion of Yeats's attempts to achieve a particular tone in this passage, see introduction, p. lxiv.

The verses to the right and below the heavy ink lines are drafts of a poem about love's anxieties; they are not related to the play.

2 "Wether" (an elderly ewe) is conjectural but would seem appropriate in relation to its shambling gait; the image partners well with that of the "Xmas goose." In the ensuing draft, NLI 8769(ii), Yeats experiments with "heavy footed," revised to "thick of the limbs" (see pp. 290–291 below). This would seem to support the reading "wether" (though "heavy footed" is equally well aligned with "heavy walker," another possible reading of Yeats's hand).

Part III. *The King of the Great Clock Tower* (Verse)

C. Second Draft: NLI 8769(ii) a

No proofs, corrected or otherwise, of the text of *The King of the Great Clock Tower* in verse, as published in *A Full Moon in March* in 1935, survive in the Macmillan archive in the British Library or amongst any collections of Yeats's papers. The final extant version of the play in draft is therefore the holograph manuscript, NLI 8769(ii) a, written in blue-black ink in an initially neat hand that grows larger and heavier as the text advances. This offers a relatively clean copy of the material in the Rapallo notebook (BC). And, with the exception of vestiges of the songs for the Queen and for the Severed Head, all the lyrical material and much of the final episode in mime is omitted. Both elements were carried over to the published text from the prose version.

The transcription that follows is collated with the first published text by Macmillan in *A Full Moon in March* (London, 1935). Stage directions are uniformly printed in italic type in *FMIM(K)*; such variations are not recorded here. In *VPl* R. K. Alspach collates the text printed in *Collected Plays* (London, 1952; New York, 1953) with *FMIM(K)* and *HEOP*.

[NLI 8769(ii) a, 1r]

The King. A year ago you walked into this house
A year ago to night – though neither I
Nor any man could tell your name or family
Nor what your country is, I made you queen;
And now before the assembled court
Courtiers, attendants, pages, men at arms
I ask for country name and family
And not for the first time, why sit you there
~~A wooden image or marble image. All~~
~~Assembled in this house fix eyes upon you~~
~~Declare that silence unendurable.~~
Dumb as an image made of wood or metal
A screen between the living and the dead
All that are assembled in this hour
Declare that silence unendurable.
~~Fix eyes upon you~~ (There is a pause The queen neither speaks nor moves.
The first attendant strikes the drum three times.)
~~Captain of the guard~~ Captain of the guard
Some traveller strikes a blow upon the gate
Open, admit him.
~~First attendant~~

First attendant (speaking as captain of the guard, without turning the head)
I admit him King.
(The stroller enters)

The King. What is your name?

The Stroller. Enough that I am called
A stroller and a fool that you are called
The king of the great clock ~~tow~~ Tower

The King What do you want?

The Stroller. A year a ago I heard a traveller say
That you had married with a woman he called
Most beautiful of her sex. I am a poet
From that day out I put her in my songs
And day by day she grew more beautiful
Strong headed men that plough the earth or sea
Sing what I sang yet I that sang her forth
Have never looked upon her face

[NLI 8769(ii) a, 1r] [*VPl*, 17–42]

The King

A year ago you walked into this house
A year ago to night. Though neither I
Nor any man could tell your name or family
Nor what your country is, I made you queen;
And now before the assembled court
Courtiers, attendants, pages, men at arms
I ask for country, name and family
And not for the first time. Why sit you there
~~A wooden, bronze or marble image. All~~
~~Assembled in this house fix eyes upon you~~
~~Declare that silence unendurab~~le.
Dumb as an image made of wood or metal
A screen between the living and the dead
All that are assembled in this house
Declare that silence unendurable.
Fix eyes upon you / There is a pause
(^The Queen neither speaks nor moves.
The first Attendant strikes the drum three times).

~~Captain of the Guard~~

Captain of the Guard

Some traveller strikes a blow upon the gate
Open, admit him.

~~First Attendant~~

First Attendant

(speaking as Captain of the Guard, without turning his head)
I admit him King.
(The Stroller enters)

---

3 name or family] your family, *FMIM(K)*
4 Country or name, I put you on that throne. *FMIM(K)*
5 court, before *FMIM(K)*
6 Neighbours, attendants, courtiers, men-at-arms, *FMIM(K)*
7 ask your *FMIM(K)*
14 All persons here assembled, and because *FMIM(K)*
15 They think that silence unendurable, *FMIM(K)*
16*sd* There is a pause. The Queen neither / speaks nor moves. First Attendant strikes / the drum three times. *FMIM(K)*
17 gate. *FMIM(K)*
18 Open. Admit *FMIM(K)*
18*sd* (speaking as Captain of the Guard, / without turning his head) . . . (The Stroller enters) *FMIM(K)*

9–11, 12–15 First Yeats attempts a variation on BC, 43r, ll. 18–20, but then replaces it with a slightly emended version of the two-line revision that forms the sole entry on BC, 42v, giving dramatic emphasis to the word "dumb" and establishing economically the twin themes of the Queen's silence and the metaphysical complexity inhering in her very presence.

[NLI 8769(ii) a, 1r]

The King. A year ago you walked into this house
A year ago to night – though neither I
Nor any man could tell your name or family
Nor what your country is, I made you queen;
And now before the assembled court
Courtiers, attendants, pages, men at arms
I ask for country name and family
And not for the first time. They set you there
~~A wonder image of marble image. All~~
~~Assembled in this house fix eyes upon you~~
~~Declare that silence unendurable.~~
Dumb as an image made of wood or metal
A screen between the living and the dead
All that are assembled in this house
Declare that silence unendurable.
~~Fix eyes upon you~~ (There is a pause. The queen neither speaks nor moves.
The first attendant strikes the drum three times).
~~Captain of the guard~~ Captain of the guard
Some traveller strikes a blow upon the gate
Open, admit him.
~~First attendant~~
First attendant (speaking as captain of the guard, without turning her head)
I admit him King.
(The stroller enters)
The King. What is your name?
The Stroller. Enough that I am called
A stroller and a poet that you are called
The King of the great clock ~~[illegible]~~ Town
The King What do you want?
The Stroller. A year ago I heard a traveller say
That you had married with a woman he called
Most beautiful of her sex. I am a poet
From that day out I put her in my songs
And day by day she grew more beautiful
Strange heard men that through the earth I see
Sing what I sang yet I that song her fame
Have never looked upon her face

[NLI 8769(ii) a, 1r, continued] [*VPl*, 17–42]

19 The King. What is your name?
The Stroller Enough that I am called
20 A stroller & a fool that you are called
21 The King of the Great Clock ~~tow~~ Tower
The King What do you want?
22 The Stroller A year a ago I heard a brawler say
23 That you had married with a woman he called
24 Most beautiful of her sex. I am a poet
25 From that day out I put her in my songs
26 And day by day she grew more beautiful
27 Strong hearted men that plough the earth & sea
28 Sing what I sang yet I that sang her first
29 Have never looked upon her face

---

20 A Stroller and a fool, *FMIM(K)*
21 King *FMIM(K)*
23 woman called *FMIM(K)*
24 poet. *FMIM(K)*
26 beautiful. *FMIM(K)*
27 Hard-hearted . . . and *FMIM(K)*
28 Sing what I sing, *FMIM(K)*
29 never seen *FMIM(K)*

[NLI 8769(ii) a, 2r]

The King. ~~Whe~~ Have you no lips
Mistress, [?] friend to put out a song?

The Stroller I had a wife; this image in my head
Made her appear ~~as a fat country wench~~
~~In all her move~~
Made her appear, fat slow, ~~a heavy footed~~ thick of the limbs
In all her movement like a country goose.
I [?] her, but a night or two ago
I ate my sausage at a tavern table
A stroller and a man of no account
I dined among the ganders; a gander scoffed,
Said I would cry and drink myself and sleep
My head among the dishes on the table
Because of a woman I had never seen.

The King But what have I to do with it.

The Stroller Send for the queen
The ganders cannot scoff when I have seen her

The King. He seems a most audacious [?] man
Not caring what he speaks of nor to whom
Nor where he stands

The Stroller Never have I said
Bigger audacious, disrespectful words
Of the image in my head, but call her in
That I may look on its original.

The King. She's at my side.
The queen of the great clock tower.

The Stroller —

The King The queen of the great clock tower is at my side

[NLI 8769(ii) a, 2^{r}] [*VPl*, 42–63]

<u>The King</u>. ~~Who~~ Have you no wife
Mistress, or friend to put into a song?
<u>The Stroller</u> I had a wife; the image in my head
~~Made her appear but a fat country wench~~
~~In all her mov-~~
~~that~~ thick of the limbs
Made her appear, fat slow, ~~& heavy foote~~d
In all her movements like a country goose.;
I ~~fe~~ left her, but a night or two ago
I ate my sausage at a tavern table
A stroller & a man of no account
I dine among the ganders; a gander scoffed,
Said I would cry and drink myself to sleep
My head among the dishes on the table
Because of a woman I had never seen.
<u>The King</u> But what have I to do with it.
<u>The Stroller</u> Send for the Queen
The ganders cannot scoff when I have seen her
The King. He seems a most audacious brazen man
Not caring what he speaks of nor to whom
Nor where he stands
<u>The Stroller</u> Never have I said
Brazen audacious, disrespectful words
Of the image in my head, but call her in
That I may look on its original.
The King. She's at my side.
The Stroller – The queen of the great clock tower.
The King The Queen of the great Clock Tower is at my side

1 wife, *FMIM(K)*
2 Mistress or *FMIM(K)*
3 wife. The *FMIM(K)*
5 limbs, *FMIM(K)*
6 Michaelmas goose. *FMIM(K)*
8 table - *FMIM(K)*
9 and *FMIM(K)*
10 ganders - *FMIM(K)*
11 would drink myself to sleep, or cry *FMIM(K)*
12 table, *FMIM(K)*
15 her. *FMIM(K)*
17 of, . . . whom, *FMIM(K)*
18 stands. . . . But never *FMIM(K)*
19 Brazen, *FMIM(K)*
20 head. Summon her *FMIM(K)*
22 She is . . . The Queen of the Great Clock Tower *FMIM(K)*
22 Great . . . side. *FMIM(K)*

4–5 Yeats revises the description of the Stroller's wife beyond the work in the Rapallo notebook.

Th Stroller.

Neither so red, nor white, nor full in the breast
As I had thought. What matter for all that
So long as I proclaim her everywhere
As the most beautiful.

Th King.

Go now that you have seen her

Th Stroller.

Not yet for on the night the ~~gander trussed~~ gander gabbed scuffed
I swore that I would see the queen and that —
My god but I was drunk — the queen would dance
And dance to me alone.

Th King.

What?

Th Stroller.

When she has danced
I shall grow grateful and grow ~~gab~~ grateful sing,

Th King, Sing loud you may
~~You shall sing but~~ but ~~not for great birds~~ ~~in darker fashion~~
Guards flog this man.

Th Stroller.

~~But who dare flog a~~
What flog a sacred man!

Th King,

How sacred

Th Stroller.

I went to the Boyne water
And where the ~~gannets and the salt winds howl~~
sea mew & salt ~~winds yelp~~ sea mew [illegible]
~~Godhead~~
~~Villa~~
~~Then~~ Godhead ~~Lay upon a round green hillock~~
on
upon a round green ~~[illegible] I lay~~ hillock lay

[NLI 8769(ii) a, 3r] [*VPl*, 64–77]

1 The Stroller Neither so red & white nor full in the breast
2 As I had thought. What matter for all that
3 So long as I proclaim her everywhere
4 As the most beautiful.
The King Go now that you have seen her

gander gabbed
5 The Stroller. Not yet for on the night the ~~gander hissed scoffed~~
6 I swore that I would see the queen & that -
7 My god but I was drunk – the queen would dance
8 And dance to me alone.
The King. What?
The Stroller. When she has danced
9 I shall grow grateful & grown ~~gal~~ grateful sing

Sing loud you may not from gratitude
10 The King ~~You shall sing out~~ but ~~in another fashion~~
11 Guard flog this man.
The Stroller ~~But who dare flog a~~
What flog a sacred man!
12 The King
How sacred
The Stroller I went to the Boyne Water
13 And where the ~~gannets and the salt winds howl~~
sea mew ~~&~~ & salt ~~winds yell~~ sea wind
14 ~~God head~~
Yell~~s~~ on
~~There~~ Godhead ~~lay upon a round green hillock~~
~~upon~~ a round green ~~hill I lay~~ hillock lay

---

1 red, nor white, nor *FMIM(K)*
4 Most beautiful! . . . seen! *FMIM(K)*
5 yet, *FMIM(K)*
6 Queen, and *FMIM(K)*
7 Queen *FMIM(K)*
8 Dance, and dance *FMIM(K)*
9 Till I grow *FMIM(K)*
10 Sing out *FMIM(K)*
11 Guard, . . . man! *FMIM(K)*
12 A sacred man? . . . I ran *FMIM(K)*
13 a sea-mew and the salt sea wind *FMIM(K)*
14 Yelled Godhead, on *FMIM(K)*

nine day days I fasted there
~~Lay fasting for nine~~ days but that is a secret
— A secret between you & me & she —
upon the ~~ninth~~ ninth day, Aengus & the gods appeared
and when I said what I had sworn, all there
should approve — then great Aengus spoke
— O listen for I speak his very words —
('At midnight when the old year dies
At the last stroke of the bell the queen
Shall kiss ~~your mouth~~ that mouth' — Let there be no mistake
Your queen, my ~~mouth~~, mouth & she kiss my mouth.

The King —
when the old year dies upon the stroke of midnight
~~Yes at the very stroke~~
yes on that stroke, the tolling of the bell
The queen shall kiss your mouth — drunk on the words
Your queen my mouth & she shall kiss my mouth.

The King.
Come captain of the guards
First attendant (speaking as captain of the guards) King, I am here.

The King
This man insults me & insults the queen
Bring me his head

First attendant (speaking as captain of the guards)
I take him King,

The stroller
I go but that will happen (counting on his fingers) First, the queen
will dance before me, second, I shall sing.

The King. What sing without a head
The stroller I ~~sing with~~ I sing when I am grateful

[NLI 8769(ii) a, 4r] [*VPl*, 78–92]

nine day days I fasted there
~~Lay fasting for nine days~~ but thats a secret
– A secret between you & me & she –
Upon the ~~nineth~~ ninth day Aengus & the gods appeared
And when I said what I had sworn, all there
Shouted approval – Then great Aengus spoke
– O listen for I speak his very words –
‘ At midnight when the old year dies
At the last tolling of the bell the queen
that
Shall kiss ~~you on~~ the mouth! – Let there be no mistake
Your queen, my ~~moth~~ mouth & she kiss my mouth.
~~The King~~.
When the old year dies upon the stroke of midnight
~~Yes on the very stroke~~
Yes on that stroke, the tolling of that bell
The queen shall kiss your mouth – drink in the words
Your queen my mouth & she shall kiss my mouth.
The King.
Come Captain of the Guards
First Attendant (speaking as Captain of the Guards) King I am here.
The King
This man insults me & insults the queen
Bring me his head
First Attendant (speaking as Captain of the Guards)
I take him King
The Stroller
I go but this will happen (counting on his fingers) First, the queen
Will dance before me, second, I shall sing.
The King. What sing without a head
The Stroller ~~I sing whe~~ I sing when I am grateful

---

1 Nine . . . there—but that's *FMIM(K)*
2 Between us three—then Aengus and the Gods *FMIM(K)*
4 Appeared, and when I said what I had sworn *FMIM(K)*
5 approval. . . . spoke— *FMIM(K)*
6 O listen, *FMIM(K)*
7 ‘On stroke of midnight *FMIM(K)*
8 Upon that stroke, the tolling of that bell, *FMIM(K)*
9 The Queen shall kiss your mouth,'—his very words— *FMIM(K)*
10 mouth, the Queen shall kiss my mouth. *FMIM(K)*
15 Come, . . . Guard. Direction (speaking as Captain of the Guard) . . . King, *FMIM(K)*
16 and . . . Queen. *FMIM(K)*
17 Take him and bring Direction (speaking as Captain of the Guard) . . . him, *FMIM(K)*
18 go; . . . happen: Direction (counting on his fingers) First the Queen *FMIM(K)*
20 What, . . . head? . . . Grateful I sing, *FMIM(K)*

[NLI 8769(ii) a, 5r]

Then grateful in her turn the queen shall kiss
The singer on the mouth.

The King   Slain where you are
Stand, all from the beginning has been ~~lie~~ lies
All mummery and lies. Who is this man?
Perhaps if you will speak & speak the truth
I may not kill him. What you will not speak?
(Then strike him captain of the guard ~~& strike him~~
First attendant (speaking as captain of the guard) I strike him.
The King. The king has heard no evidence of his death
If he was not your lover in this place
You come from, if ~~nothing~~ the nothing that he dreams
A stroller or a fool, a rambling rogue
That has insulted you, laugh, dance or sing
Do something, anything I care not what
So that you move — But why those ~~[illegible]~~ staring eyes
Second attendant (singing as queen & in a low voice)
O what may come
Into my womb
The King. Ah this is better — let the voice ring out
Let everybody hear that song [illegible]

Second attendant (singing as queen
He longs to kill etc

[NLI 8769(ii) a, 5r] [*VPl*, 93–111]

1 Then grateful in her turn the queen shall kiss
2 The singer on the mouth.
The King Stand where you are
3 Stand, all from the beginning has been ~~bl~~ lies
4 All mummery and lies. Who is this man?
5 Perhaps if you will speak & speak the truth
6 I may not kill him. What you will not speak?
7 Then ~~sta~~ take him Captain of the guard ~~I take him~~
First Attendant (speaking as Captain of the guard) I take him.
8 The King And bring his head as evidence of his death
9 If he was not your lover in that place
10 You come from, if ~~nothing~~ the nothing that he seems
11 A stroller and a fool, a rambling rogue
12 That has insulted you, laugh, dance or sing
13 Do something anything I care not what
staring
14 So that you move – but why those ~~string~~ eyes
Second Attendant (singing as queen) in a low voice)
15 O what may come
16 Into my womb
17 The King. Ah this is better – Let the voice ring out
18 Let everybody hear that song of joy
Second Attendant (singing as queen
19 He longs to kill Etc

---

1 Then, . . . turn, the Queen will kiss *FMIM(K)*
2 My mouth because it sang. . . . are! *FMIM(K)*
3 Stand! All . . . lies, *FMIM(K)*
4 Extravagance and *FMIM(K)*
5 speak, and . . . truth, *FMIM(K)*
6 What? You *FMIM(K)*
7 him, . . . Guard. Direction (speaking as Captain of the Guard) *FMIM(K)*
8 death. *FMIM(K)*
10 seems, *FMIM(K)*
12 sing, *FMIM(K)*
13 something, anything, *FMIM(K)*
14 eyes? Direction (singing as Queen in a low voice) *FMIM(K)*
16 womb? *FMIM(K)*
17 Ah! That is better. . . . out. *FMIM(K)*
18 joy. *FMIM(K)*
19*sd* (singing as Queen) *FMIM(K)*

The King. I do not know the meaning of that word
But they have a scornful sound.
(The King goes to steps & returns with the head, & he stands on steps or stands upon the [?] throne & [?] never audience)
Sing strollers & fool
Open this mouth; my queen wants a song
(The queen begins to dance)
Dance; turn him out mocker, with a dance;
No woman ever had a better thought;
All here applaud the thought; dance woman dance
Neither so white red nor which not fall in the heart)
That's what he said; dance; give him scorn for scorn;
Display your beauty spread your peacock tail —
(The queen dances. Then stands in the centre of the stage, facing audience, her head upon her shoulder)
His eyelids tremble, his lips begin to move
The First Attendant (singing as head in a low voice)
Clip, o lip & long for more.
The King. O, O; they have begun to sing

The First Attendant (singing as head)
The women rest of lyre

The stage dark and then Clock tower
First Attendant sings, which ends play

[NLI 8769(ii) a, 6[r]] [*VPl*, 119–130]

1 The King. I do not know the meaning of those words
2 But they have a scornful sound.
(The King goes to right & returns with the head of the Stroller and lays it upon the cubical throne to right nearest audience)
Sing stroller & fool
3 Open that mouth: my queen awaits a song
(The queen begins to dance)
4 Dance; turn him into mockery with a dance;
5 No woman ever had a better thought;
6 All here applaud that thought; dance woman dance
7 Neither so ~~white~~ red nor white nor full in the breast
8 Thats what he said; dance; give him scorn for scorn:
9 Display your beauty spread your peacock tail –
(The ~~da~~ queen dances. Then stands in the centre of the stage, facing audience, his head upon her shoulder.)
10 His eyelids tremble, his ~~e~~ lips begin to move.
~~O – O~~
The First Attendant (singing as head in a low voice)
11 Clip, & lip & long for more
12 The King. O; O; they have begun to sing
[~~?~~]
13 The First Attendant (singing as head)
Then comes rest of lyric

[NLI 8769(ii) a, 7[r]]

Then stage directions as in Great Clock Tower &
First Attendants song, which ends play

---

2 That have *FMIM(K)*
2*sd* The King goes to right and returns with / the head of the Stroller, and lays it upon / the cubical throne to the right nearest / audience. Sing, . . . and fool. *FMIM(K)*
3 mouth, my Queen, . . . song. *FMIM(K)*
3*sd* (The Queen begins to dance) *FMIM(K)*
4 Dance, . . . dance! *FMIM(K)*
5 thought. *FMIM(K)*
6 thought. Dance, woman, dance! *FMIM(K)*
7 red, nor white, . . . breast, *FMIM(K)*
8 That's . . . said! Dance, . . . scorn, *FMIM(K)*
9 beauty, . . . tail. *FMIM(K)*
9*sd* The Queen dances, then takes up the / severed head and stands in centre of the / stage facing audience, the severed head / upon her shoulder. *FMIM(K)*
11*sd* The First . . . voice)] First . . . (singing as Head in a low voice) *FMIM(K)*
11 Clip and lip and . . . *FMIM(K)*
13*sd* The First . . . head)] First . . . (singing as Head) *FMIM(K)*

7[r] The final lyric is described here as the "First Attendant's song," even though the four stanzas are set in the published text to be sung by both attendants, alternating a stanza each, with the First Attendant leading (as in the prose version). This intimates that the further section, comprising "Why must those holy, haughty feet descend," was to be omitted, since that lyric is conceived as predominantly a solo for the Second Attendant. In the clutch of manuscript sheets that include NLI 8769(ii) a, this version of the play is followed by a draft of the Preface, NLI 8769(ii) b, that introduces the Macmillan publication by outlining the compositional history of this play in relation to *A Full Moon in March*; it is dated "May" in the manuscript but more precisely "May 30, 1935" when printed (see pp. 335–339).

Appendixes

Yeats introduced and commented on his plays to guide and interpret their performances. The first four appendixes present these prose materials in their probable chronological sequence. For the most part the text as revised is what appeared in print. The printed version of the program note is transcribed below; for the printed versions of the other three prose texts the reader is referred to Russell Alspach's *The Variorum Edition of the Plays of W. B. Yeats* (London: Macmillan, 1966), pp. 1008–1011 and 1309–1312.

Besides the prose materials, a remarkable number of materials are extant that allow one to piece together a near-complete performance text of the first production in 1934 of *The King of the Great Clock Tower* (prose version). If the appendixes here are read in relation to Lennox Robinson's annotations to NLI 29,550(2) regarding the blocking for the principal characters at crucial moments in the action (see above, pp. 55–70) and to the subtle changes to the stage directions for the stages of the danced sequence from the manuscripts to the text published by Cuala (see above, pp. 76–86), then it is possible to attempt a virtual recreation of the Abbey production. We lack only a detailed insight into the precise choreography devised by Ninette de Valois in the style she termed "abstract expressionism" and Arthur Duff's score for the dance, neither of which survives. The score for the dance, if it should turn up, may give an indication of the length of the sequence and the pacing of its climactic moments. However, all other features of the design scheme (setting, costumes, masks) are extant, together with Duff's music for the sung lyrics; all are included here.

Appendix I

Prose Materials: The Evolution of the Program Note: NLI 30,336 b, 1^v, 2^r

NLI 30,336 b offers a draft version of the untitled note, which was designed to follow the cast list and production credits in the program of the initial production for the prose version of *The King of the Great Cock Tower* at the Abbey Theatre (July 30, 1934). It shows Yeats wrestling with an issue of potential plagiarism and with defining the ritual background to the play and its relation to Irish legend (though he does not yet draw parallels with his early tale, "The Binding of the Hair").

Dissatisfied with his opening sentence, Yeats drafted an alternative on the verso of the previous page of the notebook but did not clue it into the main text. Finally, this rephrasing was integrated succinctly into the text to create the finished program note, transcribed at the foot of p. 305.

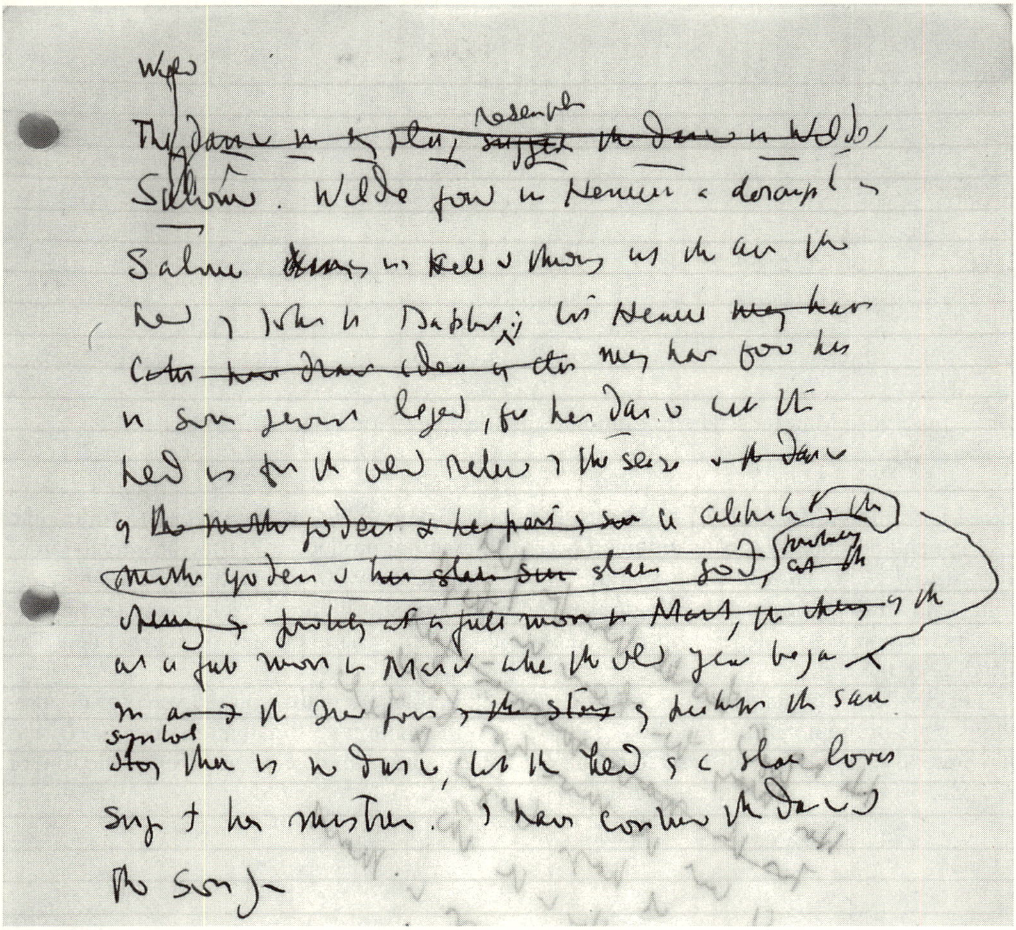

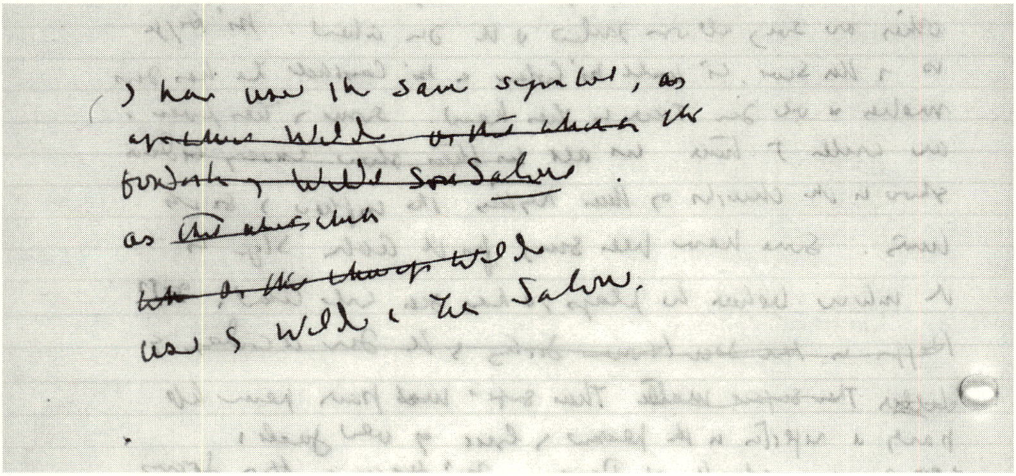

[NLI 30,336 b, 2r]

Wild
resembles
~~The dance in my play suggests the dance in Wildes~~
Salome. Wilde found in Heiner a description of
Salome ~~dancing~~ in Hell and throwing into the air the
head of John the Baptist; but Heiner ~~may have~~
~~taken have drawn idea of this~~ may have found her
in some Jewish legend, for her dance with the
head is from the old ritual of the seizon ~~& the dance~~
~~of the mother godess & her part in some~~ a celebration of the
probably
Mother Godess & ~~her slain son~~ slain god, ~~at the~~
~~opening or probably at a full moon in March, the opening~~ of the
at a full moon in March when the Old Year began
In ~~an I~~ the Irish form ~~of the story~~ of perhaps the same
symbol
~~story~~ there is no dance, but the head of a slain lover
sings to his mistress. I have combined the dance and
the song.

[NLI 30,336 b, 1v]

I have used the same symbol, as
~~upon which Wilde or that where on~~ that
~~found in the of Wilde's Sam Salome.~~
as ~~that whics~~ which
~~like as that whereupon Wi~~lde
used by Wilde in his Salome.

[Program Note for the Performance of *The King of the Great Clock Tower*]

I have used in 'The King of the Great Clock Tower' the symbol used by Wilde in his 'Salome'. He had found in Heine a description of Salome dancing in Hell, throwing up into the air the head of John the Baptist. Heine may have found her in some Jewish legend, for her dance with the head is from the old ritual of the seasons, a celebration of the Mother goddess and her slain god, enacted probably at a full moon in March at the opening of the new year. In an Irish form of perhaps the same symbol there is no dance, but the head of a slain lover singing to his mistress. I have combined dance and song. W.B.Y.

2r, ll. 2, 4 For "Heiner" read "Heine".
Program Note Transcribed from the original in the editor's collection.

Appendix II

Prose Materials: Draft of the Preface to the Cuala Edition of *The King of the Great Clock Tower*: BC, 9^v, 10^v

The Rapallo notebook, BC, 9^v and 10^v, contain Yeats's drafting of the Preface to the Cuala edition of the prose version of *The King of the Great Clock Tower*, published in October 1934. The Preface is reprinted in *VPl*, pp. 1309–1310.

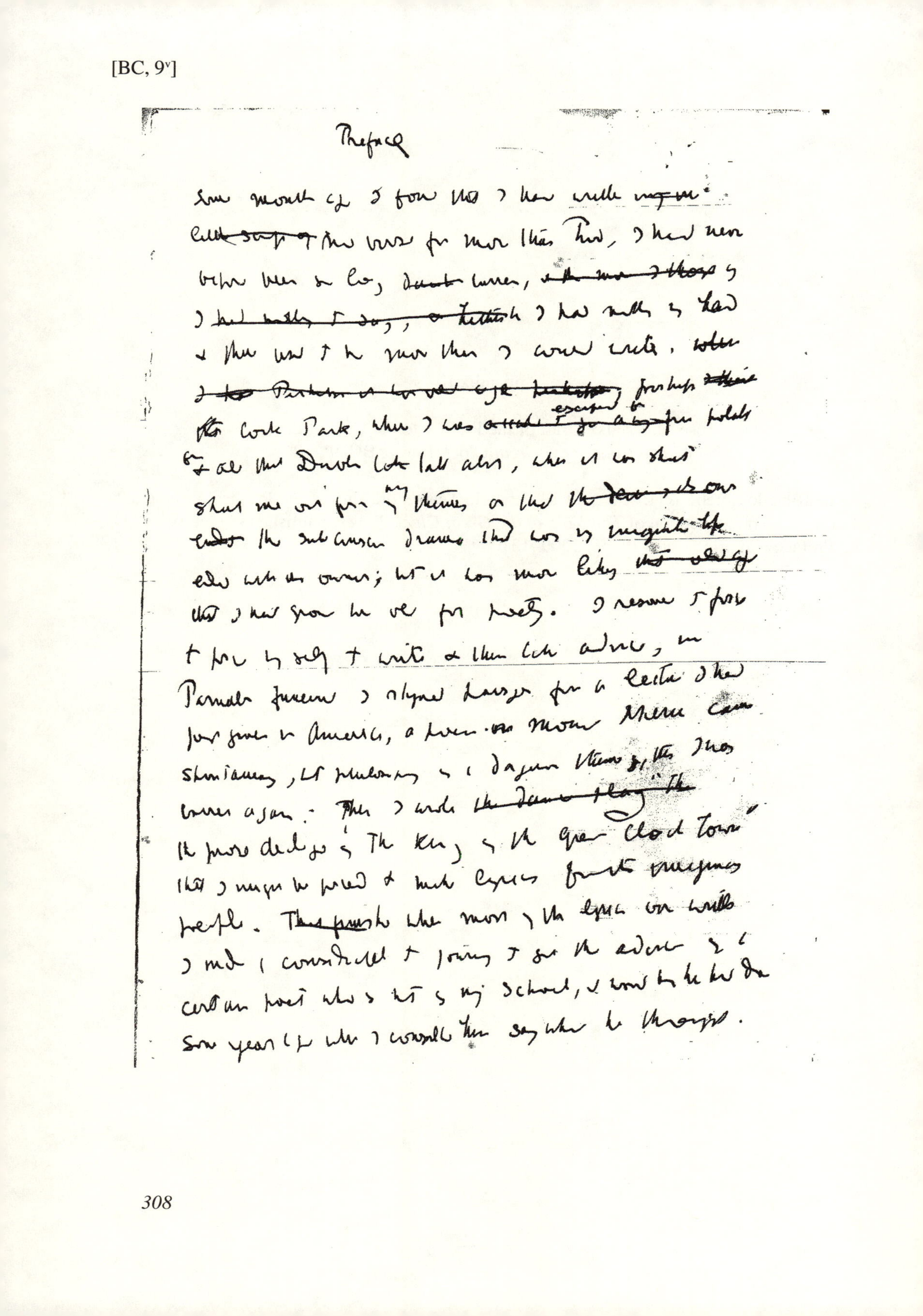

Preface

[BC, 9[v]]

Preface

1 Some months ago I found that I had written ~~very no~~
2 li~~ttle scraps of~~ no verse for more than two, I had never
3 before been so long ~~dumb~~ barren, ~~& the more I thought in~~
4 I ~~had nothing to say, & nothing in~~ I had nothing in hand
5 & there used to be more than I could write. ~~When~~
6 ~~I had Perhaps in my old age perhaps~~; perhaps ~~I think~~
escaped from
7 ~~that~~ Coole Park where I was ~~[?accustomed] to go away from~~ politics
from
8 ~~&~~ all that Dublin ~~lik~~ talked about, when it was shut
my
9 shut me out from my themes or that ~~the death of its owner~~
10 ~~ended~~ the subconscious drama that was my imaginative life
11 ended with its owner; but it was more likely ~~that old age~~
12 that I had grown too old for poetry. I resolved to force
13 to force myself to write & then take advice, in
14 Parnell's Funeral I rhymed passages from a lecture I had
15 just given in America, a poem on mount Meru came
16 spontaneously, but philosophy is a dangerous theme~~;~~, then I was
17 barren again. Then I wrote ~~the dance play "The~~
18 the prose dialogue of 'The King of the Great Clock Tower'
19 that I might be forced to make lyrics for its imaginary
20 people. ~~That finished~~ when most of the lyrics were written
21 I made a considerable journey to get the advice of a
22 certain poet who is not of my school, who would as he had done
23 some years ago when I consulted him say what he thought.

7–11 Lady Gregory's daughter-in-law, Margaret Gregory, sold the house and demesne to the Forestry Commission in 1927, but Lady Gregory retained a life-tenancy. She died at Coole on May 22, 1932. Margaret apparently observed to Yeats the night before the funeral: "Yes it is your home too that is broken up." See R. F. Foster, *W. B. Yeats: A Life*, vol. 2: *The Arch-Poet* (Oxford: Oxford University Press, 2003), p. 438.

15 Yeats made his last lecturing tour of America from October 1932 to January 1933.

17–20 Not perhaps strictly true: the opening lyric is the first recorded evidence that survives of *The King of the Great Clock Tower*, while the composition of *A Full Moon in March* suggests that the lyrics were all completed before Yeats began work on the dialogue.

21 Yeats and his wife went to Rapallo in Italy in June 1934 but with the express intention of disposing of their flat in the via Americhe. The play was by this date sufficiently complete to have been circulated among the Abbey personnel who would eventually stage it.

22 certain poet] Ezra Pound.

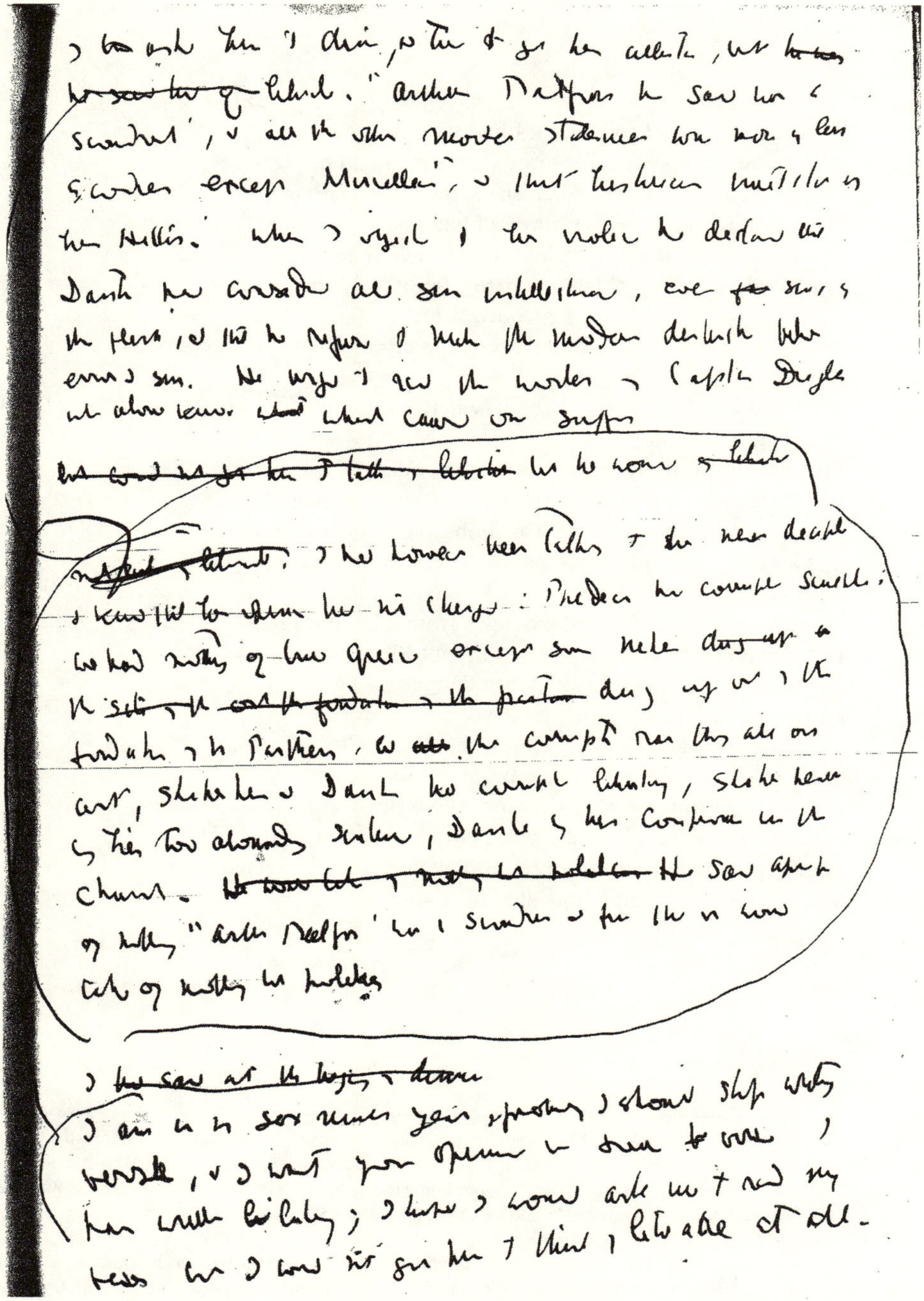

[BC, 10r]

I ~~tried~~ asked him to dine, and tried to get his attention, but ~~he was he scorned talk of~~ literature. "Arthur Balfour he said was a scoundrel', & all the other modern statesmen were more or less scoundrels except Mussolini", & that histerical imitator of his Hitler.' When I objected to his violence he declared that Dante had considered all sin intellectual, even ~~for~~ sins of the flesh, & that he refused to make the modern distinction between error & sin. He urged to read the works of Captain Douglas who alone knew ~~what~~ what caused our suffering

~~but could not get him to talk of literature~~ but he would ~~of literature~~

~~not talk of literature.~~ I had however been talking to his newest disciple & knew that his opinions had not changed: Phidias had corrupted sculpture; we had nothing of true Greece except some Nike ~~dug up o that sits in the out the foundations of the Parthenon~~ dug up out of the foundations of the Parthenon, and ~~all~~ that corruption ran through all our art, Shakespeare and Dante had corrupted literature, Shakespeare by his too abounding sentiment, Dante by his compromise with the Church. ~~He would talk of nothing but politics~~. He said a propos of nothing "Arthur Balfour was a scoundrel & from that on would talk of nothing but politics

~~I had said at the beginning of dinner~~
I am in my six ninth year, probably I should stop writing verse, & I want your opinion on some ~~b~~ verse I have written ~~li~~ lately; I hoped I would ask me to read my verses but I could not get him to think of literature at all.

---

2 Was this a gibe at Yeats's expense? Balfour as an influential politician had been invited to dine with Yeats at the behest of Lady Cunard in 1915, when she was trying to organize some public recognition of Yeats in England, possibly a knighthood, although Yeats had informed her that he would have to refuse such an honor.

8 Captain Frederick Douglas wrote on monetarist reforms but was generally deemed a crank.

11 Possibly Basil Bunting (though he was a long-term resident in Rapallo) or maybe one of two young American acolytes who were now associated with Pound's stable of writers: Robert Fitzgerald or James Laughlin.

11–20 The repetition of the outburst about Balfour in ll. 19–20 shows how the new material was to be ordered in sequence with what had already been written. This is the order observed in the printed text.

22–25 These lines are bracketed in the left-hand margin and then clued to the beginning of l. 11. Given the confusion of insertion marks, it is not altogether clear that these four lines are designed to precede lines ll. 11–20, though the printed text locates them directly after "tried to get his attention".

[BC, 10^{v}]

He took my manuscript and went away ~~denouncing~~ denouncing as as reactionary backward place because I had said that I was re-reading Shakespeare, and would go on to Chaucer & ~~prefer to get the modern world from~~ & found all I wanted of modern life in detection & the wild west. Next day his judgement came & that in a single word "putrid." Then I took my verse to a friend of my own school & he begged me to go on just like that ~~you have~~ like ~~upon themes This new has~~ " plays like 'The Great Clock Tower' will always seem unfinished, but that is no matter. Begin ~~developing~~ plays without knowing how they are to end ~~You find subjects I once wrote a play~~ for the sake of the lyrics. I once wrote a play & ~~fil~~ after I had filled it with lyrics abolished the play. Then I ~~asked~~ brought my work to others until I was like Panurge consulting oracles as to whether he should get married and always giving their answers the sense he wanted.

1–2 For "denouncing / as as" read "denouncing Dublin as".

5 George Yeats regularly had to quest for such fiction to meet Yeats's high demand.

7 friend] Probably F. R. Higgins, Yeats's protégé and staunch, if somewhat obsequious, companion.

15 Panurge is a character in Rabelais' novel, *Pantagruel* (1532–1533); he is at times crafty and at others a buffoon; as a companion to the hero on his travels, he functions as a kind of medieval Odysseus. The episode Yeats refers to is one of the great comic set pieces of the novel.

17 With the thick ink line Yeats marked the completion of his draft of the Preface; below this are sets of astrological calculations for October 1934, including a lunar calendar. In *KGCT* the Preface concludes with Yeats's poem, "God guard me from those thoughts men think," which in *FMIM* would stand independently with the title, "A Prayer for Old Age." The poem had been drafted on BC, 7^{v}–8^{r}, and first published as "Old Age" in *The Spectator* (November 2, 1934).

Appendix III

Prose Materials: Drafts for the "Commentary on 'The Great Clock Tower'": NLI 30,546, 4^{v}–8^{v}, and NLI 30,306

NLI 30,546 is a bound notebook containing the draft of the "Commentary on 'The Great Clock Tower'" for the Cuala edition of *The King of the Great Clock Tower*. NLI 30,306 is a single sheet containing an adaptation of the program note to form section IV of the "Commentary." The commentary is reprinted in *VPl*, pp. 1008–1011.

[NLI 30,546, 4v]

Note upon the great Clock Tower

When I was a young man I [...] lost my
[...] singers [...] because I could not hear [...] my [...]
[...] is [...] "if you cant say unutterable sort
I said sing a recipe from a cooking book of something
[...] you you cant [...]. But sing no change – I can hear the word
produces [...] this language with honey & oil, cannot sing poets
[...] art three centuries ago, hardy perhaps such as the Itsn poet
[...] unknown Tudor Clerk than poet
who wrote upon "Lais & false Surper"

A little wild bird sometimes at my ear
Sings his own verses very clear;
Others sing louder that I do not hear
For singing loudly is not singing well,
But ever by the song that's soft & low
The master singer's voice is plain to tell
Few have it & yet all are masters now
And each of them can shout out what he calls
His ballads, canzonets, & madrigals.

Now when a singer sets by words I say "coop up my
words into such an elaborate pattern of notes, that the

[NLI 30,546, 4v]

Note upon the Great Clock Tower
I

~~I hi~~ When I was a young man I ~~said disreputable things lost my~~ ~~*lose my*~~ *lost my*
I said to singers
~~temper because I could not hear words of my poetry when~~
unintelligible sounds
it ~~was set su~~ng: "If you want to sing ~~inaudible~~ words
I said sing a receipt from a cookery book ~~or~~ something
get by heart singing has changed. I can hear the words
~~else that you~~ you want to ~~remember~~." But ~~I was all wrong;~~
~~*intelligible*~~
~~now the words are audible~~ & I put my fingers in my ears
to keep them out. A singer ~~trained by some voice producer to~~ turn
~~language into honey & oil~~, shrill from conflict with the violins,
loud from the strain of great concert halls, trained by some voice
producer to turn language into honey & oil cannot sing poetry
that art died centuries ago, hardly perhaps survived the ~~Italian poet~~
~~whose songs were the 13th century It~~ unknown thirteenth century Italian poet
who wrote upon "true & false singing"

A little wild bird sometimes at my ear
Sings his own verses very clear;
Others sing louder that I do not hear
For singing loudly is not singing well,
But ever by the song that's soft & low
The master singers voice is plain to tell
Few have it & yet all are masters now
And each of them can thrill out what he calls
His ballads, canzonets & madrigals.

musician
Now when a ~~singer~~ sets my words I say "Cover up my
words with such an elaborate pattern of notes, that those
words may remain a secret between musician singer &
~~leave~~ ~~words~~
poet. ~~Do not allow a single intelligible syllable to~~
~~the audience~~
~~reach for they can read me afterwards I know what I want:~~
Not one word must be intelligible."

1–22 With minor emendations these lines became the opening section of the published "Commentary," cited here as *KGCT(C)*.

23–28 These sentences in the expanded form in which they were later redrafted on 8r–8v were ultimately transferred to the second paragraph of the third section of *KGCT(C)*.

[NLI 30,546, 5v]

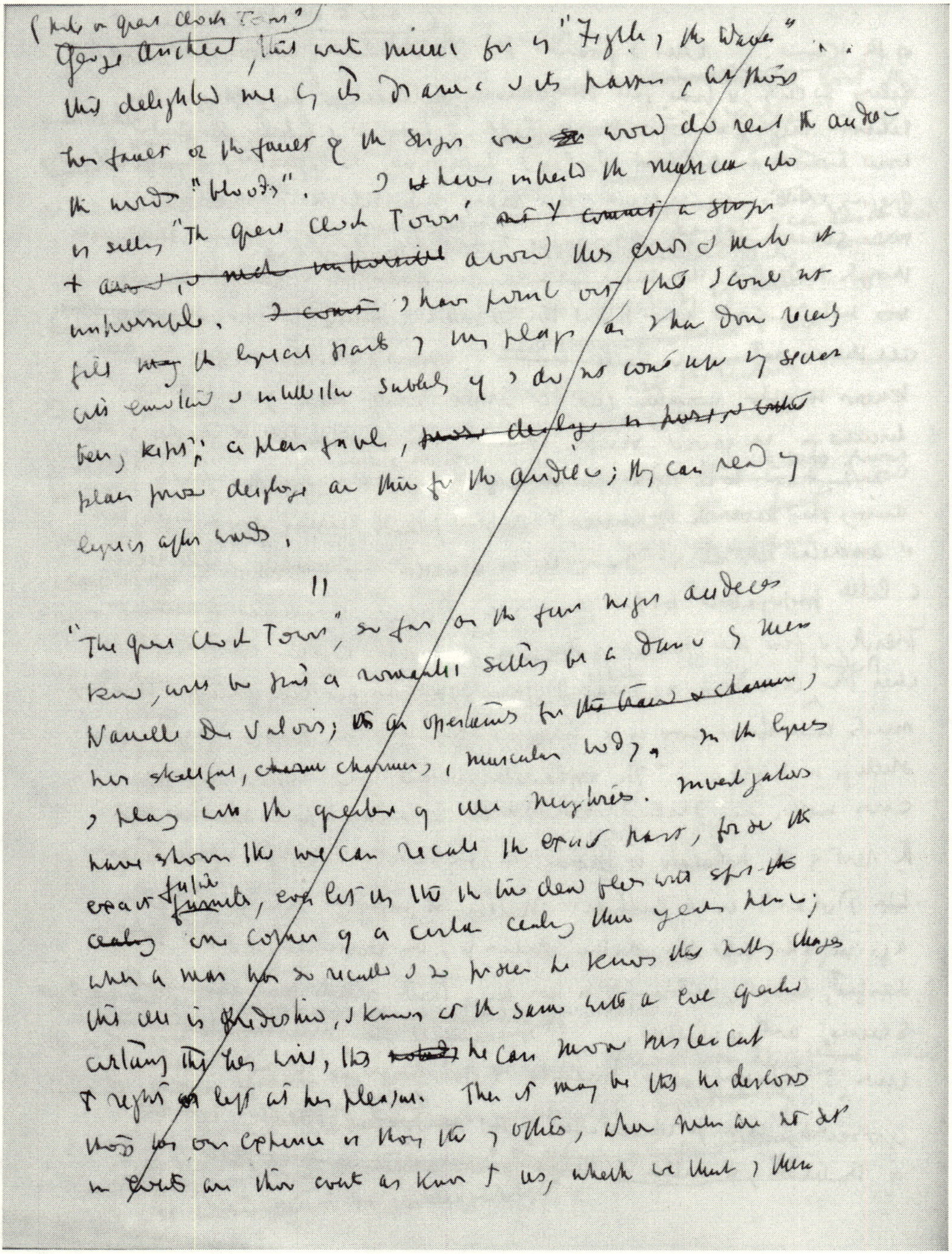

[NLI 30,546, 5^{v}]

Note on "Great Clock Tower"

George Antheil, that wrote music for my "Fighting the Waves" that delighted me by its drama & its passion but through his fault or the fault of the singer one ~~sen~~ word did reach the audience the word "bloody". I ~~in~~ have intreated the musician who is setting "The Great Clock Tower" ~~not to commit a singer to about & make impossible~~ about this error & make it impossible. ~~I count~~ I have pointed out that I could not fill ~~my~~ the lyrical part of my plays as I have done recently with emotional & intellectual subtlety if I did not count upon my secret being kept; a plain fable, ~~prose dialogue in prose and without~~ plain prose dialogue are there for the audience; they can read my lyrics afterwards.

II

"The Great Clock Tower", so far as the first night audiences know, will be just a romantic setting for a dance by Miss Nanette De Valois; ~~the~~ an opportunity for ~~the trained & charming~~ her skilful, ~~charm~~ charming, muscular body. In the lyrics I play with the question of all mysteries. Investigators have shown that we can recall the exact past, for see the

future

exact [?~~future~~], even let us that the two dead flies will spot ~~the cealing~~ one corner of a certain ceiling three years hence; when a man has so recalled & so forseen he knows that nothing changes that all is predestined, & knows at the same with an even greater certainty that his will, that ~~nobody~~ he can move his tea cup to right or left at his pleasure. Then it may be that he destroys through his own existence or through that of others, when men are not set in events as those events are known to us, whether we think of them

---

title This abbreviated title, which recurs on 6^{v}, 7^{v}, 8^{r}, and 8^{v}, is to distinguish this note from the draft of "Note to Three Songs," which occupies 5^{r}, 6^{r}, and 7^{r}.

1 *Fighting the Waves* was staged at the Abbey Theatre on August 13, 1929, and was the first occasion in which Ninette de Valois in the role of Fand performed in one of Yeats's plays. George Antheil, an American composer, was a protégé of Ezra Pound.

4 The reference is presumably to l. 26 of the opening lyric: "What wounds, what bloody press / Dragged into being / This loveliness." The "musician" was composer Arthur Duff (see appendix VIII).

15 For "Nanette" read "Ninette". (Yeats regularly misspelled the dancer's name.)

16–26 Though Yeats was to attempt a second draft of this passage on 8^{v}, he eventually dropped it entirely from *KGCT(C)* as published.

[NLI 30,546, 6^{v}]

[NLI 30,546, 6v]

Note on "Great Clock Tower"
as momentary or as timeless but as completed & perfected & that completion
incompletion, perfection, imperfection coexist, & may draw the conclusion
past ages have drawn, that we "return to the ~~lv~~ lovely"
in life and after life through the nobility of passion
such are my riders from mountain to mountain
~~what~~ that though the Great Clock Tower chimes
cannot abate their speed.

& she said
When I had written these sentences I read them to my wife ~~who~~ ^
& ~~she said "you have never heard singers~~, had you heard Elena
Gerhardt or Campbell McInnes or Gervase Elwes
you would know that is all nonsense". "But I have heard so & so,
answered "their
& so & so," I ~~said that though every word audible~~ words ~~were~~ though
^ if think
audible they were more bloodless than veal. "O^you ~~think~~
they can sing" said my wife & disgusted with my ignorance
~~she~~ would have gone off to bed ~~& left me alone at the study fire~~
had I not changed the subject.

II

I am not musical; I have the poets exact time sense & only
the vaguest sense of pitch, & yet I get the greatest pleasure from certain
combinations of singing & speaking voices, with ~~dur drums & flutes &~~
gong
drum ~~and~~ flute & string, ~~where~~ provided that some or all of the words
keep their natural passionate rhythm. ~~Thirty years~~ Thirty years ago
I persuaded Florence Farr, beautiful woman, incomparable elocutionist to rediscover
with the help of Arnold Dolmetsch what seems to be the ancient art
of singing or speaking poetry to notes, Greek music if Greek music was
as some authorities think "regulated declamation". Many people came to learn
but she had only one serious pupil & I think her name was Tailor I
have not heard of her for many years, all others had ~~the pitch, without~~
the sense of pitch, ~~without an~~ without the understanding of words, or ~~were lovers~~ of
~~poetry & had no sense of pitch~~ understood words & had no sense of

---

8–16 In a compressed form these lines were added in parentheses following the material retained from 4v to complete what eventually became the first section of *KGCT(C)*.

21–25 For a more detailed account of this formative episode in Yeats's theatrical career dating from November 1901, see his essay "Speaking to the Psaltery," written with Farr's help, first published in *The Monthly Review*, May 1902, and again in *Ideas of Good and Evil* (London: A. H. Bullen, 1903). Florence Farr had directed both Yeats's *The Land of Heart's Desire* at the Avenue Theatre, London, in 1894, and *The Countess Cathleen* for the Irish Literary Society in 1899, when she also took the role of Aleel. Margaret Campbell in *Dolmetsch: The Man and His Work* (London: Hamish Hamilton, 1975) quotes both Arnold and Mabel Dolmetsch's view that, though Farr was impressive when she matched the psaltery to "the thrilling tones of her low voice," she never sufficiently mastered the technique of playing the instrument so that, if "she raised the pitch of her voice," she could "follow it on the psaltery" (p. 144).

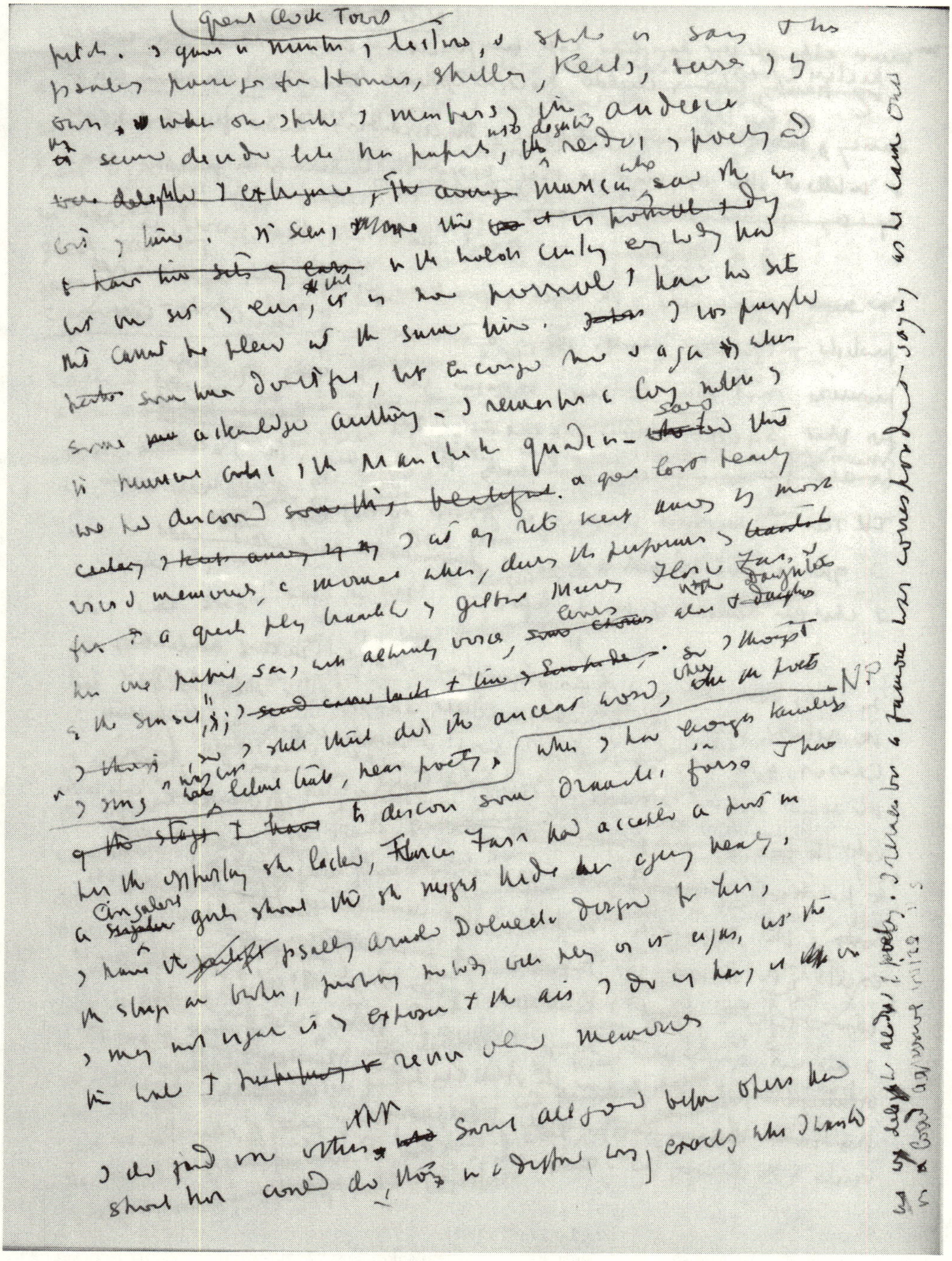
(Great Clock Tower)
pitch. I gave a number of lectures, [illegible] spoke or sang [illegible]
passages from Homer, Shelley, Keats, verse of my
own [illegible] audience
[illegible]
[illegible]

[NLI 30,546, 7v]

(Note on "Great Clock Tower")
pitch. I gave a number of lectures & spoke or sang to her
psaltery passages from Homer, Shelley, Keats, verse of my
.
own,} ~~&~~ when one spoke to members of the audience
they into delighted
~~and~~ seemed divided like her pupils, ~~the~~ readers of poetry and
who
~~were delighted to extravagance, the average~~ musician said she was
out of tune. It seems ~~to have~~ that ~~was~~ ~~it is possible to try~~
~~to have two sets of ears~~ in the twelfth century everybody had
~~&~~ that
but one set of ears, it is now possible to have two sets
that cannot be pleased at the same time. ~~I was~~ I was puzzled
~~perhaps~~ some times doubtful, but encouraged now & again ~~by~~ when
some ~~fam~~ acknowledged authority – I remember a long notice by
said
the musical critic of the Manchester Guardian – ~~who held~~ that
we had discovered ~~some thing beautiful~~ a great lost beauty
~~Certainly I keep among my m~~ I at any rate keep among my most
vivid memories, a moment when, during the performance of ~~translat~~
~~from S~~ a Greek play translated by Gilbert Murray Florence Farr &
lines "The Daughters
her one pupil sang with alternating voices ~~some chorus~~ about the ~~daughters~~
of the Sunset"; ~~I seemed carried back to time of Euripides~~; so I thought
where
~~I thought~~, and I still think did the ancient world, ~~when~~ the poets

---

1 The published text clarifies the meaning here by inserting "Miss Farr" before the word "spoke."

2 The psaltery was made by Dolmetsch; Yeats described it as containing "all the chromatic intervals within the range of the speaking voice" (*Essays and Introductions* [London: Macmillan, 1961], p. 16).

15–18 The reference is to a production by Granville Barker of Euripides' *Hippolytus*, staged in Murray's translation at the Lyric Theatre from May 26 to June 3, 1904. Yeats attended the first and last performances.

[NLI 30,546, 7v]

[NLI 30,546, 7ᵛ, continued]

sang but
"I sing" ~~were~~ literal truth, hear poetry. When I had enough knowledge NP
~~of the stage to have~~ to discover some dramatic forms to have
her the opportunity she lacked, Florence Farr had accepted a post in
Cingalese
a ~~singalese~~ girls school that she might hide her ageing beauty.
I have the ~~beautiful~~ psaltery Arnold Dolmetsch designed for her,
the strings are broken, probably nobody will play on it again, but that
I may not injure it by exposure to the air I do not hang it ~~up~~ on
the wall to ~~perpetuate &~~ revive old memories

~~III~~

I did find one other, ~~who~~ Sarah Allgood before opera had
spoilt her could do, though in a different way, exactly what I wanted

and we delighted readers of poetry. I remember a famous war correspondent saying as he came out
in a loud aggressive voice "S

21–22 For "have / her" *KGCT(C)* reads "give her," which clarifies the idea.

28–29 Yeats canceled the start of a new section to add a final paragraph to section II about Sarah Allgood. He later amplified his characterization of Allgood into a full sentence that reads: "I doubt if she could do so now for she sings in opera."

[NLI 30,546, 8r]

[NLI 30,546, 8[r]]

\Great Clock Tower/
The dirge in my Deirdre 'Eagles have gone into their cloudy bed'
sung
~~sing~~ by her, & one other, perhaps her sister ~~made poignant that~~
~~kept~~ preserved the utmost poignancy of speech. ~~Her~~ Her method ~~is allied~~
to "folk singing", ~~she all that her mind had her mind humble & simple~~
or allied to it, ~~her mind humble & simple~~ beautifully humble & simple
whereas Florence Farr was Greek & arrogant.

III

~~When~~ I gave up the fight & began writing little dance plays founded upon
a Japanese model, ~~saw~~ that need scenery or properties & can be performed
in ~~private~~ studio or private drawing room, thinking that some group
of musicians or art students might make a little money playing them &
gradually elaborate a ~~musical~~ technique that would respect both literature both
literature & music. When ever I produced one of these plays I asked my
singers for no new method, nor even talked to them upon the subject.
When the Abbey School of ballet was founded, ~~it see~~ I tried these plays
musician
upon the Abbey stage where they seemed out of place. Why should actor ~~walk up~~
fold & unfold a cloth, when the proscenium curtain was there why carry on
orcestra
the stage gong, drum & flute, when the ~~ocestra~~ was there. ~~In~~ "Fighting
the Waves" ~~art~~ & in the present play I ~~have adapted the No form~~
imitate the Japanese model
~~to the ordinary stage are No plays~~, they climax in a dance

1 *Deirdre* was first published by A. H. Bullen in 1907. The quoted words form the concluding line of the lyric sung by the Two Musicians during the moments when, unseen by the audience, Deirdre kills herself after Conchubar's murder of her lover, Naisi. The Allgood sisters played the Musicians in early performances (1906–1907).

1–6 With some additional punctuation these lines were incorporated into *KGCT(C)*.

2 Molly Allgood, Sarah's sister, whose stage name was Maire O'Neill, appeared as a Musician in *Deirdre* when it opened in November 1906.

8 The model was Noh drama. The text in *KGCT(C)* introduces a negative absent from the manuscript, which clarifies the austere nature of this genre that Yeats found particularly attractive: "no scenery, no properties".

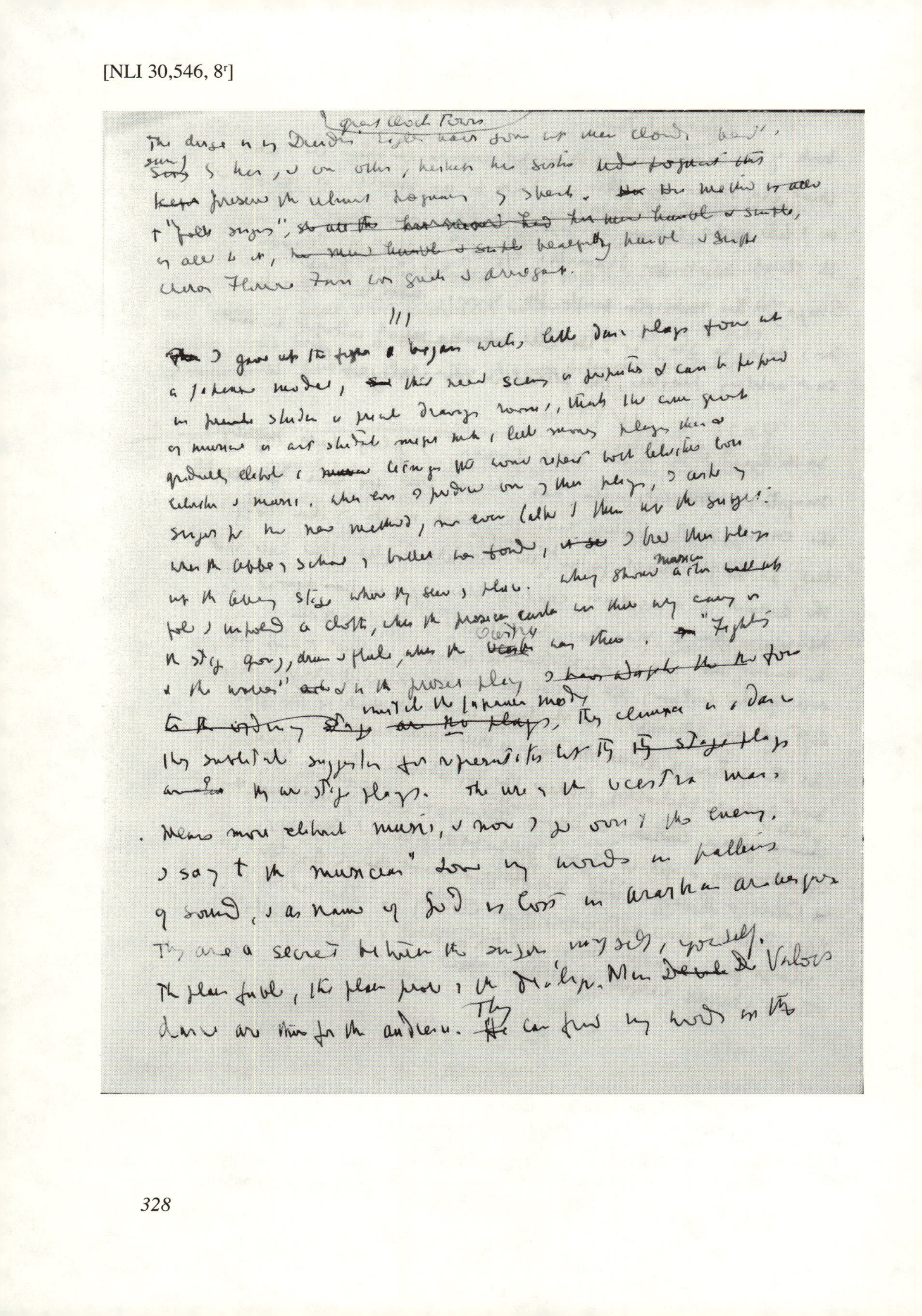

[NLI 30,546, 8r]

[NLI 30,546, 8[r], continued]

they substitute suggestion for representation but they ~~they stage pl~~ays
~~are Eur~~ they are stage plays. The use of the orcestra mans
means more elaborate music, & now I go over to the enemy.
I say to the musician "Lose my words in patterns
of sound, & as name of God is lost in Arabian arabesques.
They are a secret between the singers, myself, yourself.
The plain fable, the plain prose of the dialogue, Miss ~~Deval~~ De Valois
They
dance are there for the audience. ~~He~~ can find my words in the

21 The final word "mans" was an error immediately corrected on the following line but not canceled here.

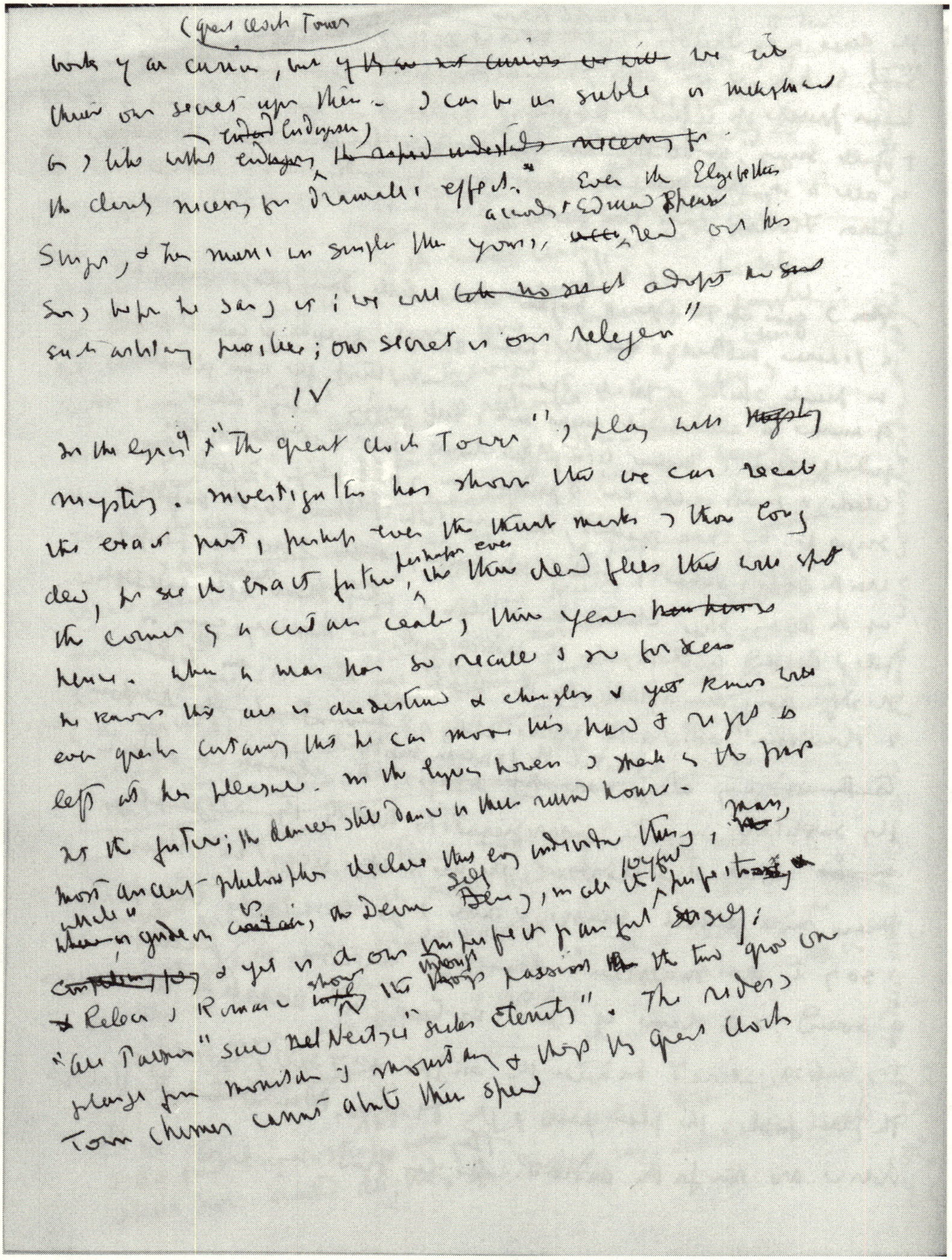

[NLI 30,546, 8v]

\Great Clock Tower/
book if are curious, but ~~if they are not curious we will~~ we will
thrust our secret upon them. I can be as subtle or metaphysical
~~endand~~ endangering
as I like without ~~endangering~~ ^ ~~the rapid understanding necessary for~~
the clarity necessary for dramatic effect. Even the Elizabethan
according to Edmund Spenser
singer, & his music was simpler than yours, ~~acco~~ ^ read out his
song before he sang it; we will ~~take no such~~ adopt no ~~such~~
such arbitrary practice; our secret is our religion."

of IV
In the lyrics ~~to~~ "The Great Clock Tower" I play with ~~mystry~~
mystery. Investigation has shown that we can recall
the exact past, perhaps even the thumb marks of those long
perhaps even
dead, for see the exact future, ^ the three dead flies that will spot
the corner of a certain ceiling three years ~~hen hence~~
hence. When a man has so recalled & so for seen
he knows that all is predestined & changeless & yet knows with
even greater certainty that he can move his hand to right or
left at his pleasure. In the lyrics however I speak of the past
not the future; the dancers still dance in their ruined house.
Man,
Most ancient philosophers declare that every individual thing in ~~me~~
which is is Self joyful
~~where is~~ guide or ~~contains~~ the Divine ~~Being~~, makes its ^ perfection,
~~completion of joy~~ & yet in its own imperfect painful ~~Sel~~ self;
show through
~~and~~ Relics and Romance ~~imply~~ ^ that ~~thoug~~ passion ~~that~~ the two grow one.
"All Passion" said ~~Net~~ Nietzsce "seeks Eternity". The riders
plunge from mountain to mountain & though the Great Clock
Tower chimes cannot abate their speed.

1 For "if are" read "if they are". *KGCT(C)* reads: "we will not / thrust" for "we will / thrust".

4–7 Incorporated with some revisions as the concluding lines of section III in *KGCT(C)*.

8–24 Yeats attempts to redraft the material he canceled on 5v and 6v. The ideas are more cogently expressed now; but, although this passage is not canceled in the manuscript here, it was not published. Instead *KGCT(C)* offers as section IV a revised version of the material that went into the shaping of the program note (see appendix I above); this revision was effected in NLI 30,306 (see pp. 332–333 below).

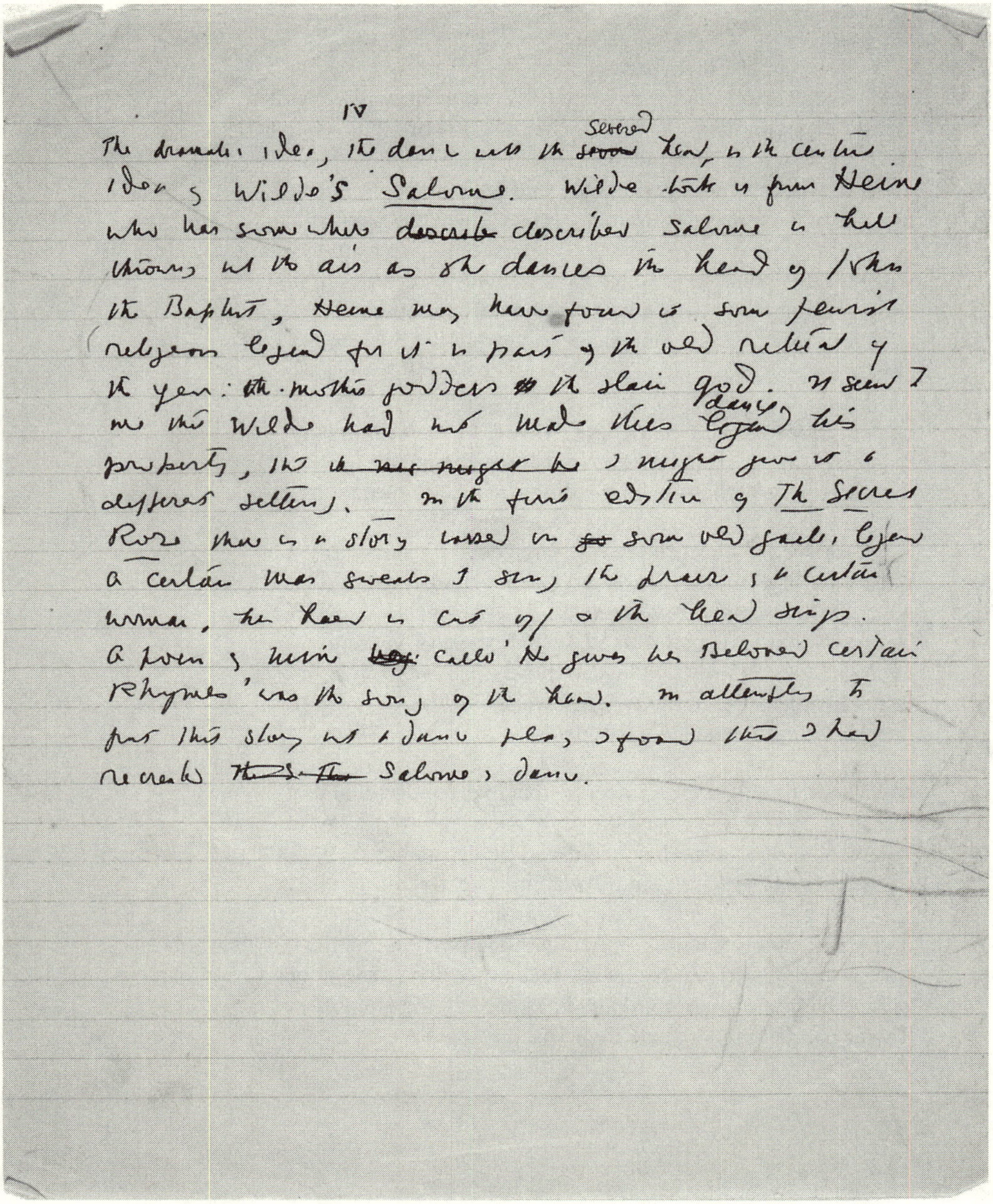

IV

The dramatic idea, the dance with the ~~sword~~ severed head, is the central idea of Wilde's Salome. Wilde took it from Heine who has somewhere ~~describe~~ described Salome in hell throwing into the air as she dances the head of John the Baptist. Heine may have found it in some Jewish religious legend for it is part of the old ritual of the year: the mother goddess ~~&~~ the slain god. It seems to me that Wilde had not made this dance legend his property, that it ~~was might be~~ I might give it a different setting. In the first edition of The Secret Rose there is a story based on ~~go~~ some old Gaelic legend. A certain man swears to sing the praise of a certain woman, his head is cut off & the head sings. A poem of mine ~~bag~~ called 'He gives his Beloved certain Rhymes' was the song of the head. In attempting to put this story into a dance play, I found that I had recreated ~~the the~~ Salome's dance.

[NLI 30,306]

IV

severed
The dramatic idea, the dance with the ~~sevred~~ head, is the central
idea of Wilde's <u>Salome</u>. Wilde took it from Heine
who has somewhere ~~describ~~ described Salome in hell
throwing into the air as she dances the head of John
the Baptist. Heine may have found it some Jewish
religious legend for it is part of the old ritual of
the year: the mother goddess ~~&~~ the slain god. It seemed to
dance
me that Wilde had not made this ~~legend~~ his
property, that it ~~mig might be~~ I might give it a
different setting. In the first edition of <u>The Secret
Rose</u> there is a story bassed on ~~so~~ some old Gaelic legend
A certain man swears to sing the praise of a certain
woman, his head is cut off & the head sings.
A poem of mine ~~beg~~ called 'He gives his Beloved Certain
Rhymes' was the song of the head. In attempting to
put this story into a dance play I found that I had
recreated ~~the S this~~ Salome s dance.

---

17 The attribution is tempered in *KGCT(C):* "gone close to Salome's dance in Wilde's play. But in his play the dance is before the head is cut off."

Appendix IV

Prose Materials: Draft of the Preface to *A Full Moon in March*: NLI 8769(ii) b

Yeats's draft of the Preface to Macmillan's edition of *A Full Moon in March* (London, 1935) is transcribed and annotated below; the Preface is reprinted in *VPl*, pp. 1310–1311, where it is followed by the slightly modified version printed in *The Herne's Egg and Other Plays* (New York: Macmillan, 1938), p. 1311–1312.

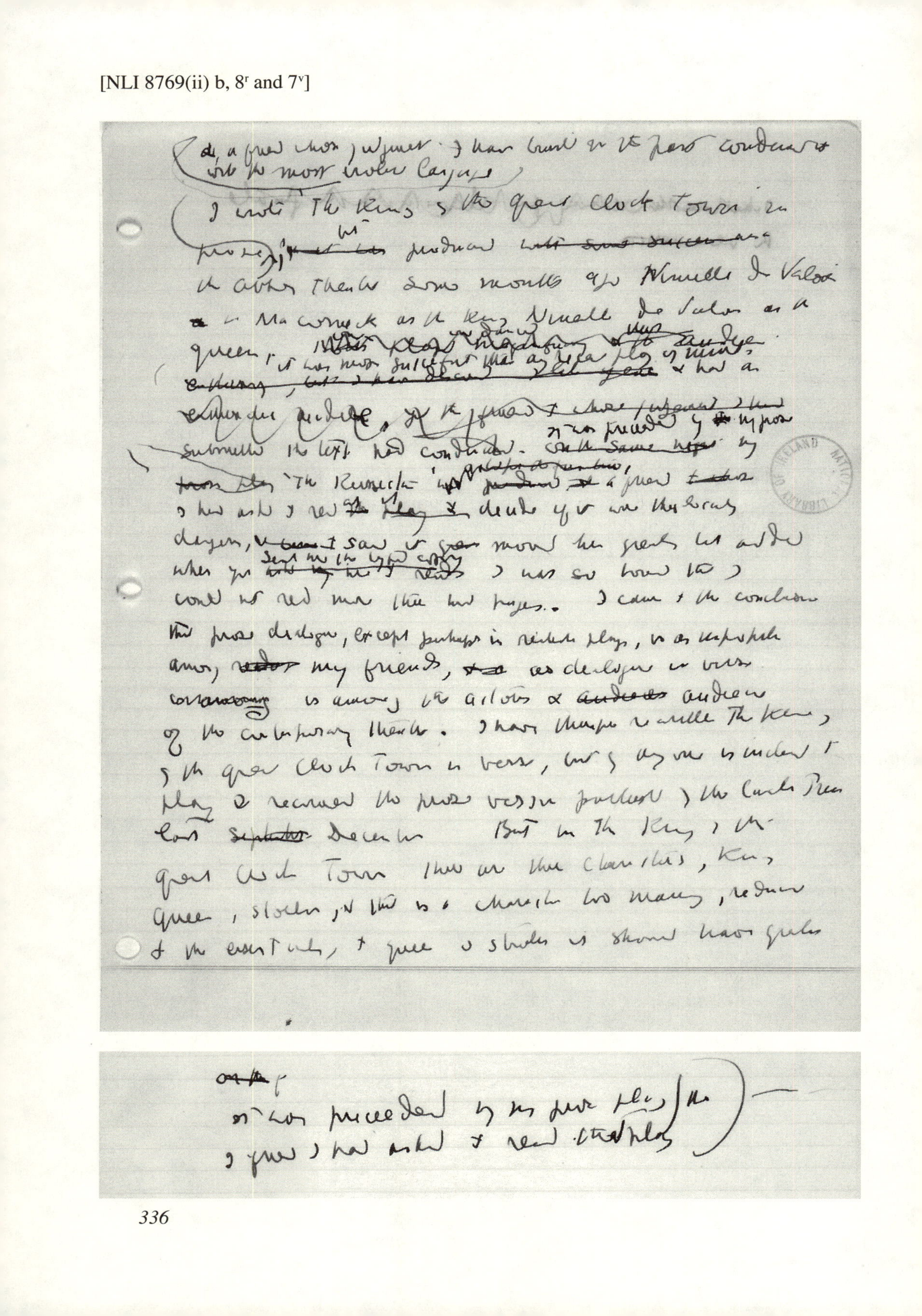

[NLI 8769(ii) b, 8^{r} and 7^{v}]

[NLI 8769(ii) b, 8r]

~~di~~ a friend whose judgment I have trusted in the past condemned it
with the most violent language
I wrote 'The King of the Great Clock Tower' in
but
prose; ~~& it was~~ produced ~~with some success~~ in
the Abbey Theatre some months ago Ninette de Valois
~~as~~ – McCormick as the King Ninette de Valois as the
~~and~~ ~~and danced~~ ~~their~~
Queen,. ~~Both played magnificently and the audience~~
it was more successful than any recent play of mine.
~~enthusiastic, but I have~~ [~~?discerned~~] ~~the~~ [~~?like~~] [~~?before~~] & had an
~~enthusiastic audience. Yet the friend to whose judgement I had~~
It was preceded by ~~the~~ my prose
~~submitted the text had condemned it.~~ ~~On the same night~~ my
~~acted for the first time~~,
~~prose play~~ 'The Resurrection' ~~was~~ ~~produced~~ ~~the~~ a friend ~~to whose~~
over it
I had asked to read ~~the play~~ to decide if it were theologically
dangerous, ~~& came~~ and said it ~~grea~~ moved him greatly but added
sent me the typed copy
when you ~~asked my me to read~~ I was so bored that I
could not read more than two pages. I came to the conclusion
that prose dialogue, except perhaps in realistic plays, is as unpopular
among ~~readers~~ my friends, ~~& a~~ as dialogue in verse
~~is among~~ is among the actors & ~~audiences~~ audience
of the contemporary theatre. I have therefore rewritten The King
of the Great Clock Tower in verse, but if anyone is inclined to
play I recommend the prose version published by the Cuala Press
last ~~September~~ December. But in The King of the
Great Clock Tower there are three characters, King,
Queen, Stroller, and that is a character too many, reduced
to the essentials, to queen and stroller it should have greater

[NLI 8769(ii) b, 7v]

[~~?on the p~~]
it was preceded by my prose play though
a friend I had asked to read that play

8r, 1 As in the Preface to the Cuala edition of *KGCT*, the identity of the "friend" (Ezra Pound) is not revealed.
12 The lines on facing 7v are clued in here, marked to show where to insert the play's title.
23 The date of publication of the Cuala edition was December 14, 1934.

[NLI 8769(ii) b, 9r]

[NLI 8769(ii) b, 9r]

intensity. I started afresh & called the new version
<u>A Full Moon in March</u>. Then quote from 'The
dance with the severed head' etc from P 19
down to cut off on page 20. ~~The first two~~
~~songs~~ "That blond girl there" "I would I were a
blind man" are songs re-written for the sake of their
tunes from songs 'The Pot of Broth' & 'The Player Queen'
~~& supernatural songs~~ in the Ribh in Supernatural Songs is
an imaginary contemporary of St Patrick. His Christianity
come perhaps from Egypt like much early Irish Christianity
may
^ reflect ~~some more ancient religion~~ pre Christian
thought.

WBY.

May

2–4 The reference is to section IV of the "Commentary on 'The Great Clock Tower'" in the Cuala edition, which includes the text for these two pages. The text in *FMIM(K)* and *HEOP* omits the sentence refering to Yeats's poem, "He gives His Beloved Certain Rhymes." It concludes: "But in his [Wilde's] play the dance is before the head is cut off."

5–6 Yeats has merged the first and second lines of the song from *The Player Queen*: "I would that I were an old beggar / Rolling a blind, pearl eye." See W. B. Yeats, *"Parnell's Funeral and Other Poems" from "A Full Moon in March": Manuscript Materials*, ed. David R. Clark (Ithaca: Cornell University Press, 2003), pp. 105–111.

7 For "songs 'The" read "songs in 'The".

Appendix V

The Floor Plan of the Setting for the Abbey Staging: NLI 29,550(2)

The image shown on the following page was inserted between the list of characters and the opening page of text of *The King of the Great Clock Tower* in NLI 29,550(2). It shows a stage floorplan, which realizes Yeats's prescriptions for the setting and the disposition of the actors within the playing space. Characteristic of Abbey practice, the scheme redeploys elements from earlier productions in the theatre: the fore-curtain that is parted by the attendants during their opening lyric is to be that used formerly for *Oedipus*, also directed by Robinson in December, 1926 (it was of a pale gray with a mauve-like hue), while the Craig screens had often been used in settings for heroic plays since their appearance in a revival of Yeats's *The Hour Glass* in 1911. What the setting reveals, unlike the stage directions in the text, is that the semicircle of half-foot screens ended at either side in tower-like structures, presumably made with wider screens to give the main curve greater stability. This effectively forms a second frame within that already provided by the proscenium, the parted curtain, and the two attendants, so that the action is firmly contained and focused on the relation of the masked figures and the arrangement of the four cubical thrones. Initially the pair of thrones situated at what is designated stage right [R] of the curving screens would have been empty opposite the seated figures of King and Queen; later King and severed head would have confronted from that space an isolated Queen at stage left [L]. The disposition of curving screens, the two framing towers, the placing of the two attendants all create a sense of mathematical precision, which admirably evokes by spatial means a sense of the King's need for complete order within his realm.

Yeats's letters during the play's composition, rehearsal, and staging and his prefaces to the printed texts show that he was throughout anxious not to appear to be reworking Wilde's *Salome*. He was perhaps right to claim that his play bore little textual or structural relation to Wilde's tragedy; and yet the floor plan shows that there are marked parallels between the plays in terms of their deployment of stage space. Salome appears on the terrace of Herod's palace where the action is set: it is the tetrarch's space and he has absolute command over the ordering of it and the movement of persons within it. By overriding his instruction that Jokanaan is not to be removed from the cistern where he is imprisoned and later by taking complete possession of the space as her dance floor, Salome undermines Herod's rule, marginalizing him to the periphery of the space as, out of desire for her, he comes more and more under her power. For much of the action of Yeats's play the King is situated centrally within a space that is decidedly his; but, once the Queen begins to move in a dance that resists his attempts to objectify her, she takes complete possession of what has been his masculine space, making it absolutely hers as she becomes its centralizing focus. The King attempts to recover his domain but ends like Herod totally marginalized, as his abasement before the Queen in the final tableau makes clear. Despite its stylized simplicities, the setting admirably conveys an audience straight to the dynamic inner significances of the stage action: it allows for a metaphorical and symbolic use of stage space.

[NLI 29,550(2), 2bis^{r}]

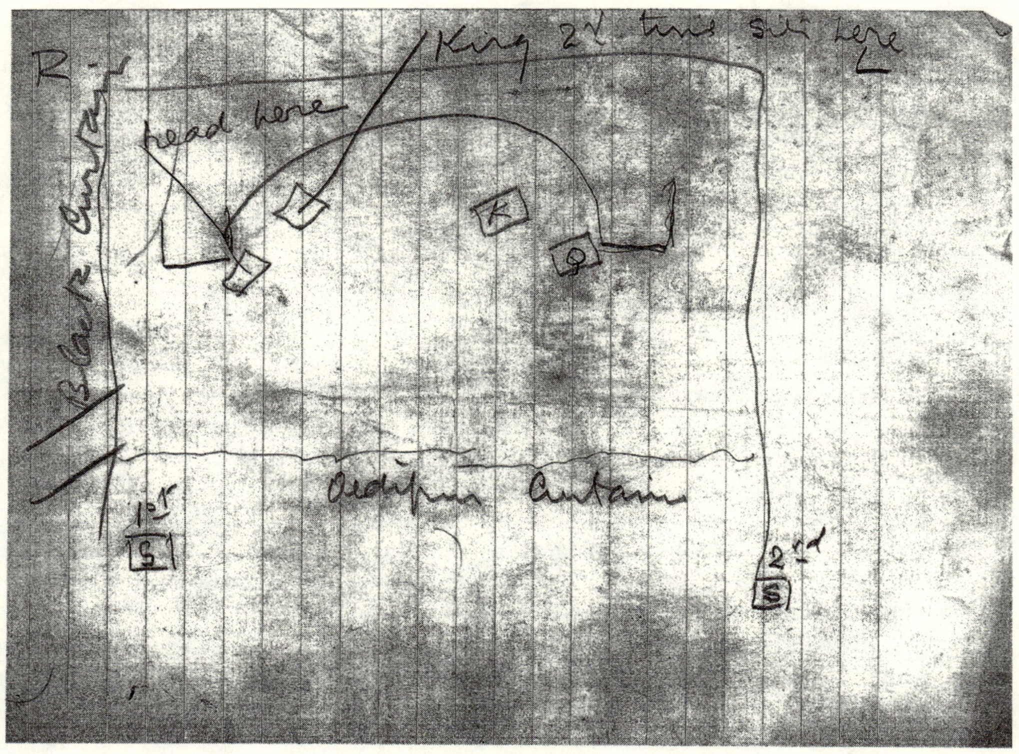

Appendix VI

Evolution of Yeats's Design for the Four Thrones

The four pen-sketches shown on the following page are found on the verso of page 9 of the typescript SIUC 76/1/7; they are drawn in the same blue-black ink that Yeats used for making his holograph revisions to the play text and were entered with the sheet inverted. The designs show him thinking through ideas about how he wished the four thrones to appear, which are required in the action. The first large and ornately decorated double throne with its mandala-inspired back and richly draped seat is akin to ones often seen in ballet, such as that usually devised for the King and Queen in *The Sleeping Beauty* (a favored work of de Valois, who was in the process at this date of making it one of the signature works of her new Vic-Wells Ballet Company). The connotation of unity suggested by the double throne is clearly out of keeping with the relationship of King and Queen as defined by the action. Moreover, its Bakst-inspired appearance invests it too precisely with orientalist resonances in a manner that would constrict imaginative engagement with the play within too limiting a set of associations. The play is neither a fairytale nor an escapist fantasy. What is impressive is the leap from such an elaborate design to ones of utter simplicity: first the stool-like structures, where two are placed side by side as if to gauge how successfully the pairing would achieve an effect of physical proximity and emotional distance; and then the further refinement of that idea to a plain cube, which is wholly functional and carries no resonances whatever, cultural, historical, or aesthetic. Within the designs one can see Yeats working out a set of principles, which also govern his scheme for the costumes as outlined in the various redraftings that he made to the opening list of characters on the first page of this typescript. Nothing visual was to distract an audience's attention from the play's preoccupation with issues of power, gender, and sexuality. It is fitting that primary colors (red, orange, and black costumes seen with absolute clarity against—at this stage in Yeats's invention—a curtain of "pale ivory") should be deployed for stage action that through continual revision has become increasingly primal in its thematic significance. Interestingly the scheme adheres exactly to the prescriptions for an ideal stage design, which Yeats had outlined in one of his earliest manifestos about theatrical reform: "it is necessary to simplify both the form and colour of scenery and costume. As a rule the background should be but a single colour so that the persons in the play wherever they stand, may harmonize with it, and preoccupy our attention. In other words it should be thought out . . . as if it were the background of a portrait. . . . There must be nothing unnecessary, nothing that will distract the attention from speech and movement" ("The Reform of the Theatre," *Samhain: An Occasional Review* [Dublin], ed. W. B. Yeats, September 1903, pp. 9–10).

[SIUC 76/1/7, 9v]

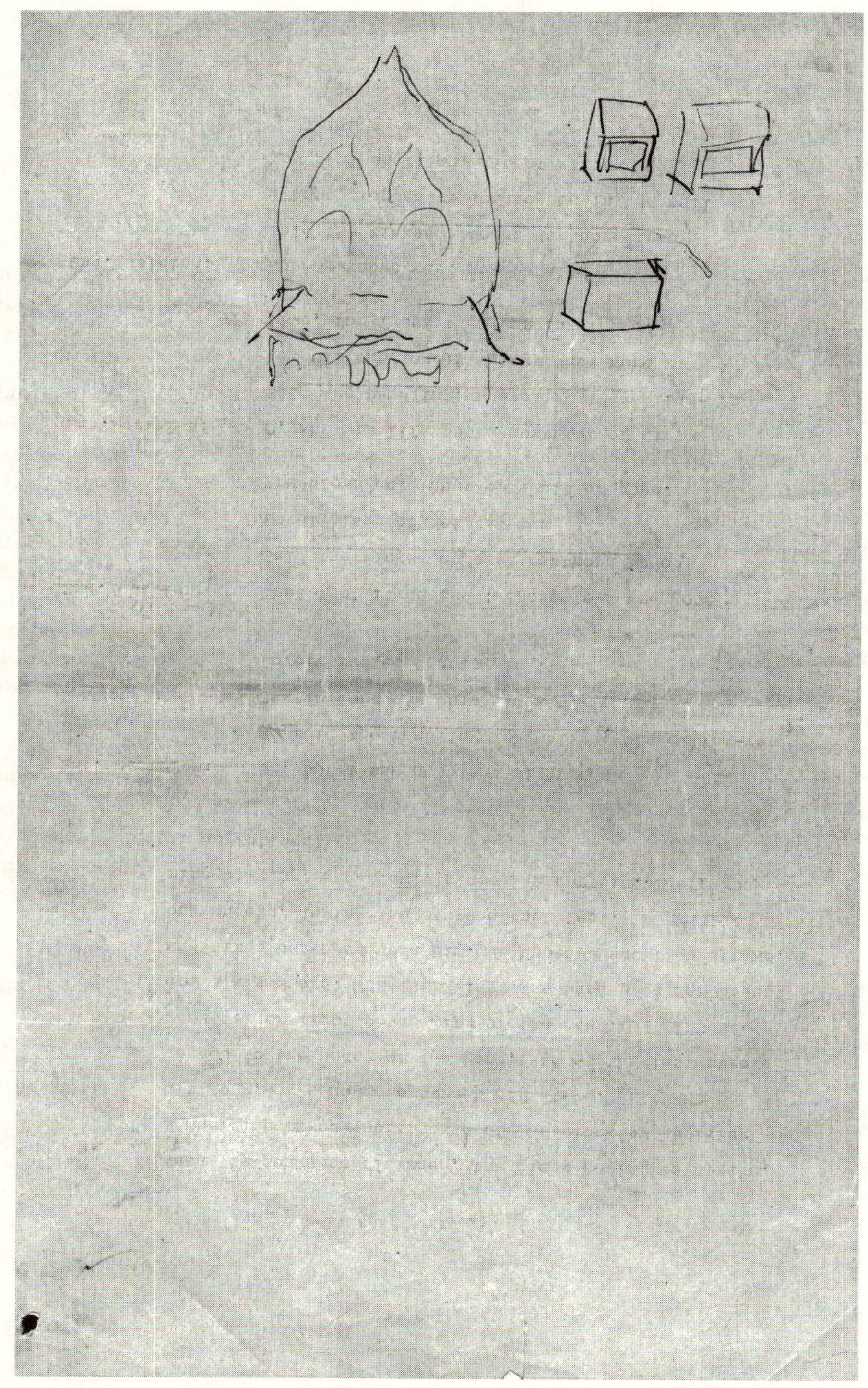

Appendix VII

Photograph of the Original Cast

Reproduced on the following page is a photograph of the production of *The King of the Great Clock Tower,* the only one known to survive. It is an informal shot of the three main characters posed backstage in costumes and (in the case of Queen and Stroller) in their masks. The actors are from the left: Denis O'Dea as Stroller, Ninette de Valois as Queen, and F. J. McCormick as King. The costumes for the Stroller and the King by Dorothy Travers Smith followed Yeats's prescriptions closely: the former being, according to de Valois in conversation with me, predominantly black over a red jerkin; the latter predominantly a red surcoat over a longer black gown with a black cape and white full cuffs, which much accentuated the play of McCormick's hands. Both men are heavily bearded; it is almost as if the one has been conceived as the inverse image of the other. The King's sword was a skilfully painted, wooden shape suggestive of blade and hilt. De Valois' dress was not, however, of the orange tone Yeats indicated but rather in a hue shading more towards pale gold with an undershirt, visible at the neckline, and an unusual decoration at the waist in a red, which matched that in the costumes for King and Stroller. The change to the colors of the Queen's dress may have been occasioned by the decision to have a blue-gray background to the action (Yeats described it in the published text as "pale purple") rather than the ivory curtain he specified in the typescript SIUC 76/1/7, though it is conceivable that the old-gold tones of the dress showed orange under Udolphus Wright's lighting. What is noticeable about the costume designs is how Travers Smith has sought to avoid either a precise period or a precise stylistic idiom. The full-head mask for the Queen by George Atkinson evokes the simplicities of a doll, unmarked by emotion or outward definitions of "character"; that for the Stroller avoids intimations of caricature or grotesque elements: though evidently marked by experience, his features are not without a distinctive, rugged beauty and appeal. What the photograph beautifully evokes is the diminutive stature of de Valois between the two men, a fact that would make her gradual empowerment and final dominance over both the entire stage space and the prostrate figure of the King a highly potent image: one that would effectively "dominate memory".

[Cast of *The King of the Great Clock Tower*]

Dennis O'Shea, Ninette de Valois, and F. J. McCormack in costume; the photograph is from the editor's personal collection.

Appendix VIII

Arthur Duff's Score for the Lyrics

It was long believed that Duff's score was lost in the Abbey fire of 1951, except for a piano rendition of the accompaniment to the final lyric, which had been printed as part of one of the Cuala Press broadsides (new series) in 1935 (see appendix IX). We have Sam McCready to thank for locating the music for all the lyrics in the possession of Robert Irwin, the actor who originally performed the role of the First Musician. Irwin emigrated to Canada, taking the manuscript of his songs with him, where McCready tracked him down. Irwin generously gave the material to McCready, who included it in his unpublished master's thesis, "The Stage Director's Approach to the Presentation of the Plays of W. B. Yeats" (University of Wales, Bangor, 1975). McCready, generous in his turn, has allowed the music to be published with this edition so that, properly, it will be in the public domain. Unfortunately, to date the score for the dance is lost; and it is galling to find at the close of the song for the severed head ("Images ride—I heard a man say") the instruction "dance follows" but no accompanying music.

The style of the music is what one might term *classicized* Irish folk in its idiom, supported at times by surprisingly romantic harmonies. The exceptions to this general tenor are the song for the Queen ("O what may come / Into my womb"), which has a powerful Handelian shaping of the melodic line, and the setting for the inserted stanzas from "Why must those holy, haughty feet descend," which develops an aptly incantatory quality, especially in the hauntingly unresolved treatment of the refrain. The few variants in wording of the lyrics are not thought to be authorial.

["They dance all day that dance in Tir-na-nogue"]

The King of the Great Clock Tower.

W. B. Yeats.

Second Attendant – Tenor.

First Attendant – Bass.

"They dance all day that dance in Tir-na-nogue."

Arthur Duff.

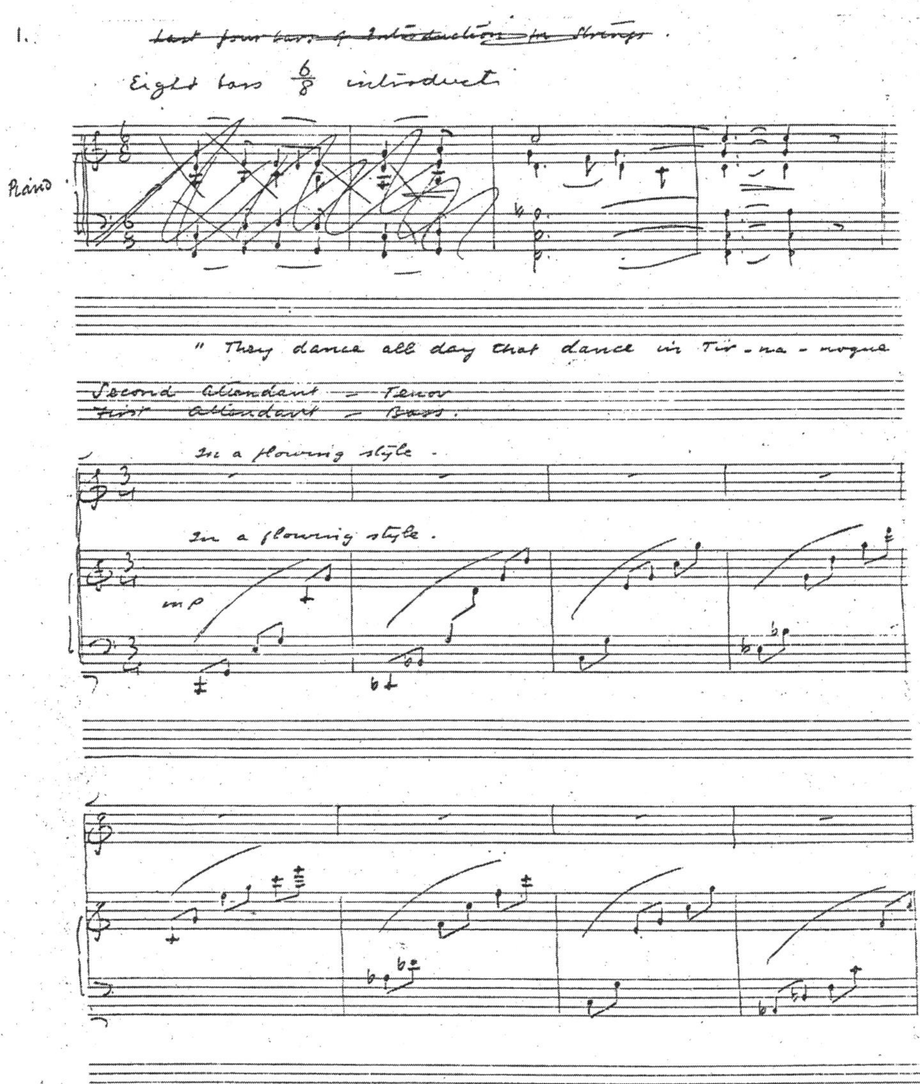
1.
Last four bars of Introduction for Strings.
Eight bars 6/8 introduct.
Piano
" They dance all day that dance in Tir-na-nogue
Second Attendant – Tenor
First Attendant – Bass.
In a flowing style.
In a flowing style.
mp

["They dance all day that dance in Tir-na-nogue"]

3.

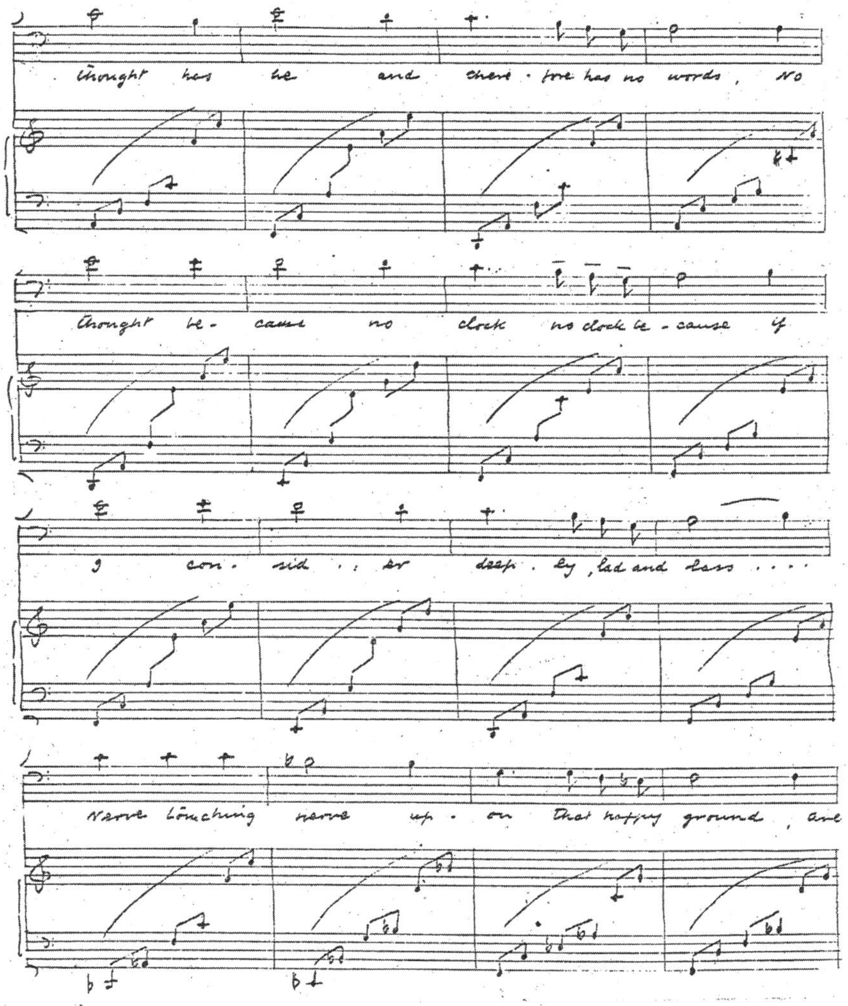

thought has he and there - fore has no words, No

thought be - cause no clock no clock be - cause if

I con - sid - er deep - ly, lad and lass . . .

Nerve touching nerve up - on that happy ground, are

["They dance all day that dance in Tir-na-nogue"]

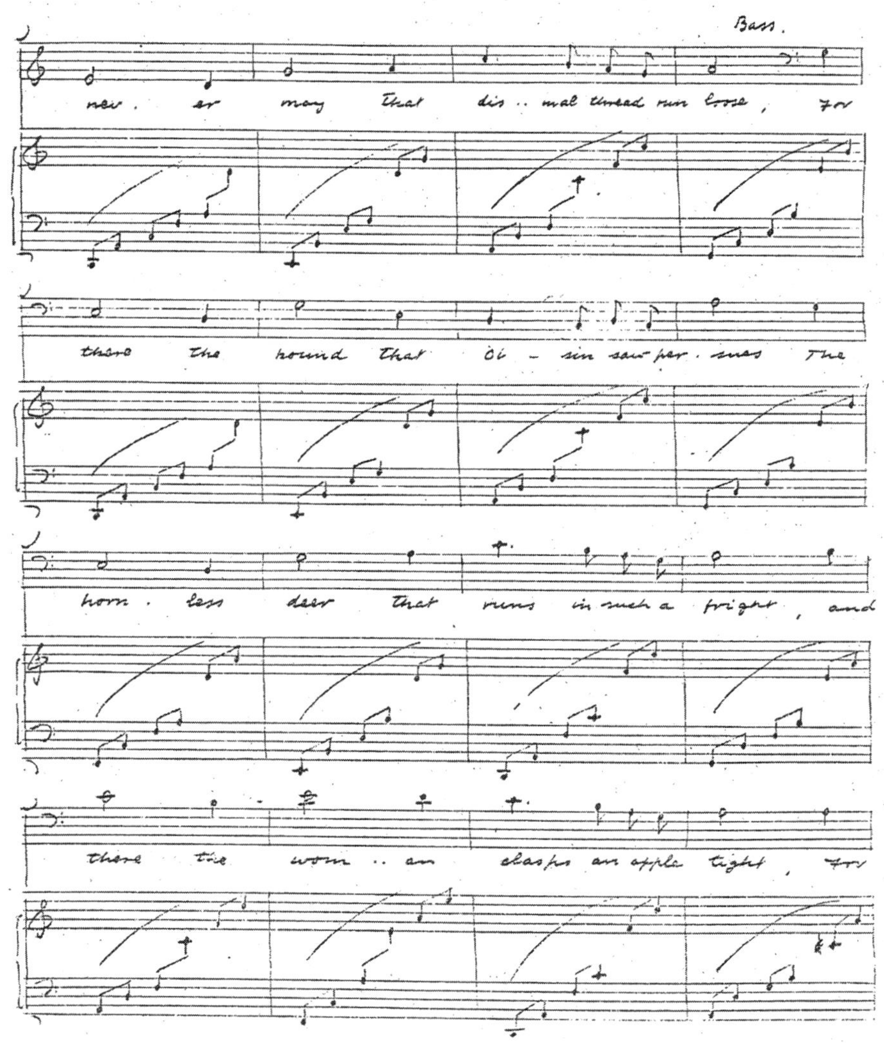
Bass.
nev. er may that dis.. mal thread run loose, for
there the hound that Oi - sin saw pur. sues The
horn. less deer that runs in such a fright, and
there the wom.. an clasps an apple tight, for

all the clam ... mer of a famished man, They
run in foam, and there in foam they ran . . .
Nor can they stop to take a breath that still
Rall
Hear in the foam the beat . . ing of a
Rall

tempo

The Queen's Song

from

"The King of the Great Clock Tower"

by

W. B. Yeats

The music by

Arthur Duff.

The Abbey Theatre 193

1. "He longs to kill my body
Slowly
Slowly.
p
P. Oh, what .. may
come .. in - to my womb
He longs to kill my

body, un til that sudden shudder and limbs lie
still. Oh, what may come .. in - to my
womb, what cat .. ter .. pillar my beauty con
sume.

The King of the Great Clock Tower. Robert Irwin

W. B. Yeats.

First attendant – Bass. (singing as Head.)

"Images ride – I heard a man say."

Arthur Duff

["Images ride—I heard a man say"]

First Attendant: (singing as head.)

Images ride – I heard a man say –
Out of Benbulben and Knockareagh,
What says the Clock in the Great Clock Tower?
Out of the grave, saddle and ride
But turn from Rosses crawling tide,
The meet's upon the mountain side
A slow low note and an iron bell.

What made them mount and what made them come;
Cuchulain that fought night long with the foam;
What says the Clock in the Great Clock Tower?
Niam that rode on it; lad and lass
That sat so still and played at the Chess –
Oh high, heroic wantonness.
A slow low note and an iron bell.

Aleel his Countess; Hanrahan
That seemed but a wild wenching man;
What says the Clock in the Great Clock Tower?
How can a phantom ride among these;
Grip the saddle tight with your knees;
Image, ride among images.
A slow low note and an iron bell.

First attendant.
"Images ride – I heard a man say."
With a steady rythm.
With a steady rythm.
mf
Images ride – I heard a man say.
[The King: O, terror, it has begun to sing.]
f
Rall
f
Images ride – I heard a man say – Out of Benbulben and Knockarea
tempo
mf
What says the clock in the Great Clock Tower? Out of the grave, saddle and ride but
rall
tempo

Slowly
turn from Rosses crawling tide, The masts upon the mountain side. a
slow low note and an iron bell . . . .
slowly.
p
tempo
What made them mount and what made them come, Cu-chulain that fought night long with the foam;
tempo. mf
What says the clock in the Great Clock Tower? Niam that rode on it; lad and lass that
rall . . .
tempo .

slowly
sat so still and played at the chess, O High hero-ic wantonness a
slow low note and a iron bell . . . .
slowly
p
tempo
Alleel his Countess; Hanrahan that seemed but a wild wenching man;
tempo mf
What says the clock in the Great Clock Tower? How can a phantom ride among these
rall . .
tempo .

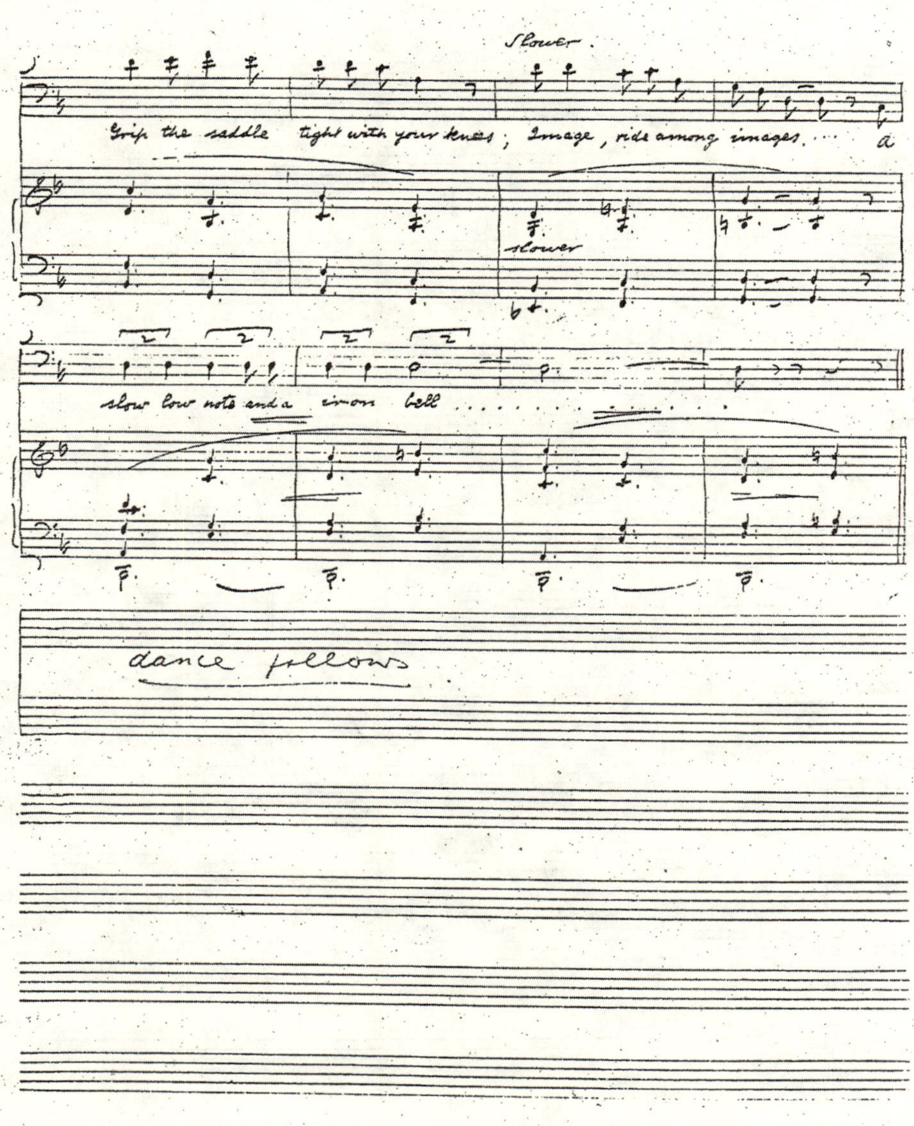
Slower.
Grip the saddle tight with your knees; Image, ride among images. ... a
slower
slow low note and a iron bell ....
dance follows

The King of the Great Clock Tower.
W. B. Yeats.
Robert Irwin
"Oh, but I saw a solemn sight."
First attendant - Bass.
Second attendant - Tenor.
First attendant - Bass.
Voice.
Piano
mf
mf Oh, but I saw a
sol - emn sight, said the rambling, shambling travelling man;
Castle Dar - gan's ruin all lit love - ly ladies
B.C. No. 29c.
Made and Printed in England by Bosworth & Co., Ltd.

Rit.
Second attendant - Tenor
dancing in it.
Rit.
what tho' it danced, those days are gone, said the wicked crooked
hawthorn tree. Love-ly la-dy or gallant man are
Rit
blown cold dust or a bit of bone.
Rit.

First attendant - Bass.
Oh what is life but a mouth - ful of air said the
rambling, shambling travelling man, Yet all the love - ly
things that were live for I saw them dancing
Rit.
Rit.
Second attendant - Tenor.
there
No - body knows what
B.C.
No. 20c.
Made and Printed in England by Bosworth & Co., Ltd.

["Oh, but I saw a solemn sight"]

W. B. Yeats.
"Why must these holy, haughty feet descend"
Broadly
First Attendant
Voice
Piano
Why must these
ho-ly, haughty feet descend From em-blem-at-ic niches, and what
hand ran such a qui-et raddle through their white? My heart is broken,
yet . . . must un-der-stand. What are they seeking?

["Why must these holy, haughty feet descend"]

2.

Second Attendant

why do they des - cend . For desec - ra - tion and the

Rall.

Rall.

lov-er's night . . .

First att. a little quicker.

I cannot

tempo

face that emblem of the moon, nor eye lids that the un - mixed heaven

dart, Nor stand up - on my feet, so great a fight descends upon my -

rit.
savage, sunlit heart.
What can she lack whose
Second att.
emblem is the moon?
But desec-ra-tion and the
Rall.
lover's night . . .
First att.
(Impassioned)
Delight my
tempo
heart with sound; speak yet a-gain, I
look on feet but not upon a
3

["Why must these holy, haughty feet descend"]

Appendix IX

The Cuala Press Broadside of "The Wicked Hawthorn Tree"

The Cuala Press issued a new series of broadsides in 1935, the second of which comprised Arthur Duff's melody for the final song of *The King of the Great Clock Tower* together with the words of Yeats's lyric (shown on the following page). The accompanying illustration by Victor Brown shows the tree in winter starkness rising out of dark, shaped stones, suggestive of a ruined building, though Castle Dargan is seen on the far horizon, surmounting a hill. A few osiers, briars, and ragged grasses grow through the stones but only to emphasize the bleakness of the scene. Each printed image was hand-painted to give the tree touches of light tan, while the grasses were a bluish, dark green and the stones variously tinted buff, tan, and a faint maroon. The hill was colored blue-green and the dominant sky an ethereal, creamy lemon tint to give a decidedly spectral atmosphere to the scene. The resulting publication was more sombre and sophisticated than many in the series. Victor Brown (1900–1953), an admired illustrator of books, contributed designs to some six of the twenty-four broadsides published in 1935 and more for the series issued in 1937; and he designed settings for Austin Clarke's *The Kiss* at the Peacock Theatre in 1942. But, according to Theo Snoddy's entry on Brown in his *Dictionary of Irish Artists: 20th Century* (Dublin: Merlin Publishing, 1996; rev. 2002), p. 57, he was perhaps best known for his political cartoons for the *Irish Times* under the pseudonym "Bee."

[*A Broadside*, no. 2, n.s., February 1935]

NO. 2 (NEW SERIES) FEBRUARY, 1935.

A BROADSIDE

EDITORS: W. B. YEATS AND F. R. HIGGINS; MUSICAL EDITOR, ARTHUR DUFF. PUBLISHED MONTHLY AT THE CUALA PRESS, ONE HUNDRED AND THIRTY THREE LOWER BAGGOT STREET, DUBLIN.

THE WICKED HAWTHORN TREE.

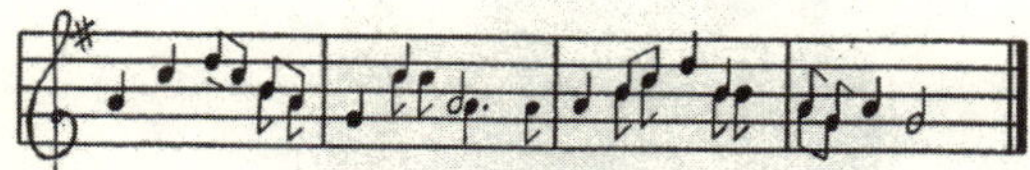

O, but I saw a solemn sight;
Said the rambling, shambling travelling-man;
Castle Dargan's ruin all lit,
Lovely ladies dancing in it.

What though they dance; those days are gone;
Said the wicked, crooked, hawthorn tree;
Lovely lady and gallant man
Are blown cold dust or a bit of bone.

300 copies only.